TIMBER TRADE PRACTICE

TIMBER TRADE PRACTICE

Jack H. Leigh, F.I.W.Sc.,
Technical Consultant to the Price & Pierce Group,
Examiner for the Institute of Wood Science in Timber
Economics and Administration,
Timber Trade Federation Arbitrator

Alan G. Randall
Former Manager of Price & Pierce Group Technical Services,
Timber Trade Federation Arbitrator and Authorised Stress Grader

Fourth Edition

First edition 1950
Second edition 1953
Third edition 1965
Reprinted 1973, 1974
Fourth edition 1981

Published by
THE MACMILLAN PRESS LTD
London and Basingstoke
Companies and representatives
throughout the world

Typeset in 10/11 Press Roman by
Cambrian Typesetters, Farnborough, Hants
and printed in Hong Kong

ISBN 0 333 23885 0

Contents

Preface to the Fourth Edition

The authors wish to express their appreciation for the help and co-operation which has been extended to them by the Price and Pierce Group, without whose readily available facilities this book could not have been written. In particular, we thank our Chairman, Mr H. C. Gilbert, for his encouragement by ensuring that the comprehensive experience of the Group's wide knowledge could be utilised.

The third edition of *Timber Trade Practice* was published in 1965 and it is possibly true to say that in the intervening period of some 15 years more changes have taken place in the timber trade than in the previous 100 years. There are now at least 30 TTF Contract Forms and, in addition, charter parties have been revised, and we have seen the introduction of metrication, decimal currency, stress grading, unitisation in the form of packaging and truck-bundling, changes in the method of marketing, new forms of documentation by way of computerised specifications and changes in shipping procedure.

All these developments are subject to constant negotiation and revision. This book can only review them as they exist at the time of writing and point out the principles that should be understood by the reader. Changes between writing and publication − often quite extensive − are likely but cannot be anticipated.

Jointly, we have served the trade for a total of about 92 years, and during that time we have been involved in practically every, if not every, aspect of trade procedure. In latter years we have been principally employed in the agency business − so becoming very familiar with the problems which arise between both the shippers and the buyers. These are considerable, and while it is often merely a question of language misunderstanding, they are sometimes due to changing methods of marketing and interpretation of contract terms which do not always satisfy the changes in trade structure or the quite extraordinary marketing conditions which have developed in recent years.

We trust that readers will appreciate the difficulty of producing this book, in which we have tried to anticipate possible future changes and at the same time have endeavoured to avoid expressing personal opinions by merely stating the facts as we understand them at the present time. We should like to quote from the Preface to the third edition: 'there is no substitute for reading contracts, charters and documents carefully before signing and ensuring that they agree with each other as well as being correct in themselves'.

J. H. LEIGH
A. G. RANDALL

Acknowledgements

It would not have been possible to prepare this book without the generous and whole-hearted co-operation of many people and authorities, both outside and inside the trade. To all these the authors tender their sincere appreciation for the valuable assistance which they have received. In particular, they wish to thank the following for their permission to reproduce the material mentioned:

Benn Publications Ltd (extracts from *Shipping Marks on Timber*); Chamber of Shipping of the United Kingdom (extracts from and copies of Nubaltwood and other charters); Institute of London Underwriters Association (extracts from and copies of insurance clauses); Timber Trade Federation of the United Kingdom (extracts from and copies of contract forms and statistics); Finnish Sawmill Owners Association and the Association of Finnish Sawmillmen (Softwood Grading Rules).

The authors' thanks are due to the following, who supplied much detail, information and statistics in the preparation of the text:

Chapter 2 — Geographical Background. Colleagues in the various companies of the Price and Pierce Group.
Chapter 3 — The Imported Timber Trade — Mr P. T. Dransfield, Brewster and Co. (Woking) Ltd; Mr Tim Spencer, Tim Spencer and Co. Ltd, Westgate-on-Sea.
Chapter 4 — The Softwood Trade. *Timber Trades Journal* articles.
Chapter 5 — Shipping. Mr Eric Hawkes, Leafe and Hawkes (Chartering) Ltd, Hull.
Chapter 6 — Marine Insurance. Mr A. P. Mayne and Mr E. R. Lawson, Sedgwick Forbes Marine Ltd, London.
Chapter 7 — Timber Contracts. Legal Aspects Mr G. A. Clifton, William Crump and Son, London; Timber Trade Federation of the United Kingdom.
Chapter 11 — Arbitration. Mr H. Gordon Craig, Chairman of the Timber Arbitrators Association.
Chapter 13 — Transport, Handling, Storage and Office Routine. Mr W. J. Hall, Freight Marketing Services, British Rail.
Chapter 15 — Measurements, Calculations and Units of Sale. Mr Victor Serry, Chairman of the BSI Metrication Committee.
Chapter 16 — Grading Rules. Mr Jack A. Baird, The Swedish Finnish Timber Council, Retford; Mr Paavo Miettanen, Finnish Sawmill Owners Association.

Chapter 18 – Home Grown Trade. Mr J. R. Aaron, Forestry Commission.

Chapter 19 – Specialised Branches of the Trade (Stress Grading): Mr H. Gordon Craig.

Chapter 20 – Trade Associations and Authorities. Mr H. J. Bocking, Mr A. J. Garratt and Mr C. K. Norman, Timber Trade Federation of the United Kingdom; The Timber Research and Development Association; The Princes Risborough Laboratory; The British Wood Preserving Association; The Institute of Wood Science.

To all others who have assisted in many ways, our grateful thanks.

List of Tables

List of Figures

1 A Short History of the Timber Trade

The history of the timber trade is as old as the history of commerce. Timber was perhaps the first building material used by man. It is mentioned in Biblical times; the Egyptians were acquainted with the finer techniques of the use of veneers; and the buying and selling of timber in the history of man has been as important as the buying and selling of foodstuffs and clothing.

The British Isles at one time were covered with forests and these provided the material for building dwellings and ships; at the same time the clearance of the forests provided the ground on which food was grown and cattle grazed.

By the seventeenth century a fair amount of timber was already being imported into the country and very substantial quantities came in from Norway to satisfy the rebuilding of London following the Great Fire in 1666. Samuel Pepys in his Diary has recorded the considerable business the Navy placed for Baltic timber. During the seventeenth century substantial quantities of 'Spanish' mahogany were imported (coming from Spanish colonies in the New World) to satisfy the needs of the cabinet makers of the seventeenth and eighteenth centuries.

In the eighteenth century the imported timber trade was fairly well established, with four and six month bills of exchange as an accepted practice in the trade to assist in the financing of it. At the end of the eighteenth century the bulk of the softwood that was imported into the British Isles came from the Baltic, with a very small amount coming from the new North American colonies.

At the start of the nineteenth century an important change occurred. The domination of Napoleon over the European continent closed many of the Baltic ports to British ships and as a result the country turned to North America. Table 1.1 shows not only the increase in timber consumption as an average over the years shown, but also the switch from Baltic suppliers to North America.

Table 1.1

Average per year	Imported from Baltic	Imported from North America
1788–1792	73 132 standards	866 standards
1803–1807	77 392 standards	5 511 standards
1829–1833	40 927 standards	134 227 standards

Until the middle of the nineteenth century the Baltic ports Danzig, Memel and Riga were the principal suppliers of oak to this country, but after the middle of the nineteenth century the countries of Central Europe and also the USA became the main sources of imported oak. The early nineteenth century saw the start of the Industrial Revolution and with it the great expansion of population in the UK and the rapid development of building. The home-grown timber trade was quite unable to cope with the demands upon it and, in fact, imported timber was often cheaper. As the nineteenth century went on, a reversal in the pattern of trade took place. From 1850 to 1875 the value of Swedish exports of timber was raised by a factor of 5. By 1870 Baltic exports to the British Isles had passed the Canadian exports and another 70 years were to pass before the Canadians regained their preeminent position in supplying the UK with timber.

By 1875 the Russian exports of softwood to the United Kingdom were already equal to the exports from Finland. At that time, as on many occasions since, the prices of Russian timber were considerably below those of other Baltic countries. At that time also the structure of the trade that we accept today — agents for foreign principals selling to a limited number of established importers who in their turn had their own inland merchant customers — was firmly established. This trade structure had developed naturally over the years as the most suitable assembly of organisations for handling a complex material such as timber.

At the end of the nineteenth century the first plywood mills were being established in the Baltic, their early outlets being principally for the manufacture of tea chests.

The beginning of the twentieth century saw another important new hardwood source being developed in the form of shipments of oak from Japan.

The nineteenth century and the early part of the twentieth century were periods of great prosperity for the timber trade, with occasional difficult trading times of comparatively short duration.

From the middle of the nineteenth century to the early days of the twentieth century many of the well-known firms in the timber trade were established. A limited number of firms can trace their history back for two centuries but they are comparatively rare.

With the First World War came a rise in the price of timber and a very sharp rise in sea freights. Government control was introduced during that war and government purchasing for its own requirements.

In 1921 there was a very sharp fall in the price of timber following the general trade slump. After this slump, which was of short duration, a period of calm set in until the general depression of the 1930s.

In 1931 the Ottawa Conference was held, at which a 10 per cent duty was introduced for most goods being imported into the UK, and the principle of 'Imperial Preference' was established for goods shipped from and originating in the British Empire.

When the Second World War broke out in 1939, arrangements for the purchase and control of commodities such as timber were far better organised and were put immediately into operation. A 'Timber Control' was established, manned by timber men from the trade. Supplies of timber were no longer available from Russia or the Baltic, so Canada once again became the main supplier, with increasing quantities coming from the West African colonies.

Government import of timber and licensing of its consumption continued for some years after the war, being released slowly.

In 1946 the Government gave some freedom to timber importers by permitting them to bring in new woods from new sources in the world, provided that they did not require the expenditure of hard currency dollars. The enterprise of the trade in this period resulted in many new excellent timbers being imported and marketed in the UK. By 1949 hardwood licensing had been abolished, although the Government still controlled dollar purchases.

By 1951 softwood importers were able to undertake a large measure of their own buying, although they were still restricted by consumer licensing, which was not abolished until 1953. In the same year the plywood trade were allowed to start some measure of their own imports, and by 1954 they were free to import what they required, with the exception of plywood, from hard currency dollar countries (USA and Canada). By 1955 hardwood importers were allowed a restricted quota from the USA and Canada, and in 1959, with the liberalisation of Canadian and American dollars, imports of hardwood, softwood and plywood became freely available from both these countries.

To bring this short history up to date, it is of interest to record that since 1959 the importation of wood products of all types has undergone a considerable change of pattern. Not only have new sources of supply been introduced which have, in the softwood and hardwood trade, meant new species, but also there have been quite wide fluctuations in volume and values. In terms of volume, hardwood has declined, particularly in log imports, whereas particle board has increased in a spectacular manner. Needless to say, values have risen since 1972 to heights never contemplated by the trade. A striking example of this is the fact that in 1974 the softwood import was approximately the same as in 1960 but its average value had increased by more than $3^1/2$ times. The circumstances of these changes are described in greater detail in Chapters 2 and 4, with tables giving statistics.

Since softwood represents the principal import of wood products, the changes in leading sources of supply are shown in Table 1.2. The predominant countries exporting to the UK are shown, with their respective percentages of total import; it will be seen that leadership in volume has changed many times over the years, which illustrates the fluctuations already mentioned.

Figure 1.1 shows the annual average price index based on 1970 on imported wood goods. This has not gone back further than 1968, because prior to that year prices had remained reasonably stable with very slight fluctuations.

Finally, but by no means least, the trade has adopted the metric system of measurement. After some 300 years this change must be regarded as being of the greatest significance. The subject is dealt with in detail in Chapter 15.

It will be seen, therefore, that the timber trade has developed as a result of the natural circumstances of supply and demand, the structure of the trade

Table 1.2 Softwood sources of supply – percentage of total UK import

Country	1960	1961	1962	1963	1964	1965	1966	1967	1968	1969	1970	1971	1972	1973	1974	1975	1976	1977
Canada	17	18	19	20	23	26	22	23	15	10	18	14	10	12	21	12	19	22
USSR	21	21	23	26	25	25	25	23	24	26	22	19	19	18	15	22	22	21
Finland	28	30	27	24	21	19	21	20	21	22	21	23	24	21	20	18	16	17
Sweden	22	19	17	16	16	14	15	21	25	26	23	28	32	33	28	30	24	23
Poland	3	3	5	5	6	6	6	6	6	5	6	5	6	5	3	6	5	4
Portugal	1	2	2	1	2	2	2	2	2	3	4	4	3	4	5	4	5	6
Brazil	2	2	2	2	2	2	3	2	3	2	2	2	2	2	1	2	1	1
Czechoslovakia	2	1	2	2	2	2	2	2	2	2	2	1	1	1	2	3	2	3
Norway	1	1	1	1	1	1	1	1	1	1	1	1	1	3	2	1	2	1

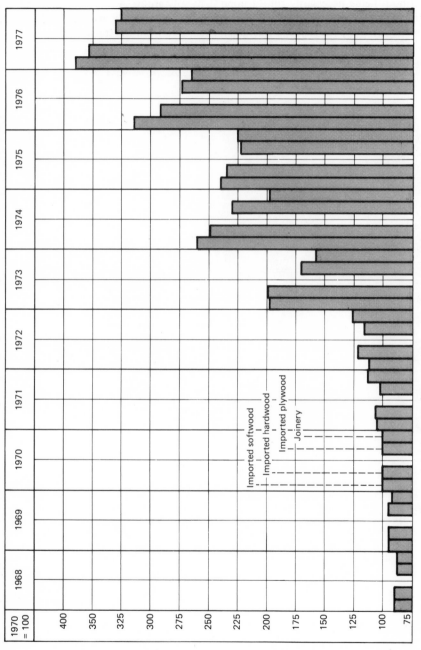

Figure 1.1 Wholesale price index, annual averages. Basis: 1970 = 100

emerging naturally as the most useful to satisfy the conditions of the trade without being necessarily forced upon it by any group. At the same time the timber trade, as many other trades, has been considerably affected by both economic and political consequences far removed from the trade itself. Sometimes these have been for the benefit of the trade, but in many cases they have been to its detriment.

2 Geographical Background

2.1 General

Forests cover a quarter of the earth's land surface, although only a proportion are in positions where it is economical and practical to fell and extract the timber, and for this reason only a fraction of these resources is being utilised. The volume of roundwood being removed from the forests is steadily increasing, owing to the development of industries, improvement in transportation, growth in population and rise in the level of living in most regions. The trees from which we obtain our timber vary considerably in size and quality, depending upon their environment. The many varied conditions of weather, soil, altitude and location each has its effect on the growth of the tree and, hence, on the quality of the timber it produces.

It is fortunate that, unlike most other raw materials, the forests of the world are relatively inexhaustible, provided that trees are harvested as a crop and the forests are properly managed. Of the 8000 million acres of the world's forests, it is estimated that about 3000 million acres are being commercially exploited, which leaves vast areas relatively untouched.

Over 40 000 species of woody plants have been botanically identified, and of these some 10 000 are trees of some commercial importance − at least in their local environment. Obviously, only a minority of these are of commercial importance in terms of world trade, and there are many factors which influence quality of growth and resulting value. Among these are the variations between climatic conditions, the effect of latitude, rainfall, temperature and the effects of mountain ranges, deserts and the Gulf Stream. Moreover, many tree genera are represented by a number of species, which between them have a very wide natural distribution.

It may be desirable to define more clearly what is meant by the description 'softwood' and 'hardwood'. The description is a poor one and has no connection with the density of the wood. It is a broad classification which is commercially understood but gives rise to many anomalies, as some softwoods, such as yew, are hard and some hardwoods, such as balsa, are soft. Softwoods are derived from a class of trees known as conifers (Coniferae), which are cone-bearing, have needle- or scale-like leaves and are usually evergreen. Hardwoods, on the other hand, come from a class of trees which bear broad leaves − that is a definite flat surface area. These trees are more highly developed plants than the conifers, and whereas species of the latter are numbered in hundreds, there are many thousands of species of broad-leaved trees. In temperate climates such trees are usually deciduous, but there are evergreen hardwoods.

SOFTWOODS (Conifers)

Softwoods are found principally in a broad belt stretching across the North American continent, Scandinavia, Europe, Russia and Siberia.

The coniferous species account for the bulk of the extractions in these regions and in 1959 represented 54 per cent of the world's timber harvest. The commoner softwoods, such as European redwood and whitewood, when grown in different parts of Europe, produce very different grades of timber.

Generally speaking, the farther north a conifer grows the better the timber it will produce, as the rate of growth is slower than in the warmer southern climates. The 'annual rings' are narrower, and the timber is more even in texture and more valuable. It must, however, be borne in mind that altitude may compensate for latitude; also that trees growing in the north may develop different defects from those growing in the south, such as the black knots in North Scandinavian whitewood. For instance, the Scots pine (*Pinus sylvestris*), while but one species to the botanist, may produce any one of five or six commerical timbers to the timber merchant. It might be 'Archangel redwood', 'Leningrad redwood', 'Finnish redwood', 'Swedish redwood', or 'home-grown Scots pine', each of which will be different in quality and have its own value.

Earlier many of the northern ports were completely frozen over during the winter months, which restricted the period each year during which timber could be shipped from these ports. The date when the port was declared open for shipping was known as 'first open water' (f.o.w.). This depended on whether it was a mild or severe winter. Today highly efficient ice-breakers of an entirely new design have changed this long-established pattern and most ports which were hitherto closed are now open throughout the year. Because mills are now less dependent upon air-drying and have changed to kiln-drying, they are able to take advantage of this development and ship their goods all the year round.

HARDWOODS

There are two general categories of hardwoods: Temperate hardwoods, from Europe and North America; tropical hardwoods, from Central and South America, Africa, India, S.E. Asia and Australasia.

Hardwoods of the same species vary greatly according to local conditions of temperature, rainfall, etc., which affect the structure of the wood during growth. It is necessary, therefore, when one studies the timber trade to have a broad geographical background of the various producing and exporting countries.

In most cases timber is graded, named and priced according to the port from which it is shipped. Very often the timber is given the name of the port — for example, as a prefix 'Archangel' redwood, 'Memel' whitewood, 'San Domingo' mahogany, etc. When the timber comes from sawmills some distance inland from a port, it will usually take the name of the district where it was produced — for example, 'Slavonian' beech or 'Appalachian' oak.

At the end of this chapter there are maps which show the principal districts and ports from which the countries listed in the following sections export their wood goods. Statistics are also given to indicate the total volume of imports and the importance of each country in relation to UK imports.

2.2 USSR

Nearly one-third of the world's forest resources are in the USSR. In these northern forests there are large pine trees of slow growth from which is produced redwood of fine texture and close grain and a large proportion of high-quality wood which is especially noticeable in the boards which are cut from the outer part of the log. These high-quality boards have in the past been much sought after and have commanded a very high price, but owing to the fact that the general quality requirements for joinery are not so high as they used to be, there is no longer quite the same demand for expensive boards.

The sapwood of the redwood is close-grained and of an attractive creamy colour. This well-grown wood is much less liable to warp and twist than sappy open-grained wood and is therefore specially suitable for joinery purposes. The finest redwood comes from the Kara Sea, which, owing to ice hindrances, has a very short shipping season, since the loading port, Igarka, lies far up the Yenisei river. The whitewood shipped from the White Sea ports is also of fine quality, that shipped from the Leningrad area is more similar to the south Finnish productions. Exports consist of sawn softwood (redwood and whitewood), poles, pit-props, sleepers and plywood, with a small proportion of planed softwood, mainly to countries other than the UK.

There are vast forest resources in Siberia still largely untouched, and, even with possible over-mature logs, there is great potential expansion for removals. Although the enormous distances to the main consumption areas and the severity of the climate create special problems, these are slowly being overcome by new projects which will help this area to become an increasing source of supply in the future.

In regard to plywood, the Soviet Union is the largest producer — mainly of birch — but with an increasing use of softwood species. Formerly its plywood was all of interior quality but now the production of WBP exterior grade is quickly increasing. Exports are made to all the West European countries.

2.3 Finland

In the years up to 1939 Finland was the largest single exporting country of timber to the UK. The loss of territory to the USSR, including some of the finest forest areas, at the end of the Russo-Finnish war in 1940 reduced the forest resources of Finland, but notwithstanding this reduction it remains one of the largest and most important timber-exporting countries in the world.

There is a great variety of growth, the product of the northern and eastern parts being close-grained, fine-textured wood, much in demand for joinery. The pine trees producing redwood in the north of Finland are not so large as in Russia, so that the dimensions produced are not so wide, but the narrower boards are usually of very fine quality and the wood of a pleasing reddish colour. The whitewood is also close-grained and fine-textured, but that grown in the north usually contains many small black knots. In other parts of Finland the wood is generally more quickly grown and consequently more sappy and open-grained. The so-called 'second-grade' stocks consist almost entirely of this sappier wood, while the better productions, even from the south of Finland, contain a high percentage of close-grained wood quite suitable for joinery.

Exports are principally sawn and planed softwood (redwood and whitewood), poles, pit-props, box-boards, etc., plywood and blockboard, with moderate quantities of hardwood, mainly birch, from the south of Finland.

Finland has a commercial forest area of about 19.7 million ha* and in 1976 produced 5.85 million m³ − of which at least 20 per cent was exported to the UK.

2.4 Sweden

Sweden has always been one of the most important suppliers of timber to the UK, the redwood shipped from the more northerly ports comparing favourably with redwood from the White Sea. There is considerable diversity of growth and manufacture, as the large forest areas of the northern half of Sweden are well cared for and are operated on a large scale, with all of the latest technical improvements in manufacture, etc. In the southern half of the country, while there are some fine forest areas in the interior, there are also coastal areas with a more scattered growth converted in small rotary sawmills and obtainable at a lower price. The best grades of Swedish redwood and whitewood are close-grained, and are of even texture and easy to work. Swedish redwood has always been a favourite of the joiner, and its pinkish colour is distinctive, something between the darker reddish-brown colour of the North Finland wood and the creamy colour of South Finland wood.

Exports consist mainly of sawn and planed softwood (redwood and whitewood), poles, pit-props, box-boards, etc., and plywood.

Since 1968 Sweden has been at the top of the UK import table, the goods coming mainly from South Sweden. The country has a commercial forest area of about 23.5 million ha and in 1976 produced 11.3 million m³ − of which at least 24 per cent was exported to the UK.

2.5 Norway

Norway has not been an important supplier of timber to the UK for many

---

* 1 ha (hectare) = 10 000 m²

years, owing to severe over-exploitation of the forest resources of the country in the nineteenth century. The need for conservation of the Norwegian forests to-day limits very greatly the amount of timber available. The Norwegians make the best of their difficulties by specialising in exports of planed goods and box-boards. They even import timber for the purpose of machining and exporting it. Other exports include telegraph, ladder and scaffold poles.

Norway has a commercial forest area of about 6.5 million ha and in 1976 produced 2.15 million m³ − of which about 2 per cent was exported to the UK. This figure has remained steady for many years, except for 1973, when it increased to 3 per cent. It is interesting to note that the annual consumption per capita is 0.9 m³, which is greater than that in the UK.

2.6 Lower Baltic States

This description covers Poland and the areas that up to 1940 were Estonia, Latvia and Lithuania. The redwood from these areas is generally more open-grained and resinous than that from more northerly areas. Although less suitable for joinery, it is often preferred for general constructional purposes, as it is cheaper than the higher grades from other countries. The lower grades of whitewood in the past have provided much of the cheaper carcassing timber for houses as well as case-making and box-making timber.

Poland has a commercial forest area of about 8.5 million ha and in 1976 produced 7.1 million m³ − of which 5 per cent was exported to the UK. This figure has remained constant since 1962, except for 1974, when it dropped to 3 per cent. The annual consumption of the country is about 0.7 m³ per capita.

2.7 Other European Countries

Yugoslavia, Czechoslovakia, Romania, Austria and Germany all provide soft-woods and some hardwoods, which are usually shipped from Rotterdam, Hamburg, Gdynia and Stettin, having been brought across Europe by rail or barge. There are large forest areas in and around Yugoslavia, Austria and Czechoslovakia producing whitewood which is well manufactured and generally of larger sizes than the North European wood. The wood itself is more brittle than the northern wood and often contains a brown streak which gives it an unhealthy appearance. It is a very useful wood for many purposes and is competitive in price with Scandinavian and Baltic timber.

The principal hardwoods produced in central Europe are beech and oak. Only the better qualities are exported, and these are known as Austrian oak, Slavonian beech, etc., depending upon the area from which they come. A pre-war feature of this trade was the export of high-grade billets, from which the centre plank of the log, containing the heart, was retained and not ex-ported. Quantities of beech are exported from both Denmark and Italy.

In 1950 French hardwoods occupied a dominant position in UK hardwood imports, providing nearly a third of the total hardwood import in a year which surpassed all previous records of hardwood imports.

Much of this was caused through currency restrictions which curtailed purchases from 'hard currency' areas, principally the USA and Canada, but openly permitted purchases from sterling currency areas.

In recent years the export has declined and in 1976 it was only 5 per cent of the total UK import and only 50 per cent of the volume of 1973.

Softwood has also been exported from France, principally the Landes pine or Maritime pine, grown in the Landes district and shipped from Bordeaux. This is a poor timber compared with other European pine and is produced in short lengths and comparatively small sizes. The standing tree, *Pinus pinaster*, produces turpentine, and the wood is hard and resinous. However, it is inexpensive and there has been a considerable demand for it in the UK for the packing-case industry.

A limited amount of softwood has been exported from Corsica.

2.8 Canada

As will be seen in Table 1.2, the volume of lumber exported from Canada to the UK has fluctuated quite considerably. Since the war years and de-restriction of timber control, the annual import has varied between 10 per cent and 26 per cent — the latter in 1965. In 1977 it was 22 per cent.

Although, in the past, freight rates have been higher from Canada than from Scandinavia, the position has changed somewhat, owing to the fact that the introduction of bulk carriers and packaging or rationalisation have made costs competitive. Additionally, one should bear in mind the abolition of Imperial Preference or freedom of import duty since the introduction of EEC tariffs which impose no duty on sawn softwood.

The commercial forest volume is immense, some 19 000 million m³ with an area of 310 million ha. Much of this has been inaccessible in the past, but modern methods of communication and transportation are now opening up areas which have not been exploited before. Canada has a very high home consumption, and the 1976 annual figure per capita was 5.8 m³.

EAST COAST

Eastern Canadian forests produce primarily three commercial softwood species or species grouping: the spruce/pine/fir group; white pine; and red pine.

The species group spruce/pine/fir covers softwood occurring throughout eastern Canada on varying degrees of latitude. The group may include white spruce (*Picea glauca*), red spruce (*Picea rubens*), black spruce (*Picea mariana*), jack pine (*Pinus banksiana*) and balsam fir (*Abies balsamea*).

White pine (*Pinus strobus*) is known in the UK as Quebec yellow pine or Ottawa pine and is used a great deal for pattern-making on account of its even texture and ease of working. Red pine (*Pinus resinosa*) is commonly marketed as a separate species and not in combination with white pine.

The most common import from the east coast Maritime Provinces is *Picea glauca* — known as eastern Canadian spruce, western white spruce, Quebec spruce and Maritime spruce. It may be rotary- or band-sawn, the latter being a superior product, as rotary-sawn lumber is sometimes very uneven. The best qualities are usually regarded as being shipped from Nova Scotia.

Eastern Canada contains more than 142 million ha of commercial forests suitable for harvesting on a sustained yield basis. The region has approximately 1000 sawmills, which produce about 12 million m³ per annum. Most of the larger mills have kiln-drying facilities, and about 75 per cent of the production is marketed in a planed (surface) condition — lumber which is uniform in thickness and width. Needless to say, the majority of these mills are small, and do not export but supply local needs.

WEST COAST

The largest and formerly most important Canadian tree was the Douglas fir (*Pseudotsuga taxifolia*), exported from the west coast through Vancouver and other British Columbian ports. In addition to the normal dimensions of lumber, the Douglas fir provides the exceptionally large dimensions up to 600 mm x 600 mm and the great lengths that are required for heavy constructional work and are unobtainable elsewhere. Since many of the more accessible stands of this species were logged in earlier days, Pacific coast hemlock (*Tsuga heterophylla*) and Western white spruce (*Picea glauca*) have now assumed greater importance. In addition, clear grades are obtainable in Western red cedar (*Thuya plicata*) and occasionally in Sitka spruce (*Picea sitchensis*). That is to say, they are available as straight-grained and virtually free from knots. These grades command higher prices than the best European softwoods, as they are only obtainable from this area. Other softwoods from the west coast are Western white pine (*Pinus monticula*) or Idaho which is very similar to *Pinus strobus* and *Picea sitchensis*, all being fine-textured, long-fibred and very strong for their weight. They used to produce large dimensions of high-quality wood and provided Aero grades required for aircraft construction but they now find an outlet for piano sounding-boards. Production from the interior of British Columbia — principally Western white spruce with a small volume of lodgepole pine and Alpine fir — now exceeds the volume of the coastal mills.

Plywood is manufactured on a large scale in British Columbia from Douglas fir but increasingly from hemlock and Western white spruce. The Pacific Lumber Inspection Bureau published in 1951 a set of Grading Rules called the 'R List' which was adopted by the lumber associations in both the west coast and the USA and is still in use today for export of many items to world markets.

In more recent years rationalisation has resulted in National Grading Rules being established in the USA with visual stress grades included, and these have been incorporated into virtually all the Grading Rules published by the various bodies in both Canada and the USA, including National Lumber Grading Association (NLGA), West Coast Lumber Inspection Bureau (WCLIB), Southern Pine Inspection Bureau (SPIB), Quebec Lumber Inspection Bureau (QLIB), etc. The basis of the stress grading paragraphs in the National Grading Rules is to establish visual grades which allow stress ratings to be established for each size and grade. (See chapter 16.)

2.9 USA

For many years the traditional exports from the USA had been pitch pine and hardwoods. Pitch pine export had declined to almost nothing by 1960, when the best long-leaf and short-leaf forest stands became exhausted. Substantial new forests established first by natural regeneration and also since the last war years by extensive planned replanting have re-created a substantial new source of Southern yellow pine (*Pinus palustris*), with new sawmills providing kiln-dried, planed material principally for the USA market in smaller sizes, but they are likely to play an increasing part in the overall pattern of world supply and demand.

In regard to hardwoods, economic restrictions in the post-war years forced the UK to seek new sources of supply, but relaxation of dollar expenditure in 1958 renewed this market. However, it cannot be said to have regained its former position in respect of volume. The hardwood lumber industry of the USA is one of the most highly productive organisations in the world, with very high standards of selection, grading and marketing. There are over 30 species of hardwood being exported from the country, but by far the most important is oak, which is sold as white or red, according to species. Other important species are ash, gum, walnut, hickory and poplar. The mills producing hardwoods are grouped in two areas — mainly north and south. Oak, beech and ash from the north, particularly the Appalachians, is better-grown and more valuable than southern productions.

The commercial forest area is slightly smaller than that in Canada, but in 1976 the volume of industrial roundwood harvested was greater — more than double. The reason for this is not clear, since the annual consumption figure per capita was only 1.5 m^3.

In regard to plywood production, the real growth has been confined to the Southern States, where Southern yellow pine constitutes the raw material. This plywood has proved to be an acceptable alternative to Douglas fir within the States and its further expansion into overseas markets would appear to be inevitable.

2.10 Central and South America

This vast continent, which is often referred to as Latin America in forestry publications, has immense areas of tropical hardwoods, much of which are unexploited owing to communication and transportation difficulties and the great distances between the source of raw material, processing plants and loading ports. Brazil is South America's largest country and occupies nearly half of the continent. Of this area, nearly half is taken up by the mighty Amazon Basin in the north and west, with its many tributaries. The vegetation in this area is more luxuriant than anywhere else on earth, and, in terms of forest wealth, production and exports, Brazil is of principal importance.

As far as the UK is concerned, the softwood which has always been the most significant import is Parana pine (*Araucaria angustifolia*). In 1968 the import was over 283 000 m³ but has gradually declined until in 1976 it was only 95 000 m³. This is not because its popularity has faded, since it is an outstanding softwood obtainable in large dimensions – especially boards – with grades practically free from all defects, including knots. The reason for the decline in availability is that former vast natural forests in the southern states of Brazil have become depleted and replaced with plantations of imported species which reach maturity in a remarkably short time. The trend is now towards providing fast-growing raw material for the rapidly developing industry producing pulp, paper, particle board and allied products. The principal species are *Pinus caribaea* and a hardwood, *Gmelina arborea*, which has a long fibre and is suitable for pulping.

It is calculated by the FAO that no less than 67 per cent of the world's total forests are hardwoods and that Latin America as a whole has over 25 per cent of them. New developments giving enormous advantages over traditional methods are narrowing the enormous gulf which has hitherto prevented the opening up of untouched virgin forests. A typical example of this is the new Trans-American highway, which is providing greater access to Amazonia.

In past years, the exports from Central and South American countries principally consisted of the various mahoganies, with a small quantity of other tropical exotic or unusual species. In recent years the pattern has changed and as will be seen in table 2.2, the UK import from this area has increased considerably. The following timbers are now popular: American mahogany (known by a variety of names, mainly prefixed by the country of origin – British Honduras, Costa Rica, Nicaraguan, Panama, etc.), *Swietenia macrophylla*, which is perhaps the best known; South or Central American cedar (Cedro, Peruvian, Brazilian, Honduras, Nicaraguan, etc.) *Cedrela* spp.; virola, *Dialyanthera* spp.; guatambu (Pau Marfim), *Balfourodendron riedelianum*; tatajuba (similar to iroko), *Chlorophora tinctoria*; andiroba (Brazilian, Para, British Guiana mahogany), *Carapa guianensis*; imbuia (Brazilian walnut), *Phoebe porosia*; sucupira (black), *Bowdichia nitida*; cordia (laurels), *Cordia trichoioma*; freijo, *Cordia goeldiana*; rosewood (jacaranda), *Dalbergia nigra*; Ipe peroba rosa (red peroba), *Aspidosperma* spp.; greenheart, *Ocotea rodiaei*; purpleheart, *Peltogyne* spp.; *balsa, Ochroma* spp.

Not only has the production of hardwoods increased in recent years; but also other allied industries have expanded. Large pulp mills are under construction with schedules up to 1980 and other projects to follow with government encouragement for a massive export pulp capacity. One of the widely ranging projects is a pulp mill built in Japan on two large rafts. These were towed across two oceans to the mouth of the Amazon and up its tributary the Jari River, where it is anchored in a nest of piles. This is a classic example of new techniques to overcome communication and transportation difficulties by converting fast-growing raw material *in situ*, with advantage being taken of the already existing transportation facilities. In addition, the production of allied commodities such as paper and panel products is rapidly developing and there is no doubt that supply will exceed domestic demand, so providing considerable extension of export potential.

Plywood and blockboard is manufactured principally in the Parana region, close to the Parana pine growing area. Owing to increasing shortages of peeler logs for veneers, some mills are producing plywood and blockboard of 'Folhoza' — a vernacular name for several mixed hardwood species which have been found suitable for peeling.

2.11 The African Continent

The African continent has vast supplies of tropical hardwoods that have not yet been exploited. During the last few years the political and economic situation in so many countries in the continent has changed very considerably. so affecting and, in fact, completely altering the pattern of the timber industry. Countries such as Nigeria and Ghana have reduced their exports of logs and sawn hardwoods, whereas others such as Ivory Coast, Liberia and Cameroon have increased production and exports. There are a number of reasons for this. To take Nigeria as an example, with a population now exceeding 76 million and new-found wealth from oil, the domestic timber requirements are greater than production and even have to be supplemented by imports of many different wood products. Ghana, which was formerly a principal supplier of West African hardwoods, has suffered from a high rate of inflation which is mainly due to the increase in price of Middle East oil and the Government's refusal to devalue its currency, which is tied to the US dollar.

All the countries involved have extensive plantation plans, and in 1976 it was reported that 75 000 ha had been reforested. Many problems have yet to be overcome, since some of the best supply areas are so far from ports of loading and transportation development is slow. Zaire is a typical example of the tragic situation of a country incapable of capitalising on its enormous untapped forest wealth following the military action which started in 1977 and which, to date, has virtually stopped all commercial progress. It is stated that the country possesses the largest volume of forest resources in the continent and can be equated with Brazil's potential.

In the past a particular feature of the African trade has always been hardwood logs exported to the UK. In recent years this trade has declined, owing to the fact that economic development and outside financial help has made it more attractive to convert logs at their source. Between 1973 and 1976 the volume dropped 53 per cent and the volume of sawn hardwoods by approximately the same percentage.

An overall appraisal of Africa's forest industries has to take account of four types of situations in which various countries are now found to be: log export; transition from log export to domestic processing (primarily for domestic consumption at the present time); establishment of plantation resources — either to replace depleted natural forest or to create forest resources for the first time; and development of processing capacity to handle new plantation-derived raw materials. To dismiss Africa as a production region because its volume of log exports has diminished is to overlook an intensity and complexity of activity the region has never had before. Its exports of processed products are likely to make a significant impact on world markets very soon.

There are many hundreds of hardwood species grown in Africa, principally in the west. The commercial names of these are rather confusing, since there are sometimes several local names for the same species and one local name may apply to more than one species. For this reason the following popular imports to the UK are given with their botanical names: utile (sipo), *Entandrophragma utile*, afro+mosia (kokrodua), *Afro+mosia elata*, sapele (aboudikro), *Entandrophragma cylindricum*; obeche (wawa), *Triplochiton scleroxylon*; African mahogany (this has many local names, often prefixed by the source — for example, Ghana, Ivory Coast, Takoradi, Lagos, Benin, etc), *Khaya ivorensis*; agba (Nigerian cedar, tola), *Gossweilerodendron balsamiferum*; iroko (African teak, mvule, odum), *Chlorophora excelsa*; makore (baku, douka), *Tieghemella heckelii*; African walnut (this has many local names, often prefixed by the source — for example, Benin, Nigeria, Ghana, etc.), *Lovoa trichilioides*.

As far as softwood is concerned, the Republic of South Africa is possibly the most significant producer. The country is not naturally endowed with indigenous wood of a type required by commerce and industry. During the last century a considerable plantation programme of imported species has been successfully evolved and today ever-increasing volume of softwood satisfies 90 per cent of the country's structural needs and 80 per cent of its paper and packaging requirements. The principal species are those introduced from North and Central America, and *Pinus* spp. is South Africa's most important commercial timber. The plantations are mainly concentrated on the eastern coastal regions, and the predominant species are *Pinus radiata*, *P. taeda*, *P. patula*, *P. pinaster*, *P. elliottii* and *P. canariensis*. Exports have not been significant so far but it is expected that the time is soon coming when home demand will be more than satisfied, with, therefore, a surplus for export. Even in 1977 the UK imported over 20 000 m³, whereas in previous years the volume had hardly been worth recording. When one considers the freight involved and the competition with, say, south Sweden, this is quite an achievement.

2.12 Australasia

It is difficult to differentiate between 'Australasia' and 'Oceania', which is the term used by the very informative publication *World Wood*, and 'Asia/Pacific', used by the UKTTF *Year Book of Statistics*. For this reason, the most important countries involved in business with the UK are mentioned separately. As with all the countries within the area, the significant factor is freight.

AUSTRALIA

The forests of Australia are very large and contain a wide variety of excellent softwoods and hardwoods.

The main sources of hardwoods exported to the UK are *Eucalyptus* spp.: jarrah, *E. marginata*; karri, *E. diversicolor*; Tasmanian oak, *E. delegatensis*; Southern blue gum, *E. glodulus*; and saligna gum, *E. saligna,* (also grown in South Africa and elsewhere). Certain species known for their decorative features are Queensland walnut, *Endiandra palmerstonii*; silky oak, *Cardwellia sublimis*; and black bean, *Castanospermum australe.*

Softwoods include Queensland kauri pine, *Agathis* spp., and bunya pine, *Auracaria bidwillii.*

Australia has a commercial forest area of over 22 million ha, and the volume of industrial harvest is in excess of 12 million m^3. The annual average consumption per capita is about 1.25 m^3.

NEW ZEALAND

This country has never been significant in exports to the UK, even though it exports substantial amounts of timber to other countries. The principal softwood grown is radiata pine (*Pinus radiata*), which accounts for almost 95 per cent of the current plantations. It has a commercial forest area of about 1.5 million ha, and the volume of industrial harvest is in excess of 8 million m^3. After the domestic timber market has been satisfied, a very high percentage of the resources are converted for pulp and paper together with panel products such as plywood, particle-board and fibre-board.

PAPUA NEW GUINEA

This island is one of the largest in the area and is rapidly developing its considerable forest resources. It has some 40 million ha of forest, of which half is accessible at the present time. The species involved are similar to those of Indonesia, and exports have so far been mainly to Japan and Australia – the former taking about 60 per cent of the total. Many new projects sponsored by international forest interests are in hand, and it can be expected that the country's contribution to world trade will be significant in the future. This involves not only timber, but also pulp and paper, together with plywood and other panel products.

2.13 South-East Asia and the Pacific

This massive area is now the most important supplier of tropical hardwoods and wood products to the UK and elsewhere. It is impossible adequately to cover under this heading all the countries contained in the area, and only those of real significance in terms of production and export are mentioned. These countries are as follows: Burma, Taiwan, India, Indonesia, Korea, Malaysia, the Philippines and Thailand. In recent years not only have sources of hardwood in log or sawn form increased very considerably, but also some of the countries have developed the production of panel products – particularly plywood – to a degree which was unthought of in the past. UK imports of plywood and blockboard from this area have quadrupled between the years 1969 and 1976, whereas, for the same period, hardwood volume remained fairly stable except for 1973, which was a boom year in all sections of the industry. However, despite the fact that volume has not changed very much, the pattern has changed in that sources of supply have declined from some countries and increased from others.

The principal species of hardwood produced in this area are as follows:

Teak (*Tectona grandis*)	Burma, Thailand and India
Shorea spp.	
meranti – light and dark red, yellow and white	Malaysia (including Sarawak and Sabah), Brunei, Indonesia
seraya – light and dark red and yellow	as above
lauan – red and white (also known as Philippine mahogany)	Philippines
Dipterocarpus spp.	
keruing, gurjun, yang and apitong	Malaysia, Indonesia, Thailand, Burma and Philippines
Leguminosae spp.	
sepitir, (*Pseudosindora palustris*)	Sarawak
Apocynaceae spp.	
jelutong, (*Dyera costulata*)	Malaysia and Indonesia
ramin, (*Gonystylus macrophyllum*)	Malaysia (including Sarawak)

In regard to plywood and blockboard, some of the manufacturing countries mentioned above have become dependent upon Indonesia for the supply of logs. This applies to Malaysia, where, owing to severe cutting of standing trees for peeler logs in excess of regeneration, importation is necessary. Korea, being situated in higher latitudes than many countries in S.E. Asia, has no indigenous species for plywood and imports every log from Indonesia and the Philippines. Already there is some anxiety about the future of their raw material, as, not unnaturally, those few countries with abundant supplies of logs are in a strong position to dictate terms.

2.14 Japan

Considering the size of the islands, the overall population and industrial development, it is surprising that this country has such a large commercial forest area — over 9 million ha. The 1976 production of sawn timber was in excess of 34 million m³, and so great have been the needs for domestic consumption that exports have been less than imports. Traditionally, the UK has always been a major importer of Japanese oak, and in the years 1975 and 1976 Japan accounted for half the UK's oak import. Nevertheless, the UK import of hardwood from Japan was halved in total between the years 1973

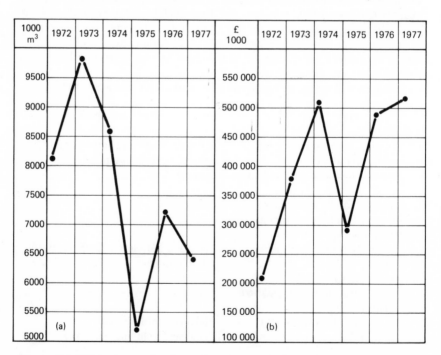

Figure 2.1 UK imports of softwood — sawn and planed: (a) volume; (b) c.i.f. value

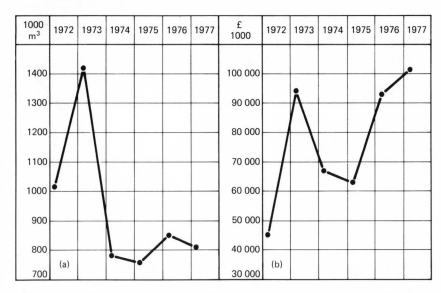

Figure 2.2 UK imports of hardwood — lumber and logs: (a) volume; (b) c.i.f. value

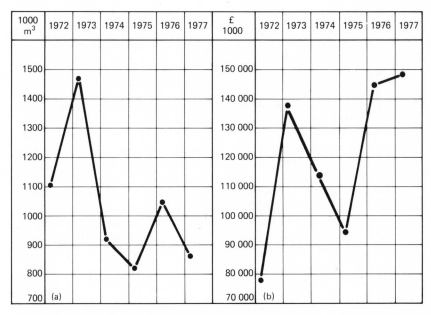

Figure 2.3 UK imports of plywood (blockboard, etc.): (a) volume; (b) c.i.f. value

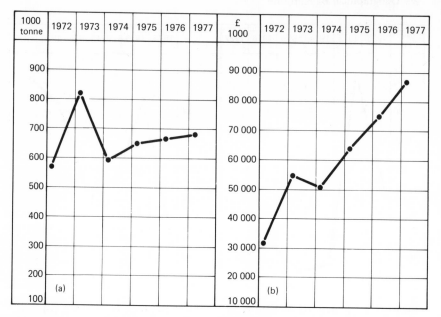

Figure 2.4 UK imports of particle board (flaxboard, etc.): (a) volume; (b) c.i.f. value

and 1976, and in the same period the import of plywood and blockboard decreased even more, dropping to about 22 per cent of the 1973 figure.

2.15 Statistics

Figures 2.1—2.4 illustrate in graph form UK imports during the period 1972—1977. Softwood imports by countries of consignment are shown in table 2.1. It had been hoped to provide similar tables for hardwood but it proved impossible to include them all, as there are over 50 countries involved; tables 2.2—2.5 list areas of consignment and tables 2.6—2.11, for panel products, list the principal countries.

All the data in these tables have been obtained from publications issued by the UKTTF. These are available to the trade and are, indeed, the only reliable source of information which is circulated to all members in monthly bulletins and a *Year Book of Timber Statistics* which covers all wood products. Permission to use this information is gratefully acknowledged.

2.16 Shipping Ports

Figures 2.5—2.12 show the principal ports from which the UK imports are shipped.

Table 2.1. UK Imports (1000 m³) of Softwood – Sawn and Planed: Countries of Consignment

Country	1969	1970	1971	1972	1973	1974	1975	1976	1977
Canada	815.6	1463.0	1099	810.8	1217.4	1761.1	617.7	1367.9	1401.0
Soviet Union	2029.1	1725.6	1567.8	1578.2	1806.1	1288.2	1159.8	1599.1	1316.3
Finland	1708.3	1666.4	1892.2	2009.5	2027.8	1744.7	947.1	1172.6	1084.5
Sweden	2064.7	1873.3	2296.1	2617.8	3193.8	2397.2	1547.9	1749.3	1479.2
Norway	77.9	56.7	67.0	75.6	276.9	199.5	77.4	114.2	55.1
Poland	429.0	489.0	391.3	461.2	458.0	271.5	327.2	385.8	250.7
E. Germany	35.3	40.3	35.1	34.6	40.6	32.9	33.6	47.9	42.8
W. Germany	18.6	11.5	4.5	14.6	32.6	43.5	10.3	40.9	27.6
France	6.4	8.1	3.2	1.8	8.2	10.8	2.1	0.5	0.4
Austria	1.1	–	0.2	0.1	4.2	6.5	1.0	12.3	6.8
Czechoslovakia	164.9	129.1	127.5	116.3	99.6	156.7	144.9	142.5	163.2
Yugoslavia	1.1	0.5	0.1	–	3.6	–	–	–	–
Romania	0.2	0.2	–	–	–	1.5	–	–	–
Portugal	219.5	281.3	290.6	274.2	373.9	436.8	206.7	326.9	369.9
USA	30.0	57.7	46.9	40.1	80.4	65.3	45.6	102.1	55.9
Brazil	167.2	149.8	187.5	186.9	177.4	78.8	79.5	94.6	68.5
Other countries	40.0	55.1	79.7	21.2	14.9	34.6	14.6	24.3	58.5
TOTAL	7808.9	8007.7	8088.7	8242.9	9815.5	8529.7	5215.4	7181.2	6380.2

Table 2.2. UK Imports (1000 m³) of Hardwood Timber: Areas of Consignment

Area	1969	1970	1971	1972	1973	1974	1975	1976	1977
Europe and USSR	243.6	233.9	235.8	252.8	263.1	194.0	165.7	165.8	183.4
Asia and Pacific	237.6	282.1	245.2	265.4	485.9	197.5	223.6	274.1	274.3
Africa	237.3	228.7	195.7	207.5	244.8	135.7	127.7	133.6	98.5
North America	40.8	46.9	56.6	40.0	45.4	47.8	39.3	27.0	30.7
Central and South America	11.3	11.9	12.0	20.5	40.1	31.7	24.8	40.3	46.7

Table 2.3. UK Imports of Hardwood Timber: c.i.f. Value (£1000)

Area	1969	1970	1971	1972	1973	1974	1975	1976	1977
Europe and USSR	6916.1	7053.5	7910.3	9456.8	14 186.9	14 941.7	13 018.6	16 024.1	20 968.0
Asia and Pacific	8998.5	11 103.5	10 358.2	11 905.9	34 231.0	18 290.1	19 465.9	30 892.8	33 956.2
Africa	9593.4	10 317.4	8154.8	9897.3	19 710.6	13 965.9	11 727.2	18 199.2	16 560.1
North America	2443.7	3322.2	4317.7	3110.3	4070.9	5955.7	4988.2	4109.1	4789.1
Central and South America	652.4	650.2	563.9	928.1	2513.7	2865.3	2498.6	5751.6	7465.6

Table 2.4. UK Imports (1000 m³) of Hardwood Logs: Areas of Consignment

Area	1969	1970	1971	1972	1973	1974	1975	1976	1977
Europe and USSR	21.8	19.0	17.1	27.7	41.9	24.2	26.2	32.9	18.6
Asia and Pacific	8.7	6.6	6.9	5.4	7.0	4.1	4.4	9.2	10.9
Africa	253.5	187.4	226.2	239.4	285.6	137.8	128.7	150.7	136.1
North America	4.8	2.0	1.3	0.9	1.0	3.5	4.4	4.9	3.9
Central and South America	2.2	3.4	2.8	4.0	5.1	2.2	2.5	2.3	5.3

Table 2.5. UK Imports of Hardwood Logs: c.i.f. Value (£1000)

Area	1969	1970	1971	1972	1973	1974	1975	1976	1977
Europe and USSR	575.5	625.0	524.1	817.9	2017.2	1195.1	1585.8	2386.6	1641.6
Asia and Pacific	721.7	548.3	665.4	518.3	874.8	750.2	490.2	1258.3	2014.1
Africa	7554.1	6034.1	6232.8	7767.2	16 413.3	8791.7	8488.7	14 231.7	14 639.9
North America	128.9	109.4	78.8	69.7	74.5	196.4	210.9	349.7	281.2
Central and South America	83.0	156.7	130.2	139.7	267.2	137.1	218.5	219.9	644.5

**Table 2.6. UK Imports (1000 m³) of Plywood (Blockboard, etc.)
Countries of Consignment**

Country	1972	1973	1974	1975	1976	1977
Canada	211.9	280.2	213.6	182.0	161.4	187.3
Finland	305.9	315.5	170.4	133.2	156.8	99.7
Malaysia	111.4	162.2	55.5	67.9	93.3	67.8
Singapore	61.6	150.2	56.7	95.8	106.7	83.4
Soviet Union	87.1	118.6	104.3	61.1	67.0	95.4
USA	28.8	44.6	64.4	78.9	150.3	53.5
Korea (Rep.)	5.1	10.2	10.3	17.2	85.0	96.7
Taiwan	14.3	42.1	45.4	26.3	32.6	35.9
Philippines	6.8	12.6	21.7	11.8	27.4	19.9
Sweden	23.1	34.9	12.2	14.5	12.9	6.6
Romania	19.8	18.6	9.4	12.5	12.5	13.0
Brazil	16.8	23.9	11.3	13.3	24.8	13.8
Poland	4.2	9.5	7.0	13.2	20.8	20.8
Others	215.6	246.9	136.1	94.3	95.3	74.0
Total	1112.4	1470.0	918.3	823.0	1046.8	867.8

**Table 2.7. UK Imports (£1000) of Plywood (Blockboard, etc.): Countries of
Consignment**

Country	1972	1973	1974	1975	1976	1977
Canada	13 948	23 532	20 680	17 874	19 413	25 600
Finland	22 509	29 555	25 737	19 355	27 105	23 359
Malaysia	7027	16 207	7361	7464	12 531	10 977
Singapore	3960	16 005	7826	11 329	16 196	15 865
Soviet Union	5387	8311	11 083	6290	6729	11 158
USA	1557	3362	4871	6708	15 915	6565
Korea (Rep.)	481	1317	1310	2078	11 818	17 613
Taiwan	1281	5271	6279	3363	6439	8001
Philippines	439	1267	2841	1298	3734	3520
Sweden	1260	2534	1153	1359	1558	981

Table 2.7. continued

Country	1972	1973	1974	1975	1976	1977
Romania	1031	1331	1063	1004	1233	1687
Brazil	1039	1888	1246	1457	3131	2112
Poland	257	734	809	1175	2267	2716
Others	18 214	27 612	21 617	13 961	18 082	16 942
Total	78 390	138 926	113 876	94 715	146 151	147 096

Table 2.8. UK Imports (1000 m³) of Particle Board (Wood, Flax and Other): Countries of Consignment

Country	1972	1973	1974	1975	1976	1977
Finland	225.0	358.7	218.2	147.1	140.5	106.3
Belgium	132.3	217.6	207.8	310.1	276.9	258.7
Sweden	80.0	126.8	114.0	117.2	130.0	115.6
Norway	81.5	111.4	60.5	49.8	65.9	39.5
Canada	87.5	102.7	93.4	2.3	15.9	4.6
Austria	47.9	87.0	54.8	87.0	65.6	63.4
Romania	55.4	55.6	29.6	55.7	29.3	24.5
Irish Rep.	48.0	40.0	35.4	26.9	45.8	48.8
Portugal	44.8	33.4	12.3	15.3	21.9	16.5
Poland	15.6	23.6	10.0	14.4	15.8	12.9
West Germany	8.5	18.3	28.5	47.4	77.6	83.5
Netherlands	11.5	14.6	20.9	36.7	28.3	34.2
Spain	9.8	14.0	4.0	6.2	20.5	82.6
Denmark	15.1	13.9	15.5	32.0	20.5	12.5
France	1.3	8.1	13.2	18.9	20.5	48.4
Switzerland	1.1	0.8	1.9	29.3	45.4	50.6
Others	21.2	25.4	8.1	6.9	10.7	50.0
Total	886.5	1251.9	928.1	1003.2	1031.1	1052.6

Table 2.9. UK Imports (£1000) of Particle Board (Wood, Flax and Others): Countries of Consignment

Country	1972	1973	1974	1975	1976	1977
Finland	7558.1	14 039.6	11 906.6	9606.5	9472.1	8756.8
Belgium	3360.7	6862.8	8461.8	14 344.8	17 165.7	18 827.7
Sweden	2814.0	5725.0	6355.7	7512.7	9066.5	11 213.8
Norway	3644.7	5753.6	4035.3	3028.8	4045.4	3062.5
Canada	2100.5	3317.2	3563.1	150.7	1204.1	504.9
Austria	3749.0	8782.0	6429.3	10 296.1	8177.5	9364.6
Romania	1289.6	1478.1	1052.9	2033.3	1179.1	1249.7
Irish Rep.	1889.7	1883.9	1911.3	1676.8	3012.6	3705.9
Portugal	1449.4	1253.2	688.1	853.3	1169.8	1208.4
Poland	320.8	567.6	321.6	478.1	546.5	555.0
West Germany	615.5	1461.1	2225.8	3789.2	7291.4	9616.6
Netherlands	610.1	1160.2	1779.6	3727.3	3496.4	4158.6
Spain	237.4	397.3	154.6	309.7	1184.3	4475.6
Denmark	511.5	567.1	828.6	1768.1	1344.9	984.4
France	47.3	528.8	1001.9	1640.4	2000.1	4326.2
Switzerland	59.6	46.9	132.9	1954.7	3847.7	4704.1
Others	665.5	1093.7	414.1	438.4	731.3	607.4
Total	30 923.4	54 918.1	51 263.2	63 608.9	74 935.4	87 322.2

Table 2.10. UK Imports (1000 tonnes) of all Fibre Building Boards: Countries of Consignment

Country	1972	1973	1974	1975	1976	1977
Sweden	136.2	155.7	121.2	83.3	93.5	66.7
Finland	52.6	63.2	44.3	37.4	30.3	24.7
Poland	15.0	33.0	24.2	23.2	29.1	25.6
South Africa	20.6	32.4	27.1	12.7	19.5	8.9
Norway	18.9	26.2	29.2	21.6	18.9	9.8
Belgium	–	–	0.2	4.2	15.2	11.8
Irish Rep.	14.2	13.1	9.8	7.0	11.7	7.2
Brazil	0.7	1.5	2.5	8.3	10.5	11.9

Table 2.10. continued

Country	1972	1973	1974	1975	1976	1977
Netherlands	0.8	0.7	1.1	7.3	9.0	9.4
Portugal	9.2	9.4	5.9	12.5	8.7	6.4
Romania	6.1	0.4	1.1	4.4	7.0	5.3
France	3.4	4.1	5.3	2.8	4.7	4.9
Spain	—	—	0.4	0.4	4.2	9.6
Soviet Union	0.1	3.0	3.9	1.1	3.2	5.1
Czechoslovakia	1.7	1.3	1.3	1.8	2.0	4.9
Others	9.1	9.9	6.3	4.5	3.8	13.1
Total	288.6	353.9	283.8	232.5	277.1	225.3

Table 2.11. UK Imports (£1000) of all Fibre Building Boards: Countries of Consignment

Country	1972	1973	1974	1975	1976	1977
Sweden	7695.4	11 351.1	11 127.9	9588.8	12 130.0	10 115.5
Finland	2866.2	4308.0	4281.6	4501.0	4278.7	3963.1
Poland	580.4	1513.4	1616.1	1716.9	2462.4	2708.3
South Africa	891.4	1626.7	1820.1	972.2	1726.9	961.3
Norway	1411.8	2025.8	3055.3	2664.2	2834.2	1954.6
Belgium	—	—	24.9	426.7	1592.3	1331.4
Irish Rep.	703.3	837.4	917.3	689.6	1256.1	1038.6
Brazil	37.5	135.6	274.2	843.1	1432.5	1864.6
Netherlands	102.7	118.9	166.9	926.0	1441.9	1592.6
Portugal	413.5	552.4	441.0	1026.2	795.3	818.0
Romania	174.1	21.3	77.1	273.3	449.5	414.1
France	200.6	312.9	428.9	275.1	568.3	760.3
Spain	—	—	37.3	27.8	321.4	850.2
Soviet Union	5.4	132.8	257.3	67.6	246.5	507.3
Czechoslovakia	62.5	65.8	94.8	143.5	196.4	488.1
Others	734.7	1036.0	292.2	770.9	1630.1	2512.2
Total	15 879.5	24 038.1	25 632.2	24 912.9	33 362.5	31 880.2

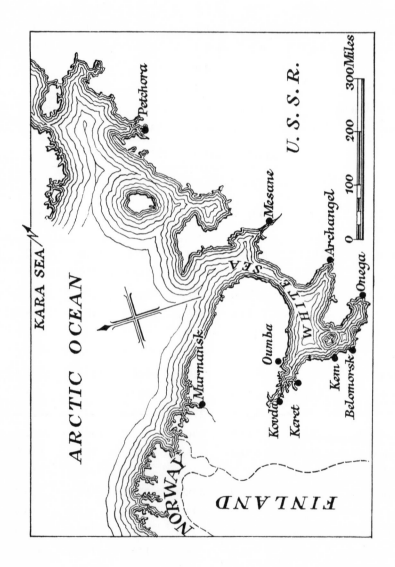

Figure 2.5 Map of White Sea ports

Figure 2.6 Map of Finnish ports (the Finnish–Swedish frontier is the river between Haparanda and Tornio)

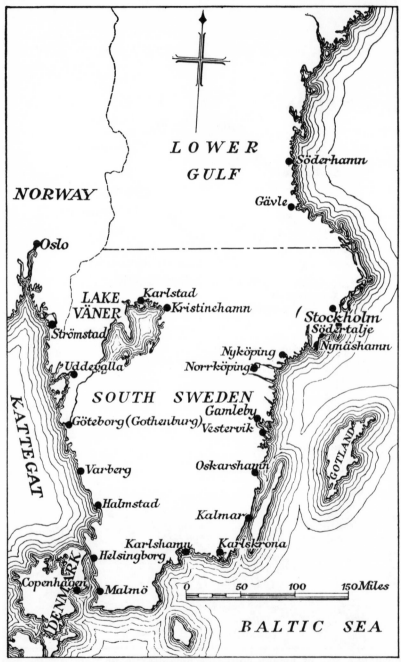

Figure 2.7 Map of south Swedish ports

Figure 2.8 Map of Sweden — Upper, Middle and Lower Gulf ports

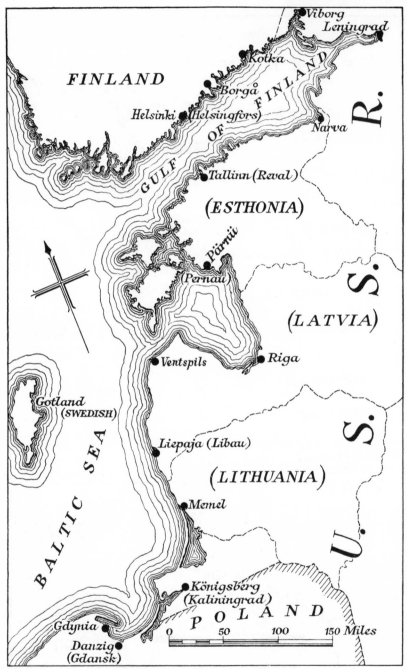

Figure 2.9 Map of Lower Baltic ports

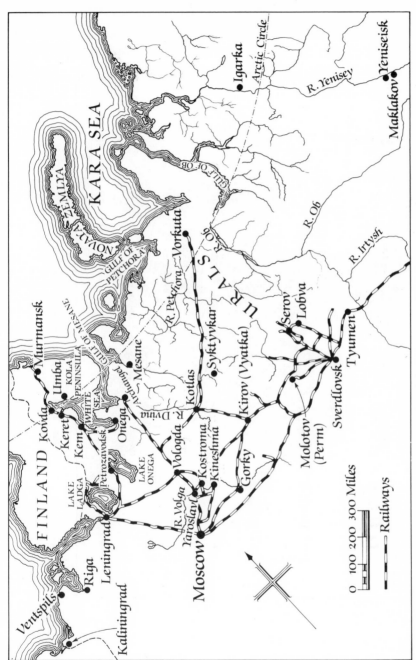

Figure 2.10 Map of USSR ports

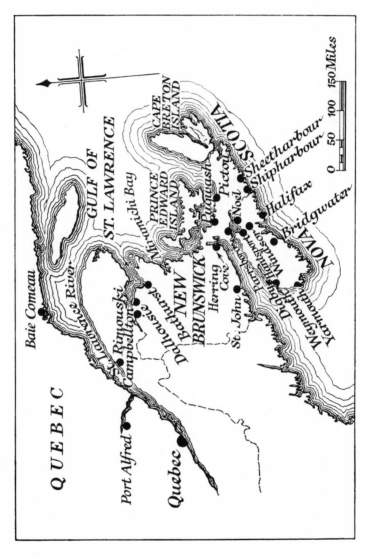

Figure 2.11 Map of east coast ports of Canada

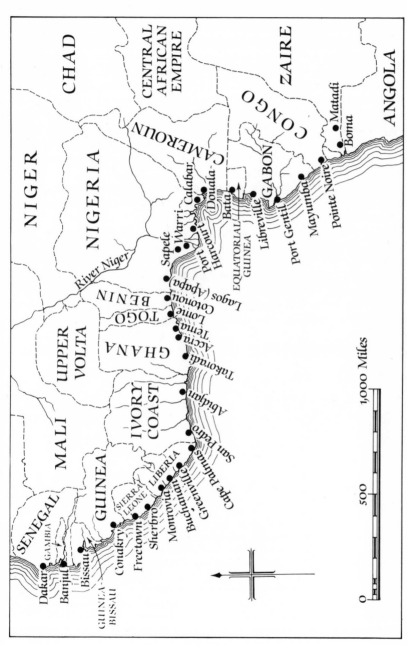

Figure 2.12 Map of West African ports

2.17 Importing Ports

To complete the geographical background, the various ports in the UK through which timber is imported must be considered. All the major ports and many minor ports are used for importing timber, but the class of trade varies in each. Liverpool has always been a great hardwood port, with its natural trade and shipping routes to America and Africa, and in conjunction with Manchester and Preston it has been one of the principal ports for Eastern Canadian spruce.

The major trade through Hull and the east coast ports has always been from Scandinavia. The freight rates from Scandinavia to Hull are very much cheaper than from Scandinavia to Liverpool or Manchester, since the journey is much shorter. On the other hand, the west coast ports enjoy advantageous freight rates with Canada and the USA.

The dock facilities and trade practice at each port vary quite a lot, but a regular feature of the trade for the east and south coasts is the arrangement of cargoes for 'small ports' to be carried in 'small ships'.

With different labour rates, dock dues and other charges, there are considerable differences between one port and another in the cost of importing timber.

Table 2.12 gives the names of the Port Authorities at each major port in the UK and table 2.13 the percentage of wood goods imported through each port in 1970–1977. The total amount imported through any particular port during one year varies with the total amount imported into the UK. However, these figures will suffice to show the relative importance to the timber trade of the various major UK ports.

Table 2.12. Major UK Ports of Entry for Wood Goods, with Port Authorities

London	Port of London Authority
WEST COAST	
Liverpool	Mersey Docks and Harbour Company
Garston	British Transport Docks Board
Manchester	Manchester Ship Canal Company
Preston	Port of Preston Authority
EAST COAST	
Hull	British Transport Docks Board
Grimsby	British Transport Docks Board
Tyneside	Port Authority for the River Tyne
Hartlepool	Tees and Hartlepool Port Authority
Yarmouth	Great Yarmouth Port and Haven Commissioners
Boston	Port of Boston Authority
King's Lynn	King's Lynn Conservancy Board
Felixstowe	Felixstowe Dock and Railway Company
Scarborough	Scarborough Borough Council
Gunness	British Transport Docks Board
Whitby	Scarborough Borough Council

Table 2.12. continued

London	Port of London Authority

BRISTOL CHANNEL

Bristol	Port of Bristol Authority
Avonmouth	Port of Bristol Authority
Cardiff	British Transport Docks Board
Gloucester	British Waterways Board
Sharpness	British Waterways Board
Swansea	British Transport Docks Board
Newport	British Transport Docks Board

SOUTH COAST

Southampton	British Transport Docks Board
Plymouth	British Transport Docks Board
Portsmouth	Portsmouth City Council
Poole	Poole Habour Commissioners
Shoreham	Shoreham Port Authority

SCOTLAND

Glasgow	Clyde Port Authority
Clydebank	Clyde Port Authority
Leith	Forth Port Authority
Grangemouth	Forth Port Authority
Aberdeen	Aberdeen Harbour Board
Dundee	Dundee Port Authority

N.IRELAND

Belfast	Belfast Harbour Commission

Table 2.13. Percentage of UK Imports by Ports of Entry

	1970	1972	1973	1974	1975	1976	1977
SOFTWOOD (all classes)							
London	23	21.5	21	19	22	23	25
Scotland	8	8	8	7	10	9	7
N.Humber	5	6	6	6	5	4	5
Humber	14	17	17	16	17	15	15
Grimsby and Immingham	6	5	5	5	6	4	4
E.Anglia	8	9	9	9	9	9	8
Kent	2	2	2	3	3	3	3

Table 2.13. continued

	1970	1972	1973	1974	1975	1976	1977
S.Coast	6	7	7	7	6	8	7
Hants and Dorset	3	3	3	3	3	2	2
W.Counties	2	3	2	2	2	2	2
Bristol Channel	7	8	10	13	7	10	11
Liverpool	9	4	5	4	5	5	5
Manchester	4	3.5	3	3	3	3	2
N.Ireland	3	3	2	3	2	3	4
UK Total	100	100	100	100	100	100	100

HARDWOOD (all classes except logs)

	1970	1972	1973	1974	1975	1976	1977
London	45	44	37	35	34	33	27
Scotland	6	6	8	7	6.5	3	2
N.Humber	2	1.5	3	2	2	3	2
Humber	10	8.5	9	8	7	6	6
Grimsby and Immingham	0.5	1	1	2	1	1	1
E.Anglia	2	3	3	6	7	5	6
Kent	1	2	1	2	2	2	3
S.Coast	3	4	4	4	6	8	9
Hants and Dorset	1	1	1.5	2	2	1.5	3
W.Counties	—	—	0.5	1	0.5	0.5	0
Bristol Channel	6	8	19	16	19	17	18
Liverpool	18.5	16	9	9	9	15	18
Manchester	3	3	2	3	2	2	2
N.Ireland	2	2	2	3	2	3	3
UK total	100	100	100	100	100	100	100

PLYWOOD, BLOCK-
BOARD, ETC.

	1970	1972	1973	1974	1975	1976	1977
London	53	50	43	44	51	50	47
Scotland	5	7	9	6	5	5	3
N.Humber	2	2	1	3	3	4	4

Table 2.13. continued

	1970	1972	1973	1974	1975	1976	1977
Humber	10	10.5	13	13	9	7	6
Grimsby and Immingham	—	0.5	1	0.5	1	0.5	1
E.Anglia	2	3	3	6	4	3	3
Kent	2	3	5	4	5	5	4
S.Coast	2	2	1	0.5	1	2	1
Hants and Dorset	1	3	7	5	13	11	11
W.Counties	1	—	—	—	—	—	—
Bristol Channel	3	4	7	6	3	4	13
Liverpool	14	10	6	8	2	6	4
Manchester	3	3	3	3	2	0.5	1
N.Ireland	2	2	1	1	1	2	2
UK total	100	100	100	100	100	100	100

PARTICLE BOARD

	1970	1972	1973	1974	1975	1976	1977
London	26	23	14	11	12	12	11
Scotland	4	3	3	3	1	2	1
N.Humber	1	3	2	3	3.5	4	4
Humber	7	8	10	9	11	12	11
Grimsby and Immingham	7	6	11	10	10	9	7
E.Anglia	13	16	16	14	18	19	16
Kent	22	18	24	31	37	31	34
S.Coast	1	2	1	0.5	0.5	2	3
Hants and Dorset	1	—	—	0.5	2	4	6
W.Counties	1	1	1	—	—	—	2
Bristol Channel	5	12	10	12	1	1	1
Liverpool	3	—	1	1	1	2.5	3
Manchester	8	7	6	4	2	0.5	0
N.Ireland	1	1	1	1	1	1	1
UK total	100	100	100	100	100	100	100

3 The Imported Timber Trade

3.1 Structure of the Trade

GENERAL

The timber trade must surely be one of the most intricate of trades, dealing as it does with hundreds of species of timber, each of which can be supplied in three variable dimensions of thickness, width and length. Timber is not a homogeneous product like woodpulp or steel, and it requires an elaborate system of shippers, agents, importers, merchants and brokers to arrange its transport and distribution.

As a matter of essential convenience, the trade is divided into a number of sections — softwoods, hardwoods, plywood, fibre-board and other panel products, home-grown, etc. Many commercial enterprises may produce or trade in several or all of these products. Apart from the purely commercial aspect of selling and buying, these sections are represented by trade organisations whose functions are to protect, promote and develop common interests, to support research and development and to provide publicity. (See Chapter 20.) Since there are many hundreds of species commercially involved in world trade, all of which vary in quality from piece to piece, and a very wide range of sizes, it is not surprising that a complex organisation is required to effect transfer from the forest to the ultimate consumer, who may well be on the other side of the world. Each country has its own custom of the trade, but, in general terms, the pattern is the same, with only minor changes to suit specific local requirements. The structure given in the following pages has existed for more than a century, and that in itself is some proof of its efficiency in satisfying all the needs of the various sections of the trade.

The three main classes of trader are the overseas principal, known as the shipper; the shipper's agent, who is normally resident in the importing country; and the importer, who is normally the first owner of the goods. The importer may sell direct to the consumer or to a fourth class of trader, the non-importing merchant, who, in turn, sells to the consumer.

In recent years there have been a number of changes in this traditional structure. Overseas shippers have formed their own sales organisations in the importing countries, and importers have made direct contact with shippers and negotiated for their requirements — thus eliminating the need for the services of the agent. Agents have extended their services by operating import terminals and providing direct delivery to the importer or even his customer. Without exception, these developments have been inspired by economics, and only time will tell whether they can be coupled with greater efficiency. It is too early to say whether the advantages of selling by this method outweigh those obtained by operating by the well-tried and traditional way through an agent.

THE SHIPPER

The shipper is the man who ships the timber from the sawmills. He may have forests of his own, or he may purchase his logs from landowners or from State forests, take them to his sawmill and convert them into sawn goods for shipment. In the African hardwood trade he may ship the logs to the UK without further conversion. Timber is a product of Nature, not a man-made article of guaranteed size, shape and quality. The economic conversion of logs to sawn goods results in a large number of sizes of deals, battens and boards, depending upon the diameter of the tree. Each of the sizes of deals, etc., produced will require grading for quality according to the number of defects in it. As a result of the conversion of trees of one species the shipper may therefore, have a mixture of sizes varying from, say, 22 mm x 75 mm up to, say, 100 mm x 275 mm in two or three qualities. Certain sizes after many years have come to be the sizes of choice because of most constant demand. These sizes are the centrepiece of stocknotes covering all the sizes produced, and they are used as an attraction to the buyer to take the less popular sizes.

The shipper aims to sell his complete output, not merely the choice sizes that are in greatest demand, and therefore appoints agents in the UK, and perhaps elsewhere, to find buyers for his production. Alternatively, he may offer goods through his own selling organisation.

THE AGENT

The agent acts for the shipper, usually under the authority of an agency agreement. In the course of his business he is well acquainted with the importers who are his customers, as well as the shipper who is his principal. This creates a two-way confidence between the shipper and the importer which is not always possible in the other systems of selling. The shipper knows that the agent will only make contracts with reputable importers of some standing. The importers know that the agents would not accept a contract of agency without having first ensured that the principal is a reliable shipper.

The agent works on a small selling commission, and for an additional commission he may become a 'del credere' agent, when he will guarantee to the shipper the solvency of the buyer under certain circumstances. The agent may be a man working on his own, or he may be a large firm of great wealth with a network of overseas connections. The agent fulfils a vital role in arranging finance for his shipper at times when his resources are stretched, thus enabling him to cover his log requirements, which can involve very heavy outlays of cash.

The agent may also finance the importer by arranging to grant him credit, usually over a period of 4 months. This is of particular importance when prices are high — in fact, without the credit facilities granted by an agent many importers in times of high prices would find themselves unable to finance their purchases.

The term 'agent' is used here, as in the timber trade generally, to describe the selling agent in the UK for a foreign shipper. There are also agents in foreign countries, particularly Finland, who act as selling agents for the smaller sawmills. For the purpose of considering the structure of the trade these may be regarded as shippers.

THE IMPORTER

The importer normally buys from the shipper through an agent or his direct-selling organisation. He will buy a general specification covering a number of sizes and qualities which the shipper produces. The price will depend not only on current market conditions, but also on the proportion of choice sizes and qualities in the specification offered. His contracts for the goods will be made in most cases without his having seen the goods he is buying. He relies, there-fore, upon an accurate description of the goods in his contract and upon his confidence in the shipper built up over a period and his trust in the agent.

Contracts for wood goods are sometimes placed many months ahead, and the importer may buy from, say, Scandinavia at the end of one year for shipment at f.o.w. (first open water), which means as soon as the ice clears from the port in question, enabling shipping to load and leave without risk or damage. At one time virtually no goods were shipped from the more northerly ports during the coldest months of winter. Nowadays, when most productions are kiln-dried and more powerful ice-breakers are in use, mills are able to keep up supplies during most of the year. This tends to give a more evenly spaced import to the UK and elsewhere, which is a major advantage to all involved.

THE MERCHANT

The importer sells to the merchant. In practice the importer is often a merchant himself as well. The merchant has a stock yard of his own, or he may use a Public Storage Yard operated by a Port Authority or Docks Executive. He buys in smaller quantities from the importer, who may resell one shipment of timber among several merchants. From his yard he sells specific sizes and qualities to the consumer. Not all sales are quite as simple as this, for the importer may resell his timber to another importer while it is on the high seas, or the merchant importer may sell timber to large consumers direct from the quay, thus avoiding additional labour and storage charges.

THE CONSUMER

Almost every factory at some time or other in the course of its operations requires wood goods of some size or quality. In addition to the well-known users such as builders, furniture manufacturers, joinery manufacturers, etc., new users of timber are still developing. For example, pallet manufacture, which at one time was a comparatively small industry, has in the last decade grown out of all proportion. Additionally, a new use for timber which has currently developed is the manufacture of laminated container floors, now much in demand owing to the change in transportation methods. By purchasing from various merchants, the consumer can obtain just those sizes and qualities he wants. In his turn, the merchant depends on a wide clientele of customers, each with varied interests and requirements, so that he can sell the whole of his stock.

It will now be seen how essential is this system of shippers, agents, importers, merchants and consumers. If the consumer were to short-circuit this system and buy direct from the shipper, he would have to take a more general specification of sizes and qualities, including those which he did not really want. Consumers do sometimes buy direct from shippers, but unless they use really large quantities of a range of sizes (e.g. large joinery manufacturers), more often than not they find themselves in trouble. Having bought their requirements from importers or merchants for so long, they expect to receive the same treatment from the shipper, which, of course, is not possible. This is particularly evident when the question of a claim arises. When dealing with a merchant, they have been accustomed to telephoning and asking him to collect and replace anything containing the slightest defect; more often than not, the merchant does so in order to maintain goodwill and not lose a valued customer. When dealing direct with a shipper, such procedure is quite impossible, and the consumer feels aggrieved at being saddled with a parcel which is useless to him with his very limited requirements.

THE BROKER

The broker is often an agent as well, but this is not invariable. For a small commission he finds buyers for stocks belonging to an importer or merchant which they have difficulty in selling. In the same manner he will find sellers of special sizes or stocks that a merchant or importer requires and cannot easily find himself. Both these functions are carried out without any great financial outlay, and are made possible by the broker's day-to-day connections with the principal importers and merchants.

Some brokers sell both hardwood and softwood by auction publicly. This has always been a great feature of the mahogany trade, where logs are rarely sold by description but are usually landed and sold by auction, which the buyer, importer or merchant can inspect the logs before bidding or purchase.

CONSIGNMENTS

Although not exactly a proper part of the structure of the trade, the question of 'consignments' may best be dealt with here.

The normal structure of the trade outlined above applies to the great majority of the transactions that are made. There are some cases, however, when shippers find their goods difficult to sell, possibly owing to some market having failed them, and perhaps have their yards overstocked or want to clear sizes for which there is little or no demand, where the shipper ships the goods without having an order for them. These are then said to be shipped 'on consignment', and the agents and brokers have to do their best to sell them while they are still on passage and find storage accommodation for them if unsold.

In recent years some agents have set up permanent storage facilities at arrival ports and arrange regular shipments of unsold goods, which they sell in small quantities as and where they can. This method of trading is most usually done with Canadian goods, where bulk carriers bring several thousand cubic metres at a time.

3.2 Grading and Shippers' Marks

SHIPPING MARKS

All imported timber and panel products are graded for quality. The grading rules for softwood, hardwood and panel products differ greatly from country to country, with the exception that all grading is based primarily on the number of defects present. The higher grades of sawn goods that are practically free from wane, knots, shakes, heartcentre, etc., command higher prices.

The grading of timber is of great importance to the trade and is the basis of all sales. With the exception of the consumer buying timber from the merchant, all purchasers of timber will buy it on description only, without an opportunity to inspect the timber beforehand.

After it has been graded for quality, it is usual for the timber or plywood to be marked or branded with the *shipper's mark*. For sawn softwoods and hardwoods this is usually done on the end of the deal, board or plank by different colours of paint and a stencil. Plywood shippers' marks are stamped on to one face, or may be in the form of a small gummed label.

Shippers' marks are in the nature of trade marks, and each shipper will have a selection of marks covering the qualities of timber or panel products he produces. Each mark will consist of a series of letters, figures or other symbols, such as crowns, stars, crosses, etc.

A reference book, *Shipping Marks on Timber*, is published by Benn Publications Ltd. This is most comprehensive, and gives the marks of world shippers of softwood and hardwood, plywood and other panel products. It shows their normal shipping ports, production — both volume and qualities — and their selling agents. Also, there is a glossary of trade terms and maps of ports and loading places. With the publisher's permission examples from this book are reproduced in figures 3.1 and 3.2.

FINLAND

European Shippers and Their Marks

Name of Shipper	Description	Average Annual Production in m³	Unsorted	IV	V	VI	Sawfalling	Stress-graded G.S./S.S.
Ukkola O/Y., Ukkola								
Ukkola Mill	Sawn and	70,000	M ♔ W	...	MWW	...	...	
Ship from Hamina or Kotka	planed and finger-jointed							
Hyrynsalmi Mill	Sawn	16,000	♔ MW ♔	...	M * W	...	...	
Ship from Toppila								
Valtion Polttoainekeskus	Sawn	100,000						
(VAPO), Jyväskylä								
Hankasalmi Sawmill	...	...	♔ VAPO ♔ and	...	* VAPO *	...	VAPO	VH▮GS
			♔VAPO♔					VH▮SS
Mikkeli Sawmill	...	...	VA ♔ PO	...	VA * PO	...	VAPO	...
Siuro Sawmill	...	...	VA ♔ PO	...	VA * PO	...	VAPO	...
Röykkä Sawmill	...	...	VA ♔ PO	...	VA * PO	...	VAPO	...
Autioniemi Sawmill	...	...	★ VAPO ★	...	· VAPO ·	...	VAPO	...
Rahkee Sawmill	...	...	★ VAPO ★	...	· VAPO ·	...	VAPO	...
Peuravuono Sawmill	...	...	★ VAPO ★	...	· VAPO ·	...	VAPO	...
Tuomilahti Sawmill	...	...	★ VAPO ★	...	· VAPO ·	...	VAPO	...
Veitsiluoto Osakeyhtiö								
Sales Office, Veitsiluoto								
Veitsiluoto Sawmill	Sawn	140,000	FENNIA ♔	...	FENN	F — N	...	FS ▯ GS
Ship at Veitsiluoto Quay						FNNA		FS ▯ SS
Kevätniemi Sawmill, Lieksa	Sawn	90,000	SUOMI ♔	...	SUOMI	S * I	...	SF ▯ GS
Ship at Veitsiluoto Quay, Kotka and Hamina						S = I		SF ▯ SS
Vepsäläinen, Puutavaraliike Eero,	...	...	E ♔ V	...	E × V	...	...	
Eero, Varkaus								
Verksalon Saha, Alpua	Redwood	600/800	VE ♔ SA	...	VE — SA	Mixed		
Ship from Rahja and Toppila	and whitewood					VE * SA	...	
Vienti-Export Ltd., O/Y., Turku	Sawn	10/12,000	VEL	...	V — L	...	...	
Ship at Turku	and planed							
Vierumäen Teollisuus O/Y.,	Sawn	60,000	♔ KOLLI ♔	...	* KOLLI *	...	♔ KOLLI *	...
Vierumäki								
Ship from Walkom, Hamina, Kotka, Sörnäinen								
Virsunen, Puutavaraliike A.,	...	...	A ♔ V	...	A × V	...	...	
Tohmajärvi			or		or			
			TT		AV			
Visuvesi Oy., Visuvesi	Sawn	15,000	E ♔ L	...	E — L	...	...	
Ship at Mäntyluoto, Kotka and Helsinki								
Vuotunki Oy, Kuusamo	Sawn,	...	KU ♔ HA	...	KU — HA	...	KU · HA	...
Ship from Toppila, Kotka, Hamina, Mäntyluoto	planed							
Yhtneet Paperitehtaat Osake-								
yhtiö,								
Ship from all South and South-West Finnish ports								
Olkkolan Saha	Sawn	110,000	Y ♔ P	...	Y — P	YP	...	...
Nurmisen Saha	Sawn	30,000	Y ♔ P	...	Y — P	YP	...	...
Vihavuoden Saha	Sawn	25,000	VEL	...	V — L	VL	...	...
Loimaan Saha	Sawn	15,000	VEL	...	V — L	VL	...	...
Kettulan Saha	Sawn	65,000	♔ MK ♔	...,	M — K	MIKKO	...	...
Teuron Saha	Sawn	40,000	♔ MK ♔	...	M — K	MIKKO	...	...

Figure 3.1 Reproduction from *Shipping Marks on Timber* — softwood

With this book a timber merchant can identify any stock that he inspects. The marks are quoted in contracts, sale notes, invoices and specifications, and become part of a description of the timber.

The discriminating buyer of timber soon learns that certain marks of timber represent a higher quality than others. These marks enjoy the prestige accorded to a trade mark for any goods that have been established on quality.

MALAYSIA

Countries Outside Europe—Shippers and Marks

Name of Shipper	Description	Average Annual Production in m³	Marks	Quality
Federal Timber Trading Co., Kuala Lumpur Ship from Port Kelang and Singapore	Hardwood and softwood including wagon planks sleepers	...	FTT End marks: Brown/green	All qualities
Federated Kilning and Exporting Sdn. Bhd., Kuala Lumpur	All commercial species of Malaysian timber, rough sawn, kiln dried, chemically treated, machine processed (dressed timber), knock down furniture and housing components	35,400		Sawn timber end markings yellow/brown Mouldings Grapestakes (chemical treated)
Fidvi Corporation Sdn. Berhad, Kuala Lumpur Ship to Basrah, Cardiff, Newport, Tilbury, Amsterdam, Rotterdam, Grangemouth, Kuwait	Keruing sawn timber, keruing railway sleepers and crossings, dark red meranti—fullsawn, jelutong L.T.N.D.—fullsawn	...	FIDVI Red/white/blue ends	...
Finewood Export Agencies Sdn. Bhd., Kuala Lumpur Ship from Port Kelang	Malaysian species generally, sawn lumber	...	FEA Purple/red/brown	...
Finewood Products Corporation Sdn. Bhd., Kuala Lumpur Ship from Port Kelang	Mouldings and machined	4,000 tons	FINEWOOD	High quality
Furniland Timber Industries Sdn. Bhd., Selangor Ship from all ports	Sawn timber of all species, e.g. D.R.M., L.R.M., nyatoh, keruing, kempas, etc.	8,000	F.T.I. End mark Green/white/red	...
Genagco Sendirian Berhad, Pahang and Kuala Lumpur Ship from Port Kuantan and Port Kelang	Malaysian sawn timbers, shipping dry and kiln dry, and railway sleepers	28,317	GENAGCO and G.A.C. Brown/blue/green	All grades
General Sawmills (M.) Sdn. Bhd., Petaling Jaya Ship from Penang, Port Kuantan, Port Kelang and Singapore	Hardwoods sawn, kiln dried or Celcure pressure impregnated, railway sleepers	100,000 tons of 50 cu. ft.	GSM Brown/black end	All grades under Malayan Grading Rules
M/S General Timber Processing Co. (M) Sdn. Bhd., Selangor Ship from Port Kelang, Penang, Singapore, Kuantan	Mouldings	14,000	GTR MALAYSIA	...
M/S General Trading Corporation (M.), Sdn., Bhd., Petaling Jaya Ship at Port Kelang, Penang, Singapore, Kuantan	Hardwoods	150,000	GTC White/Blue end	All grades under Malayan Grading Rules
Golden Harvest Sdn. Berhad, Selangor Ship from Port Kelang	Sawn timber, all species	20,000	...	...
Gomez, J. M. & Co., Malacca	...	...	GOMEZ/MALACCA Ends painted Black/blue/purple	All grades as per Malayan Grading Rules
M/S Good Harvest Sdn. Bhd., Kuala Lumpur Ship to Antwerp, Rotterdam, Le Havre, Cardiff, Newport, Grangemouth, Amsterdam, Leghorn	Full sawn timber—dark red meranti, light red meranti, sepetir, merbau	2,119	GH	...

Figure 3.2 Reproduction from *Shipping Marks on Timber* — **hardwood**

GRADING – NORTH EUROPEAN COUNTRIES

Softwood from Russia, Finland, Sweden, Poland and the Baltic States is graded as follows:

I, first	IV, fourth
II, second	V, fifth
III, third	VI, sixth, *utskott* or *wrack* (not Russia)

Finnish and Swedish mills normally mix first, second, third and fourth grades together and sell these as Unsorted (abbreviated U/S), but Russian Unsorted grade includes only first, second and third grades, Russian fourth grade being similar to the fifth grade of high-class Finnish stocks. Russian fifth grade is equal to good-quality Finnish or Swedish sixth productions.

During the past few years some of the better-quality Finnish and Swedish mills have departed from this long-established system and sell on their marks only. An example of this is for their top-quality mark to contain first, second, third and the better fourths; the next lower mark to contain the lower fourths and better fifths and the lowest quality mark to contain the low-quality fifths and the better sixths.

The commercial grades of North European wood, in order of quality, are as follows:

Russia	Finland	Sweden	
U/S = III and better	U/S = IV and better	U/S = IV and better	the normal grade for joinery and high-class work
IV	V	V	for carcassing timber, constructional work, floorings, etc.
V	VI	VI	low-grade rough carcassing timber, box and packing-case timber: for underground or temporary work or for reconversion

Polish timber follows the Swedish and Finnish grading (U/S = IV and better) and Baltic States timber follows the Russian grading (U/S = III and better).

The rules for grading or bracking of timber are not hard and fast and are not consistent between countries, ports or shippers, and it is here that the knowledge of the geographical background of the trade becomes essential, as this greatly affects the quality and description of the goods. This is dealt with in greater detail in the chapters on Grading.

The experienced buyer appreciates fully the differences between timbers of the same grade such as 'U/S Archangel redwood', 'U/S Swedish redwood' and 'U/S Finnish redwood'. As a general rule, one particular grade of soft-wood will vary from port to port as follows, with the best-quality goods at the top of the list:

(1) Kara Sea
(2) White Sea

(3) Sweden: Gefle and northwards

(4) Finland: north and east   (7) Sweden: south of Gefle
(5) Leningrad   (8) Baltic States and Poland
(6) Finland: south

Usually it is found that Swedish grades are slightly superior to the equivalent Finnish grade (e.g. V Swedish redwood will often be superior to V Finnish redwood from the same latitude, as, although the grading for defects will be the same, the texture of the wood will generally be closer and finer). Generally speaking more wane is permitted in Swedish goods than in Finnish of the same grade.

Torrack is the product of trees which have died standing — it is sold sawfalling, usually at about the same price as sixths.

This list can only be an approximate guide and it must not be assumed from it that Polish timber, for instance, is of particularly poor quality, as this is not the case, Polish whitewood, in particular, being excellent material.

In South Sweden and parts of Finland it has now become popular to sell a sawfalling quality of fifths and better. In this case sixth quality is usually excluded and sold separately. Planed goods from Scandinavia are usually sold as U/S and fourth quality, the fourth quality for all intents and purposes being approximately the same as sawn fifths.

GRADING – CANADA, WEST COAST

Canadian grading rules for timber are much more complicated and explicit than their European counterparts, and are set out in both export and domestic rules, the latter being very detailed.

The most recent classifications are defined in the Standard Grading Rules for Canadian Lumber, first published in 1970 by the National Lumber Grades Authority and known as the NLGA Rules. These were revised in 1973. Hitherto the long-established 'Export R List', published by the Pacific Lumber Inspection Bureau (PLIB) in 1951 and revised in 1956, had covered the classification of all the west coast species — Douglas fir, Western hemlock, Sitka spruce and Western red cedar. The need for rationalisation and the establishment of structural stress grades brought about this revision in 1970. Greater detail is given in chapter 16.

A true comparison with equivalent European grades cannot be given, since the dimensions produced in Canada are often larger and are certainly produced from much larger logs. Also, the Canadian grading is applied with reference to the suitability for use or uses for which the grade was developed. One important difference between Scandinavian and west coast Canadian grading rules is that Scandinavian goods are usually sawn with sufficient overmeasure to hold up to the nominal thickness after normal seasoning, while the Canadian goods are sawn to the nominal thickness and permit not only specified variations in sawing, but also natural shrinkage within specified limits. In spite of this, it may be desirable to give comparative values of the different grades when landed in the UK, if only for historical reasons. They are approximately as follows:

R List.   No. 2 Clear and better   =   Russian I and II
          No. 3 Clear   =   best Swedish
          Selected Merchantable   =   good Scandinavian Unsorted
          No. 1 Merchantable   =   south Swedish
          No. 2 Merchantable   =   Scandinavian fifths
          No. 3 Common   =   Scandinavian sixths

At one time shipper's quality marks for Canadian timber were not so widely used as in the north European countries. To a certain extent, this has changed with the introduction of the NLGA Rules, and identification of grades is now clearer.

GRADING – CANADA, EAST COAST

As will be seen in Chapter 16, there is no longer the wide difference between the grades of east and west coasts of Canada. At one time the eastern Canadian spruce followed the north European pattern of dividing the qualities into Unsorted and fifths. The NLGA Rules mentioned in the previous section now apply to the east coast exports, and the species in the spruce/pine/fir group now conform to these rules. This is why, in Chapter 16, the west and east coast Canadian goods are combined under one heading.

GRADING – USA, SOFTWOODS

As will be seen in chapter 16, the Pacific coast softwoods of the USA follow the species and grades of the NLGA Rules. This is explained in more detail in that chapter, but it must be remembered that there are Southern Pine Inspection Bureau Rules of 1977 (SPIB) which are to all intents and purposes in line with the NLGA Rules.

GRADING – BRAZIL, SOFTWOODS

The grading of Parana pine in Brazil differs from both the Canadian and north European systems. New rules were published in December 1951 detailing defects permitted in the four qualities, broadly speaking as follows:

Firsts may contain slight defects, including some wane on one edge only and small knots on one side only.
Seconds may contain rather more defects, including some wane on both edges, knots on both sides and a few wormholes.

Thirds may contain still greater defects, including some sap-rot on one side. Fourths are the former 'Refugo' or 'Inferiors'.

Prime quality is a combined grade of 80 per cent I and 20 per cent II, and may be guaranteed free from wormholes.

GRADING – HARDWOODS

In the USA there is one set of grading rules, issued by the National Hardwood Lumber Association, that covers all American hardwoods.

The standard grades are:

Firsts	No. 2 Common
Seconds	Sound Wormy
Selects	No. 3A Common
No. 1 Common	No. 3B Common

Firsts and seconds are usually combined as one grade, abbreviated F.A.S. Selects and No. 1 Common may be combined as one grade, and No. 3A and No. 3B Common may be combined as one grade called No. 3 Common.

Canadian hardwoods follow the American grading.

The grading of African hardwoods also follows the NHLA Rules to a certain extent, whereas European hardwoods do not follow any hard and fast rules. The normal export grades of square-edged hardwood are Prime and Selects, while logs are generally classified as Fair Average Quality, sometimes abbreviated F.A.Q. There is no set definition of the grade Prime, but, in general, it is composed of firsts and seconds with a preponderance of firsts. Hardwoods from Malaya and Sarawak are normally shipped in accordance with the Malayan Grading Rules. These are explained in greater detail in chapter 16, together with the British Standard rules for home-grown hardwoods.

GRADING – PLYWOOD

Plywood grading is based upon the method of manufacture and the number of defects on each face of the sheet. The usual symbols adopted to indicate this are: A, B, S, BB, CP, C and WG, the last merely indicating well-glued.

Intermediate grades are indicated by combinations of these symbols, such as B/BB, in which one side of the sheet is B grade and the reverse side is of a lower-quality BB grade.

The grading of plywood varies from shipper to shipper, but no geographical rule can be applied for quality as for softwoods. Finland and the Soviet Union are our main sources of birch plywood, and their grades vary to a certain degree, as explained in more detail in chapter 16. Central Europe provides mainly beech plywood and the Far East provides the widest range of species.

North America — once almost exclusively associated with Douglas fir plywood — has simplified its grading rules to include other coniferous species. These are also explained in detail in Chapter 16.

3.3 Methods of Importing Timber

GENERAL

In importing timber the buyer may purchase it at any one of several stages of its journey from the mill where it was produced to the port where it enters the UK.

The earlier the stage of the journey, the cheaper the timber will be but the greater are the risks undertaken. The method adopted largely depends upon the buyer's experience and judgment.

F.A.S. (FREE ALONGSIDE)

The buyer may contract to purchase timber f.a.s. The shipper will deliver the timber alongside the vessel. The buyer is responsible for chartering the ship to load and carry the goods delivered alongside, and for arranging the insurance of the goods on passage.

F.O.B. (FREE ON BOARD)

The term 'f.o.b.' indicates that the seller has to put the goods contracted for, free of cost to the buyer, on board the vessel the buyer charters to receive and carry them.

The term 'f.o.b.' here differs considerably from its use in exporting goods from the UK. In exporting, say, textiles, f.o.b., the seller or shipper is responsible for the dock labour charges putting the goods 'on board'. In the timber shipping ports of the world there are rarely the same craneage and dock facilities that are found in the big ports of the world, and generally the goods have to be loaded from a lighter, using the ship's tackle.

It is convenient to use the term 'f.o.b.' in the trade, particularly since 'f.a.s.' is a term regularly used in the grading of hardwoods in a different sense altogether — namely a combined grade of firsts and seconds.

In an f.a.s. or f.o.b. contract the buyer is taking the risk of the freight market. His contract may be made in February for shipment in June, and he must anticipate the freight market and decide when and at what rate to charter. In times when freight is difficult to charter the buyer is incurring further risks, since if he cannot find a ship to lift his timber, he still has his contract obligations to discharge and may have to pay for the timber while it is still lying in the shipper's yard.

Note that the TTF 'Uniform' contract, generally referred to as an f.o.b. contract, is in fact partly f.a.s. inasmuch as the seller only has to put the goods free of cost alongside the vessel which the buyer has to provide to load the goods. At one time most contracts were closed on a f.o.b. basis but nowadays nearly all such contracts are closed on a f.a.s. basis.

C.I.F. (COST, INSURANCE, FREIGHT)

The contract price here will include the first cost of the timber (the f.a.s. price), the insurance convering the passage from the shipper's yard or warehouse to the destination in the UK and the freight for that passage.

In general, the c.i.f. price will be a little higher than the f.a.s. price plus insurance and existing freight, as under a c.i.f. contract the shipper undertakes the business of chartering and either charters immediately or takes the risk of what rate he must pay. If the buyer is making a c.i.f. contract in January for goods that are to be shipped in June, the shipper, if he does not charter immediately, will now have to bear (within certain limits) the increase of freight that may occur in the intervening period. It is only natural that in these circumstances the shipper will cover himself for any possible rise in freight at the time of shipment.

A contract is completed, not by the delivery of the timber, but by the delivery of certain essential commodities that represent the timber. These documents are in effect a set of title deeds to the timber, and possession of them is equivalent to ownership of the timber. If the ship and cargo are lost on voyage, the buyer is adequately protected by the insurance policy that has been taken out as a necessary part of the contract.

A c.i.f. contract may be made on a 'freight basis', in which a basic rate of freight is stated in the contract upon which the c.i.f. price has been calculated. Any increase or decrease in the freight rate at the time of chartering is passed on to the buyer, who thereby is put in much the same position as if he had purchased f.a.s. There are, however, advantages in this, since the responsibility for chartering freight space still rests with the seller, and if it is impossible to charter freight, the buyer incurs no liability.

C. & F. (COST AND FREIGHT)

This is a variation of the c.i.f contract, in which the contract price includes cost and freight only, the buyer arranging insurance.

C.I.F. RESALE

Since the timber on passage in a c.i.f contract is represented by negotiable documents, it can be bought and sold merely by transferring the documents.

An importer may buy timber c.i.f from another importer, who, in his turn, will have bought it f.a.s. or c.i.f. from the shipper. In this case he may be making a contract to buy the timber while it is still on passage -- that is to say, only a week or so before it arrives in the UK. The risk here is much smaller and not so much judgement is required, since he is not having to work so far ahead. On the other hand, the timber will be more expensive, since he will be paying a little extra in the way of profit to the other importer who has made the original contract with the shipper.

The remarks only cover the purchase and sale of timber up to the UK port. Methods of purchase and sale of timber after it has arrived in the UK are dealt with in Chapters 13, 14 and 15.

3.4 Supply and Demand

THE SUPPLY

In countries with a large forest area, such as Finland, which is taken here as an example, the export of wood and wood products is one of the main sources of national income. For instance, from 1947 to 1951, taken together, the export of wood, wood goods and wood pulp amounted to almost 70 per cent of the total export. It is therefore of national importance that the forests should be conserved so as to supply as high a yield of suitable logs as possible and that the logs should be used to the best advantage. It is, of course, the aim of all sections of the trade to do their part profitably.

The natural supply of logs on a 'sustained yield' basis can be calculated fairly closely, but the effective supply is a different matter, as it depends on demand. For instance, the forests are variously owned by the State, or communities, companies or private persons, and when demand is strong and prices comparatively high, all these owners are anxious to sell and the effective supply is stimulated; but when demand weakens and prices fall, the forest owners, if they are not particularly in need of money, prefer to leave their logs standing in the forest, where they increase in volume, while awaiting an improvement in market value. The matter, however, is not so simple as this in practice, as shippers who are sawmillers and have to purchase logs must often do so a year or two before the sawn product comes on the market, since felling, floating, ponding, sawing and seasoning may occupy many months, during which market prices may rise or fall very considerably.

THE DEMAND

Assuming that the shipper has bought his logs, he then has to decide how to convert them, and in this he will be guided by his estimate of which markets are likely to show the strongest demand and his experience of the particular sizes which those markets normally require. For instance, the UK usually wants a preponderance of batten sizes, while the Continent requires a good proportion of narrow boards, and so on. But all the time he is limited by what his logs can produce economically. He knows that technically, logs of a certain diameter give the best yield when cut to certain sizes, and if he is to depart from that, he must get a better price to compensate for the waste in conversion. For this reason, if for no other, it is advantageous for shippers to make sales of sawn goods in the autumn as soon as they know what the bulk of their log supply consists of, and they can cut during the winter as nearly as possible to buyers' requirements. This is not to say that the sawmills do not operate all the year round, but the new season's logs are usually available for cutting during the winter following that in which they are felled. In estimating market requirements the shipper will consult his agents in various countries as to any changes which may have taken place in their particular market; for instance, in the UK market there has sometimes been less demand for 63 mm x 175 mm, and more for 100 mm x 175 mm and at one time it was expected that 38 mm x 100 mm would displace 50 mm x 100 mm as a favourite dimension, and so on.

THE STOCKNOTE

Having collected all the information available, the shipper converts his logs on paper to sawn goods and issues his stocknotes showing what he will have available for shipment, properly seasoned, at various shipping dates in the following year. The agent then enters upon his main task of selling by ascertaining what the importers are open to purchase and the price they are willing to pay. In passing, it may be mentioned that the agent does a good deal towards stabilising the market for the benefit of all concerned by declining to submit to shippers any offer which he considers unreasonable.

THE NEGOTIATION

There are three main factors in any negotiation — specification, price and date of shipment, in that order of importance. Unless the importer wants what the shipper can supply, no business can result, but the price may vary according to whether the specification is a difficult one or not. The date of shipment may not always be so very important. As a matter of convenience negotiations are usually based on the f.o.b. price for 175 mm. Unsorted battens, it being understood that anything wider than 175 mm will cost more and narrower something less. These variations from the basis price are usually fairly stable over a period of time, and there is general agreement as to extras for wider widths and for boards and reductions for narrower widths and for fifth quality. Of late years there has been a tendency for wide widths and especially wide boards to cost comparatively more than formerly and the under 175 mm to be hardly anything less. This is probably to be accounted for by the average log dimension having diminished in the course of years, old forests of large trees being replaced by younger growths. The extras for board sizes do not apply to fifths, in which quality all thicknesses are charged alike, and the price only varies with the width, and even then not so much as in Unsorted.

THE IMPORTER'S OFFER

Having obtained an offer from an importer of a reasonable price for a reasonable specification, the agent telexes or telephones it to the shipper for his consideration. If he accepts it, the business is closed and contracts are exchanged; but if he demands a change in the specification or an increase in the price, the matter is still in the negotiation stage and the importer is no longer bound by his offer: he may either accept shippers' counteroffer, or renew his offer, or improve or withdraw it. It is always understood that there are no special conditions attaching to an offer unless they are mentioned when the offer is made. The current Albion, Uniform or other contract conditions will be assumed to apply, including the description of the goods as 'Sellers' usual'; while in such specialities as slating battens, where lengths are shipped 'as falling', one importer may want as many ends as possible to get the advantage of the reduced price and another may want as few as possible because his particular customer has less use for them, in which case shippers would probably make no difficulty about agreeing to a minimum percentage of ends in one case and a maximum percentage in the other.

THE TRANSMISSION OF THE OFFER

While it is the shipper who decides what he will sell and at what price, the agent's task as negotiator is not always an easy one, especially if, on a falling market, he is instructed by his shipper to 'try to get an advance in price of so-and-so, but do not risk losing the business'. Nothing annoys an agent more than to receive from his shipper in reply to an offer a laconic 'decline', or words to that effect. The agent wants to know why, and so does the importer. Is it specification, price or date of shipment that is unacceptable? No agent can serve his principals efficiently unless he has their support, and a bare refusal of an offer, without an explanation, stifles the chance of the negotiation leading to business which an explanation might well bring about. With the wider use of telephone and telex it is now extremely easy for a shipper to keep his agent fully advised of his exact feelings as to price, shipment date, specification, etc., which was not often possible in former times, when the usual method of communication between then was the Zebra Code book.

THE DATE OF SHIPMENT

The date of shipment is that on which the shipper undertakes to have goods of the contract description ready for loading, properly seasoned. In an f.a.s. contract, if the goods are not removed within a fixed period, usually 6 weeks from that date, they have to be paid for as overlying. It is, however, a mistake to suppose that specific goods are allocated to a particular contract in such a way that if one lifts the goods a month later, one may expect them to be a month drier: the shipper is not even obliged to carry the same goods over from one season to the next unless this is specifically agreed. The term 'f.o.w.' is seldom used nowadays in contracts as the shipping date, since it is much more satisfactory to have an actual calendar date. Some ports which used to be closed for weeks or months on end during the winter are now kept open by ice-breakers all the year round.

In a c.i.f. contract the date of shipment will be based upon the same considerations, but if the goods are not shipped within a stated period of the stipulated time (6 weeks in the case of the Albion c.i.f. contract), the buyers have the option of cancelling the contract as far as it concerns those goods.

In the Albion contract there is an obligation on the shippers as sellers to secure freight space 'in due time' in order to effect shipment by the date named in the contract. The shipper must take account of this obligation in arriving at the c.i.f. price at which he is prepared to sell the goods, since his obligation is to ship the goods irrespective of the rate of freight he has to pay (with the exception of increases in freight rate due to war, etc.).

HARDWOOD NEGOTIATION

While much of the above is also true of the shipment of hardwoods, this is generally much more an all-year-round business. Furthermore, the grading, range of lengths, etc., is more closely defined in the respective grading rules, and there is less room for negotiation as to specification.

Although the specification is important, the greater widths and lengths will always command the better price, the fact that hardwood is rarely used in the dimension in which it is imported, as is softwood, but is usually sawn down to smaller sections and sizes, emphasises this difference in specification between hardwood and softwood. In Chapter 16 the grading rules of hardwood based upon this same consideration are compared with the softwood grading rules. The specification of imported squares and other hardwood 'dimension stock' is a rather different matter, being a specialised business of its own.

On the other hand, the date of shipment assumes a greater importance. Practically all hardwood sales are on a c.i.f. basis, with the goods being carried by liners (see Chapter 5) on regular services. Apart from those countries and out-of-the-way places that are badly served with liner services, the shippers can be fairly certain of securing freight space easily and so are in a position to match the dates of shipment on their stocknotes (which are issued the whole year round) with their production.

4 The Softwood Trade

4.1 General

Importing softwood is the largest section of the UK timber trade, in numbers of firms engaged, in volume of timber handled and in overall finance involved. (It accounts for approximately 54 per cent of the value of all timber imports.) The seasonal nature of the trade introduces its own problems, which are not reproduced to the same extent in the hardwood and plywood panel products importing trades. It is useful, therefore, to consider the special problems of the softwood trade.

For many years it has been an undercapitalised trade, but very significant changes in trade structure have helped to create a different situation. Above all, the reduction in the number of small importers, who have been taken over by the large concerns, has been a contributory factor. At the present time the importing trade is largely in the hands of a relatively small number of extremely powerful companies, who have the advantage of available finance and the possibility of buying in bulk at realistic prices. Such companies usually buy their needs under a centralised system and allocate the goods to their various branches, who, in turn, indicate their requirements for their particular area. Furthermore, most importers of softwood have diversified by importing or trading in panel products of all types, plastics and general building materials. In many cases they have extended their marketing down to retail shops selling a multitude of items which appeal to the growing 'do it yourself' demand.

It is difficult to generalise, but there is no doubt that for many years the position has been aggravated by relatively modest profit margins, the high cost of money (that is to say, the high terms of interest on borrowed money) and the penal rates of taxation, which have militated against the building up of adequate reserves. Weakness of prices and associated profit margins could usually be traced to too much softwood immediately competing for a limited market. For a considerable number of years the softwood trade has always been seasonal, but in recent years this factor has been mitigated by the increase — particularly in the Baltic countries — of seasoning by kiln-drying, which has meant that goods could be shipped at a much earlier date after sawing than in the days of air-drying. Additionally, as mentioned earlier, many ports which closed owing to ice in the winter months are now open all year round since the introduction of superior ice-breakers. Thus, the long-established term 'f.o.w.' does not apply to the same extent today. It means the expansion of all-the-year-round shipping from most of the Baltic, which can now compete with shipments from other countries such as Canada.

At one time it was always accepted that approximately one-third of our softwood imports arrived in the first 6 months of the year and two-thirds arrived in the last 6 months. While there is a tendency for this situation to remain, the reasons for it are not so much dictated by former circumstances as by importers' desire to purchase their requirements on a 'little and often' basis, depending upon their customer's demands to ensure that they have adequate stocks towards the end of the year. It is still true to say that stocks at the end of the year are at their highest. The key to the softwood trade, therefore, is to purchase the right quantity, of the right goods, at the right price, for delivery at the right time.

The importer will make his purchases of softwood from his own assessment of his future requirements, which will be based on past experience and estimation of available statistics. In present years the speculative aspect of buying based on intuition and the less essential need to become involved too far ahead has been aided by a clearer interpretation of readily available statistics, which are now published monthly. The TTF circulates a monthly statement of the import situation and an annual *Yearbook* of a very comprehensive nature. HMSO also publish monthly statistics in a publication called *Business Monitor*, which is obtainable from the Stationery Office by subscription. There are five sets of figures the intelligent interpretation of which can help the importer. They are: Arrivals; Contract Balances; New Contracts; Stocks; and Apparent Consumption. Before we examine these headings in greater detail, it is necessary to remark on the quite extraordinary situation which has developed in recent years.

In 1973, for some unexplained reason, the trade was of the opinion that there was a world shortage of softwood. This applied not only to the UK, but also to the Continent. In time of shortage we know that prices will rise, but it is difficult to understand why the trade — not only softwood — came to this conclusion. It was an erroneous conclusion, because there was no shortage of trees in any of the countries from which we imported softwood, but there appeared to be a shortage of supply or reduction in production. In other words, it appears that the crux of the matter was unhealthy competition of conflicting interests between the various enterprises involved. Commercial or economic interests dictate most of the situations of this kind, and forest owners had been slow in harvesting their saw logs for softwood producers until a profitable relationship had been established between the purchase price and value of the finished product. Competition between sawn goods and chips for pulp and panel products contributed, the forest owners asking themselves — quite naturally — whether they should harvest the smaller trees for chips or wait until they qualified for saw logs.

The so-called law of supply and demand is capable of being abused to suit circumstances. In times of true shortages it is accepted that prices rise, and it is reasonable to assume that owing to the high prices now prevailing, there will be a natural inclination to increase production wherever possible. If there is an increase in supply to meet demand, it may be realistic to expect that prices will drop.

It will be seen from figure 2.1 that the volume and value of softwood imports was as follows:

1972	8 243 000 m³	£206 242 000 =		£25.00
1973	9 815 500 m³	£356 053 000 =		£36.00
1974	8 529 700 m³	£508 393 000 =	valued at	£60.00
1975	5 215 400 m³	£288 723 000 =		£55.00 per m³
1976	7 181 200 m³	£484 510 000 =	average	£67.00
1977	6 380 200 m³	£521 611 000 =		£82.00

It is illustrated that between 1972 and 1977 the price of softwood more than trebled, dropping in 1975, when the trade realised the true implications of the situation. This was because, rightly or wrongly, the state of panic buying was recognised and there was no fear of it being ignored. To some extent the situation was understandable, since no importer can exist unless he has stocks to sell, and everyone followed the others' lead.

At this stage it is pertinent to study the Wholesale Price Index, which covers the most important items used in the building and construction industry. If we bear in mind that this industry is the trade's most important customer, taking about 80 per cent of its import, the figures are very significant. It is well known that this industry has not exactly been flourishing for a number of years, with building in both the public and private sector well below estimates. It is difficult for many to establish where the highly priced soft-wood is being consumed, especially since the average dwelling only consumes about 10 m³, of which only 1 m³ is joinery.

Table 4.1 gives the price indices of the most common materials used by the industry. It will be seen that softwood and its allied products are well in the lead as far as price is concerned.

In retrospect, it may be that wood goods can now be accepted as having reached a realistic level and have been undervalued. If one studies the import and price levels for the 20 years prior to 1973, it will be seen that these have fluctuated very moderately. As with other essential raw materials, the prices have remained reasonably static. Perhaps it is unfortunate that the quite unprecedented rise over such a short period of time should have taken place and that it would have been easier to explain if the price had risen yearly by a reasonable amount rather than in one year. However, it should be remembered that there is some justification for this. Materials such as cement, bricks, steel, aluminium, plastics, etc., are home-produced, and had it not been for govern-ment control through the Prices Commission, it could be that the prices of these would have increased proportionally. Since our wood goods are mainly imported from overseas, they were outside this control. For this reason wood goods are not shown in a favourable light, pricewise.

It is of interest to note that when prices rose so much in 1973 and 1974, Canada increased its exports to the UK quite considerably and the volume more than doubled from 1969 to 1974.

Until the Second World War softwood was an undervalued commodity

Table 4.1. UK Wholesale Price Index Numbers. Basis: 1970 Average Price = 100

Commodity	Jan. 1972	Jan. 1973	Jan. 1974	Jan. 1975	Jan. 1976	Jan. 1977	Jan. 1978
Imported softwoods	106	129	258	248	246	382	352
Imported hardwoods	113	144	241	230	246	336	364
Imported plywood	108	132	225	228	223	325	325
Home-grown hardwood	113	131	212	225	228	272	320
Bricks	120	145	156	217	244	288	335
Joinery	120	143	178	208	240	312	339
Precast concrete products	116	128	135	168	217	261	304
Steel bars and sections	113	119	144	236	236	334	331
Plastic building materials	108	116	147	186	204	257	291

Reproduced by courtesy of the Price and Pierce Group – *Market Reports*

purchased by rule of thumb interpretations of 'supply and demand'. Statistics of imports were available, and some figures of sales from exporting countries to the UK were published from time to time, but there was little serious work on the true relationship of statistics and the interpretation of them in planning purchasing.

4.2 Consumption

There are two figures of consumption which will show considerable variation between each other. 'Actual consumption' is the actual amount of wood used by the packing-case maker, the joiner, the builder, etc., over a given period. It is not possible to collect this figure accurately over short periods of time, as this would obviously entail a written return being made by every softwood user in the country. The more readily obtainable figure is 'apparent consumption', which is the volume of wood which is passing on its way to consumption. Variation between it and 'actual consumption' occurs through the stock in the yards of the consumers. This may be a substantial item.

'Apparent consumption' can be obtained from the monthly statistics produced by the TTF from returns made by importers. It is most important to remember that while goods may leave an importer's yard, this does not necessarily mean that they have been actually consumed. They may have been placed in stock for future use and do not really come under the heading of consumption but rather that of stock. It follows that the available statistics are the best that can be provided but are not always accurate. It is well known that over the past 20 years the actual consumption of softwood has not varied to any significant extent annually. Obviously there is a potential limit to the volume of softwood which any country can consume, and this figure is known. Proof of the folly of buying excessive quantities at any price is illustrated by our import volume and prices in 1974, which left the UK with one of the highest stocks ever recorded.

An important fact is that arrivals of softwood (that is to say, the imports into the country) over a given time are related to the 'apparent consumption'. If the amount of softwood imported in a given month is high, the 'apparent consumption' will be high, because both importers and merchants will tend, in general, to make greater deliveries in that period. If the importer has some indication of the year's potential consumption, the monthly figures of arrivals of softwood should give him an indication as to how that estimated yearly consumption is being met.

Without doubt one of the most useful functions of the Economic Commission for Europe has been the interchange among European countries of statistics of consumption and production. Reports of meetings of this Commission are published in the trade press and give the importer an insight into future estimates of production in the shipping countries and consumption in the importing countries.

In the assessment of possible consumption in the UK reference can only be made to the major users of timber. Housing figures are the most readily available. Figures of new construction by public authorities are published in advance, together with estimates of future private building, the latter, incidentally, having a higher softwood content per dwelling. To this must be added the very considerable trend towards the building of timber-framed houses, which require 50 per cent more softwood than the traditional style. This form of utilisation is growing annually, since it has at last been recognised that dry construction has so many advantages over the traditional wet construction and problems associated with 'drying out' and its associated 'snags'.

The other large user of softwood is the packing-case industry. Here the amount of softwood likely to be consumed in a given period is controlled by our export trade, itself at the mercy of international politics and many other external forces.

4.3 Purchases

Statistics are available of the amount of timber purchased but not shipped. It is not possible to learn precisely when the timber may be expected to arrive, but the statistics do give a picture of the total forward commitment. They certainly give advance notice of the movement month by month of arrival figures.

The actual time at which purchases are made depends upon the offers of

stock from the shippers. They may be early in the season or late in the
season, as the various shippers try to assess the market.

The offer of Russian wood for sale here assumes considerable importance,
as instead of individual shippers approaching the market there is only one
organisation with a substantial quantity of wood available.

4.4 Arrivals

The arrivals of stock are firm figures produced from statistics of HM Customs
and Excise. They can usually be anticipated from the statistics of purchases
put out. The arrivals month by month affect 'apparent consumption' (as mentioned above) and also, of course, stock. The arrivals figure, therefore, is an
indication to the importer of at once both 'apparent consumption' and stock.

4.5 Stock

Figures are often available of timber stock held at various docks. Even if the
figures themselves are not available, the physical presence of the stock is there
to be seen. When dock stocks are high, it may be assumed that importers'
stocks are high. The overflow from the importer's yard has remained in the
docks. When deliveries from dock stocks are high, equally it may be assumed
that deliveries from private yards are high. When the importers themselves
are overstocked, it may be assumed that merchants and the consumers themselves are overstocked.

These are simple truths but not always fully appreciated.

The real importance of the figure of stock held lies not so much in the
volume of timber as in *the number of weeks of 'actual consumption' that it
will take to be liquidated.*

4.6 Prices

From all the above the importer must try to ensure that the price at which he
is closing his contract is that which will show him an adequate profit.

If there is an over-estimation among importers of the rise in 'apparent
consumption', this will result in pressure on the market and, as a consequence,
an increase in prices. When that rise in 'apparent consumption' does not take
place, there may be a fall in prices, and the importer can be caught. On the
other hand, a change to the buyers' market does not necessarily mean a drop
in prices. It may entail stability of prices, but enable the buyer to be more
selective in his specification, shipping dates and other terms.

Most statistics on prices are based upon c.i.f. value of Finnish V and U/S
quality of redwood on a 175 mm basis. Since 1968 Sweden has been the
largest exporter of softwoods to the UK with the USSR and Finland competing
for second place.

Prices depend upon the amount of softwood on offer and the amount which the importers wish to buy. Prices may be weak or strong. In general, when prices are strong (that is, when shippers are able to pick and choose the contracts they will close and to hold the prices up to the level they desire), these conditions are not so readily passed along through the softwood importing trade to the ultimate consumer. On the other hand, in a weak market the weakness in shippers' prices is all too often passed straight to the consumer. While on the face of it, from the consumer's point of view, this is a very good thing, it hardly makes for stability in a trade which must commit itself so far ahead.

Weaknesses in price often occur through last-minute offers of timber by shippers at the end of a shipping season. A comparatively small number of transactions of this nature can weaken not only the prices between shipper and importer, but also the prices between importer and merchant and merchant and consumer, and this although the importer and merchant have possibly committed themselves much earlier to contracts at higher prices. This is, in fact, the crux of the instability in prices from time to time in the softwood trade since weaknesses at the end of a shipping season will often be carried forward to the early part of the following season.

No one can pretend that there is an easy and immediate solution to this problem. The entrepreneur must take his chance. Nevertheless, from the information now available to him he may calculate the risk a little more closely.

The sources of supply shown in table 2.1 shows the trend over the years from 1969 to 1977 of the import of softwood from the principal supplying countries.

5 Shipping

5.1 Elementary Definitions

The imported trade is bound up closely with shipping and marine insurance, which must be fully understood if pitfalls are to be avoided. The following simplified definitions will help to explain the clauses and conditions appearing in shipping and marine insurance documents.

TYPES OF VESSEL

Liners are vessels that sail on scheduled journeys between specific ports. *Cargo vessels* — more commonly called 'tramps' or 'freighters' — are in the nature of 'free lance' carriers. They will load and carry almost any cargo between any ports in the world suitable to their capacity and type.

TONNAGE

This word occurs in many documents and can have any one of the following meanings:

Gross register tonnage (G.R.T.). The total internal capacity of the ship based upon the calculation 100 ft³ of capacity = 1 ton.
Net register tonnage (N.R.T.). The tonnage available for cargo or passengers. This represents the earning power of the ship, and is a measure of capacity calculated as 100 ft³ of capacity = 1 ton. It is the basis on which port and canal dues are paid.
Dead weight tonnage (D.W.). The tonnage available for cargo, passengers and fuel. This is the actual carrying power of the ship in tonnes of 1000 kg.
Displacement tonnage. The weight of the vessel, including the weight of crew and supplies but *not* including weight of cargo, fuel or passengers. Given in tons of 2240 lb, and actually the weight of the volume of water displaced by the ship. Used for warships but not for freighters.

General cargo (other than normal timber cargo) is carried on a tonnage basis, either actual weight or based on the measurement, 40 ft³/ton, whichever is the greater.

CLASSIFICATION

For marine insurance purposes, all the more important vessels in the world are classified as to their condition and seaworthiness. The most important classification is that carried out by:

Lloyd's Register of Shipping, for British tonnage and many foreign-flag vessels
Germanischer Lloyd, chiefly German vessels
American Bureau of Shipping, chiefly American vessels, and for vessels of other leading maritime nations
Bureau Veritas
Nippon Kaiji Kyokai
Norske Veritas
Registro Italiano Navale
Register of Shipping of the USSR
Hellenic Register of Shipping

The highest classification that is granted by Lloyd's Register is   100 A1.
    The   signifies that the hull was built under Lloyd's supervision; the 100 reveals that the ship has a steel hull; the A shows that the state of the hull and the 1 that the state of the rigging (a relic from the days of sailing ships) are first-class. A1 has thus become an everyday expression for anything first-class. Vessels on Lloyd's Register undergo inspection at frequent intervals, and the older the vessel, the more rigorous the inspection.
    The insurance of the hull of the ship depends upon the classification: the higher the classification, the lower the insurance premiums. The importer who buys timber f.a.s. and arranges his own insurance (for goods) is affected by the classification in this way. Suppose that a very cheap freight rate is offered by a shipowner, and the importer takes this up without checking on the classification of the ship. He may find that if the vessel is not classified by one of the recognised classification societies, as detailed above, the insurance companies would not be willing to insure the goods in transit. Furthermore, all underwriters now have an agreement that extra premium is paid if goods are carried on vessels over 15 years old. The current extra premium for such vessels, known as 'overage tonnage', is minimal, but rises steeply if the carrying vessel is over 20 years old.
    In addition to the classification, the vessel will be registered at a 'port of register', the official document being the 'Certificate of Registry'.
    The 'Plimsoll line' is the white line within a circle painted on the side of the hull to show the safe loading level. The level is fixed by Department of Trade and Industry inspectors, and varies slightly for different oceans, waters and seasons. It is required by the Merchant Shipping Act. If a vessel is over-loaded beyond the Plimsoll line and founders during the voyage, any claim made on the insurance policy covering the goods may be disallowed, unless provision is made to cover this risk, which is effected by Clause 9 of the TTF clauses regarding seaworthiness, etc.

The phrase ' . . . loaded down to her marks' is the common way of expressing that a vessel has been loaded to full capacity down to the level of the Plimsoll line applicable to the voyage and time of year.

In addition to the Plimsoll line (which is also known as the load line), certain vessels which are so constructed as to enable them to trade as open or closed shelter deck vessels have a tonnage mark in the form of an inverted triangle cut in the ship's side at a lower level than the Plimsoll to indicate which set of tonnages, according to whether the vessel is trading as an open shelter deck or a closed shelter deck, will apply.

For vessels regularly employed in the carriage of timber, a further timber load line may be allocated, allowing the vessel to load even more deeply when carrying wood, to take into account the relatively high stowage factor and the natural buoyancy of the cargo.

SHIP'S PAPERS

Each ship carries the following documents relating to the vessel, the crew, the cargo and the voyage:

(1) The agreements with the crew and a description of the voyage for which they are engaged.

(2) Certificate of registry.

(3) International load line certificate.

(4) Safety radio certificate (vessels above 300 G.R.T.).

(5) Safety equipment and safety construction certificates (vessels above 500 G.R.T.).

(6) Classification societies' survey report covering hull, engines, etc.

(7) Certificates of competency of the master and officers.

(8) Pilotage certificates.

(9) Light dues certificates.

(10) De-ratisation exemption certificates.

(11) Certificate of 'entry outwards', stamped and issued at the port of departure. This is issued by the authorities at the port in exchange for notification of the vessel's departure.

(12) Bills of lading, manifests, passenger lists, etc., giving full details of cargo and passengers being carried.

(13) Charter party.

(14) Department of Trade and Industry certificate covering the inspection of ship's gear and tackle must be available for inspection if the ship is going to discharge at a port in the UK and ship's gear is being used. It must be renewed at stated intervals. If it is not available, or is out of date, the stevedores may refuse to unload the ship. Similarly, the vessel must carry a certificate covering the testing and inspection of the slings being used, when the cargo is being carried 'pre-slung'.

SHIP'S LOGS

The three log books carried on board make up a complete diary of the life of the ship. The official log book contains a list of the crew and report of character. Disciplinary offences are noted in it and also details of births, deaths, etc. The deck and engine-room log books record details of arrival and departure at each port, with details of freeboard and draft on each occasion the vessel goes to sea. Speed, course, wind, engine movements, etc., are shown at regular intervals, as are also the names of lookouts and watches, with their reports. The deck and engine-room log books are written up into 'fair copies', but in a court of law reference would be made to the actual 'rough' log books in daily use.

The log book may be inspected by a bill of lading holder when the ship reaches port, and the master of the ship must produce it if reasonably required, or provide extracts of entries having a material bearing on a matter in dispute. In inspecting the ship's log particular attention should be paid to any entries concerning rough weather and the effect of weather and storms on the deck cargo. Sometimes part of the deck cargo may have to be thrown overboard if the vessel is in very heavy seas; on other occasions the violent movement of the ship may displace part of the deck cargo. References to 'battening down deck cargo' usually indicate disturbance during the voyage.

If part of a parcel or cargo is shipped on deck, and entries in the ship's log state or imply that part of the deck cargo has been lost or disturbed by rough weather, then the importer is forewarned. A shortage in the deck cargo may be expected, and the evidence of the ship's log can be used to support the claim for the shortage.

ARRIVAL PROCEDURE

Under revised boarding procedure introduced on 1 April 1978, HM Waterguard employ at their discretion a selective system of boarding vessels after arrival in a UK port. All vessels from a foreign port will receive at least one visitor from HM Customs.

Certain forms are to be completed by the master, with assistance from his agent, and deposited with HM Customs within three hours of arrival. These forms include: general declaration; declaration of ship's stores on board; crew declaration; small parcels list; deck cargo declaration. After all necessary papers have been lodged with HM Customs, the unloading of the ship may commence.

If the ship has encountered really rough weather on its voyage, the master will take the precaution of 'noting a protest', which is done before a notary. The protest gives a brief account of the voyage and the weather encountered. While the value of a protest as evidence of the facts it contains is by no means conclusive in the English courts, protests, in general, do have their importance; for instance, the fact that no protest as to bad weather was noted may be an indication that no bad weather was experienced. On the other hand, the fact that a master protests the loss of cargo due to heavy weather does not necessarily mean that this explanation will be accepted. However, foreign courts and some underwriters place greater reliance upon the existence or otherwise of a protest, and its contents.

5.2 The Charter Party

The contract by which a ship is chartered to load and carry goods is known as a 'charter party' (abbreviated to C/P or merely 'charter'), and is usually prepared by the shipbrokers who have arranged it. If timber, or any other bulk commodity, is to be shipped from one port to another, shipbrokers are approached and given the details of quantities, the voyage, ready date, and so on. Being in close touch with the shipping world, the shipbrokers are able to offer various possibilities of freight which are available by different shipowners.

It may take more than one ship to lift the cargo, but the shipbrokers can arrange for whatever is required. When the shipbrokers have found suitable freight space at a rate of freight which the charterer is willing to pay and the owners to accept, they draw up the charter party or booking note.

If the cargo be a part-cargo only, or even a small parcel, then often a booking note is issued which, however, will still incorporate the full terms, clauses, conditions and exceptions of the charter party.

The charter party is a very ancient document dating back many centuries. The word is derived from 'charter', which is a 'document bestowing certain rights and privileges' (a historic example is the well-known Magna Carta), and 'party', which is derived from the Latin and means 'parted' or 'divided'. It is said that in olden days the charter party was torn into two parts after being signed, one part being held by the shipowners and the other by the merchants, called the charterers, and that to complete the document both parts had to be brought together. It has also been thought to signify that it is not merely a 'bestowal' by one party on another, but a contract in which the 'rights and privileges' are 'divided' between the parties. Nowadays, however, the word has become abbreviated to 'charter', as in the Nubaltwood charter itself, and is so referred to in the contract forms.

There are two principal types of charter party: (1) time charters; (2) voyage charters.

In a time charter the vessel is chartered for a particular period and during that period is under the direction of the charterer. The shipowners are paid an agreed amount per day, per week or per month for the hire of their vessel, irrespective of the amount of cargo it is carrying. Time charters are made by companies with large amounts of goods to be carried by sea. When shipping lines cannot provide shiproom for all the goods they have to carry, they will often charter other vessels on time charter to supplement their own fleet. The vessel flies the flag and is operated by the crew of the shipowner, but the time charterer is able to deploy the ship where he wishes and pay all port expenses, disbursements, fuel, etc., and appoint and pay the port agents.

A variation of the time charter is the demise or bare boat charter, where the charterer hires only the vessel for a given period and provides his own crew supplies and services. A bare boat charterer even has the right in many instances to change the name of the ship.

In a voyage charter the vessel is chartered for a particular voyage to be performed between specified ports. By mutual agreement between shipowner and charterer the vessel can be arranged to load at more than one port and discharge at more than one port, by the payment of extra freight.

The rate of freight on a voyage charter may be calculated in one of two ways:

(1) A rate of an agreed amount per cubic metre, usually varying with one rate being agreed for length packaged goods and another for truck bundled goods, or a single negotiated flat rate for a declared description of cargo, perhaps limiting the proportions of each kind. In the charter party the size of the cargo to be carried is clearly stated in the current Nubaltwood charter party; provision is also made for separate rates for loose deals, battens, boards, slatings, etc., but in effect the carriage of loose timber with freight being paid in this way is practically non-existent.

(2) A lump sum covering the voyage. The estimated carrying capacity of the vessel is declared at the time the freight is negotiated.

Of these two forms of freight, the first one, based on a rate per cubic metre, is by far the safest for the importer. He is only required to pay freight on the goods carried and delivered (presuming no dead-freight arises) and he does know beforehand how much freight per cubic metre he will have to pay. This information may be vital to him if he is selling his goods forward — that is, before they have been shipped.

The lump sum freight at first sight may appear attractive and cheaper than a fixed rate per cubic metre, but there are many pitfalls. All too often it has been found that the vessel was not able to lift the full quantity of goods expected and that the capacity of the vessel for carrying timber has been overestimated by the shipowners, particularly in the case of vessels not regularly used as timber carriers. This overestimation is difficult to prove, the shipowners usually claiming that the goods were insufficiently seasoned or were otherwise heavier than calculated. As a result, as soon as the vessel has been loaded so that it is down to its 'marks' (i.e. the Plimsoll line), the master stops loading and sails with only a part of the cargo. On arrival at the port of destination the lump sum freight is payable in full, irrespective of the amount of cargo carried. In such a case what may first have appeared to be a very cheap freight is seen to have cost much more than freight based upon a rate per cubic metre. If the difference between the amount of goods carried and the estimated capacity of the vessel is very great, the charterer may have a claim against the shipowners for overestimating the capacity of the vessel, negligence in stowing the cargo, etc., but in any case it is likely to entail some form of legal proceedings, and these should be avoided if possible.

The charter party contains the following details:

(1) Names of the contracting parties – that is, the shipowners and the charterers.

(2) Name, flag, class, age, registered tonnage, normal carrying capacity and/or deadweight tonnage of the vessel and position at time of chartering.

(3) Expected loading date.

(4) Description and size of cargo, giving maximum and minimum details and margin allowed to the shipowner for loading.

(5) Rate of freight and how it is to be paid.

(6) Time allowed for loading and discharge and the amount of demurrage chargeable if these periods are exceeded. As far as the carriage of cargo on Nubaltwood terms is concerned, the rates for loading, discharging and demurrage are agreed from time to time between the United Kingdom Timber Trade Shipowners Mutual Association, the Timber Trades Federation of the United Kingdom, the Finnish Sawmill Owners Association, the Swedish Wood Exporters Association, the Chamber of Shipping of the United Kingdom and the Baltic and International Maritime Conference. The Nubaltwood charter party merely stipulates that the rates as agreed will apply, without specifically detailing them, and reference must be made to the current Schedule published by the United Kingdom Timber Trade Shipowners Mutual Association Ltd for full details.

(7) Name of the loading port(s) and the discharging port(s).

(8) Clauses protecting the shipowner against various events for which he is not responsible. (In Scandinavian charter parties the ice clause is particularly important in autumn and winter, as it can give the shipowner the option to cancel a charter party if the port is ice-bound or not reachable.)

(9) The undertaking to load, carry and deliver the goods detailed in the charter party but 'free discharge' places the obligation of taking from the ship's hold upon the bill of lading holder.

With reference to (4) above, it is extremely important that the cargo shall be correctly and fully described, as otherwise serious difficulties may arise. The standard Nubaltwood charter party is basically for the carriage of mill-sawn red and/or whitewood described in the purchase contract as being properly seasoned for shipment to the UK, and it is desirable that such items as 'planed goods' are declared when fixing or booking, as extra loading, handling and discharging costs may be incurred. If length packaged goods are being supplied in units of four, and if the length packaged or truck bundled goods are being supplied on bearers, it should be declared when fixing or booking, otherwise shipowners may be able to claim dead-freight or damages, if vessels' intake can be proved to be lower than expected.

It is also important to ensure that any 'unseasoned goods' are correctly described in the charter. Charterers have escaped responsibility when shipping goods which have been proved to be 'not fully seasoned', because the Nubalt-wood charter party calls for goods to be 'described' as properly seasoned, and not necessarily requires that they are in fact so properly seasoned. Nevertheless, it is wise always to fully describe the cargo which is not properly seasoned for shipment to the UK in such a way as is stated in the purchase contract, viz. as 'not fully seasoned', 'not shipping dry', '60 days in stick', etc., to prevent troubles.

'Demurrage' is a sum paid or agreed to be paid to the shipowners as pre-agreed or agreed or liquidated damages for delay in loading or discharging beyond certain stipulated times. These stipulated times vary in each form of charter, from a 'reasonable time' qualified by such phrases as 'in accordance with the custom of the port', to 'fixed lay-days'.

The 'custom of the port' is difficult to define exactly, but nevertheless is one of those terms that in the past has been well understood by charterers, shippers and shipowners without much difficulty or dispute.

In some charters the fixed lay-days are calculated to start from the date when the vessel arrives at the port, as opposed to the date when the vessel arrives at a *berth* in the port. The former is known as a 'port charter', the latter as a 'berth charter'. The difference is important in ports subject to congestion and delay, where vessels may be kept several days awaiting a berth. In such a case a period of time, say 24 hours, is permitted after the vessel has reported at the port, after which the shipowners notify the charterers that they regard the vessel as an 'arrived ship', irrespective of the fact that there is no berth available.

For example, the Nubaltwood charter states in clause 6 that '. . . time for loading shall commence at 2 p.m. if the vessel be ready to load (whether in berth or not), etc. . . .'.

Other charters may contain the words '. . . time lost waiting for berth to count as loading time . . .'. This makes a great deal of difference to the financial outcome of a berth charter.

Demurrage is calculated usually at a certain sum per day or part thereof. It is payable by the charterer, but the importer is usually protected by clauses in his contract with the seller by which the seller agrees to pay any demurrage caused by him at the loading port. An important exception to this is the Nubaltwood charter (and Uniform contract), since with these documents the charterer is protected by the demurrage equalisation scheme (see page 83).

Where the importer/charterer/bill of lading holder has resold the bills of lading and the property in those bills of lading has passed to the new buyer, the latter, as the last consignee, is liable for demurrage at the port of discharge and may also be liable for demurrage at the loading port (see page 93).

In some charters provision is made for an incentive to be paid by the ship-owners to the shippers for working time saved in loading or discharging the vessel. This is known as 'despatch money' and may be at half the agreed rate for demurrage.

The current Nubaltwood charter party contains provision for 'incentive money' being paid to bill of lading holders, where goods are chartered with

Nubaltwood clause 15 (b) (free discharge to the ship), or Nubaltwood 15 (c) (fixed discharging cost guaranteed to shipowners) applying. Nubaltwood clause 15 (d) also provides for incentive money payable, but in practice the clause is not used and can be ignored.

If the charterer does not provide sufficient cargo, within the quantities and margins set out in the charter, the shipowners may claim dead-freight. Dead-freight is damages for the unoccupied cargo space and is payable at the same rate of freight as if that space was used, less 'savings' in respect of costs which shipowners would have become liable to pay if in fact the goods had been loaded.

The provision of the cargo is largely out of the control of the importer buying goods on f.a.s. or c.i.f. terms. Protection is given in the Uniform f.a.s. or Albion c.i.f. contract by which the sellers agree to pay any dead-freight admitted or proved to have been caused by them at loading port (see page 148).

Demurrage and dead-freight do not arise in a time charter, since the charterers themselves are the only party to suffer loss; the shipowners are not affected, being paid in any case for the full period the vessel is under time charter.

The undertaking to load and deliver the cargo (paragraph 9 above) refers particularly to charters for carrying timber from Scandinavia and North America. There are, however, other charters, such as f.i.o. (free in and out) charters, in which the shipowners, for the freight named, only carry the goods from port to port, all costs of loading and discharging being paid by the charterers and nothing at all by the shipowners.

It is now a common practice that under Nubaltwood terms the vessel is fixed 'free discharge', which means that while the shipowners pay for the loading and stowing of the cargo, they make no contribution towards the cost of discharge, which is borne entirely by the charterers/receivers/bill of lading holders, according to the agreement made when chartering.

In a c.i.f. contract the sellers are the charterers; in an f.a.s. contract the buyers are the charterers.

The charter for shipments from Norway and the Baltic to the UK and the Republic of Ireland is known as the Nubaltwood charter, published in 1973.

5.3 Nubaltwood Charter Party, 1973

Figure 5.1 is a reproduction of the Nubaltwood bill of lading. It will be seen that it contains the General Paramount Clause, which incorporates the rules contained in the Brussels Convention of 1924.

This charter party has been agreed between the Chamber of Shipping of the United Kingdom and the Timber Trade Federation, the Finnish Sawmill Owners Association and the Swedish Wood Exporters Association. It has also been agreed and adopted by the International Shipowners Organization of

COPYRIGHT PUBLISHED BY THE CHAMBER OF SHIPPING OF THE UNITED KINGDOM, LONDON.

Shipper

B/L No.

Reference No

Consignee

Master for this present voyage

Date of Charter party

Notify address

'NUBALTWOOD' BILL OF LADING

(The Vessel has liberty to sail without pilots, to proceed via any route, to proceed to and stay at any port or ports whatsoever in any order in or out of the route or in a contrary direction to or beyond the port of destination once or oftener for bunkering or loading or discharging cargo or embarking or disembarking passengers or any other purposes whatsoever, and to carry the within cargo into and then beyond the port of discharge named herein and to return to and discharge the said cargo at such port, to tow or to be towed, to make trial trips with or without notice, to adjust or calibrate compasses or to repair or drydock with or without cargo on board, all as part of the contract voyage.)

Vessel | Port of loading

Port of discharge

Specification

AUTHORISED PRINTERS: S. STRAKER & SONS LTD., 49 FENCHURCH STREET, LONDON

of which pieces on deck at Charterers' risk

All the terms, conditions, clauses and exceptions including Clause 30, contained in the said Charter party apply to this Bill of Lading and are deemed to be incorporated herein. Further, notwithstanding anything to the contrary contained in the said Charter party and notwithstanding the transfer, indorsement or negotiation of this Bill of Lading to any person, the Shippers but no other person shall pay any demurrage at loading port calculated in accordance with the terms of the Agreement concerning Loading Port Conditions agreed between The United Kingdom Timber Trade Shipowners' Mutual Association Ltd., and the Finnish Sawmill Owners Association and the Swedish Wood Exporters' Association. In the case of other than Finnish or Swedish Shippers the Loading Port Conditions shall be those agreed between The United Kingdom Timber Trade Shipowners' Mutual Association Ltd. and the Shippers' organisation of the country concerned recognised by The Timber Trade Federation of the United Kingdom, or failing such agreement the Loading Port Conditions set out in the schedule of The United Kingdom Timber Trade Shipowners' Mutual Association Ltd. In all cases the rates shall be those current at the date of the said Charter party.

GENERAL PARAMOUNT CLAUSE

This Bill of Lading shall have effect subject to the provisions of any legislation relating to the carriage of goods by sea which incorporates the rules relating to Bills of Lading contained in the International Convention, dated Brussels 25th August, 1924, and which is compulsorily applicable to the contract of carriage herein contained. Such legislation shall be deemed to be incorporated herein, but nothing herein contained shall be deemed a surrender by the Carrier of any of its rights or immunities or an increase of any of its responsibilities or liabilities thereunder. If any term of this Bill of Lading be repugnant to any extent to any legislation by this clause incorporated, such term shall be void to that extent but no further. Nothing in this Bill of Lading shall operate to limit or deprive the Carrier of any statutory protection or exemption from, or limitation of liability.

The goods described above have been shipped on the above-mentioned vessel in good order and condition and are to be delivered at the above-named port of discharge in the like good order and condition to the consignees and/or his or their assigns subject to the terms and conditions set out in this Bill of Lading.

In WITNESS whereof the Master or Agent of the said ship hath signed Bills of Lading all of this tenor and date, any one of which being accomplished the others shall be void.

AGREED (1973) WITH THE TIMBER TRADE FEDERATION OF THE UNITED KINGDOM, THE BALTIC AND INTERNATIONAL MARITIME CONFERENCE, THE SWEDISH WOOD EXPORTERS' ASSOCIATION, THE FINNISH SAWMILL OWNERS' ASSOCIATION

Received upon account of freight ....

Pounds and .... Pence

from which a charge of 2% has been deducted.

£ ....

....

Freight payable at | Place and date of issue

Number of original B/L. | Signature

QUALITY, CONDITION and MEASURE UNKNOWN

Figure 5.1 Nubaltwood bill of lading

The Baltic and International Maritime Conference. It became effective as regards fixtures and contracts made on and after Monday, 17 September 1973.

The Nubaltwood charter party, 1973, has been updated and is now in a box layout form for ease of completion, with main details on a separate front sheet and the general terms, conditions and warranties set out on a fold of three separate pages. The unit of measurement used is a cubic metre, and as shipments of Baltic timber are now carried almost entirely in length packages or truck bundles, the charter party is worded accordingly.

The reverse of the separate front sheet is for the use of the United Kingdom Timber Trade Shipowners Mutual Association only, and is used as a fixture report form. The reverse of the agreement sheet also explains concisely the separate items usually being carried on Nubaltwood terms.

The front page of the charter party contains 24 boxes, each referring to a clause in the general terms, conditions and warranties, which are as follows:

(1) Name of shipbroker (i.e. usually the shipbroker through whom the charter party was concluded).
(2) Place and date of issue of charter party.
(3) Name of owners or disponent/time charter owners.
(4) Name of charterers.
(5) Name of ship's manager or chartering agent.
(6) Name and telegraphic address of shipper(s).
(7) Name of vessel.
(8) Position of vessel at the time of fixing charter party.
(9) Date of build of vessel.
(10) Nett registered tonnage of vessel.
(11) Carrying capacity of vessel in cubic metres.
(12) Maximum sets of bills of lading to be issued.
(13) Number of hatches of the vessel and their dimensions.
(14) Previous discharging port, if agreed.
(15) Lay-days (i.e. the earliest day on which lay-days can commence).
(16) Cancelling date (i.e. the date on which charterers have the option to cancel if the vessel does not comply with its loading date as per clause 3 of the charter party.
(17) Loading port and name of ship's agent.
(18) Discharging port and name of ship's agent.
(19) Description of cargo.
(20) Freight rate.
(21) Method of discharge.
(22) Whether or not fixed price agreed for discharging.
(23) Brokerage rate (payable by the shipowners).
(24) To whom brokerage to be paid.

PREAMBLE

This refers to the boxes listed above and to vessels' carrying capacity. It is not a clause as such but contains the conditions precedent to the charter party. A margin of 10 per cent more or less on the cargo quantity is allowed to owners, with a maximum margin of 250 m^3. However, a greater margin than 10 per cent may be allowed on cargoes over 2500 m^3 if specially agreed. It is important to remember that the general rule is that shippers must be prepared to supply a margin of 10 per cent upwards, while the shipowner must be able to lift a minimum quantity of 10 per cent less than the quantity stated. Failure by either party to comply could result in a claim for dead-freight or damages, respectively. Failure by shippers to supply the cargo required which results in a claim for dead-freight being made against charterers is covered in clause 14 of the Uniform contract. Failure by owners to lift the minimum quantity under the charter party may result in owners being faced with a claim for damages resulting from charterers' costs of arranging for the shipment of any outshipped cargo to the charter party destination.

Furthermore, it is important that the margin allowed by charterers to shipowners coincides with the margin allowed by shippers to buyers in their purchase contract — a special alteration being made to the charter party if necessary. Frequently shippers sell on the basis of a maximum quantity, with a downwards margin only in the shipowners option, necessitating a specific amendment to the charter party.

GENERAL TERMS, CONDITIONS AND WARRANTIES

Clause 1

This clause provides that the vessel is to proceed to the loading port named in box (17), load the cargo described, thereafter proceed to the discharging port named in box (18) and there deliver the cargo in the same good order and condition. It is important to name the loading port(s) exactly as stated and described in the purchase contract. Provision is made for the vessel to be provided with a deckload at full freight, carriage to be at charterers' risk, and quantity of deckload not to exceed that which the vessel can reasonably stow and carry. The phrase 'a full and complete cargo' applies where there is only one charterer for the vessel. If there are several charterers, each with only a part cargo, these words are amended to read 'a part cargo of . . . cubic metres', the special inclusion of which in the charter party will prevail over the printed terms of the Nubaltwood general terms and conditions and warranties, 1973. Where part cargoes are carried, it is usual to include the words 'proportionate deckload', unless the cargo is specified as being 'all on' or 'all under' deck. Any of the clauses in the charter party may be amended in this way by mutual agreement, the amendment prevailing over the printed term.

The clean form of the Nubaltwood charter party requires that the goods presented for shipment shall be 'described in the Purchase Contract as properly seasoned for shipment to the United Kingdom'. Both the Uniform and Albion contracts provide (clause 2 in each) for the goods being properly seasoned for shipment, etc., but if the importer is buying goods that are not so described (for instance, 'unseasoned goods'), it is vitally important to see that the phrase 'properly seasoned etc.' is deleted from the charter by an overriding clause, and the cargo properly described. Failure to do this can only cause disputes and claims for dead-freight. Reference is made in this clause to the loading and discharging ports being ports where vessels may safely get and lie always afloat. There are a number of ports, particularly where timber cargoes are discharged, where vessels are not always able to be afloat. These are described as n.a.a. b.s.a. ports, the abbreviation generally accepted as standing for 'not always afloat but safe aground where vessels of similar size and draft are accustomed to lie in safety'. The abbreviation n.a.a. b.s.a. should be shown after the name of the port in the appropriate box on the front page of the charter party, if the vessel is not to lie always afloat. If the vessel is to load and/or discharge at a specified dock or wharf, then this should be shown clearly on the front of the charter party. Alternatively, a vessel may be fixed to load and/or discharge at a place within a port 'as ordered on arrival'. In this case, after the proper declaration of the loading and/or discharging place required within the port it is as if that place had been stipulated in the original charter party.

Clause 2

Under this clause shipowners are to give shippers at least nine consecutive days' notice of probable date of arrival of the vessel to the place of loading. However, this clause is invariably amended to coincide with the general requirement of Baltic shippers, who need ten working days' notice (excluding Saturdays) to be given, and so stipulate in the Uniform contract. Holidays as listed in this clause shall not count when the consecutive days' notice is calculated. Owners are also required to inform shippers by telegram (or telex) when the vessel leaves her last port for her first port of loading. If the ship-owners do not give the required notice, lay-days are extended and the shippers agree to accept responsibility for any costs incurred on lighters or trucks at loading port by their failure to give this notice.

Clause 3

The charterers are given the option of cancelling the charter if the vessel is not ready to load within a certain period. Shipowners will on occasions seek an extension of the cancelling date, if the vessel cannot be ready to load on time.

Considerable care must be exercised by the charterer in giving an unqualified extension, since when this has been granted, *all* rights, obligations and exceptions contained in the charter are extended for both parties. If an unconditional extension is granted towards the end of the shipping season, the shipowners may be able to take advantage of the exceptions permitted to them under the 'Ice' clause 8, enabling them to cancel, whereas by not being ready to load on time they were in breach of the charter, with the charterers having the option of cancelling and claiming damages. Consequently, when an extension is asked for, charterers should grant this only on a clearly written understanding that they are treating the shipowners as being in breach of charter and fully reserving their rights to claim damages by reason of the delay. Whatever form of qualified extension is given, it must be agreed by both parties, as it is a variation of the original contract.

Clause 4

This clause covers the situation where, due to fire, goods are destroyed or cannot be provided before any loading takes place. Where all the goods are destroyed by fire, or fire prevents their being provided, charterers have the right of cancelling the charter, giving immediate notice to owners. Where, however, part of the goods only is destroyed or cannot be provided, the charterers must give immediate notice to owners of the quantity left available for shipment are liable to ship such quantity only. However, if the quantity of the remaining cargo is less than 50 per cent, the shipowner can, if he so wishes, cancel the charter party. Should the shipowner not exercise his latter option, he is at liberty to take on other cargo at the same or other port, not necessarily one in the course of the chartered voyage.

Clause 5: Option of the master to carry ballast

Clause 6: The loading clause

This clause provides that the master 'on arrival at the loading port, shall give written notice to the shipper or his agent of the approximate quantity of cargo required'. It is also stated that the master shall exercise due care in giving such notice and in adjusting this quantity as soon as loading of the holds is completed. This covers the 'chartering' clause of the Uniform contract (see Chapter 8). So if goods are purchased on a Uniform contract, it is important that no other charter than the Nubaltwood is used.

The clause proceeds to state that 'the cargo shall be brought alongside the vessel in the customary manner at charterer's risk and expense'. The Uniform contract stipulates that the goods are to be delivered 'all free alongside the vessel', and the Timber Trade Federation Insurance clauses protect buyers against risks from the time the goods leave the shipper's wharf.

The rate of loading for deals and battens, boards, etc., is per 'weather working day'. This excludes holidays, Saturday afternoons, Sundays and those periods in working days when weather conditions prevent loading. All the time during working hours when weather permits loading is counted.

These rates are calculated on the basis of the number of workable hatches given in the description of the vessel in the preamble, and a schedule of rates of loading *per day per hatch* agreed between the Chamber of Shipping and the shippers' associations. These schedules of rates are amended from time to time and are published by the Demurrage Association (see page 83). By clause 20 the rates of loading in the schedule current at the time of signing the charter apply.

The last paragraph of this clause provides for disputes at the loading port to be settled before the bills of lading are signed, but failing this, claims (which will generally be for demurrage or dead-freight) are to be endorsed on the bills of lading or, if the master is prevented from so doing, notified to charterers by telegram. Against this, however, is the undertaking by shippers in the Uniform contract to pay all *dead-freight* admitted or proved to have been caused by them at the loading port and the undertaking by the shipowners in clause 18 of this charter that neither they nor the master will endorse any bill of lading with a *demurrage* claim or clause.

Clause 7: Advance freight

A proportion of freight, not to exceed one-third of the total freight, is to be advanced to the master at loading port to cover ordinary disbursements if required. The amount of the advance must be endorsed on the bills of lading and is subject to a charge of 2 per cent to be deducted by shippers.

Clause 8: Ice hindrance

The first part of this clause gives shipowners the option of cancelling the charter if ice setting in at the end of the year prevents the vessel from loading or continuing to load. The last paragraph covers charterers for the ice hindrance clause of the Uniform contract, which limits seller's liability to supply cargo at f.o.w. (first open water) until 48 hours *after* navigation between shipper's wharf or quay and the vessel is unimpeded by ice. There are often circumstances where there is no difficulty or danger for a steamship to load while there is considerable risk of danger and damage to barges from heavy floating ice. The additional 48 hours is to cover the fact that the barges may have to come some distance down a river estuary, where the ice breaks up more slowly than in the open harbour or seaway.

Clause 9: Strike clause

The first part of this clause extends the period of loading or discharging by the period of the strike. The remainder deals with options given to the shipowners to cancel the charter if there is a strike at the loading port either just before or after arrival of the vessel. It also gives the shipowners the option of sailing with a part cargo if the strike lasts for more than six calendar days and prevents the vessel from loading the complete cargo.

Clause 10(a): Bills of lading

This clause governs all the terms, clauses, conditions and exceptions of the bills of lading which 'shall be prepared on the Nubaltwood Bill of Lading Form'. The owners shall be responsible for the number of pieces signed for by the master. The owners shall not be responsible for broken bundles unless due care is not taken in loading and/or discharging. In the event of there being only one consignee, all cargo on board shall be delivered to him.

Clause 10(b)

Allows the owner and charterer/receiver to enter into a non-tallying agreement against the payment to receivers of an allowance per cubic metre which is agreed between them. In the event of such an agreement being reached, no liability for shortage of pieces based on a tally taken elsewhere after discharge attaches to the owner.

Clause 10(c)

Provides for where such a non-tally agreement is not reached or is found impracticable, and contains the stipulation that no liability for shortage of pieces on an ex-ship tally attaches to the owners unless notified to them or their agents within eight days of completion of discharge.

Clause 11: Sets of bills of lading

This clause sets out the number of bills of lading required. It stipulates that charterers will send the goods alongside in such a manner as to enable the cargo under each bill of lading to be kept separate. The importer passes this obligation on to the shipper in Uniform bills of lading clause. Charterers are called upon to send a copy of their loading orders to shippers to the master for his information, but without obligation upon the owners. Any specific stowage requirement must be specially negotiated at the time of chartering, which stipulation will then become a contractual requirement. Otherwise, the stowage of the cargo will be entirely at the discretion of the master from the point of view of stability and seaworthiness.

Clause 12: Exceptions

This is a clause protecting the shipowners against a wide range of occurrences over which they have no control. The importer in his turn is protected by his marine insurance policy, including the TTF insurance clauses.

Clause 13: Deviation clause

A further clause protecting the shipowners that has the effect of defining the scope of the voyage in wider terms to avoid possible claims for deviation. The TTF insurance clauses again protect the importer fully.

Clause 14: War

Provides for cancellation of the charter in case of war, and protection for the shipowners if the vessel is deviated by order of the Government.

Clause 15

This clause is divided into five sub-sections, the first four dealing with various methods of discharge and the fifth dealing with calculation of laytime.

Part (a) provides for the shipowner arranging and paying for the costs of discharging from ship's hold to ship's rail or within reach of shore cranes or ship's tackle. To cover costs beyond this point, receivers pay an 'apportionment charge' as determined for the appropriate discharging port by the local Apportionment Committee.

Part (b). Receivers to arrange and pay for the discharging costs from ship's hold in full.

Part (c). The receivers arrange and pay for the discharging costs from ship's hold, but owners pay to the receivers an agreed amount per cubic metre representing the cost or being a contribution towards the cost of discharge.

Part (d) provides for a complex arrangement for the payment of discharging costs, but because of its complicated nature has probably never been used. A provision is made for receivers to be paid 'incentive money' at 50 per cent of the demurrage rate if parts (b) and (c) of the clause are used, but only 25 per cent of the demurrage rate if part (d) of the clause is used.

Clause 16: Responsibility for dock dues in a London dock

In the case of a part-cargo the words 'their proportion of' should be inserted before 'the dock dues'.

Clause 17: Demurrage Association clause

This, together with clauses 18, 19 and 20, is peculiar to the Nubaltwood charter. The shipowners undertake to become members of the United Kingdom Timber Trade Shipowners' Mutual Association Ltd (referred to in this chapter as the Demurrage Association). The charterers undertake when signing the charter to notify this association, giving details of name of vessel and name of shipowners. The shipowners also undertake to pay the voyage subscription at the current rate based on the bill of lading quantity, their right to claim demurrage being conditional on this payment.

Clause 18: Demurrage at loading port

This clause sets out the shipowners' right to claim demurrage from the Demurrage Association, and contains a waiver by the shipowners of their right to claim demurrage except from the Association.

Clause 19

This clause states that if the vessel is not discharged at the specified rate whereby the vessel is detained, then demurrage is payable at the rate provided for in clause 20. Holders of each bill of lading agree to pay contributions to the shipowners' agents when the first instalment of freight is paid by cheque in favour of the Association.

This payment is based on the bill of lading quantity but is subject to an adjustment when the final out-turn is ascertained in the same way as the final instalment of freight is payable. Any demurrage claim that shipowners may have must be proved to the Association, who then arrange settlement. Payment of this fixed charge per cubic metre is therefore the equivalent of insurance of the bill of lading holder, giving protection against liability and meeting demurrage claims, which may be heavy. Where a shipowner or his agent has reason to believe that, for reasons within the control of the receiver, discharging operations are being delayed, a warning may be sent by the ship's agent to the receiver, with a copy to the Demurrage Association. This enables that Association to pursue claims against the bill of lading holder for excess demurrage under certain circumstances. If a bill of lading holder does cause demurrage to be incurred for any reason within his control, he may be liable to pay half the cost of such excess demurrage.

Clause 20: Loading and discharging rates

This clause confirms that the rate of loading and discharging, the voyage subscription, the demurrage rates and contributions will be those set out in the

Schedule of the Association according to the terms of the charter party. The discharging rate in 1978 for pre-slung packaged timber is 1000 m³/day for Baltic cargoes and 850 m³/day for Polish cargoes. Charges are frequently made as required by current circumstances, and the latest published amendments should always be consulted as necessary.

Clause 21: Payment of freight

Freight to be paid is the full freight less advance of freight made under clause 7 plus charges (if any) payable under clause 15. Ninety per cent is paid when the vessel commences discharge and the remainder upon final out-turn being ascertained or 60 days from the completion of discharge, whichever is the earlier. Where the balance of freight becomes payable before final out-turn is ascertained, it is to be paid on the basis of the bill of lading quantity, less allowances for pieces short delivered, providing that the consignees may within six months of the completion of discharge claim refund of any over-payment on the basis of final out-turn. Most of the forms of charter party, including liner booking notes, do not permit any retention by the importer of part of the freight, but stipulate that the freight must be paid in full 'ship lost or not lost'. The freighting of timber has its own problems, and claims by importers against shipowners for shortage in delivery and pieces against bill of lading quantities are frequent. The retention of a percentage of the freight by the importer, until the final out-turn is ascertained and therefore any shortage known, greatly strengthens the position of the importer in getting his just claims met by the shipowners. This particularly applies to foreign shipowners. If the charter party is governed by English law, they are within the jurisdiction of the English courts; with an English arbitration clause, as in the Nubaltwood charter party, they can be forced to arbitrate in England, and if they lose have the award enforced on them in their own country. There are obvious practical difficulties where the shipowner is a small company operating perhaps under a flag of convenience. It is here that the right of arrest is important. The vessel may be arrested by court order, the writ being nailed to the mast of the vessel. Furthermore, in recent years the Merchant Shipping Act has provided the right to arrest sister ships of the offending ship. Such proceedings may be expensive for the importer or the bill of lading holder and will certainly take time. If, however, the freight is retained, the importer may set off part or all of this retention against the shortage or the claim against the shipowners. This forces the latter to take the initiative to prove their case and if necessary sue the importer. This must be done through the courts in the UK so foreign shipowners will straightway be placing themselves under the jurisdiction of English (or Scottish) courts, enabling the importer to pursue his claim as if it were against a British company. While the retention of freight is certainly a helpful practical measure, at the same time it must be understood that there is a substantial body of legal opinion which holds that the importer has no legal right of retention of freight against claims on shipowners. It should be noted that 'final out-turn' in this context refers to a shortage of measure, the bills of lading being claused 'Quality, condition and measure unknown'. Shortages of pieces or packages are as determined by the ex-ship tally.

Clause 22: General average

The York—Antwerp Rules, 1974, govern the proceedings for adjustment of general average and permit a statement to be drawn up in a foreign port. The New Jason clause is applicable where average adjustment is computed under American law.

Clause 23: 'Both to blame' collision clause

A further clause to protect shipowners by reason of differences in American law. Any possible liability falling on bills of lading holders is covered under the marine insurance policy.

Clause 24: Lien

The master or shipowners have an absolute lien on the cargo for all freight, dead-freight, average and charges payable under clause 15. Under this clause, if the shipowners do not receive payment or settlement of these items, they can hold the cargo, refusing to give delivery until they receive satisfaction. By order of a court, they may sell the cargo themselves to settle their own demands or under Section 497 of the Merchant Shipping Act after a defined period and in a prescribed manner they may sell the goods by public auction.

Under other charters the most common exercise of lien by shipowners is for settlement of claims for demurrage. This may be particularly hard on the owners of the last bills of lading to come out of the vessel. The first bills of lading will have been discharged and may have been moved away from the quay by the time the vessel comes on demurrage. The shipowners may then place a lien on the remaining bills of lading, until such time as the demurrage, which is for the whole vessel, has been paid. In such circumstances it is conceivable for demurrage at the discharging port, for a vessel chartered under fixed lay-days, to be paid entirely by the holders of the last bill of lading in the vessel.

Clause 25: Telegrams

This clause is self-explanatory. (Check clause 2 that telex is accepted as an alternative.)

Clause 26: Brokerage

This clause sets out the amount of brokerage and to whom payable.

Clause 27: Agency

Although this clause states that shipowners shall appoint their own brokers or agents at loading or discharging ports, there may be a stipulation in the purchase contract that brokers or agents named by the shippers shall be appointed at the loading port. In such a case it is important to see that the charter is amended to comply with the shippers' stipulation.

Clause 28: Substitution

The right is given to shipowners to substitute a similar vessel, on giving notice to charterers of not less than 14 days prior to the probable date of the vessel's arrival. It is a common practice, however, particularly with shipowners operating a large fleet, to fix named tonnage (or substitute), in which case owners are relieved of the restrictive 14 days' notice of this clause, without creating any disadvantage to charterers.

Clause 29: Overtime

This clause sets out how additional costs of overtime are to be apportioned between charterers and shipowners.

Clause 30: Arbitration

Where disputes cannot be settled amicably, provision is here made for reference to arbitration (see Chapter 11).

The Nubaltwood 1973 charter, which has been described here in detail, is normally the most used charter, covering as it does goods shipped from Norway, Sweden and Finland.

The Sovietwood charter party, 1961, is used for shipments of timber from all Russian ports. Since purchases from the USSR are on c.i.f. terms, the provisions of the charter party with regard to loading of the cargo and matters arising at loading ports do not concern UK importers, but are dealt with by the Russian 'Exportles' company as charterers and sellers.

The Sovietwood charter party follows the Nubaltwood charter party very closely, with differences in detail, particularly concerning loading at White Sea and Kara Sea ports.

Under the purchase contract the sellers (and therefore charterers under the

Sovietwood charter party) are responsible for demurrage, freight and expenses incurred at the loading port and also demurrage at the port of discharge. If shipping documents are presented indicating that there is a claim under the charter party for demurrage, dead-freight or expenses at the loading port, then these documents should not be accepted without an appropriate letter of indemnity from the sellers.

In the case of shortages from the ship a claim for shortage of pieces on ex-ship tally should be made within eight days, in the same manner as in the Nubaltwood charter.

Payment of freight is now made in much the same stages as set down in the Nubaltwood charter.

The Nubaltwood 1973 charter party provides that 'All claims must be made in writing and the Claimant's Arbitrator must be appointed within twelve months of the delivery of the goods or the date when the goods should have been delivered.' It should be noted that the former qualification was twelve months from the date of 'final discharge'.

5.4 The Bill of Lading

The bill of lading, sometimes abbreviated to B/L, is the most important document in the carriage of any goods by sea, and it is essential for importers to understand their rights and their responsibilities in connection with it.

The Nubaltwood bill of lading contains the following clauses and information:

(a)   Name of shipping port.
(b)   Name and address of shipper.
(c)   Name of vessel and master.
(d)   Date of charter party.
(e)   Description of cargo — given as number of packages and pieces, mark and description.
(f)   Number of packages and pieces of deck cargo.
(g)   Name of port of destination.
(h)   Name of consignee 'or Assigns'.
(j)   Signature of master or agent.
(k)   Receipt for freight advance.
(l)   Clauses protecting shipowner — these are usually references to clauses in a particular charter party which shall 'apply to this bill of lading'.
(m)   The clause 'Quality, condition and measure unknown'.
(n)   The reverse side will often contain the specification of the goods covered by the bill of lading.

It fulfils three main functions:

(1)   It is a receipt by the master of the ship for the goods shipped. It

must be remembered, however, that it is a receipt only for the number of packages and/or pieces shipped. The master of the ship or shipowners are only responsible for the number of packages and/or pieces signed for and acknowledged as received.

The master signs for the goods *quality, condition and measure unknown,* but first of all it is stated that the goods were shipped at the named loading port 'in good order and condition' and later the master undertakes that the goods shall 'be delivered in the like good order and condition'. It is sometimes supposed that this undertaking is cancelled by the words at the foot of the bill of lading, namely 'quality, condition and measure unknown'. But there are in effect two clauses which, while they seem contradictory, are not so but are really complementary, the first being a specific undertaking by the master and the latter a general understanding. Taking the latter (i.e., the general) clause first, it is clear that the master of the vessel has no interest in 'quality': the freight rate would be the same whatever the quality. The intrinsic 'condition' of the goods (as distinct from their apparent 'condition'), whether discoloured or otherwise, would not concern him either (except in so far as affects clause 1A of the charter (Nubaltwood) as to their being properly seasoned). The 'measure' of the goods certainly concerns the master, as the size of the cargo and the amount of freight are calculated upon it, but would be very difficult for the master to check, so it is the custom to accept the evidence of the seller's invoice as to measure, and therefore quantity, on the basis that 'what is good enough for the buyer to pay on is also good enough for the ship to be paid freight on'. 'Actual' and 'nominal' are of course another matter, as freight is always paid on 'actual' measurement. There remains, however, the master's specific undertaking to deliver the goods in as good order and condition as he received them, as he is primarily responsible for any damage that may occur to the goods during passage, from the time they were shipped to the time they are delivered, and this includes the breaking of pieces which is a common occurrence.

(2)   It is *evidence* of the terms of the *freight contract* made between the charterer and the shipowner.

Quite obviously it is not the freight contract itself, as this must be drawn up before the goods are shipped, while the bill of lading is drawn up only when the goods are actually being shipped. However, if there is no separate charter party, the bill of lading does give the necessary legal framework for evidence as to the freight contract.

The Bills of Lading Act, 1855, states that the rights and obligations under a freight contract are vested in the endorsee of a bill of lading, just as if the endorsee had made the freight contract himself. This again is an essential factor of the c.i.f. contract, as the buyer, when he acquires ownership of the goods on passage, must have the full protection of the freight contract as well as the insurance policy taken out by the shipper.

(3)   It is a *document of title* to the *goods*. Without the bill of lading, delivery of the goods at their port of destination cannot be obtained.

This can be explained in greater detail as follows:

(a)   In law rightful possession of the bill of lading is equivalent to ownership of the goods it represents.

(b)   The title to the goods can be transferred by *endorsement* and *delivery*
of the bill of lading.

(c)   To make it a negotiable instrument, a bill of lading must by its terms
be deliverable to a *named person* or to *a name left blank* followed by *'or to*
order or assigns'. It is not usual to put 'deliver to bearer'.

(d)   By the Sale of Goods Act (Section 47) the bill of lading must be
'lawfully transferred' by a person who has a right to transfer it.

(e)   The endorsee of a bill of lading acquires no better title to the goods
than was possessed by the endorser. If, therefore, a bill of lading is in the
possession of a person who had *no* title to it because the bill of lading had
been stolen or lost, any subsequent transfer of the bill of lading confers no
title on the innocent buyer. There is a considerable difference here between
the bill of lading as a negotiable instrument and, say, a bill of exchange or a
cheque: if a bearer cheque, or a cheque endorsed in blank is lost or stolen, a
person who subsequently acquires it in good faith and for value obtains a
good title, and is entitled to payment of the cheque.

The form of bill of lading used with the Nubaltwood charter has been
evolved over years of trading and presents few difficulties to the importer.
Other forms of bills of lading, that are used for all classes of merchandise, are
not so simple.

In some ports a bill of lading may be drawn up before the goods are loaded,
while they are in transit sheds or wharves. This form of bill of lading confers
a good title to the goods, but is not a clear receipt that the goods have been
loaded. In certain French ports a similar document known as a *pris en charge*,
duly stamped and sworn before a notary or consul, is used. Its chief advantage
lies in the fact that it enables the property in the goods to be transferred to
the buyers without delay. Where there is a very short sea voyage of no more
than two days, the vessel may have arrived at the port of destination before
the normal shipping documents and bills of lading have been received by the
importer to enable him to obtain possession of the goods.

Practically all shippers and importers, however, require a bill of lading
referring to the actual goods placed on board the vessel. This is known as an
'on board bill of lading' or a 'shipped bill of lading'. With the Nubaltwood
charter these phrases are not used, since the bill of lading is automatically an
'on board bill of lading' by virtue of the clauses embodied in it and the charter,
but it is wise to use this phrase when describing the type of bill of lading
required for goods being shipped from other parts of the world. In these
other forms of bill of lading the words 'on board' are sometimes endorsed on
the face of the bill of lading to indicate that the goods described in the bill of
lading were in fact all loaded.

A bill of lading drawn up on the prescribed form and signed by the master
or agent without any qualifying terms is said to be a 'clean bill of lading'. If
any qualifying terms are added, it is said to be a 'claused bill of lading'. In

recent years the growth of claused bills of lading has presented a serious problem to the timber trade. These qualifications limit the shipowners' liabilities. Although these clauses may cover any condition in which the cargo is received by the vessel, the most common qualifying clauses are '. . . pieces said to be . . .' or '. . . shipper's count said to be . . .'. Thus, although the master of the vessel is signing for a certain number of pieces, the shipowners are not accepting responsibility for that number of pieces. The only way to overcome such a clause is to institute some form of tally, to be acknowledged by the shipowners, as the goods are loaded. This is additional expense and not completely satisfactory. The use of these terms and clauses depends largely on the freight market. With present-day values of timber, the loss of a number of pieces can amount to a substantial amount of money. At the same time, shortage of freight space places shipowners in a strong position from which, to a certain extent, they can dictate terms to their own advantage.

5.5 Liner Bill of Lading

As opposed to carrying by tramp tonnage, many shipments of softwood, and the majority of shipments of hardwood and plywood, are carried by liners. If goods are carried by a liner on a scheduled journey, no charter party is necessary, since the shipowners themselves have determined the ports and dates of loading and discharge.

When freight space on a liner service is booked for the carriage of timber, this is confirmed by the shipowners on a 'booking note' which describes the cargo and voyage, usually without nominating a vessel. All other conditions are said to be 'as per bill of lading', or may refer to some other standard form of charter as 'all other terms and conditions as per Nubaltwood charter'.

The terms of the freight contract and other terms and conditions normally found in the charter party are now embodied in the bill of lading. These liner bills of lading therefore contain much more detail and many more clauses and provisions than ordinary tramp bills of lading.

In considering liner bills of lading it must be remembered that there may be as many as 500 on a particular voyage. The relationship between the shipowners and the bill of lading holders is therefore rather different. The bill of lading holder represents merely a very small part of the interest in the cargo being carried, as apart from a major interest or a total interest in the case of a tramp cargo, where the bill of lading holder is also the charterer.

The liner bill of lading holder must accept the shipowners' terms and conditions of carriage; he can rarely make his own stipulations about loading and discharging wharves, for instance. On the other hand, since small parcels only are being carried and it is presumed that the liners are making regular passages, there are not the same difficulties in arranging marginal quantities for the convenience of chartering.

A liner bill of lading will nearly always stipulate that the full freight must be paid before the shipowners will release the goods. There is no question of a retention by the bill of lading holder of a proportion of the freight to set off claims against the shipowners. Liner bills of lading are frequently claused 'freight payable ship lost or not lost', which is self-explanatory and necessitates that the charterer shall insure the full amount of freight as well as the f.a.s. value if he wishes to be fully covered against all loss in the event of the vessel being lost at sea.

Most liner booking notes and bills of lading are drawn up by the shipowners concerned, who print their own forms with their own terms and conditions.

There is a standard form of liner booking note, known by the code name 'Conlinebooking' and a liner bill of lading, known by the code name 'Conline-bill', published by the Chamber of Shipping and approved by the Baltic and International Maritime Conference, last amended in 1978.

The Conlinebooking booking note sets down the following information, and in this respect resembles a charter in the hands of the importer:

(1) Names of shipowners and bills of lading holders (referred to as 'merchants').

(2) Name of vessel (with rights of substitution).

(3) Name of loading port.

(4) Name of discharging port.

(5) Approximate time of shipment.

(6) Rate of freight – and whether prepayable or payable at destination.

(7) Whether goods to be loaded on deck or under deck.

(8) Name of bill of lading holder's representatives at loading port (will usually be the shippers).

This form of booking note then proceeds to set down extracts of the more important clauses and conditions of the Conlinebill bill of lading, on which the goods will be carried.

The Conelinebill bill of lading follows the normal bill of lading, showing a full detail of the goods carried ('weight, measure, marks, numbers, quality, contents and value unknown'), with the amount loaded on deck, together with the rate of freight payable and amount of any freight advance.

The standard clauses printed are as follows:

Clause 1. Definition of term 'merchant'—which covers the shipper, importer, etc., as holder of the bill of lading.

Clause 2. Paramount clause—standard shipping clause relating to the Hague rules.

Clause 3. Jurisdiction—unless otherwise provided, any disputes on the bill of lading to be decided in, and by the law of, the country of the shipowners.

Clause 4. Period of responsibility: this limits shipowners' liability by disclaiming responsibility for loss or damage before loading or after discharge.

Clause 5. Scope of voyage, a deviation clause which in spite of the more restricted nature of the published voyage, permits shipowners to call at other ports or omit calling at some ports.

Clause 6. Substitution: permits shipowners to substitute another vessel and also permits shipowners to tranship, land, store and reship goods if necessary.

Clause 7. Lighterage, at loading or discharging ports to be for account of merchants.

Clause 8. Loading, discharge and delivery.

No set rates of loading or discharging are laid down, but the shippers (referred to as 'merchants') must be prepared to supply the cargo without any notice as soon as the vessel is ready to load. Furthermore, they must supply cargo 'as fast as the vessel can receive', during overtime periods if necessary.

At the discharging port the importers (again referred to as 'merchants') must take delivery of the goods 'as fast as the vessel can deliver'.

The importer must accept his reasonable proportion of unidentified loose cargo (which may possibly be offered in lieu of shortage on underdeck bills of lading).

Any goods not applied for within a reasonable time (usually referred to as 'overlanded') may be resold by the shipowners.

Clause 9. States that deck cargo if carried shall be subject to the Hague rules.

Clause 10. If the importer has an option of having a part of the cargo discharged at more than one port of discharge, this option must be declared at least 48 hours before the vessel reaches the first port.

Clause 11. This deals with any charges payable on the goods and other expenses, all payable by the bill of lading holder.

Where the freight is prepaid, it is deemed to have been earned when the goods are loaded, and is not then returnable.

Clause 12. Refers to shipowners' lien on the goods for any amount due, and permits the sale of the goods without recourse to a court order.

Clause 13. Shipowners' disclaimer of responsibility for any loss sustained through delay, unless caused by gross negligence of the shipowners.

Clause 14. General average clause.

Clause 15. Both to blame collision clause.

Clause 16. Force majeure, war, strikes, etc. A clause protecting shipowners against liability if the vessel does not sail or is deviated, or if goods are discharged at another port, owing to the *force majeure* circumstances set out.

Clause 17. Identity of carrier or demise clause. This clause establishes the bill of lading as evidence of a contract between the bill of lading holder and the shipowners. It proceeds to declare that any shipping line, company or agents who execute this bill of lading for the shipowners shall not be under any liability arising out of the contract if they are not one of the principals of the transaction. This is declaratory of the law, since in such circumstances they are 'agents' for one of the principals, and their position is the same in law as the shippers' agent (see page 88).

Clause 18. Exemptions and immunities of all servants and agents of the carrier. This clause affords protection of the contract to servants and independent contractors employed by them.

Clause 19. Optional stowage. Unitisation.

The printed form then goes on to state that clauses 1–19 will not be altered, but supplementary clauses may be added.

Three optional additional clauses are given; the most important relates to demurrage.

Additional Clause A. Demurrage. This clause sets out the rate of demurrage to be paid per ton if the vessel is not loaded or discharged with the dispatch set out in clause 8 (which states that goods must be supplied as fast as the vessel can receive them), any delay in waiting for berth at or off port to count. If the delay is due to causes beyond control of the bill of lading holder, the time of demurrage will be reduced by 24 hours. The demurrage will not exceed the freight on the goods, the amount being a proportionate part of the whole. Demurrage is not payable where the delay has arisen only in connection with goods belonging to other bill of lading holders.

5.6 Liner Through Bill of Lading

A liner through bill of lading is used where the carriage of the goods from the shipper to the importer takes place by several shipowners or railway companies. The freight contract in a liner through bill of lading to carry for the complete distance is one contract made with the company signing and delivering the bill of lading. Unless there are special provisions to the contrary, that company is liable for loss occurring on any part of the journey.

The freight is usually paid in advance, but whether paid in advance or collected at destination, it is usually payable for the whole journey. Should the goods be lost on any one of the stages, the bill of lading holder is not entitled to a pro rata return of the freight for the other stages. A statement commonly used in liner through bills of lading is: 'Freight is fully earned on shipment, ship lost or not lost, at any stage of the entire transit.'

The through bill of lading will cover possible transits by rail, or barge or coastal vessel and then at some stage an ocean voyage and then possibly barge or rail or coaster at the other end.

In many cases liner through bills of lading incorporate in them all the terms of the bill of lading normally issued by the shipping company carrying out the ocean voyage, when they contain a phrase such as 'incorporating all conditions expressed in the regular form of bills of lading in use by the steamship company'. The effect here is to grant to the original carrier signing the bill of lading all the rights and exceptions available under the ocean bill of lading.

It behoves the importer, or bill of lading holder, to be acquainted with the terms and conditions of the bills of lading issued by the ocean carrier, as there may well be terms therein which are particularly significant when claims etc. are considered.

The Chamber of Shipping have a standard liner through bill of lading under the code name 'Conlinethrubil'. This follows fairly closely the terms and provisions of the 'Conlinebill'.

5.7 The Hague Rules

Before 1924 shipowners were able to clause their bill of lading in such a manner that they were able to avoid responsibility for almost every contingency that could arise. Further, as every shipping line had a different form of bill of lading, it was necessary for everybody involved — merchant, insurer, banker, agent, etc. — to be acquainted with the full terms of every bill of lading in the trades with which they were concerned.

This was clearly unsatisfactory, and in 1922 a meeting at the Hague was called by the Comité Maritime International of all the interested parties to draw up a uniform set of rules to be applied to all bills of lading. These were to set out the definite rights and responsibilities to apply to both shipowners and shippers. The Hague Rules were thus formulated in 1924 and were subsequently incorporated in the UK legislation as the Carriage of Goods by Sea Act, 1924. Eventually most maritime nations passed laws giving statutory effect to the Hague Rules.

By the late 1960s it was apparent that the 1924 Rules were somewhat dated by modern standards, and a meeting was called at Brussels in 1968, when an updated version called the Brussels Protocol was formulated. This eventually became incorporated into English law as the Carriage of Goods by Sea Act, 1971. However, for this Act to become operative, it was necessary for at least ten countries to adopt the Rules, and the Carriage of Goods by Sea Act, 1971, became effective on 23 June 1977. The Scandinavian countries had, however, decided to operate the Brussels Protocol from 1974, and the Rules are now often referred to as the Hague—Visby Rules.

Some confusion may occur in that so far only eleven countries have adopted the Brussels Protocol: Denmark, Ecuador, Finland, France, Lebanon, Norway, Singapore, Switzerland, Sweden, Syria and the UK. For shipments between these countries or shipments outward from the UK the Hague—Visby Rules will apply, but for shipments inwards to the UK from other countries the original Hague Rules 1924 apply, provided, of course, that the country of consignment has adopted the Hague Rules. Because of this a 'dual' paramount clause has been introduced which reads as follows:

'The Hague Rules contained in the International Convention for the unification of certain rules relating to Bills of Lading, dated Brussels the 25th August 1924, as enacted in the country of shipment shall apply to this contract. When no such enactment is in force in the country of shipment, the corresponding legislation of the country of destination shall apply, but in respect of such shipments to which no such enactments are compulsorily applicable, the terms of the said convention shall apply.

In trades where the International Brussels Convention 1924 as amended by the protocol signed at Brussels on 23rd February 1968 — the Hague—Visby Rules — apply compulsorily, the provisions of the respective legislation shall be considered incorporated in this Bill of Lading. The Carrier takes all reservations possible under such applicable legislation, relating to the period before loading and after discharging and while the goods are in charge of another Carrier, and to deck cargo and live animals.'

It should be noted that the Hague—Visby Rules follow closely the wording of the original Hague Rules and do not apply to deck cargo and live animals.

Under the 1924 Act the carrier could limit his liability for loss or damage in connection with goods to £100 per package or unit, provided that a larger value was not inserted in the bill of lading at the time of shipment. The 1971 Act increased this to 10 000 gold francs per package or unit or 30 gold francs per kilogram gross weight, whichever is the greater. Provision is made for the exchange conversion to be determined by law. The Merchant Shipping (Sterling Equivalent) Order, which became operative on 1 February 1978, gives official conversions of £431.15 and £1.29, respectively.

5.8 The *Caspiana* Case

In 1954 a shipment of timber was made from Canada to Hull and London on the S.S. *Caspiana*, but in October of that year at the time the vessel was due to arrive, there was a nation-wide dock strike in the UK. The S.S. *Caspiana* could not discharge at Hull or London, and so proceeded to Hamburg and discharged her cargo there.

This was one of several incidents in that period but was made the subject of a test case which was at first successful for the plaintiffs. The decision was reversed by the Court of Appeal and the reversal was upheld by the House of Lords. It was a matter of great importance for the timber trade.

The bills of lading in this case included the following phrases: '. . . for carriage to London or Hull or as near thereunto as the vessel may safely get . . .', '. . . should it appear that . . . strikes . . . would prevent the vessel from . . . entering the port of discharge or there discharging in the usual manner and leaving again . . . safely and without delay, the Master may discharge the cargo at port of lading or any other safe and convenient port . . .'.

The cargo owners claimed damage for breach from the shipowners; the shipowners claimed that they had effected due delivery under the bill of lading. It was the Court of Appeal that held that this was *not* deviation as construed in the deviation clause and that in relation to the clauses of the charter and bill of lading the discharge at Hamburg should be deemed a due fulfilment of the contract.

The position of the bill of lading holder, therefore, has been clearly established in this case. His only protection now rests in laying off the high expenses incurred in such an eventuality with additional 'strikes diversion insurance'. Special insurance clauses have been drawn up to cover this point and these are examined on page 114.

6 Marine Insurance

6.1 General

Marine insurance is a contract of indemnity whereby one party (the insurer), in consideration of a specified payment (the premium), undertakes to guarantee another party (the assured) against risk of loss through maritime perils. It dates back to the earliest days of trading between countries and the carriage of goods by sea. Since it is a contract of indemnity, the assured can only recover from the insurer the amount of loss actually sustained.

The assured must have an 'insurable interest', which may be in (1) the hull, (2) the freight or (3) the cargo.

Shipowners have an insurable interest in the hull, and importers have an insurable interest in prepaid or guaranteed freight and cargo and also an agreed sum for 'imaginary profit'. The assured must have the insurable interest at the time of the loss. If the assured has no insurable interest, it becomes a gaming or wagering contract and is void.

In cases where any possible doubt could arise as to whether the assured has in fact an insurable interest the insurers should be asked to agree the insertion in the policy of the letters P.P.I., meaning 'policy proof of interest'.

The utmost good faith must be observed in a contract for marine insurance. The assured must disclose all material facts within his knowledge as to the venture insured. If this is not done, the contract is voidable by the insurer. There are two implied warranties, the seaworthiness of the vessel and the legality of the venture, but the seaworthiness of the vessel is admitted as between the cargo insurers and the cargo owner.

Marine insurance is carried on by 'underwriters' and 'insurance companies'. The most famous name in marine insurance throughout the world is Lloyd's of London. Lloyd's is an exchange of which these private 'underwriters' are the members. It started in the seventeenth century in a coffee house kept by a certain Edward Lloyd in Lombard Street where people connected with shipping and insurance met; hence the phrase in a Lloyd's policy '... that this Writing or Policy of Assurance shall be of as much Force and Effect as the surest Writing or Policy of Assurance heretofore made in Lombard Street, or in the Royal Exchange, or elsewhere in London.'

Insurance brokers act for the merchant, importer or shipper, who approaches them to arrange the insurance of their goods for a particular voyage. The insurance brokers draw up the contract of insurance (known as the 'policy') and then 'place' the insurance with underwriters or companies, from whom they receive their remuneration.

Underwriters at Lloyd's do not always accept the whole of any risk (though a group or syndicate of underwriters may do so), particularly if the sum is a large one, but accept varying proportions of the risk, writing their names and the proportions they are accepting on an abbreviated memorandum of the risk, known as the 'original slip'. Furthermore, all large risks are in fact spread by reinsurance, but that is a matter which concerns the insurer and not the assured.

The merchant, importer or other assured person may place his business direct with an insurance company or may employ an insurance broker. If the insurance is to be placed with Lloyd's underwriters, it is necessary to do so through recognised Lloyd's brokers, for Lloyd's underwriters themselves have no facilities for dealing directly with the assured.

Sometimes an insurance company will be prepared to accept the insurance of the whole, but if the sum to be insured is substantial, it is often necessary for the risk to be spread over several companies including Lloyd's under-writers, a task which can only be undertaken by a Lloyd's insurance broker.

English underwriters and insurance companies have the highest reputation, and through their vast network of connections do business in all parts of the world. A foreign shipper requiring to insure goods in a c.i.f. sale can easily do so with a British company. If, however, he wishes to insure with a foreign insurance company, most purchase contracts stipulate that the form of insurance policy and the risks covered shall be the same as if the insurance was undertaken by a British company. Furthermore, it is usual to stipulate that a foreign insurance company must be approved by the importers, as although the majority of foreign insurance companies are of the highest integrity, there are some in certain countries whose reputation for insurance is not of the best.

6.2 The Policy

The contract of marine insurance made between the insurer and the assured is known as the 'policy', which is itself governed by the Marine Insurance Act, 1906, in which it states that the policy must show:

(1) The names of the assured or some person who effects the insurance on his behalf. It can *not* be issued blank.

(2) The subject of the insurance, such as timber, prepaid or guaranteed freight or freight advance. Where the freight is to be paid at destination on delivery of the goods, only freight advance is insured, and in an Albion c.i.f. contract the buyer is not entitled to an insurance policy covering the balance of freight. On the other hand, if the freight has been prepaid, or, as in the case of many liner bills of lading, there is a clause in the freight contract stating 'freight payable ship lost or not lost', then the full freight must be insured.

(3) The risks against which the subject is insured.

(4) A description of the voyage; it is generally sufficient now to state 'via other loading and discharging ports', without naming all intermediate stopping places.

(5) The sum or sums insured. This is usually based on the f.a.s. value plus a 10 per cent imaginary profit, plus prepaid or guaranteed freight or freight advance, as the case may be, but a larger imaginary profit can usually be insured if desired.

(6) The name or names of the insurers.

Policies are of the following kinds:

(1) *Voyage policies*, where the contract is to insure the goods for a particular voyage from one place to another. Practically all policies used in importing timber are of this nature.

(2) *Time policies*, where the contract is to insure the goods for a definite period of time (not exceeding one year).

(3) *Valued policies*, where the policy specifies the agreed value of the subject matter insured.

(4) *Unvalued policies*, where the value of the subject matter is not specified but is left to be ascertained subsequently, subject to the limit of the sum insured.

(5) *Floating policies*, where the insurance is in general terms, leaving the name of the vessel, details of voyage and goods, etc., to be defined by a subsequent declaration. These declarations may be made by endorsement on the policy, or on special declaration forms, and must be made in order of shipments. The policy is issued for a particular amount, on which an initial premium is paid and is legally binding, but floating policies are very seldom used nowadays.

(6) *Open cover*. This is not a policy, but is an agreement by insurers to issue an appropriate policy within the terms of the open cover when the necessary details have been supplied. It covers every shipment within the limit of the cover and is in force for an agreed period of time, usually a year. The relevant details for each shipment are supplied on a declaration form as for a floating policy. The premium rates are usually specified in the cover, which may also contain a limitation of the amount of goods to be insured in any one vessel.

On receipt of the declaration form, the brokers prepare a policy in the normal way.

Open cover policies are popular with importers and shippers because of their convenience and the safe assurance that any cargo within the voyage limits and other conditions is held covered automatically. This latter point is important for the importer who has purchased goods on f.a.s. terms and who will frequently have goods on passage before the relevant shipping documents for those goods reach him.

6.3 The Policy Form

One of the characteristics of marine insurance is its flexibility. It must cover every class of goods that are carried by sea, the ships that carry these goods and the value of their carriage or freight. It would clearly be impracticable to issue a fresh policy for each and every type of goods and service insured, and so a standard type of policy form is used and then amended by additional clauses to suit the class of goods insured.

The most important standard type of policy is known as Lloyd's S.G. policy, the S.G. possibly standing for 'ship—goods'; this is set out in the Marine Insurance Act of 1906. It is not obligatory to use this particular policy, but it is the policy form most used by both Lloyd's and insurance companies.

This type of policy has been in use for centuries, and the wording has changed very little throughout the years. As a result many of the phrases are archaic and some refer to perils and practices that ceased a century and a half ago. They are still retained in the policy for the very good reason that, the form having existed in its present state for so long, there is no ambiguity in any part of it. Everyone concerned in the policy is fully aware of the meaning of each of the phrases which have been tested and interpreted in the courts during this long period.

If a new, modernised form of policy were prepared, there would inevitably be some matters in dispute, and the legal meaning of many of the phrases would again have to be tested and ruled in court.

The policy takes the following form:

(1) *Name* of assured.

(2) *Description* of voyage.

(3) *Name of vessel*. It is essential that the name of the vessel be given. This is not, of course, always possible until the time of shipment, as vessels are often substituted; however, the name must be declared when notifying insurers of the sailing. The reader is referred to the New Institute Classification Clause dated 1 July 1978.

(4) *Name of master*. This is unnecessary and is very rarely inserted.

(5) *Description of goods* and value insured. This should include the information as to whether the goods are length packaged, truck bundled, containerised, loose or of any other accepted method of packaging.

(6) *Rate* of premium.

(7) *Signature* of superintendent (with seal) of Lloyd's Policy Signing Office, or, in the case of insurance companies' policies, an official of the company concerned.

(8) *Endorsement* of numbers of underwriting syndicates and in the case of a combined insurance companies' policy, a list of the individual companies.

'Lost or not lost'. These words make the contract retrospective, in as much as underwriters are liable for loss which may have occurred before the contract

was drawn up, provided, of course, that the assured was unaware of the loss when the contract was drawn up.

'*At and from*'. These words appear before the name of the loading port. In a voyage policy the attachment of the insurance (that is, the commencement) starts from the moment the goods are loaded on to the oceangoing vessel. It does not cover the transit by lighter, etc., to the vessel, and this risk has to be covered by the addition of further clauses.

The insurance continues during the voyage, but a major deviation or transhipment or other variation of the risk could nullify the policy, so these eventualities also have to be covered by additional clauses. The insurance ends when the goods have safely reached their port of discharge.

6.4 The Perils Insured Against

'*Of the Seas*'. The foundering of the vessel, collision, stranding, heavy weather damage, etc.

'*Men of War, Fire, Enemies, Pirates*'. With the exception of fire, these are now treated as war risks. They are excluded from the policy by the addition of a special exclusion clause, the 'Free of capture and seizure clause' (see below). These risks are then covered by a separate war risk insurance with a further premium.

Piracy includes passengers in mutiny and rioters who attack the vessel from the shore.

'*Rovers*'. An anachronism.

'*Thieves*'. This term refers to assailing thieves and not petty pilferers. Where goods are covered under a 'warehouse to warehouse' clause, as in the TTF clauses, it has been held that thieves who enter a place where the goods are stored by forcibly breaking through doors, etc., are within the meaning of the term.

'*Jettisons*'. The throwing overboard of goods for the safety of the vessel, as opposed to washing overboard by the sea.

'*Letters of Mart and Counter Mart*'. An anachronism.

'*Surprisals, Takings at Sea*'. Surprisals might be treated as a war risk, but takings at sea can also include actions by a shipowner which are tantamount to theft or conversion.

'*Arrests, Restraints and Detainments of all Kings, Princes and People of what Nation, Condition, or Quality soever*'. This does not include judicial arrests, riots, etc.

'*Barratry of the Master or Mariners*'. Wrongful acts wilfully committed by the master or crew to the prejudice of shipowners.

'*All Other Perils*'. This phrase is not comprehensive, it means perils of a similar nature to those already specified.

Sue and labour clauses. These are expenses incurred to minimise or avert a loss from an insured peril, and are recoverable under the policy.

Free of capture and seizure clause. This clause, known as the F.C. and S.

clause, excludes the war risks which form part of the perils included in the original form of policy. These risks are normally covered separately, the wording including the phrase '. . . to cover the perils excluded by the F.C. and S. clause . . .', but further risks are also covered. It also excludes loss or damage by strikes, etc., if the wording is F.C. and S., as S.R. and C.C. (strikes, riots and civil commotions) are risks also covered separately.

Franchise clause. With the exception of general average (see page 102) or when the vessel is stranded, sunk or burnt (see F.P.A. clause, page 108), a franchise is set on claims on certain classes of goods. This is 3 per cent in the case of ordinary cargo, also the vessel and freight. This means that in a policy for £100 no claim of less than £3 will be recognised. If the franchise is reached, the claim is paid in full. This clause will often be overridden by the addition of clauses stating '. . . to pay irrespective of percentage'.

The T.T.F. insurance clauses change the franchise to ½ per cent or £10, whichever is the less (see page 109).

6.5 Losses Covered by Marine Insurance

The main losses normally recoverable under a marine insurance policy are as follows:

(1) Total loss. (a) absolute or actual; (b) constructive.
(2) Partial loss or damage. Known as 'Particular Average'.
(3) General average loss or expenditure.
(4) Salvage loss.
(5) Other charges incurred on the goods such as (a) salvage charges; (b) particular charges; (c) sue and labour charges; (d) extra charges.

These items are discussed at greater length in the following pages.

(1a) ABSOLUTE OR ACTUAL TOTAL LOSS

This is self-explanatory. In addition to destruction, it includes loss where the goods are so damaged as to cease to be a thing of the kind insured, or where the assured is permanently deprived of the goods.

(1b) CONSTRUCTIVE TOTAL LOSS

This is loss where the goods are reasonably abandoned on account of actual total loss appearing unavoidable or else where the preservation of the goods from actual total loss appears to be more expensive than the value of the goods.

(2) PARTICULAR AVERAGE

This is any partial loss of or damage to the goods themselves caused by a peril insured against, which is not general average (q.v.). (The word 'average' here is derived from the Italian *avarigio*, meaning risk.)

Particular average occurs where there is: (a) partial loss; (b) damage or deterioration or both; (c) partial loss and damage or deterioration of what remains. Certain types of cargo are much more likely to suffer damage than others, for instance, a deck cargo of timber may easily be damaged by sea water; underwriters will usually not accept the risk of damage to such cargo unless there is a major peril to the vessel or goods, such as fire, collision or stranding of the vessel.

The exclusion of these risks is said to make this type of cargo 'free from particular average', usually abbreviated F.P.A.

(3) GENERAL AVERAGE

This is quite independent of marine insurance; it is an obligation on all parties with an interest in the vessel, freight or goods, arising out of the freight contract.

General average loss or expenditure, however, is a loss covered by marine insurance. It is a voluntary sacrifice of one interest for the benefit of all interests. It may occur when it is found necessary to jettison part of the deck cargo to lighten the vessel in heavy weather or to get the vessel off a sandbank. Without the sacrifice of this part of the cargo, the vessel would be in danger and the whole of the cargo might be lost. The value of the goods sacrificed is therefore carried by the vessel and cargo proportionately to the value of each interest, and is divided between all the holders of bills of lading and the shipowners. These are known as 'general average contributions', and they are assessed in accordance with the York—Antwerp Rules of 1974 or as per contract of affreightment. Charterers and holders of bills of lading accept responsibility for paying these contributions in the charter and bill of lading. The amount of these contributions is a loss or expense for which each holder of a bill of lading is responsible for his own share but is covered by his marine insurance policy.

If there has been a general average loss on a vessel, the shipowners may place a lien on the cargo when the vessel reaches port, until such time as security is given by cargo interests.

Holders of bills of lading may obtain delivery of their goods by signing a *general average bond*, in which they agree to pay any contributions due from them. If the amount is large, the shipowners may insist on a *general average deposit* being paid into a bank in the name of trustees, or it is customary for a general average guarantee to be accepted from reputable insurers. In either case the insurers should be consulted first and their approval obtained, so that the bill of lading holder is quite clear that he is covered.

The calculation of the general average and the apportioning of it among the interests concerned may be very complicated and not be settled for a long time, especially, for instance, if the vessel goes into a port of refuge. It is dealt with by specialists, who are certified *average adjusters.*

(4) SALVAGE LOSS

Loss where, by reason of the perils insured against, the goods are necessarily sold before they reach their destination.

(5a) SALVAGE CHARGES

Incurred to save a vessel in peril.

(5b) PARTICULAR CHARGES

Expenses incurred by the assured in the defence, safeguarding and recovery of the goods.

(5c) SUE AND LABOUR CHARGES

Sue and labour charges must be charges incurred to minimise or prevent a loss from an insured peril.

(5d) EXTRA CHARGES

These are other charges arising out of damage and claims, and they include such items as survey fees, auction charges, etc.

It should be noted that any additional charges or expenses which are not included in the insured value, such as additional expenses incurred in shipping goods to their original destination, if they have been discharged elsewhere as a result of a shipowner availing himself of the liberties clause in a bill of lading, are not recoverable.

6.6 The Timber Trade Federation Insurance Clauses

From sections 6.2 and 6.3 it will be seen that the main body of the policy is in rather open terms, covering the goods only from the moment they are placed on board the vessel, and restricted to a clearly defined voyage with little margin for deviation. Furthermore, a study of charter parties and bills of lading (see Chapter 5) reveals many additional risks that are not covered under the standard form of policy. Some of these risks are sufficiently serious to give rise to the cancellation of the policy by insurers, such as wrongful acts by the shipowners, unseaworthiness of the vessel, etc.

The TTF insurance clauses have been drawn up and agreed between the TTF and the Institute of London Underwriters and Lloyd's Underwriters Association. They are accepted by all reputable insurers and are acknowledged in practically every timber exporting country in the world. When attached to the policy, which has the words 'including Timber Trade Federation clauses' endorsed upon it, the policy is deemed to be extended to cover all the additional risks and contingencies detailed in these clauses.

Clause 1: Transit Clause

This is sometimes known as the 'warehouse to warehouse' clause and extends the cover from the shipper's yard, which may be some distance inland, right through to the 'final destination'.

The cover afforded by this clause is very wide, and it goes far beyond the cover normally given under general cargo insurance clauses – in particular, the Institute cargo clauses.

A marine insurance policy only attaches when the assured has an 'insurable interest' in the goods. In the case of an f.a.s. contract, the property (and, hence, risk) usually passes to the buyer when the goods are placed on board, and normally this is the point where the assured assumes an insurable interest. However, the Uniform f.a.s. contract clearly states that the goods are at the risk of the buyer from the moment they are loaded on to transport, etc., at the shipper's mill or wharf. Since the goods here are at the risk of the buyers, they clearly have an insurable interest in the goods, and this is conceded by underwriters.

At the same time, it must always be remembered that in spite of the wide ambit of cover given by this clause – the assured *must* have an insurable interest in the goods, and the cover will only commence at the point where that insurable interest starts. The insurable interest is always determined by the sale contract conditions. The sale contract may give a buyer a contractual obligation to insure which otherwise would not exist: for example, goods bought on f.a.s. terms but where the contract gives the buyer a contractual obligation to insure the goods from the mill of origin. This is of great importance where goods are purchased on forms of contract other than the Uniform and Albion. Importers are well advised to check with their insurance brokers that they are adequately protected in the preloading period of such contracts; if necessary, arranging for their policies to be endorsed to cover the period up to loading on board.

The words 'in transit' not only mean the period when the goods are moving in an oceangoing vessel or lighter, etc., but also cover ordinary transhipment, delays in transit warehouses, etc., beyond the control of the assured.

The words 'final destination' cover the buyer who is resident outside a port and whose goods are to be delivered to his storage yard inland from the port. They also cover the buyer who resells his goods before arrival on delivered terms to a customer who requires the goods delivered to an inland destination.

However, it is vitally important that there is no break in the journey – the goods must remain 'in transit' for the full journey. If the journey is broken at all (for instance, if the goods are sorted at some intermediate warehouse, or if the goods are stored in a warehouse at the port, for the convenience of the assured), the policy lapses where the original journey is broken. The cover to final destination does not include a further sea voyage, such as by coastal shipping. If the goods are transhipped for delivery by coastal vessel, the policy lapses at the point of transhipment.

In a c.i.f. resale the benefits and cover of the policy pass to the new buyer, provided there has been no break in the journey. In an ex-ship sale the policy lapses after the goods have been discharged from the ship. A purchaser on ex-ship terms, therefore, must ensure that his insurance covers him from the moment the goods leave the ship.

It will be seen from the following notes that when the goods are to be stored at the place at which they are finally landed, the assured or receivers must make certain that they are adequately covered by insurance against fire from the time that they are made available, or at the termination of the 15 day period, whichever is the earlier.

It is here worth recording in full clause 1 of the TTF Clauses, which reads as follows:

'Notwithstanding that the description of the voyage contained in the body of the policy may state only the ports and places of shipment and discharge, the insurance shall attach subject to the Assured then having an insurable interest at any time on or after the loading of the goods insured hereunder on land and/or water conveyances or their floating at the mill, warehouse, factory, yard or premises wheresoever, from which the despatch to the overseas vessel is made, and shall continue while the goods remain in transit until delivery by land or water into the mill, warehouse, factory, yard or premises at their final destination, whether at the port of discharge of the overseas vessel or (further sea voyage excepted) elsewhere and are there made available to the Assured or Receivers. Provided always that where the insured goods are to be stored at the place at which they are finally landed from vessel or craft, the Underwriters' liability for loss or damage by fire shall not extend beyond 15 days from midnight of the day of the completion of such final landing notwithstanding that the goods have not then been made available to the Assured or Receivers.'

In explanation of this clause the TTF have made the following comments concerning the cover afforded after discharge from the vessel:

'The title of this clause and its wording is a reminder that the TTF Clauses are attached to and set out the conditions of a Marine Insurance Policy covering the subject matter insured while it is in transit and, with certain exceptions which do not come within the scope of these notes, only while it is in the ordinary course of transit. It follows that immediately the transit ceases the insured merchant should consider his position under the insurance policy, particularly when such transit ceases on his own instructions.

'It is clear enough that the insurance terminates on delivery of the goods at the final yard or premises at destination but it is not uncommon for the goods to be held in store either at the port of discharge or at some depot short of delivery to final destination. When the goods are so stored at the instance of the Assured, whether for his convenience or otherwise and however temporarily, the Transit Insurance also terminates on delivery to that store. On occasions, although the goods have been delivered into store they are not immediately made available to the Assured or Receiver, e.g. pending completion of processing and recording by wharfinger or Port Authority; the insurance continues until they are made available.

'In that respect it will be seen that there is an important proviso to the effect that where the goods are to be stored at the place at which they are finally landed from vessel or craft and the goods have not been made available within 15 days of midnight of the day of completion of final landing, the risk of loss or damage by fire is then excluded. Other risks are still covered until the goods are made available.

'To sum up therefore the insurance remains in force against all risks insured while the goods are in the ordinary course of transit including during delays beyond the control of the Assured (such as delays resulting from strikes or congestion not attributable to the Assured).

'Two other points must be mentioned: first, although provision is made for the insurance to attach and to remain in force during the transit from the mill of origin to the yard or premises at final destination, it is emphasised that such insurance cover is subject to insurable interest. That interest depends on the terms of sale but, amongst other things, it should be borne in mind that the transit insurance does not continue for the benefit of the buyer when goods are sold ex-ship or ex-store even where there is no interruption of transit, as the goods are then the subject of a fresh contract. Secondly, Members should bear in mind that Clause 15 of the TTF Clauses makes it a condition of the insurance that the Assured shall act with reasonable despatch in all circumstances within their control, and that compliance with such condition is quite independent of the matters dealt with in Clause 1.

'If in doubt as to the position of insurance cover, consult your Broker or Insurers, or the Federation. Members are particularly recommended to obtain advice where transit is interrupted, whether such interruption is voluntary or involuntary.'

The words ' . . . Assured or Receivers . . .' covers the situation where goods are sold on delivered terms, and delivery is taken not by the Assured but by his customer.

Clause 2: Extended Cover Clause
The normal policy permits of only limited deviation from the voyage described, and does not cover transhipment, but this clause provides for contingencies outside the control of the Assured where transhipment may be necessary. The charter grants deviation liberties to the shipowners, and in any case this is well outside the control of the assured.

This clause protects the assured against these contingencies. However, it only covers the goods during the period of deviation against the risks covered by the policy. *It does not cover the goods against damage or deterioration caused by the delay itself.* Delay is specifically excluded in clause 6 (a).

For instance, where timber, shipped as seasoned for a normal voyage to the UK is delayed owing to breakdown of the ship through a peril of the sea, and is found on arrival to have discoloured and sweated badly (even to the extent of becoming rotten), the underwriters are not liable under the policy. Although the delay to the vessel was caused by a peril or risk insured against, the damage to the timber has been caused by the *delay* and so is not covered under the policy.

Clause 3: Termination of Adventure Clause
This clause protects the assured in the event of the voyage being terminated at any port other than that named in the policy, and covers the goods until they are either sold or forwarded to their original destination *provided that notice is given to the assurers and additional premium paid if required.*

Thereafter the goods are covered in accordance with the Transit clause until they are made available to the assured or receivers. Again it should be borne in mind that this clause does not extend to cover any additional expenses incurred in forwarding goods to their final destination.

Clause 4: Craft, etc., Clause
This clause is particularly to cover transit by water to the vessel at the loading port, since the standard policy form itself only covers the goods from the moment they are put on board.

Lightermen in London, under the London Lighterage clause, repudiate all liability for loss or damage to goods, in their contract with the importer. If there is loss from a lighter, the insurers, on settling the claim with the assured, are entitled to subrogation of the assured's rights of recourse against third parties. If the assured contracts out of these rights (as in the London Lighterage clause) without informing the insurer, that would amount to concealment of a material fact and would enable the insurers to void the policy. This clause protects the assured against that possibility.

Clause 5: Change of Voyage Clause
The 'Held covered at premium to be arranged' gives additional safety to the assured but it is essential that if any change of voyage occurs, or error or omission is discovered, the insurers shall be notified immediately.

Clause 6: Risks covered

(a) All risks are construed as meaning all physical loss or damage arising from any fortuitous occurrence. Therefore, they do not cover claims due to loss, damage or expenses due to delay or inherent vice of the goods themselves, which are, in fact, specifically excluded.

The question of 'inherent vice' – particularly when associated here with the question of 'delay' – is important, as this may affect claims for deterioration of cargo through sweating, etc., during voyage. It is assumed that wood goods are 'properly seasoned' as stated in the contract and charter for a normal voyage to the country of destination. If the goods when discharged are found to be damaged or stained, have commenced to rot, etc., the assured has a legitimate claim, provided that it has been caused by a risk covered. Such reasons would include among others the following: insufficient ventilation in the holds; flooding of the holds; contamination with other goods which have sweated, such as hides. If, on the other hand, there are no such circumstances as these to support the claim, the insurers may reject it on the ground that the deterioration has been caused through the goods being insufficiently seasoned for the voyage—in other words 'inherent vice,' or 'nature of the goods.'

(b) This is the *TTF Deckload F.P.A. Clause.* The deckload is not covered for particular average (that is, partial loss or damage), but the insurers pay for any portion of the cargo totally lost by jettison or washing overboard, or in the loading, transhipment or discharge.

On the other hand, insurers will pay for particular average if the vessel or craft *at any time during the voyage* suffers from the following perils; however, the goods must be on board at the time of the casualty.

If the vessel or craft is:

(1) *Stranded.* The vessel must have remained stranded for a reasonable time. The clause does not apply if the vessel merely touches the bar of a harbour when passing over. Neither does it apply in cases where it is the custom for vessels to lie on the mud in tidal harbours.

(2) *Sunk.*

(3) *Burnt.* This means a fire affecting the structure of the vessel itself.

(4) *In Collision.* Contact with another vessel or any other external substance (ice included) other than water.

The insurers will also pay any loss or damage to deck cargo, which may reasonably be attributed to fire, explosion or collision (see above); for discharge at port of distress also to pay special charges for landing, warehousing and forwarding, if incurred at port of loading, call or refuge, etc.

This clause extends the insurance cover of underdeck cargo to include 'cargo stowed in poop, forecastle, deck house, shelter deck, or other enclosed space . . .'. This is important in connection with the Pacif c.i.f. contract form (see chapter 9).

(c) This clause overrides the general franchise clause. A lower franchise limit of ½ per cent or £10 is quoted. It is possible, however, that loss from a raft, etc., might not amount to ½ per cent of the whole cargo, so by stating that each raft, etc., is to be a separate insurance, claims are payable when the amount is ½ per cent of the raft etc., in question, as opposed to ½ per cent of the whole cargo. It must not be overlooked that in spite of the ½ per cent franchise, the assured may recover a claim in full if it amounts to £10 or over, since the clause makes it clear that the ½ per cent or £10 shall apply, whichever is the lower.

Clause 7: Constructive Total Loss

This clause was introduced into the 1962 edition of the TTF clauses for the purpose of clarifying underwriters' position under marine insurance law operating in certain foreign countries, such as France, Belgium and the United States. It makes no difference, however, to the position which has always obtained in the UK, where the Marine Insurance Act of 1906 clearly defines underwriters' liability in the case of constructive total loss.

Clause 8: General Average Clause

This clause binds underwriters to accept adjustments drawn up under the York—Antwerp Rules, or foreign statements if in accordance with contract of affreightment, with a statement of general average drawn up in a foreign port if necessary.

Clause 9: Seaworthiness Admitted Clause

This clause is to cover the assured against the 'exceptions' clause in charter and bill of lading (see Nubaltwood charter clause 12).
     The seaworthiness of the vessel is a warranty implied in every contract of marine insurance; if the vessel is unseaworthy, insurers under the policy alone would be entitled to repudiate the policy. Seaworthiness, however, is another matter beyond the control of a shipper or importer and, in fact, is a matter about which the insurer will probably have more information. Since the insurers now admit seaworthiness of the vessel, if the vessel is later found to be unseaworthy, the assured's position is not prejudiced.

Clause 10: Not to Inure Clause

This clause makes it clear that the policy issued to the owner of the goods does not benefit a carrier or other bailee while such goods are in his care, custody or control.

Clause 11: Both to Blame Collision Clause

This clause protects the assured in the event of any liability falling on them under the provision of the charter (see Nubaltwood charter clause 23).

Clause 12: War Risks Exclusion Clause

This clause excludes the risks that are normally excluded anyway from the standard marine insurance policy by the F.C. and S. clause (see page 101). These war risks have to be covered separately by the addition of special war and strike risks clauses at an additional premium.

Clause 13: Strikes etc. Exclusion Clause

The same remarks apply as in the case of clause 12. The risks excluded by the Free of Strikes, Riots and Civil Commotions clause in the TTF clauses are covered as separate risks by using the Institute Strikes, Riots and Civil Commotions Clauses (Timber Trade). The normal practice is to insure war and strikes together at an inclusive additional premium, but if strikes only are insured without war risks, a separate additional premium is charged.

Clause 14: Increased Value Clause

Where the assured places an additional value on the goods due to changed circumstances (say a rise in market value between the date of placing the insurance and the date of arrival), the agreed valuation of the policy is automatically raised to the new figure. This enables the insurers to obtain subrogation rights for the increased value from the assured, after they have settled claims to the assured.

Increased value can also arise where balance of freight, import duty and other charges are payable after arrival at the port of discharge. This is of particular interest when the goods are still at risk for some time until they reach their ultimate destination. If the insured value is based on the f.a.s. value plus 10 per cent plus freight advance, there may be a substantial under-insurance after the balance of freight and other charges are paid.

The declaration for such increased value insurances should be made for the full voyage to provide for damage occurring prior to the payment of freight or duty or other subjects of the increased value of the goods.

The premium for increased value insurance is normally at a reduced rate.

Clause 15: Reasonable Despatch Clause

This clause must be read in conjunction with the note appended at the end of these clauses, which reads as follows: 'It is necessary for the assured to give prompt notice to the assurers when they become aware of any event for which they are "held covered" under this insurance at a premium to be arranged and the right to such cover is dependent upon compliance with this obligation.'

The prudent importer notifies the insurers of any event or occurrence which might give rise to a claim, not merely those items where he is 'held covered' until a new premium is arranged.

These TTF insurance clauses, first published in 1938 and last amended in 1962, follow closely other standard clauses in use by the London Institute of Underwriters, and, in particular, the Institute Cargo Clause (All Risks).

TTF ADDITIONAL CLAUSES FOR NON-ENGLISH POLICIES

Although not properly a part of the TTF insurance clauses, it is convenient to mention these additional clauses at this point.

Most TTF c.i.f. contract forms contain printed in the margin 'Additional clauses applicable to policies issued by non-English underwriters', these clauses usually being printed below the standard TTF insurance clauses; in fact, they are often assumed to be part of them.

Reference is made in the contract to these additional clauses, making it obligatory for sellers, if arranging insurance with foreign insurers, to ensure that the following conditions are complied with:

(1) Lloyd's standard form of policy with TTF clauses to be used, and to override terms and conditions of foreign policy forms which may be inconsistent therewith.

(2) All questions regarding interpretation of the policy to be settled according to English law, the assurers admitting the jurisdiction of the English courts.

(3) Names of paying bankers and/or agents who are authorised to act for insurers (accepting claims, service of writ, etc.) to be stated on the policy.

(4) If the insured amount is stated in both foreign currency and sterling, claims to be adjusted at the rate of exchange indicated by the two amounts. If the insured amount is expressed in foreign currency only, settlement shall be based at rate for sight bills in London on date of the policy.

6.7 War and Strike Risk Clauses

War and strike risks are excluded from the standard form of policy and the TTF insurance clauses. They must be covered by separate clauses for which a separate additional premium is charged. Special sets of clauses for the timber trade, adopted by the London Institute of Underwriters, are used for this purpose.

INSTITUTE WAR CLAUSES (revised 1976)

Clauses 1 (a), 1 (b)

The first part of these clauses primarily covers those risks previously excluded by the F.C. and S. clause in the TTF clauses from the standard form of policy.

This is merely putting back what has previously been taken out and at first sight appears illogical. The reason is clear to understand. War risk premiums vary very greatly, particularly in periods of political tension, whereas normal marine risk premiums remain reasonably steady always. Insurers are unwilling to calculate premiums to cover both marine and war risks together because of this difficulty. Accordingly, the war risks stated in the standard policy have been taken out, leaving the marine risks, and are quoted separately.

This clause recognises 'piracy' as a war risk.

The second part of the clauses goes on to define war risks as follows: ' . . . loss or damage to the interest hereby insured caused by:
(1) hostilities, warlike operations, civil war, revolution, rebellion, insurrection or civil strife arising therefrom, (2) mines, torpedoes, bombs or other engines of war'.

Mine risk insurance used to be a separate cover, but is now included here as a war risk. See Clause 3.

Clause 2

This clause defines the cover against war risks as restricted to those periods when the goods are on an overseas vessel, at the port of loading, during the voyage and until discharge, provided that discharge takes place within 15 days from the date the vessel arrives. If it takes longer, the risk ceases at the end of the 15 day period.

Sub-section (iii) again limits the risk at a port of transhipment to a similar period of 15 days.

Sub-section (b) makes it clear that the risk of mines is not subject to the same limitations and includes this risk when goods are loaded into craft for transhipment to the overseas vessel, and similarly covers the same risk upon discharge.

The remainder of the clause deals with the possibility of the contract of affreightment being terminated at a port other than the original destination, and in effect underwriters agree that war risks will reattach upon loading on board an overseas vessel for transit to the original destination or elsewhere, provided that prior notice is given and an additional premium paid.

It will be appreciated from this clause that insurance against war risks is only provided while goods are water-borne, and it is not possible to insure against these risks for goods on land. The reader's attention is drawn to the definition of a vessel's arrival — stated in detail in lines 53—59 of the clause.

Clause 3

This new clause excludes loss, damage or expense arising from any hostile use of any weapon of war employing atomic or nuclear fission and/or fusion or other like reaction or radioactive force or matter.

Clause 4

Insurers are not liable for delay, inherent vice, etc. The amended clause states '. . . except such expenses as would be recoverable in principle in English Law and practice under York—Antwerp Rules, 1974.'

Clause 5

The standard general average clause (see TTF clause 8, page 109).

Clause 6

The effect of the wording 'claims . . . payable without reference to average conditions' is to pay claims 'irrespective of percentage'. That is to say, no franchise limit operates.

Clause 7

This clause has the same effect as similar clauses in the TTF clauses. It states: 'Held covered (subject to the terms of these clauses) at a premium to be arranged in case of deviation or change of voyage, or other variation of the venture by reason of the exercise of any liberty granted to the Shipowner or Charterer under the contract of affreightment, or any omission or error in the description of the interest vessel or voyage.'

Clause 8

The last clause merely states: 'It is a condition of this insurance that the Assured shall act with reasonable despatch in all circumstances within their control.'

INSTITUTE STRIKES, RIOTS AND CIVIL COMMOTIONS CLAUSES (TIMBER TRADE)

Clause 1

This clause has the effect of covering those risks excluded by the Strikes etc.

exclusion clause 13 in the TTF clauses, and is extended to cover loss or damage to goods by persons acting maliciously.

Clause 2

This clause is important because it makes it clear that loss or damage caused by delay due to strikes, the shortage or withholding of labour, or inherent vice is excluded.

Clauses 3–9

The effect of these clauses is the same as the similar clauses appearing in the TTF clauses which, in fact, brings the cover for strikes risks, etc., into line with the marine risks, and is not restricted as in the case of war risks.

6.8 Strikes Expenses Insurance

It has been pointed out on page 95 that in the event of a shipowner exercising his right to divert his vessel from a strike-bound port and to discharge the goods elsewhere, the normal timber trade policy does not cover the additional expense incurred in bringing the goods back to their original destination or a substituted destination. In recent years, owing to the prevalence of dock strikes, this has become a serious problem to importers and can incur very substantial expenditure as a result. It has, therefore, become the practice to insure against such an eventuality.

In 1973 leading members of the timber trade decided to establish mutual insurance to provide coverage for diversion expenses caused by strikes. A mutual insurance called 'Diversion Insurance Timber Association', commonly known as 'DITA', was established, with a board of directors consisting of senior members of timber importing firms, with a secretariat drawn from the TTF and managed by a leading firm of insurance brokers. Full details for any member of the TTF wishing to join this mutual association can be obtained from the head office of the TTF.

6.9 Assignment, Certificate, Claims, Subrogation

ASSIGNMENT

In a c.i.f. contract the policy of insurance on the goods is taken out by the shipper as one of his responsibilities under the contract. Any benefits from the policy have to be receivable by the importer, since he becomes the owner of the goods long before they reach the port of destination.

When the importer becomes the owner of the goods, the risks on those goods automatically pass to him, although he may not have taken delivery of them (Sale of Goods Act, 1893).

It is essential, therefore, that he be covered by a policy of insurance and that there should be no gap in the insurance cover between the risk passing from shipper to importer. This is overcome by a legal assignment to the importer of the policy taken out by the shipper, by which the importer is put in the same position as if he had taken out the insurance policy himself for his own benefit and protection.

The Marine Insurance Act, 1906, gives the conditions governing the assignment of the policy, and these are summarised as follows:

(1) The policy can be assigned or transferred by endorsement and delivery.

(2) In order to be valid, the transfer of the policy must be one of the conditions of the sale. (In a c.i.f. contract this is usually covered by the inclusion of words to the effect that '. . . sellers will arrange insurance for the benefit of buyers, etc., etc., . . . ')

(3) The importer is entitled as a minimum to the benefit of all subsisting policies upon the goods other than profit policies.

(4) Assignment of the policy does not extend the scope of the voyage, which is still subject to the original limitations.

(5) The importer can demand a policy covering solely his own goods.

(6) If the assignment or transfer of the policy is *not* made a condition of the sale (2 above), the policy lapses on transfer of the ownership of the goods and cannot afterwards be resuscitated for the benefit of the importer.

CERTIFICATE OF INSURANCE

Where a shipper or his agent has an open cover or a floating policy, it is sometimes the practice to forward to the importer under a c.i.f. contract a 'certificate of insurance' in lieu of the actual policy.

This 'certificate of insurance' is issued by the insurers or brokers, certifying that insurance of the goods in question has been carried out. It must include all details normally stated on the policy itself and the description of cargo, value, voyage, etc., are usually identical with those in the policy. It must also state all the risks covered, which is normally done by stating that the insurance includes the TTF clauses, etc.

Although certificates of insurance are frequently used, their legality as a substitute for a true policy is doubtful unless the contract for the purchase of the goods expressly states that the shipping documents will include '. . . a certificate or policy of insurance . . .'. A certificate should not be accepted, for instance, in a sale on the Albion c.i.f. contract form, where no specific reference is made.

It is becoming more and more usual for shippers, when insuring with overseas insurance companies on an 'open cover' basis, to dispense with the usual insurance certificate but to include a certificate on their invoice couched in the following terms:

'The goods covered by this invoice are insured with . . . .
for a value of Sw. Kr . . . . including freight advance of . . . . . .
. . . . as per our Open Cover No. . . . . including: Timber
Trade Federation Clauses, Institute War Clauses and Institute Strike Clauses
(Timber Trade) (Extended Cover). Invoice No. also serves as Policy Number.
UK Claim Settling Agents: Messrs. . . . .'

There are slight variations of the above wording between the various mills,
but care should be taken to see that the TTF and other relevant clauses are
mentioned.

CLAIMS AND SUBROGATION RIGHTS

Claims for loss require substantiating with documentry evidence of the quantity short-delivered; claims for damage or deterioration will be subject to inspection, negotiation and approval of a qualified insurance surveyor or assessor,
who will survey and inspect the goods on arrival on behalf of the insurers.

When the claim has been admitted and paid, the insurers will then require
to be subrogated to all the rights and remedies of the assured in connection
with these goods. These subrogation rights enable the insurers to recover in
certain circumstances some of the value they have paid out to the assured.
This they do by taking action against other parties concerned, etc. (e.g., by
recovery from shipowners where the loss is one for which they are responsible).

6.10 Wood Goods, Insurance Definition and Plywood Insurance

Confusion sometimes occurs in respect of the terminology employed for describing timber when the question of insurance is considered. The expression
'wood goods' is customarily understood to mean deals, battens and boards, or
alternatively sawn goods. Lumber indicates logs, while round wood and pit-
props or poles should be described as such when insurances are arranged.

Plywood, veneers and similar interests should be described exactly, and
although the 1938 plywood clauses are still officially in force, it is customary
nowadays to insure plywood and similar interests in accordance with the
Institute Cargo Clauses (all risks) or the clauses when called for by the sale
contract. The Plycif, Plydef, Parcif and Pardel contract forms all call for TTF
clauses.

7 Timber Contracts I

7.1 Basic Legal Aspects of Sale of Goods

GENERAL

All transactions involving the purchase and sale of timber are governed by the law of the land. While the great majority of these transactions progress without difficulty, there are inevitably times when differences arise between buyers and sellers. These are settled according to the law, which provides for the protection of the interests of both buyers and sellers. It is necessary, therefore, for any party in commerce to have an understanding of the simple elements of the law affecting the transactions they make, in order that they may benefit fully from the particular protection they receive under the law, and at the same time be fully aware of pitfalls and circumstances where they are not protected.

THE LAW

Reference to 'the law' of this country is really reference to two main sources of law — both of which on occasion are involved.

Statute law consists of Acts of Parliament, and is also generally considered to include Statutory Instruments, which are orders, rules and regulations, etc., having the force of law, made by a Minister under the authority of an Act of Parliament.

Common law is an unwritten body of law, built up over the centuries, and developed by judicial decisions given in previous cases. These decisions, unless or until overruled by a higher court, have the effect of law.

Statute law being entirely written, may be said to that extent to be inflexible, whereas the common law may be considered to be more flexible, as the law develops, although it is nonetheless consistent.

The law is administered and enforced by the courts. The main courts of 'first instance' are the High Court and the County Courts.

The latter deal with cases of lesser importance, and in contract matters their jurisdiction extends only to claims not exceeding £2000 (except by agreement between the parties). The High Court deals with all other claims. The High Court has three Divisions: the Queen's Bench Division, which deals, among other things, with matters concerning commercial contracts; the

Chancery Division, which deals with such things as real property, patents and company matters; and the Family Division, dealing with matrimonial and probate matters. Within the Queen's Bench Division there are the Admiralty Court, dealing with cases concerning the salvage of and collision between ships, and the Commercial Court, dealing with disputes arising out of charter parties, bills of lading, claims for cargo damage, freight and demurrage and particularly dealing with international commerce. While most disputes are dealt with by the High Court in London, many large towns in England and Wales have a District Registry which is part of the High Court and where proceedings can be commenced when the parties reside or carry on business there.

Generally there is a right of appeal against a judgment of the High Court or of the County Court, and this appeal is heard by the Court of Appeal. If this appeal fails, then the matter may, in certain strictly limited circumstances, be taken as a final resort to the House of Lords, acting in its judicial capacity.

The Statutory Instruments previously referred to are given an official number and are published in leaflet form by Her Majesty's Stationery Office. Up to 1948 these Instruments were known as Statutory Rules and Orders. It is these Statutory Instruments which have provided the majority of detailed regulations to which the trade has been subject since 1939 — that is, consumption licensing, acquisition and disposal of timber, prices (when and where controlled), returns to be made, etc.

According to English law, the law which governs the rights and obligations of parties to a contract is that which is known as the 'proper law' of the contract. This 'proper law' is what the parties themselves have intended shall govern the contract, but in many instances, of course, the parties make no specific reference to the matter in their contract, and the English courts therefore determine the question by endeavouring to ascertain from the contract itself what the intention was, by considering such matters as the place of performance of the contract, the currency in which the price is to be paid, the language in which the contract is written, etc., in order to find out the general preponderance of one law over another. So far as timber contracts are generally concerned, however, the matter is not usually so complicated as this, because the courts also usually hold that where there is an arbitration clause in a contract, and this provides for arbitration in England, then the parties intended that English law shall apply. As a general rule, therefore, it may be said that English law governs the usual timber contracts, although the position might well be different if, for instance, a buyer visited a seller in his own country and there entered into a contract in a form other than the usual printed timber trade contract forms.

THE SALE OF GOODS ACT

The Sale of Goods Act, 1893, which codified the law that applied at that time, has recently been amended in a number of respects. The Supply of

Goods (Implied Terms) Act, 1973, has amended the undertakings given by the seller to a buyer relating to the quantity or fitness of the goods sold. The Unfair Contract Terms Act, 1977, limits the seller's rights to exclude liability for breach of contract when he sells to a consumer; where the sale is not to a consumer, a term excluding liability is rendered subject to a test of 'reasonableness'. The provisions of this Act do not, however, apply to 'international' sales — for example, where the goods are purchased from the foreign seller.

In all forms of sale of goods, the term 'goods' can have several meanings. These meanings must be clearly understood, since they influence the type of sale, the time at which payment is made and the point at which the ownership of the goods is transferred from the seller to the buyer.

Future goods are those which at the time the contract is negotiated, have either not been manufactured or acquired by the seller. Future goods are therefore sold by 'description', the description being a vital part of the contract.

The majority of the purchases of imported timber and other wood goods are therefore purchases of future goods (e.g. softwood contracts made in November for shipment f.o.w. the following year), where the goods have not been sawn or seasoned — hardwood contracts for logs which may not have been felled at the time the contract was made.

It is usual in a sale of future goods to permit the seller to have a reasonable 'margin' or tolerance in the quantities supplied, owing to the inherent difficulties in producing exact quantities from a natural product.

Existing goods are those that are owned by or in the possession of the seller at the time the sale is negotiated. These goods may either be *ascertained*, when, in fact, they become specific goods (see below) or *unascertained* (that is to say, goods that cannot be specifically identified).

The majority of sales of timber from merchants' yards are sales of unascertained existing goods — for instance, say, the sale of one standard of softwood from a stack of ten standards. The goods are existing, but not ascertained until the one standard has been measured out.

Specific goods are goods that can be identified at the time of negotiation of the sale. The sale of a specific log or logs that have first been inspected by the prospective buyer is a sale of specific goods.

In each of the above cases the ownership of the goods is defined as the 'property in the goods'. To state that the property in the goods passes from one person to another means that the ownership of the goods passes.

THE CONTRACT

In Section 1 of the Sale of Goods Act a contract of sale is defined as one '. . . whereby the seller transfers, or agrees to transfer, the property in goods to the buyer in return for a money consideration called the price'.

It should be noted that it includes not only the actual sale (which takes place only when certain conditions are fulfilled by each party), but also the *agreement to sell.* This agreement to sell covers, for instance, the sale of future goods whereby the seller agrees to transfer the property at some future date, etc.

In practice, where specific goods are purchased, the contract merely takes the form of an order made out by the buyer, or a sale note made out by the seller or his agent and signed by the buyer. Where future goods are concerned in the timber trade, the possible difficulties that may arise are greater, particularly since the buyers and sellers are in different countries. Consequently, the form of contract is much more complicated, and provision is made for all manner of circumstances that may arise, so that the interests of both buyers and sellers are adequately protected. The next few chapters examine in detail the various forms of contract in regular use in the timber trade.

The essentials of a contract for the sale of goods are (1) the offer of the goods for sale and the acceptance of the offer by the buyer; (2) the consideration or price to be paid.

THE OFFER AND THE ACCEPTANCE

The offer of goods for sale will depend upon the supply and demand of those goods. This matter is discussed in more detail in Chapter 3 so far as the details of the offer are concerned.

The offer may be made either *generally* (as, for instance, by means of stock-lists circulated to prospective buyers) or to a *definite* person or firm (as in the case of a quotation from one firm to another) or a counteroffer from a prospective buyer to a shipper.

The acceptance must be made by a *specific* person or persons. Thus, although the offer of a stock is circulated widely, the necessary circumstances for a contract to be made are not established until a definite person or firm accepts that offer together with all the terms of that offer.

The offer may be made subject to conditions, provided that all these conditions are brought to the notice of the recipient of the offer at the time when the offer is made.

The offer may be revoked at any time before acceptance, unless an option has been granted whereby the offer will remain open for a certain time. The lapse of a specified time (or a reasonable time if none is specified) or the death of the person making the offer or of the person to whom it is made, all have the effect of revoking the offer. If the revocation of an offer is to be effective, it must be communicated to the recipient of the offer before he has accepted; otherwise his acceptance of the offer creates a binding contract.

The acceptance must be unconditional. If an offer is not accepted in all its terms, but certain revisions are suggested, this does not constitute acceptance of the original offer, but is a counteroffer. It will be seen from this that the offer is not only made by the prospective seller to the prospective buyer; there are many cases, particularly where there are protracted negotiations between the two parties, where the offer will actually be made by the prospective buyer. The law concerning acceptance is applicable to both parties of course, whether it be the prospective buyer or seller who accepts. In any case, as soon as acceptance has been made, a contract exists, and the general terms of the contract, responsibilities of parties, etc., will be the same no matter who made the final acceptance of the offer.

An important point arises over the communication of offer and acceptance by post. In making an offer, or the revocation of an offer, by post, the offer or revocation are only effective when they reach the recipient of the offer. In other words, the post must be delivered. If, for instance, the revocation of an offer is lost in the post, or for any other reason is delayed in the post so that it fails to reach the recipient of the offer *before* he accepts it, the revocation is inoperative and the acceptance stands, so the contract is binding.

On the other hand, an acceptance is complete as soon as it is posted. It does not necessarily have to be delivered. Thus, if the letter of acceptance is lost in the post, or the offer is revoked before the letter of acceptance reaches the person making the offer, the acceptance is nevertheless complete and binding provided that proof of postage can be produced if necessary.

Since acceptance must be unconditional, any letters written prior to the conclusion of the contract have no standing once the contract is signed. Letters written after the date on which the contract is signed do have a bearing on it.

From the above it will be seen that it is important for a seller to exercise care in the manner in which his offer is worded. This is particularly so where a stock-list of goods for sale is circulated widely. Some of the goods offered for sale may be sold quickly, and before the stock-list can be withdrawn or amended (the equivalent of revocation) an acceptance may be posted. Since this then constitutes a binding contract, the seller must deliver similar goods to those originally offered, or be in breach of contract. To overcome such a possibility it is usual to include in the offer the wording 'Subject to remaining unsold at the time order is received', or merely the words 'Subject unsold'. Sometimes the wider phrase 'Subject confirmation and unsold' is used. This is then a condition of the offer.

Where goods have not yet been shipped, there is the added danger that if any peril were to befall them, or if shippers or shipowners were to fail in their obligations, the importer-seller might be in a very difficult position with a buyer who had accepted an open offer of goods without any qualifying condition. In these cases the sellers usually include the following wording in the offer as a protection: 'Subject to shipment and safe arrival'.

CONSIDERATION

No contract for the sale of goods can have any legal effect unless it is made for a 'consideration'. This consideration is normally the 'price' of the goods. It is possible to have a contract where the price is fixed by 'valuation', by a third party.

Where no specific price is made, or where a third party fails to make a valuation if called for, the buyer must then pay a 'reasonable' price for the goods.

TRANSFER OF PROPERTY IN GOODS

Since the very essence of a contract for the sale of goods has been defined in the Sale of Goods Act as '. . . the seller transfers or agrees to transfer the property in goods to the buyer . . .', it is very important to see how and where this transfer takes place.

It must first be understood that 'property' and 'possession' are quite different, and a person may hold the property in goods without having possession of them. This is particularly important where questions of seller's lien arise.

Unless there is any agreement to the contrary, the goods are at the risk of the seller until property passes to the buyer, after which all risks pass to the buyer. This is an important matter when the marine insurance of goods being imported is considered.

If there is no specific agreement in the contract as to when or where the property will be transferred, the transfer of property is governed by the following rules. To avoid any ambiguity on this matter, most contracts specify the time or place where the property passes. In the case of the majority of f.o.b. and c.i.f. timber contracts, the property in goods passes to the buyer when the goods have been put on board the vessel.

If there are no stipulations of this nature, the property passes according to the following rules:

(1) *Specific goods ready for delivery.* Property passes immediately the contract is made, although delivery of the goods and payment may not take place until a later date.

(2) *Specific goods not yet ready for delivery* (or where the seller is bound to do something to the goods to put them in a deliverable state). Property passes when the seller has put the goods into a deliverable state and has notified the buyer.

(3) *Specific goods ready for delivery but requiring measuring, weighing, etc.* Property passes when the seller has measured or weighed the goods, etc., and notified the buyer.

(4) *Goods sold 'on approval' or 'sale or return'.* Property passes to the buyer when he signifies approval, which may be by word or deed. Retention of the goods without giving notice of rejection within a stipulated or reasonable time may amount to approval.

(5) *Future or Unascertained goods sold by description.* Property passes when goods of the description in the contract, in a deliverable state, are unconditionally appropriated to the contract. The commmonest form of appropriation is the handing of these goods to a carrier for transit to the buyer.

As stated above, in an f.o.b. or c.i.f. contract this point is usually made quite clear by stating in the contract that the property passes when the goods have been put on board. In any case, this is the first moment in a f.o.b. or c.i.f. contract when the goods for the buyer can be determined.

It is normally not possible to determine wood goods accurately before they are loaded, owing to the margins for loading granted to the master of the vessel and the possibility of goods being lost in transit to the vessel. For this reason, although a contract may be made on f.a.s. terms, property usually does not pass until the goods are placed on board (see page 145).

In the case of an ex-ship contract, property does not pass till the goods leave the ship. Although the goods are appropriated to the contract, being recognised as certain bills of lading, they are not in a 'deliverable state' until they leave the ship.

In any of the above five cases, if the seller reserves the 'right of disposal' until certain conditions are fulfilled, *property does not pass until those conditions have been fulfilled.* The principal condition to be fulfilled is that of payment. Some contracts include specific wording to the above effect, but the seller may be deemed to have reserved the right of disposal if shipping documents are transmitted through a bank, to be released in exchange for payment.

AMBIGUITIES

If a contract is broken, and the case has to be taken to arbitration or to court, it must be remembered that the arbitrator or the judge have only the words of the contract, and other correspondence, to guide them. It is necessary to make a careful examination of the terms and conditions of a contract before it is signed, to ensure that the meaning of each party is quite clear and that no other interpretation can be put on the words in the contract.

It is a feature of English law that where two parties completely reduce the terms of a bargain to writing, either of them may not afterwards be heard to say that they 'intended to agree something different' from the written contract detail, unless the mistake is common to both parties.

It has been stated that 'a man is responsible for his ambiguities in his own expressions, and has no right to induce another to contract with him on the supposition that his words mean one thing, while he hopes the court will adopt a construction by which they would mean another thing more to his advantage.'

CONDITIONS AND WARRANTIES

The various clauses in a contract may be divided into two legal categories — 'Conditions' and 'Warranties'.

(1) *'Condition'*. This is a major stipulation of the contract, and if it is broken, either party may cancel the contract and sue the other party for damages. For instance, if the contract calls for 75 mm x 175 mm Swedish redwood and 50 mm x 175 mm redwood is shipped, a condition has been broken. The importer may reject the goods, refuse to take delivery and sue the seller for damages. It must generally be as obvious as that for a successful action for damages to be maintained. If the breach of the contract is not so obvious or clear-cut, it is generally only safe to treat it as a breach of warranty.

(2) *'Warranty'*. A warranty is a stipulated collateral to the main purpose of the contract. Breach of a warranty may give rise to a claim for damages but *not* to cancellation of the contract. A breach of condition may be treated as a breach of warranty – for example, by accepting the 50 mm x 175 mm instead of 75 mm x 175 mm in the contract and sueing for damages afterwards.

In many contracts the words 'other terms and conditions' are used. In these cases it would have been better to use the word 'clauses' instead of 'conditions', since most of them are actually 'warranties' in law.

If a warranty is broken and the seller is sued for damages, the claim for damages may be built up in two ways: (1) claim for difference in price or value between the goods delivered and those contracted for; (2) claim for damages resulting from the wrong goods being supplied. The term 'warranty' here used in a contract for the sale of goods has a different meaning when used in a contract of marine insurance. In this latter case a breach of warranty is sufficient to render the contract void.

CONDITIONS SUBSEQUENT IN THE CONTRACT

In the normal course of events a contract will be discharged by its correct fulfilment. When this has happened, all rights under the contract cease. On the other hand, there are many events that may have occurred to bring about circumstances in which the contract cannot be fulfilled. In these circumstances the contract may be rescinded by:

(1) Payment of allowance by which one party may abandon his rights under the contract.

(2) Issue of a new contract in place of the old one.

(3) Arbitration or action in law if one party fails to fulfil his part of the contract.

(4) War or government restrictions rendering the fulfilment of the contract unlawful or impossible.

(5) Provision of clauses within the contract, by which claims are mutually abandoned.

These clauses are said to be 'conditions subsequent' and in law the contract is said to be 'defeasible by conditions subsequent'.

The difference between conditions and warranties has been explained above. Conditions may be divided, in common law, under three headings.

(1) *Conditions precedent.* Conditions that shall be carried out if the contract is to be fulfilled (e.g. the goods shall be of the specification 'hereinafter specified').

(2) *Conditions concurrent.* Conditions that are carried out simultaneously by each party (e.g. 'payment on receipt of and in exchange for shipping documents').

(3) *Conditions subsequent.* Conditions whereby on the happening of a certain specified event, either or both parties are relieved of their liability to carry out the contract.

These specified events are named in detail. If these clauses are invoked to provide an excuse for not performing the contract, the specified events must either be *actual* or *operative*. Mere fear or expectancy that these events may happen is not sufficient.

THE AGENT

Contracts that are made 'through the agency of' are contracts between the agent's principal (the seller) and the buyer. The agent himself is *not* a party to the contract; he is only an intermediary whose function is to bring the buyer and the seller into contractual relationship. The agent is not permitted to make any profit other than his agreed commission and must not place himself in a position where his interests and those of his principal will clash.

The consequence is that agents cannot be held personally responsible for the carrying out of the contract by the sellers, or for the payment of claims awarded by arbitration, or by the Court, against the sellers. There is, however, one exception to this: an agent has this protection if he signs the contract as agent and for a disclosed principal; if, however, he signs a contract for an undisclosed principal, he, or his principal, may sue or be sued thereon. In this event, however, the agent would have a right to be indemnified by his principal for any liability he incurs.

The only contractual legal relationship which the agent enters into is, therefore, that of his contract of agency as between himself and his principal. An agent can only be liable personally to a buyer if he becomes in breach of his 'warranty of authority' to the buyer — that is to say, he signs a contract on behalf of a buyer outside the terms of his authority from the seller.

It is usual for sellers' agents to take the financial risk of collecting payment from the buyer, so the agent pays the seller the amount due on the invoice, less discount and commission, and collects payment from the buyer in accordance with the payment terms of the contract, which refers specifically to 'authorised agents'. For the service of relieving sellers of financial risk, the agent is given a 'del credere' commission. In undertaking 'del credere' the agent guarantees the solvency of the buyer and in effect guarantees payment for the goods as from the time when the seller parted with them, i.e. after shipment.

In the event of the buyer becoming insolvent, the 'del credere' agent of the seller, to whom the bill of lading has been endorsed, or who has himself paid, or is directly responsible for the price, is regarded by the Sale of Goods Act, section 38, as an 'unpaid seller' and has according to section 39 of the Act a lien on the goods, a right to retain them or stop them in transit and a right of resale.

Although not a 'party' to the contract of sale, the agent (whether 'del credere' or not) has an interest in the contract and is not only responsible for certain duties, such as are mentioned in par. 5 of the Insurance clause, the Payment and Freight clause, par. 2 of the War clause and par. 3 of the Arbitration clause, but also has an 'insurable interest' in the commission earned when the contract was made which is at risk in the event of cancellation under the Exceptions clause.

7.2 Bills of Exchange

In the timber trade, as in many trades, the importer is dealing with bulk quantities of goods. There will be a considerable time lag between his paying for the goods and receiving payment from the sale of them to his customers. He is probably granting his own customers 30 days' credit or asking them for payment during the month following delivery. All these factors impose a heavy burden on the financial resources or working capital of the importer.

The seller or his agent therefore makes out a *draft* on the buyer, which is a written order requiring the buyer to pay at a specified time a sum of money to a person named (which is usually the seller's agent), and attaches it to the documents which he presents against acceptance of the draft, or the cash equivalent.

The sum of money stated in the draft represents the *net* invoice price of the goods (after any discounts have been deducted) plus interest for this sum over the period in question. The value of the draft, therefore, is greater than the net value of an invoice that is settled in cash, by the amount of the interest. In some cases, however, the amount of the interest is left off the value of the draft, and is settled separately for cash.

The buyer accepts the draft by writing across it: 'Accepted payable at — (name and address of his bank)', followed by his signature. A draft may also be 'accepted payable' at the office of the acceptor. The draft has now become a 'bill of exchange' and is governed by the Bills of Exchange Acts of 1882 and 1906. The parties to a bill of exchange are: (1) The drawer — the person who draws up the bill of exchange; in this case the seller or his agent. (2) The drawee — the person on whom the bill of exchange is drawn (i.e. the buyer). He becomes the acceptor when he has accepted it. (3) The payee — the person to whom the proceeds of the bill of exchange are payable. This will usually be the same person as the drawer.

No.   *13472*   Due   Date

£*5347:50*

London,   *19 June 1980*

Four months   after   *date* pay to our Order in London
Five thousand three hundred and forty seven pounds fifty pence
Value received   *per S.S. "Landlecrag" at Manchester.*

To   *A.B.C. Timber Company Ltd.,*
          Morley Road,   For and on behalf of
          Manchester.   X.Y.Z. & Co. Ltd.
                                  J. Smith   *Director.*
                                  H. Jones   *Secretary.*

A BILL OF EXCHANGE
with (*on right*) the
crossing, written on
it vertically upon
acceptance.

Accepted   *, payable*
at Castle Bank Ltd., Birchin
Lane, London, E.C.
    For and on behalf of
    A.B.C. Timber Co. Ltd.
      R. Robinson, Director.

Figure 7.1 Specimen bill of exchange

Bills of exchange are more commonly referred to as 'bills'.

The same bill of exchange is a bill payable (B/P) to the acceptor (the buyer) and a bill receivable (B/R) to the payee.

A cheque is a bill of exchange drawn on a bank (the drawee) payable on demand.

The bill of exchange is said to 'reach maturity' or to 'mature' when the due date specified on it arrives. It must be met at maturity or arrangements must be made for it to be renewed. If a bill of exchange is renewed, a fresh bill of exchange is made out for the amount of the old bill of exchange, the acceptor paying, usually in cash, the interest for the extended period.

A bill of exchange is a negotiable instrument unless it is crossed 'not negotiable', which is not usually done. It becomes the property of any person who in good faith gives value for it. It may be negotiated by endorsement and delivery (in much the same manner as a bill of lading).

(1) *Special endorsement.* Here the bill of exchange is made payable to a definite party who must endorse it before it is valid (e.g. 'Pay to J. Smith or order').

(2) *Blank endorsement.* The bill of exchange becomes payable to bearer and may be negotiated by delivery only.

(3) *Restrictive endorsement.* This prohibits further negotiation of the bill of exchange (e.g. when made out to 'J. Smith' only).

The sum of money stated on a bill of exchange is its 'face value'.
The holder of the bill receivable has three courses open to him:

(1) To hold the bill receivable until it reaches maturity when he will receive the full face value of the bill. This he will do if he has plenty of funds and does not require money urgently for other purposes. It is a form of investment.

(2) To 'discount' the bill at a bank or discount house. To do this he sells the bill of exchange. What he gets for it will depend on the credit standing of the acceptor, if he endorses it 'without recourse', or his own credit as well if he gives a clean endorsement which makes him liable to pay at due date if the acceptor does not.

He gets his money back quickly but does not get as much as he would have done if he had kept the bill to maturity.

The bank or discount house, however, has purchased the bill for less than the face value, and will eventually collect the full face value. Alternatively, they may sell the bill of exchange before it reaches maturity. The procedure goes on and the bill of exchange, if for a large amount, may pass through many hands before it reaches maturity. In each case a further endorsement is made on the back of the bill of exchange, and, if necessary, an additional gummed slip of paper, known as an 'Alonge' is added at one end to hold further endorsements.

(3) To negotiate it in payment. If the holder of the bill receivable owes a similar or a larger amount of money, he may endorse the bill receivable over to his creditor as payment or part payment.

The buying and selling of bills forms the basis of the London Money Market, through which many transactions outside the UK are put. These foreign transactions are by bills 'payable in London' and gave London its title 'the hub of the world'.

A foreign bill of exchange — that is to say a bill not both drawn and payable within the UK — is usually drawn in two parts, known as First and Second of Exchange, each part containing a reference to the other part. First part states: '. . . this First of Exchange (Second unpaid) . . .'. Second part states: '. . . this Second of Exchange (First unpaid) . . .'. Both parts constitute one bill of exchange only, and when either part is paid on presentation, the other becomes ineffective. Each part is sent separately to ensure that at least one part reaches its destination safely.

7.3 Uniform Laws on International Sale of Goods

International sales may now also be governed by two Uniform laws governing the relations between a seller and a buyer in different countries. These Uniform laws were incorporated into the law of the UK by the Uniform Law on International Sales Act, 1967. Briefly, they provide as follows:

(1) The Uniform Law on the International Sale of Goods governs the obligations of a seller and a buyer arising from the contract. These laws apply only to International contracts concluded after 18 August 1972 and only if the parties to the contract have chosen to apply them to their contract. If the laws do apply, the seller must effect delivery of the goods and hand over any documents relating thereto, and the buyer must pay the price and take delivery, as required by the contract. The parties are also bound by any usage which has been agreed or which is reasonable. If a seller fails to meet his obligations, the buyer may require performance or declare the contract void. In each case the buyer may also claim damages. Damages recoverable cannot exceed that which the party in default ought to have foreseen as a possible consequence when the contract was concluded. If there is a delay in payment, the seller is entitled to interest.

(2) The Uniform Law on the Formation of Contracts for the International Sale of Goods applies to contracts of sale of goods which, if concluded, would be governed by (1) above. This, too, only applies to offers, replies and acceptances made after 18 August 1972. Offers and acceptances need not be in writing, and offers can be revoked unless the revocation is not made in good faith or in conformity with fair dealing or the offer states a fixed time for acceptance or otherwise indicates that it is firm or irrevocable. An acceptance consists of a declaration communicated by any means whatsoever to the offeror. An acceptance cannot be revoked except by a revocation which is communicated to the offeror before or at the same time as acceptance.

In view of the fact that both these laws are applicable only if the parties choose to apply them, and that only a limited number of other countries are parties to the Convention setting up these Uniform laws, they have not had much effect to date.

8 Timber Contracts II

8.1 General

Since the last edition of this book there have been many changes in the timber trade, each necessitating some alteration in the wording of the various contract forms.

In the case of the Albion and Uniform – the two contracts most commonly used – these have been amended a number of times since 1964 (1969 and 1973). In 1979 and 1980 these were completely rewritten and it is fortunate that most details became available in time to be included in this book but it was not known whether they would be dated 1980 or 1981. However, throughout the book they are referred to as 1980. Because of the quite considerable changes in their terms and conditions, they are described in detail in this chapter. The other TTF Contract Forms are dealt with in a later chapter.

The many contract forms produced (with copyright) by the TTF and in use in the trade at the time of writing are as follows:

(1)	Albion (1980):	c.i.f. form for Swedish and Finnish contracts
(2)	Uniform (1980):	f.o.b. or f.a.s. form for Swedish and Finnish contracts
(3)	Scanref (1964):	Specially devised for the resale of Scandinavian softwoods
(4)	Scanrex (1964):	Specially devised for the resale of Scandinavian softwoods ex ship
(5)	Trancif (1971):	c.i.f. form for sales to motor vehicles or ferry shipment and liner terms – softwood
(6)	Ligcon (1961):	c. & f. contract for Czechoslovakian softwood
(7)	Eucon (1964):	Central European c.i.f. and c. & f. contract
(8)	Russian (1952):	c.i.f. form for softwood
(9)	Rerux (1955):	Ex-ship reselling contract for Russian goods
(10)	Reruf (1955):	c.i.f. reselling contract for Russian goods
(11)	Pacif (1958):	c.i.f. Pacific coast contract for softwood
(12)	Ecancif (1958):	c.i.f. Eastern Canadian contract for softwood
(13)	Ecanref (1959):	c.i.f. Reselling Eastern Canadian contract for softwood
(14)	Pacref (1959):	c.i.f. Reselling Pacific coast contract for softwood
(15)	Ecanrex (1959):	Ex-ship reselling contract for Eastern Canadian softwood
(16)	Pacrex (1959):	Ex-ship reselling contract for Pacific coast softwood

(17) Fobra (1957):   f.o.b. and f.a.s. contract for Brazilian softwood
(18) Rebraf (1957):   Specially devised for the resale of Brazilian softwood
(19) Rebrax (1957):   Ex-ship reselling contract for Brazilian softwood
(20)   (1960):   American contract for hardwood lumber
(21) Unicif (1952):   c.i.f. contract for UK hardwood
(22) Albion (1933):   Revised 1938 and specially amended for Polish
                        softwood
(23) Parcif (1963):   c.i.f. contract for particle board
(24) Plydef (1972):   Plywood delivered contract
(25) Plycif (1957):   c.i.f. contract for plywood
(26) Pardel (1973):   c.i.f. and delivered contract for particle board
(27) Britfibre (1978): c.i.f. contract for fibre building board (not a TTF Form)

It must be appreciated that the TTF Documentary Committee sit at regular intervals to review all contracts in the light of changes which are constantly taking place within the timber and panel products trade. It will be seen that many of the contract forms were drawn up many years ago and are in the process of being amended. This is a very lengthy process as overseas associations have to be consulted. It is virtually impossible to produce an explanation of all these contract forms guaranteed to be absolutely up to date.

To quote one example, it is almost certain that there will be amendments to all softwood contracts in due course concerning the Plant Health Regulations now in force. These prohibit the importation of timber on which there is any bark in case certain beetles are introduced into the UK. This also applies to some hardwoods.

While it is customary for the above official contract forms to be used by the trade, it is not mandatory. The advantage of using them is obvious, since their terms and conditions have been carefully prepared and agreed by the associations representing overseas shippers. However, even though use of the official forms is desirable, there is no reason why the parties concerned should not draw up a contract to suit themselves, always provided that its terms and conditions are fully understood and accepted by those concerned.

The Uniform contract has always been known as an f.o.b. contract, although sellers are only responsible for placing the goods 'free alongside vessel' — the normal terms for an f.a.s. contract. In Scandinavia there have not always been facilities for the cargo to be loaded by shore cranes on to the vessel and, in fact, the Nubaltwood charter provides for the vessel to load, so the physical placing of the goods 'on board' is in any event beyond the control of the sellers. The property or ownership passes when the goods have been placed on board, and so it is generally conceded that these are f.o.b. contracts. If it had been possible for the property to pass while the goods were in lighters, or stacked alongside the vessel, it would probably have become a true f.a.s. contract. Such a position for the passing of property, extremely important when considering insurable interest, was impossible, since within the margins for chartering and loading the vessel the master may fail to load some of the goods and send them back as not required.

In the Scandinavian countries, however, the Uniform contract is known as an f.a.s. contract, which, it is maintained, is a more correct description. At one time this contract had the letters 'f.o.b.' printed at the top of the contract form. When the 1951 Contract, replacing the 1933 Contract, was negotiated, and later amended in 1955 and 1964, the arguments of the UK importers that it was an f.o.b. contract were disputed by the Swedish and Finnish delegations, who maintained that it was f.a.s. The dispute was resolved by the simple expedient of leaving the initials 'f.o.b.' or 'f.a.s.' off the top of the contract form and referring to it merely by its code name.

In other parts of the world the difference may be much more important, especially where the charter does not provide for the vessel to load the cargo. In such circumstances, a buyer on f.a.s. terms would be responsible for arranging for stevedores at the loading port for the loading of the goods.

Seller's responsibilites when selling on f.a.s. or f.o.b. terms

The seller's principal responsibilities in a f.a.s. or f.o.b. contract are:

(1) To place the goods of the description contained in the contract 'all free alongside the vessel' or 'all free on board the vessel' at the port of shipment.

(2) To advance freight, if required.

(3) To deliver to the buyer shipping documents consisting of a specification of the goods shipped, an invoice for them at the contract price and the relative bills of lading.

(4) To pay any dead-freight claims or provide indemnity as called for in the contract.

Buyer's responsibilities when buying on f.a.s. or f.o.b. terms

The buyer's principal responsibilities in a f.a.s. or f.o.b. contract are:

(1) To arrange a freight contract for the loading of the goods that the seller has undertaken to place alongside.

(2) To notify the sellers as to the manner in which these goods are to be loaded in bills of lading.

(3) To arrange insurance for the goods in transit and, if required by sellers, produce proof that this insurance has been effected.

(4) To lift the goods on or before the date named in the contract, failing which there is an obligation to pay for the goods and thereafter pay storage charges.

(5) To pay for the goods on receipt of the shipping documents.

Seller's responsibilities when selling on c.i.f. or c. & f. terms

The seller's responsibilities, once the contract has been signed in a c.i.f. or c. & f. sale, are:

(1)   To ship at the port of shipment (named in the contract) goods of the description contained in the contract.

(2)   To arrange freight to deliver the goods to the destination named in the contract.

(3)   In the case of a c.i.f. contract, to arrange insurance of the goods during their passage, such insurance to be available for the benefit of the buyer.

(4)   To make out an invoice at the c.i.f. or c. & f. price less the amount of any freight that the buyer will have to pay when the vessel reaches its destination.

(5)   To send the buyer the following documents:
>   bills of lading
>   insurance policy or certificate (in the case of a c.i.f. contract)
>   specification
>   invoice and minor documents, to enable the buyer to:
>>   ascertain that the goods shipped are those contracted for;
>>   obtain delivery of the goods when they arrive;
>>   recover the value of any goods lost or obtain compensation for damage;
>>   know how much cost, freight, and in the case of c.i.f. sales, insurance he must pay.

Buyer's responsibilities when buying on c.i.f. or c. & f. terms

The buyer's responsibilities are fewer in number than in a f.o.b. contract, but they are no less important.

(1)   To notify the seller as to the manner in which the goods are to be loaded in bills of lading.

(2)   To pay for the goods on receipt of shipping documents, provided that these are complete, agree with each other and with the terms of the contract.

(3)   In a c. & f. contract the buyer arranges the marine insurance and so this responsibility is removed from the seller to the buyer.

8.2 Albion 1980

General

The description of the goods in any contract is a vital point which is often neglected. Only on rare occasions will the buyer have seen the goods before they are despatched. Normally, the contract will be for 'future goods' which have yet to be manufactured or measured. Therefore, the buyer must rely upon the written description of the goods in the contract to protect himself. He has none of the safeguards enjoyed by the customer in the country of destination, who can go to the importer's yard and inspect the goods for quality, condition, measurement, etc., before buying.

The Sale of Goods Act, 1893, (Section 13) states that in a sale of goods by *description* there is an implied condition that the goods shall comply with the description. However, Section 14 states that in a contract for the sale of goods there is no *implied warranty* or condition as to their quality or fitness for any particular purpose. If the goods are purchased by description, the only implied condition is that they shall be of *merchantable* quality. Therefore, if the buyer wishes to ensure that the goods he is buying will be up to the standard he expects, he must strengthen the description in the contract or impose additional warranties on the seller. This will largely depend upon the individual circumstances of each contract, but, in general, it is the responsibility of the buyer to see that he is fully protected. The preamble states '. . . the wood goods of the specification and at the prices set out on the back hereof . . .'. These words of description are a condition of the contract (see Chapter 7 – section on conditions and warranties, page 123). A breach of this clause, being a breach of condition, permits the buyer to refuse acceptance of goods materially different from those specified and sue the seller for damages. It has been held in law that a buyer is under no obligation to accept a shipment of peas against a contract for beans.

The preamble on the face of the contract is more explicit than hitherto.

Shipment

'The goods are to be shipped at . . .'. The name of the port from which the goods are shipped is a part of the description of the goods. If they are shipped from any other port, the buyers have the right to maintain that these are not the goods which they purchased.

The Pacif 1958 contract states: '. . . the goods are to be shipped in the customary manner from the Pacific Coast . . .'. The Ecancif 1958 contract states: '. . . the goods are to be shipped in the usual and customary manner . . .'.

These two wordings represent a much wider tolerance for the shipper. However, in the case of North American softwood the precise port of shipment is not so important from the point of view of quality as is the port of shipment from Scandinavia in Scandinavian contracts.

Ends

'Ends of slatings and boards 25 mm and thinner x 75 mm (see Clause 2(c) of General Conditions) maximum . . . . . per cent per item/part item'.

The percentage of such ends have to be mutually agreed and inserted on the face of the contract.

Payment

'Payment to be made in accordance with Clause 10 of the General Conditions, the balance payable thereunder to be paid less $2^{1}/_{2}\%$ of the f.a.s. price, i.e. the c.i.f. price less the cost of insurance and freight, in London in cash at 3 days sight or subject to an agreement at the time of presentation of documents by approved acceptance of Sellers or authorised agent's draft payable in London at 4 months from date of Bill of Lading, rate of interest to be mutually agreed. Sellers to give notice of vessel's arrival at loading port in accordance with Clause 4.'

This and Clause 10 vary from the previous contract terms.

Claims – unseasoned goods

'Claims for condition on unseasoned goods (see Clause 18 last paragraph of General Conditions)'.

This has to be completed where any of the contract goods are specified as unseasoned.

Method of Discharge

This refers to clause 15 of the Nubaltwood charter and, unless filled in to the contrary, clause 15(a) applies.

The Albion Softwood (C.I.F.) Contract Form 1980 is adopted by the Timber Trade Federation of the UK, the Finnish Sawmill Owners Association and the Swedish Wood Exporters Association. Many of the clauses in the General Terms and Conditions have been completely revised and are given below in full.

Price Basis: Clause 1

'The prices are per cubic metre (if planed goods in nominal measure) and include first cost, freight and insurance to the port of destination'.

This wording is the same as that of the 1969 Amendments, except that British sterling is not specified.

Ends: Clause 2

'Other than as regards items for which a separate price for ends 1.8m to 2.4m is specified in the contract (in which case notwithstanding any provision of this Clause all ends on such items shall be at that specified price) Sellers to have the right to supply up to 3 per cent of ends on each item at full price (i.e. the full c.i.f. price for 2.7m and up appropriate for the goods concerned). If the percentage of 3 per cent is exceeded on any item(s) all ends (including the first 3 per cent) on such item(s) shall be at two-thirds of the appropriate contract price per cubic metre plus one-third of the freight rate and one-third of the insurance cost appropriate to the item(s).

'Notwithstanding the foregoing however unless otherwise provided in the contract, ends shall not exceed the undermentioned percentages on each and every item or part item:-

a) of Vlth quality — 10 per cent
b) of boards 25mm and thinner x 115mm and under, all qualities — 15 per cent (unless otherwise agreed)
c) of slatings and boards 25mm and thinner x 75mm — the percentage of ends as mutually agreed and inserted in the contract
d) of all other specified goods except those defined in paragraphs a), b), and c) of this Clause — $7\frac{1}{2}$ per cent.

'Buyer's right to compensation in respect of ends in excess of these maximum percentages or the maximum percentages shown in the contract, if appropriate, shall not be limited to the reduction in price referred to in this Clause. Ends to be regarded as included in the contract quantity but to be disregarded in the calculation of average length.'

This clarifies the ends situation in clearer terms than hitherto. The shipment of ends is often of assistance for the safe and economical stowage of the cargo to the ship's full capacity, although this does not have the same significance as it had in the days before packaging and truck-bundling.

Seasoning, Bracking and Loading: Clause 3

'The goods are to be properly seasoned for shipment to the UK and the Republic of Ireland. Each item to be of Shippers' usual bracking, average length and fair specification for such description of goods and delivered to the ship in accordance with the custom of the port, the Sellers not being responsible for any deterioration by circumstances beyond their control after the goods have left Sellers wharf properly protected.

'Unless otherwise specifically agreed every package shall be marked and identified with serial number as per specification. All bundled and packaged goods shall be adequately and securely bound.

'Except where otherwise specified packaged goods shall mean goods which have a single length and size in each package provided that Sellers shall have the right to combine lengths where the residue is insufficient for a complete package. Truck bundled goods shall mean goods bundled in mixed lengths of one size the dimensions of each bundle to be mutually agreed.'

Although the wording is slightly different, this clause has the same meaning as previously.

At this point it is desirable to clarify certain aspects of terms used in this clause.

Degree of seasoning. Before packaging and truck-bundling was so general, 'shipping dry' was considered to be quite satisfactory for shipments of timber from Scandinavia to the UK to ensure that it reached its destination in a bright and discoloration-free condition. This meant a moisture content of anything between 20 and 24 per cent but with packaged and truck-bundled goods being the norm, and more shippers changing to kiln-drying, this degree of moisture content is considered too high. Unless the moisture content of packaged goods is kept down to about 18–19 per cent, discoloration will almost certainly develop unless the packages are opened up immediately upon arrival in the UK.

In order to lessen the chances of discoloration taking place during the voyage, many shippers have for some time dipped or sprayed their sawn goods with an anti-stain solution. There are several solutions available, but they all seem to consist of sodium pentachlorophenate or sodium tetrachlorophenate or a mixture of both. It has often been said that these solutions were about to be banned in Scandinavia owing to the fact that they are likely to cause dermatitis to the workers, but most mills still use them. These solutions are definitely not a guarantee against unseasoned, or even seasoned, goods discolouring, but they do lessen the probability if used properly. Unfortunately there is no easy test to ascertain whether goods have been properly treated, but there is one test, known as the Beilstein Test, which can give some indication. As it involves the use of considerable equipment and several highly toxic chemicals, it is not possible for the ordinary individual to carry it out. Readers who are interested should contact TRADA, who can supply details.

The bulk of the Pacific coast softwood is sold 'green', which permits loading straight from the saw, and if contracts are made for the supply of green or fresh lumber, then care must be taken to ensure that the charter party is amended to comply with the contract; otherwise disputes and deadfreight claims may arise.

Bracking, average length. The terms of bracking, average length and specification may or may not have been founded upon what was offered by the seller prior to the contract. A definite agreement of an average length of 4.2m/4.5m becomes a part of the contract. This is not, as is sometimes argued, an average of 4.325m – if that were so, it could and must be stated – but average neither less than 4.2m nor more than 4.5m. Expressions of opinion by the seller or his agent describing the goods in glowing terms amount to nothing if not stated in the contract.

It is quite usual for battens to be somewhat shorter in average length than deals, and boards to be even shorter than battens.

Quality terms provide a description of goods that are saleable as such in the normal market; they do not refer to an absolutely perfect grade. The basis of the quality is contained in the words 'shippers usual'. Therefore, it becomes a matter of importance for the buyer to be acquainted with the stock he intends to purchase. This leads to continuity of business between certain sellers and their regular buyers. The words 'shippers usual' are for all practical purposes synonymous with 'sellers usual', although there are possible instances where sellers and shippers may not be the same.

In the present Albion and Uniform contract forms, the words 'The goods to be of Shippers usual' have been changed to 'Each item to be of Shippers usual'. This removes possible ambiguity in a dispute concerning only one part of the goods shipped.

Chartering, Delay and Cancelling: Clause 4

The wording of this Clause is unchanged from that of the 1969 amendments and reads:

'Shiproom to be secured in due time by Sellers with liberty to substitute. Sellers shall both as regards the original chartered vessel and any substituted vessel promptly advise Buyers of the fixture with name of vessel if nominated and send them a copy of the charter party which shall be on the form of "Nubaltwood" last accepted by the respective Associations as being the document on which chartering has to be effected. Sellers to advise Buyers by telegram of name(s) of vessel(s) if not stated in the charter party and dates of arrival and departure. If Owners give notice that the vessel original or substituted cannot be ready to load within six weeks after the stipulated time of shipment or if without such notice the vessel has not been ready so to load Sellers shall instantly advise Buyers by telegram stating the exact time of the receipt of Owners' notice, if any, and Buyers shall have the right to cancel the contract to a corresponding extent provided that their cancellation reaches Sellers in time to enable Sellers to cancel the charter party save that if Sellers have not advised Buyers as stipulated above Buyers' right of cancellation is subject only to prompt advice after the delay has come to Buyers' notice. Sellers' obligation to give the above notice in respect of the original vessel shall not arise if they have substituted or have the intention to substitute another vessel. Should any vessel chartered under this contract be lost after being named to Buyers and previous to loading Sellers have the option of chartering another vessel in substitution for loading within the stipulated time or six weeks thereafter or of cancelling the contract to a corresponding extent upon giving prompt notice to Buyers leaving however Buyers the right to take the goods at the stipulated c.i.f. price less cost of insurance and the rate of freight whereat tonnage lost had been secured and on the conditions and terms of the current "Uniform" contract form adopted by the respective Associations, the drawing date of approximate payment, unless goods have been removed earlier, being six weeks from date of such right being exercised. Sellers shall not be liable for any loss suffered by Buyers from delay in shipment caused by circumstances beyond Sellers' control.'

The words 'in due time' refer to the shipping date stated elsewhere in the contract, so that, for instance, sellers may not delay shipment beyond the date stipulated, in the hope that they might be able to charter at a lower rate later in the season. This notification is usually by telex or telegram and it puts the buyer 'in the picture'. He knows approximately when to expect his shipment and can make his arrangements accordingly. By keeping in touch with the shipowner's agents in this country he can follow the course of the ship and learn its expected arrival date.

In paragraph two of this clause the words 'to a corresponding extent' refer not necessarily to the full quantity of the contract but merely to the quantity that should have been shipped by this particular vessel.

This clause is a protection to the buyer; quite obviously, he must have some power to cancel the contract at the end of a determined time, as otherwise there might be circumstances in which a seller had been unable or unwilling to secure shiproom for say six or nine months, during which time the market value of timber could have fallen badly. Without the power to cancel the contract, the buyer would still be obliged to accept the timber at a much later date and bear the loss of a dropping market. However, the buyer must notify the seller in turn, within a stipulated time, that he is cancelling the contract to enable the seller to cancel his charter party.

Margins in Sellers' options: Clause 5

This is identical with the old Albion contract form as amended by the 1969 amendments, and reads:

'Sellers shall have the option to vary by 10 per cent more or less any or every item but not exceeding 100 cubic metres on any one item and to vary items of 10 cubic metres to 50 cubic metres to the extent of 5 cubic metres always provided that the total quantity is not varied except under the provisions of Clause 6. Such option shall apply also to overlying goods.'

Margin for Chartering: Clause 6

This clause reads:

'A margin of 10 per cent more or less of the total contract quantity, but not exceeding 200 cubic metres is to be allowed to Sellers for convenience of chartering only, but when two or more shipments are made under the same contract such margins shall only apply to the quantity by the last vessel. Should Sellers under this clause give an increase of total contract quantity, such increase is to be in contract sizes and not more than 25 per cent increase or 25 cubic metres, whichever may be the greater, on any item over 50 cubic metres, or 50 per cent increase on any item of 50 cubic metres or under. Where a "minimum/maximum" quantity is stipulated in the contract, chartering shall be on a minimum/maximum basis and this clause shall not apply.'

The only difference between this clause and the terms of the old 1964 Albion contract is in the first line, where it is stated that the margin must not exceed 200 cubic metres; in the old contract this was 250 cubic metres. Although the old contract form did not mention the last clause about minimum/maximum chartering, this was introduced in identical form in the 1969 amendments.

Quantity Overshipment and Undershipment: Clause 7

This clause is identical with that in the 1964 Albion contract and reads:

'In the event of over-shipment of any item(s) of the contract (subject to Clause 5 hereof) Buyers shall not be entitled to reject the entire shipment but shall have the option to be exercised without delay of taking up the Bills of Lading and paying for the whole quantity shipped or of taking up the Bills of Lading and paying only for the contract quantity rejecting the balance. The same conditions shall apply if the excess is not apparent from the Bills of Lading but is discovered only on arrival of the goods at their ultimate destination. If Buyers elect to take the contract quantity only, Sellers shall pay all expenses whatsoever incurred by Buyers in consequence of the over-shipment. In the event of under-shipment of any item(s) of the contract (subject to Clause 6 hereof) Buyers are to pay for the quantity shipped but have the right to claim compensation for such under-shipment.'

It will be seen from this clause that if the total quantity shipped is less than the quantity purchased, the buyer must accept and pay for the goods shipped at the contract price, but may claim compensation for the undershipment. This clause excludes the provisions of the Sale of Goods Act, which are mentioned later.

If the quantity shipped is more than the quantity purchased, the buyer has two alternatives: (1) to accept the whole shipment, in which case he must pay the full contract price, or (2) to accept only the purchased quantity and reject the remainder. Where the overshipment is obvious from the bills of lading, the course for the buyer to adopt, if the overshipment is not to his advantage, is immediately to notify the seller's agents that he rejects the overshipment. Simultaneously he may offer to take the excess quantity at a reduced price, being in a strong position to gain such a concession from the seller. The clause quoted is quite clear, but there are other types of contract in which this position is not covered in the same detail. Under these circumstances an undershipment or overshipment is covered by the Sale of Goods Act, 1893, Section 30.

Insurance: Clause 8

This clause reads:

'Sellers shall insure the cargo for the c.i.f. value plus 10 per cent, at Sellers' option with a first class company registered in Buyers' country or with Underwriters carrying on business in the United Kingdom or with a first class company registered outside the United Kingdom as named in the contract as per Lloyd's form of Policy together with current Timber Trade Federation Clauses and in the case of policies issued in Sellers' country, including additional clauses as per Clause 9 hereof, losses payable in London and subject to the sub-clauses hereunder, against the risks covered by the Institute War Clauses (Timber Trade) and Institute Strikes Riots and Civil Commotions Clauses (Timber Trade) in force at the time of attachment of the insurance.

'Any premium for war risk insurance in excess of 0.125 per cent, shall be for account of Buyers, except that if owing to the Flag and/or ownership and/or condition of the vessel, there is at the time of chartering or, if chartered before the date of the contract, at the date of the contract, an increase over the general rate for such insurance such increase shall not be chargeable to Buyers.

'If sellers are unable to effect War Risk Insurance on the goods for a premium not exceeding 2 per cent or at all they shall give immediate telegraphic advice to Buyers stating the premium if any, at which such insurance could be effected by Sellers and the date when the vessel is expected to commence loading the contract goods, and thereupon Buyers shall have the option of:-

(a) Accepting the premium (if any) and paying the excess, or
(b) effecting such insurance themselves, or
(c) calling upon Sellers to ship the goods uninsured against War Risks, or
(d) (if such premium is not less than 10 per cent or if the Sellers are unable to effect such insurance at all) cancelling the contract to the extent of such uninsured shipment.

'Buyers shall exercise such option by telegram as promptly as possible. Unless Sellers receive notice of Buyers option before the said expected loading date then Buyers shall be deemed to have:

(i) accepted the excess if the premium quoted is less than 20 per cent and shipment shall be made accordingly, or
(ii) exercised their option (d) above, if the premium quoted is not less than 20 per cent or if Sellers are unable to effect such insurance at all.

'If any such insurance, whether effected by Sellers or Buyers shall be cancelled by Underwriters before the expected loading date, then Sellers or Buyers, as the case may be, shall give to the other immediate telegraphic notice thereof, whereupon, unless before the said expected loading date Sellers receive notice that Buyers require the goods to be shipped uninsured, the contract shall be cancelled to the extent of such intended shipment.

If Buyers call upon Sellers to ship the goods uninsured they shall provide, before the goods are put on board, such security for payment as may be required by Sellers or their Agents and goods lost or not lost, shall pay against presentation of documents the value of the goods shipped at contract prices less unpaid freight.'

The buyer is not entitled to an insurance policy on the full amount of freight (i.e. including the freight to be paid only on right delivery at destination) but the amount of freight advanced by seller must be covered. By the warehouse to warehouse clause in the TTF Insurance Clauses (see Chapter 6) the cover extends till the goods reach their 'ultimate destination'. As this may be some distance inland, it is possible for the goods to be underinsured after arrival by the amount of the balance of destination freight, import duty and other charges payable at port of destination. This is covered by an 'increased value' policy which extends the insured amount to cover the additional charges, etc., paid. Since there is little risk of total loss, other than by fire, after the goods arrive at the port, the premium for the increased value policy is much less than the normal cargo insurance policy.

Regarding the reference to war risks, it is obvious that during conditions in which war risk insurance on the goods is likely to be heavy, the buyer will probably not object to the heavy premium, since his goods under those conditions will usually be much more valuable. The second part of this war risk section is a protection for buyers, in case the sellers charter a very old vessel or a vessel belonging to a nation at war. The security for payment demanded by sellers if the goods are shipped uninsured against war risks is only reasonable. War risks can only fail to be covered when shipping in a particular area is in imminent war danger. In such circumstances, if the goods reach their destination safely, they become greatly enhanced in value, to the benefit of the buyer. The security given to sellers or their agents will usually be in the form of a bank credit or guarantee.

Policies issued outside the UK: Clause 9

This clause is identical with Clause 9 of the old Albion contract form, and reads:

'Where it is intended to tender policies outside the United Kingdom there shall be an obligation upon Sellers to ensure that they contain the following clauses:- Lloyd's standard printed form of Policy together with the current Timber Trade Federation Clauses shall be deemed to be the basis of this insurance and, notwithstanding anything to the contrary herein contained, shall override all terms and conditions of this Policy inconsistent therewith. Any question as to the interpretation of this Policy shall be settled according to English Law, the parties hereto agreeing that the English Courts, or in the case of a claimant resident in Scotland, the Scottish Courts shall have jurisdiction to the exclusion of all other Courts to deal with any disputes arising under this Policy.'

This clause is really a further qualification of Clause 8 and has not been altered from the wording in the 1964 Albion contract form. Clearly, the reason why this clause only appears in the c.i.f. contract is because it is the responsibility of the overseas seller to arrange the insurance.

Payment and Freight: Clause 10

'Buyers shall pay freight less advances, if any, according to Charter party or Bill of Lading and shall pay to Sellers or their Authorised Agents the balance of the invoice value after deducting total freight, in London, on receipt of and in exchange for shipping documents including policies of insurance as per Clause 8.

'Any freight advance in accordance with Charter party to be paid to Sellers or their authorised agents in net cash against Master's receipt endorsed upon the Bill(s) of Lading. The deduction of freight in the invoice shall be at the net rate only and shall not include the charges which are payable under the Charter party for delivery beyond the ship's rail or tackle, unless otherwise provided for in the contract.

'If the documents are not presented to Buyers prior to the arrival of the vessel, Buyers shall nevertheless take up the documents on presentation, but any charges incurred through delay in presentation of documents unless due to causes beyond Seller's control shall be payable by Sellers unless previous sufficient particulars of shipment have been supplied to enable the consignment to be handled without delay or extra expense.'

This clause amplifies the mention of payment in the preamble mentioned earlier. The wording is unchanged from that of the previous Albion terms, except that it does not stipulate that any freight advance must be paid in sterling. Under this clause the buyer must pay the shipowner the freight due as per charter party or bill of lading before he can obtain delivery of the goods from the ship. The freight contract covers the carriage of the goods to the port in the UK but it does not cover any labour charges in handling the goods beyond the ship's rail or ship's tackle. The buyer is responsible for charges for any additional work, and Clause 15 of the Nubaltwood charter party shows how these charges are made up. The freight contract must cover the whole of the journey from the loading port to the discharging port. If the actual point of discharge is specified, such as 'buyer's own wharf', this must be fulfilled exactly.

The Nubaltwood charter party uses the phrase 'or so near there unto as she can safely get, and deliver cargo, always afloat'. The Albion preamble states: 'to . . . always afloat'. If the cargo is to be delivered to a particular quay, these two phrases must be altered to an exact description of the wharf or quay concerned.

Clause 10 also makes the point quite clearly that the buyer pays for complete shipping documents, and provided that these documents are in order, under the terms of the contract, the seller must be paid. It may happen that the vessel is lost at sea or the cargo destroyed by fire; nevertheless, on presentation of correct documents, payment must be made and a claim under the insurance policy proceeded with.

Only too often a buyer, finding something wrong with the cargo, makes a claim on the shipper and deducts the amount of the claim from his payment for the goods. He may consider this an effective way of forcing acceptance of a claim, but more often than not payment in full has already been made to the shipper by his agent in this country, who is left in the position of having to resolve the matter with his shipper in the best way possible. Contract clauses work both ways, and a buyer cannot complain should a shipper fail in some way to comply with a contract term if he himself ignores his own obligations. The procedure for dealing with claims is clearly laid down, and the buyer's interests are fully protected; but if payment has not been made in the correct manner, this would no doubt be considered to his disadvantage should the dispute eventually end in arbitration.

Exceptions: Clause 11

This clause reads:

'In case the manufacture and/or shipment and/or sea transport of any of the goods specified in the contract should be delayed or hindered by reason of fire or through an accident to the mill and/or timber yard and/or yard at port of loading, or through drought, ice, flood or lockout, mobilisation or through any other cause beyond Sellers' control, Sellers, provided they give prompt notice to Buyers by telegram of the delay or hindrance, shall not be responsible for any damages resulting to Buyers therefrom. If shipment of the whole or part is thereby effectively rendered impossible within six weeks of the stipulated time of shipment, Sellers shall give prompt notice to Buyers and the contract shall be cancelled to the extent of any unshipped portion, but if within 7 days of the receipt of such notice Buyers so elect they shall have the right to take the goods that are available at the stipulated c.i.f. price, less the cost of insurance and freight at the rates ruling when the contract was closed, and on the conditions and terms of the said current Uniform contract form the drawing date of approximate payment, unless the goods have been removed earlier, being six weeks from the date such election is exercised.'

There has been a very slight change in the wording of this clause as compared with the old Albion form. Whereas the former clause referred to 'accident to the sawmills', the new one extends this to 'accident to the mill and/or timber yard and/or yard at port of loading'. This amendment defines quite clearly what was somewhat anomalous in the former terms. In the past there have been disputes, especially where the mill has been inland and some distance from the port. Under these circumstances it is usual for the goods to be stored in a yard or warehouse at the loading port, and under the new terms they are covered against fire etc.

The 'stipulated time of shipment' mentioned in this clause is inserted in the preamble on the face of the contract — 'ready to load about a certain date . . . . .'. If it is not filled in, it is taken that it is six weeks from the ready date. This clause differentiates between delay or hindrance and prevention. Circumstances causing delay or hindrance give sellers the option of extending the shipment. If the delay or hindrance prevents shipment within the extended time, buyers have the option of cancelling or putting back the goods for later delivery, but not later than the following f.o.w. In the case of prevention of manufacture or shipment, sellers have the option to cancel the contract. Two factors will work against the shipment of goods in time. In the first place, in a rising freight market the shipowner may try to evade his obligations to the charterer when he finds that he can sell his tonnage more dearly in another market. Secondly, in a rising timber market there are certain sellers who may hope to extricate themselves from one commitment made while prices were low in order to sell later at a higher price. (See Clause 18: Claims.)

War, etc.: Clause 12

'Should prohibition of export or import (other than export or import conditional only upon licence) war or blockade at any time prevent shipment within the time stipulated or within such extended time as provided in Clause 4 or 11 or as otherwise mutually agreed upon, the contract or any unfulfilled part thereof, to be cancelled.

'If through any of the reasons enumerated in this Clause, a rise in rates of the sea freights should occur exceeding 10 per cent as compared with the rates ruling when the contract was closed Sellers have the right of cancelling the contract if Buyers do not declare themselves willing to pay the extra freight over and above the 10 per cent and any extra insurance. Such declarations to be given to Sellers directly or through their Agents, within three working days of receipt of Sellers notice of the said increase.'

The only significant change in the wording of this clause is that it stipulates a percentage increase in rate of sea freight of not more than 10 per cent, whereas the former terms were based on a definite sum based on volume. Otherwise, the wording is unchanged.

Passing of Property: Clause 13

'Property in goods to be deemed for all purposes, except retention of Vendor's lien for unpaid purchase price, to have passed to Buyers when goods have been put on board the vessel.'

The wording of this clause is unchanged. In timber contracts and many other forms of sale there is a right of the seller to keep possession of the goods sold until payment for them has been made. This is known as seller's 'lien' on the goods. Although the 'property' in the goods (including accidents) passes to the buyer when they are put on board the vessel, the seller's lien or right to hold the goods, if he is not paid, remains.

While the TTF Insurance Clauses include a 'warehouse to warehouse' protection (see Chapter 6), the cover of insurable risk is not as nicely tied up as one would wish. There are two legal rights in considering these aspects of contracts:

(1) Right of property or ownership in the goods. As will be seen above, this passes to the buyer on shipment, subjecting him to the risk of any accident that befalls the goods — against which risks he is of course insured.

(2) Right of possession of the goods. This normally follows the right of property but it can be defeated if the buyer does not carry out his part of the contract by making payment to the seller in exchange for the shipping documents. The seller's lien can pass through three possible stages:

(a) A period of absolute control by the seller over the goods. Although the 'property' has passed to the buyer on shipment, so long as the seller still holds the bills of lading made out 'to order' or in his agent's name, the right of possession still remains in his hands. Simply by endorsing the bills of lading, he could transfer the property back to himself.

(b) The stage when the seller forwards the bills of lading to the buyer subject to the payment of the price of the goods. If the buyer refuses acceptance of the goods, or refuses to pay for them, he has no right to retain the bills of lading representing them. The seller's lien permits the seller to hold the goods pending the issue of a court order enabling them to be resold to reimburse the original seller, who can then recover any loss sustained by action against the original buyer. However, if the buyer does not hold an endorsed bill of lading, and a further endorsement passes it to an innocent person for value (that is, for money, services rendered, etc.), under Section 47 of the Sale of Goods Act, the last holder of the bill of lading obtains a good title to the goods which will defeat the seller's lien for unpaid price.

(c) A possible final stage in which, provided that possession of the goods has not been lost, the seller's lien revives by reason of non-payment by the buyer. The seller has now become an 'unpaid seller' (defined by Section 38 of the Sale of Goods Act).

As soon as possession passes to the buyer, the seller's lien lapses, but it can be revived again on the insolvency of the buyer, provided that the seller still retains possession of the goods in transit, if the buyer becomes insolvent and cannot pay. A person is deemed to be insolvent who has ceased to pay his debts in the ordinary course of business, or cannot pay them as they become due, whether he has committed an act of bankruptcy or not.

Goods are said to be in transit from the time they are delivered to the carrier, by land or water, for the purpose of transmission to the buyer, until the buyer takes delivery of them from the carrier. Where part delivery of the goods has been made, the remainder of the goods may be stopped in transit. The carrier is bound to act upon the notice to stop the goods sent to him by the seller. There is no special form for this notice.

Again, the only time when an unpaid seller's right to stop goods in transit can be defeated is when the buyer has obtained *possession* of the endorsed bill of lading and *pays* for it. If the last buyer pays for the goods but does *not* obtain possession of the endorsed bill of lading, his rights are subservient to the rights of the original seller.

Loading Orders, Bill of Lading: Clause 14

'Buyers undertake that full loading orders shall be in Agent's hands not later than 15 working days before the time of shipment stipulated in the contract. The number of Bills of Lading shall not exceed 10 per 500 cubic metre unless otherwise agreed prior to the issue of the loading orders, the additional cost of which to be mutually agreed at the same time.

'If Master calls for margin, Buyers authorise Sellers to load such margin on separate Bills of Lading.

'The cargo shall be sent alongside in such a manner as to enable Master to keep separate the cargo under each Bill of Lading. Quantities of 250 cubic metre or less for which a separate Bill of Lading is required shall be delivered to the vessel at one and the same time so as to enable Master to make one stowage of that Bill of Lading in the vessel unless part is stowed on deck.

'If it is apparent from the Bills of Lading that the Master has failed to load the vessel in accordance with Buyer's loading instructions, Sellers shall forthwith advise Buyers of all variations therefrom and make protest to the Master, sending a copy thereof to Buyers.

'If it should come to Sellers notice that packaged goods have been broken open during loading they shall forthwith advise Buyers and make a written protest to the Master sending a copy to Buyers.'

This clause has been reworded to quite a considerable extent, and is now more explicit than hitherto. The number of days for presentation of loading orders has been increased from 12 to 15, and the cost of additional bills is not stipulated but left to mutual agreement.

The number of bills of lading required by the buyer will depend to a certain extent on the nature of his business. If he does a large trade selling goods 'on passage', reselling them on a c.i.f. basis or selling goods 'ex quay', he will be selling complete bills of lading of timber. The method of handling timber at his port may require a special arrangement of bills of lading, particularly if the timber is being taken direct from ship to road or any other form of inland transport. This latter method saves many of the dock labour charges, but it can only be worked with complete bills of lading. All these points, therefore, affect how the buyer wishes the timber to be shipped.

It is the seller's duty to send the bills of lading to the buyer before the vessel reaches the port of destination, but this is not a definite commitment on the seller's part, and if he fails to do this, the buyer, although he may be seriously inconvenienced, has no redress. The seller will send the bill of lading as quickly as possible in his own interest, in order to collect payment against it.

It must be borne in mind that in spite of the wording of this clause, the shipper has no control whatsoever over the actual loading of the goods and stowage in the vessel. The most that the shipper can do is to send the goods alongside the vessel in such a way as to enable the vessel to load the goods in accordance with the charter party and the loading orders. He is in no way responsible for seeing that the vessel carries out these orders, and frequently the master may decide that for the safety of his vessel it is necessary to load goods specified in the loading orders 'to be loaded underdeck', on deck, and the specified 'on deck' bills of lading underdeck. In such matters the master has the final say and the shipper cannot be held responsible for such deviations from the loading orders. However, it is the shipper's duty to protest should there be a deviation from the actual loading orders and advise the buyer, sending him a copy of the protest.

The sellers must receive the buyer's loading orders in time to split the specification into bills of lading before the goods are sent to the ship. This period of time is defined in the contract.

Dead-Freight: Clause 15

'Sellers guarantee to pay all dead-freight admitted or proved to have been caused at the loading port by their default. If there is any such claim made against Buyers or Bill of Lading holders, Buyers shall give prompt notice thereof in writing to Sellers or their Agents. Sellers shall, within ten days after receipt of such notice, either pay the claim or give Buyers an approved guarantee to indemnify them for any amount and costs which may be awarded to the Shipowners in respect of such claim and for interest at 2 per cent above the Bank of England's Minimum Lending Rate for the time being in force if higher on any deposit in respect of such claim made to release the goods. In case of arbitration or lawsuit on such claim Buyers to follow the reasonable instructions of Sellers with regard to the defence and Sellers shall supply all necessary evidence and documents in support thereof.'

The reference to the bank rate no longer applies in the UK, since we now have the minimum lending rate, and the lowest at which banks will lend is 2 per cent above this rate.

In practice, many shippers are reluctant to give the required guarantee on dead freight claims but buyers should not fail to press agents to obtain it on their behalf. It is not unusual for some agents to give such guarantee on behalf of their shippers.

Demurrage: Clause 16

'Sellers undertake to bring the cargo alongside the vessel in the customary manner as fast as the vessel can receive and stow during the ordinary working hours of the port, in Sweden one shift only and in Finland one or two shifts as specified below (Saturday afternoons, Sundays, general and local holidays excepted unless used in which case actual time used to count) but shall not be bound to bring alongside more per weather working day than the appropriate quantities set out in the schedule agreed between the United Kingdom Timber Trade Shipowners' Mutual Association Ltd, the Finnish Sawmill Owners' Association and the Swedish Wood Exporters' Association and current at the date of the charter party. "Weather working day" shall mean a calendar day of 24 consecutive hours when work would normally be undertaken weather permitting. If weather interrupts loading the period of such interruption shall not count as laytime.

'Subject to the provisions of Clauses 3(b) and 8(e) of the charter party laytime shall commence when the vessel is ready to load and written notice of readiness has been given to sellers or their agents whether in berth or not.

'If when the harbour is working in one shift only, the notice is given before 10.00 time shall commence at 14.00 and if notice is given after 10.00 time shall commence at the commencement of the next working day. If, when the harbour is working two shifts the notice is given before 10.00 time shall commence at the commencement of the second shift and if notice is given after 10.00 time shall commence at the commencement of the first shift next working day.

'Notice may only be given in ordinary office hours. If the vessel arrives at the loading port earlier than the date notified, Sellers are not compelled to have the cargo brought alongside before 14.00 when the harbour is working one shift or before the commencement of the second shift on the notified day of arrival, if not otherwise agreed upon between Sellers and the Master of the Vessel.

'Laytime shall not run during the period of any delay in loading due to shortage of stevedores or to the vessel's inability to receive and stow at the rate at which Sellers are bound to bring the cargo alongside in accordance with the first paragraph of this Clause, or to any cause whatsoever beyond Sellers' control. If the laytime is exceeded demurrage shall be paid by Sellers at the rate set out in the Schedule previously referred to in this Clause.

'Buyers shall pay or cause to be paid the demurrage contribution payable under Clause 19(b) of the Nubaltwood charter party.'

The terms of this clause are very similar to those of the 1973 amendments but the wording has been slightly changed to make the provisions more explicit.

Licences: Clause 17

The wording of this clause is unchanged from that of the Albion (1964) contract form and reads:

'The obligation to make application for and the cost of obtaining any export or import licence and to pay any export or import duty, charges or taxes which may be payable in respect of the export or import of the goods shall be upon Sellers and Buyers respectively. If either party having made application has failed to obtain the requisite licence by the date stated in the contract, he shall have the right to cancel the contract provided prompt notice is given to the other party. If a party has not notified the other party by the above date that the requisite licence has been granted, the last mentioned party has the right of cancelling the contract subject to prompt notice being given. If any requisite licence has been refused to a party or if a licence although granted is subsequently cancelled prior to shipment, such party shall forthwith advise the other party by telegram and either party shall have the right of cancelling the contract provided that notice of cancellation is given, in the case of the first mentioned party, in the said telegram, and in the case of the other party, promptly on receipt thereof.'

The date mentioned in the second sentence is filled in on the face of the contract. The amplification of a clause covering the granting and cancelling of export and import licences has been brought about by the 'licence-ridden' conditions in which all world export and import trades work today. Provision is made for cancelling or postponement for a number of reasons in addition to the normal war and *force majeure* clauses.

Claims: Clause 18

'No claim for quality and/or condition will be recognised by Sellers unless reasonable particulars are given to Agents within three months from date of vessel's final discharge. The onus shall be upon Buyers to show that proper care has been taken of the goods during this period. No other claim will be recognised by Sellers on any goods shipped under this contract unless reasonable particulars are given to Agents within six months of vessel's discharge.

'No claim for quality shall be recognised on any item or part item shipped which has been broken into, but otherwise Buyers shall be at liberty to deal with any item or part item on which there is no such claim without prejudice to their right to claim on any intact item or part item under the arbitration clause. An item or part item shall be considered to be intact if it can be produced to the Arbitrator(s) and Umpire in its entirety as discharged.

'An item shall mean all goods of the same dimension, quality and description. Where an item is split up on different Bills of Lading the part of the item shipped on each Bill of Lading is referred to as a part item.

'On any claim for condition including discoloration Buyers are at liberty to deal with any portion of the goods on which there is no claim, the claim for condition including discoloration being confined to the quantities which the Buyers can produce to the Arbitrator(s) and Umpire.

'Reasonable particulars shall mean a statement as to whether the claim is for quality and/or condition together with a statement of the sizes complained

of and an estimate of percentages and of the amount claimed. All such statements are without prejudice and conditional on the facilities for inspecting
the goods.

'Sellers shall be liable in damages to Buyers in respect of all loss damage
and expense suffered by Buyers as a consequence of non-delivery for which
Sellers are liable, provided that in any case where Sellers can establish that
such non-delivery did not result from a deliberate act on their part, then such
damages shall be deemed to be equal to 10 per cent of the contract price of
the goods the subject matter of the claim. Where the claim is in respect of the
non-delivery of any complete item or items of the contract the mean quantity
shall be taken for the basis of a claim without regard to margins.

Claims for condition on unseasoned goods shall be as specified in the
contract.'

In producing bulk quantities of a natural material such as timber, it is
inevitable that there will be many variations in the quality of the goods.
Added to the variations in the quality and manufacture are the many factors
that can affect the condition of the goods before and during their journey to
the UK. These variations may result in claims by the buyer against the seller
for poor quality or condition, and it is for this reason that the procedure for
dealing with such claims is set out so clearly in both the Albion and Uniform
contract forms.

There are many pitfalls in formulating and presenting claims, and for this
reason it is proposed to deal with them at some length.

The time factor. In the Albion (1964) contract, amended by the 1969
amendments, the period for the presentation of claims was different for
loose goods and truck-bundled and length-packaged goods. The former was
14 working days from vessel's final date of discharge, while 3 months from
the date of final discharge of the vessel was allowed for truck-bundled and
length-packaged goods. In the new Albion (1980) contract form 3 months
from vessel's final date of discharge is allowed on all goods, loose, truck-
bundled or length-packaged.

A buyer is required to supply 'reasonable particulars' with his claim; this
means under what heading the claim is made – i.e. excessive knots or shakes,
etc., or faulty manufacture, excessive discoloration, etc. It is necessary to give
details of the quality, sizes, quantity and bills of lading concerned. It is also
necessary to detail the percentage of pieces claimed to be defective and the
monetary amount claimed for the defect. If any other charges are involved
by way of opening up packages, sticking the goods or machining (involving
conveying into mill and repackaging), these costs must also be included and
shown in the claim. If these particulars are not given within the stipulated
time, a buyer may find it difficult to pursue satisfactorily any claim against
a shipper.

Under the contract terms a buyer undertakes to take proper care of the
goods during the period allowed for the presentation of claims – i.e. 3 months
from discharge of vessel. If, for instance, it is suspected that the goods are not

properly seasoned, some of the packages must be opened up and inspected, and if discoloration is developing, the shipper's agent should be advised at once and shipper's permission sought through him for goods to be piled in stick to prevent further discoloration. A shipper is not likely to agree that leaving kiln-dried goods in the open without proper protection constitutes 'taking proper care of them'.

Breaking bulk. The contract regulations regarding the use of goods on which a claim has been made differ between a 'quality claim' and a 'condition claim'.

In the case of a quality claim each item on which the claim is being made must be kept intact for inspection by the shipper's agent and possibly arbitrators. An item can be taken to mean a definite quality and size on a given bill of lading. If the same quality and size is shipped also on other bills of lading, and these goods appear to be satisfactory, then it is in order for the buyer to use such goods, keeping intact only the goods on the bill of lading found to be faulty.

The contract regulations regarding condition claims are quite different. A buyer may use goods from a particular 'item' where, for instance, bad discoloration has developed, putting aside the faulty pieces and claiming only on what he can produce as faulty.

In a quality claim there is no obligation on a buyer to keep the goods on which he is claiming all at one place and, provided that it can be established that the item is intact, as discharged, the goods can be in a customer's yard or elsewhere. The same applies to a condition claim, except that the claim can only be pursued on the number of pieces which can be produced as discoloured.

The breaking of bulk causes considerable trouble with some buyers, who frequently ask the shipper's agent for his permission to break bulk before the claim has been agreed with the shipper. No agent is in a position to give such permission without reference back to his shipper. It is always in order, however, to ask an agent to obtain his shipper's permission to break bulk, and in many cases this will be granted, especially if the goods have been inspected by his agent.

Claims for non-delivery. The basis for settlement on claims for non-delivery has caused confusion in the trade for a very long time.

The Albion (1964) contract stated: 'Sellers shall pay to Buyers in full and final settlement as liquidated damages a sum equal to 10% of the c.i.f. value of the goods the subject matter of the claim'. It is the phrase '10% of the c.i.f. value' which has caused confusion. Some buyers said that this should mean 10 per cent of the c.i.f. price as stated in the contract, while others maintained that it must mean 10 per cent of the market value at the time that the non-delivery took place. With market fluctuations, this could mean a very different thing. It is understood that Counsel's opinion was taken on this point, and that the opinion given was that it must mean 10 per cent of the c.i.f. value of the goods at the time the non-delivery was established.

The new contract form, however, leaves no doubt at all on the point and establishes that, as far as the timber trade is concered, it means '10 per cent of the c.i.f. price as per the contract'. The alteration to this clause is important, as it would appear to cut right across the intention of Clause 51 para. 3 of the Sale of Goods Act.

The contract procedure for dealing with claims is very comprehensive, and if followed exactly, gives the buyer the fullest protection with the ultimate choice, if necessary, of taking the dispute to arbitration.

Rejection: Clause 19

'Buyers' right of rejection shall not be exercised where the claim is limited to questions of dimension and/or quality unless the shipment or Bill of Lading as a whole (if the claim is to reject such shipment or Bill of Lading) or the item or part item (if the claim is to reject such item or part item) is not in respect of such heads of claim a fair delivery under the contract from a commercial standpoint of which, the Arbitrators or Umpire are to be the sole and final judges'.

Rejection of a shipment or part shipment is limited to those circumstances whereby a 'condition' of the contract has been broken. This means generally that the goods supplied are essentially different from those described in the contract.

The occasions on which a rejection can be justified, and the documents returned, are few. If grounds do exist for the goods to be rejected outright, then the documents in their entirety must be returned at once to the shipper's agent, the reason for the rejection being stated. If, however, there is any doubt whatsoever regarding the basic facts of the rejection, it is almost inevitable that the shipper will, as is his right under the contract, refer the matter to arbitration.

Arbitration: Clause 20

'Any dispute and/or claim regarding shipped goods which it may be found impossible to settle amicably shall be referred to arbitration to be held in the country of destination of the goods and except as otherwise herein provided to be conducted according to and governed by the law of that country and the application of the Uniform Law on the International Sale of Goods to this contract is hereby entirely excluded. Where the claim is for quality and/or condition and has not been settled amicably within ten days after receipt of claim as stated in the first paragraph of Clause 18 either party may at once proceed to arbitration.

'If agreed by the parties the reference shall be to a sole arbitrator but failing such agreement the reference shall be to two Arbitrators one to be appointed by each party.

'If the parties fail to agree on the person who shall be appointed sole

Arbitrator or where the reference is to two Arbitrators either party fails to appoint their Arbitrator within seven days after being requested through the Agents under the Contract so to do, then the Arbitrator shall be appointed by the President or failing him by the Vice-President of the Timber Trade Federation on the application of either party. The said Arbitrators shall be members of the timber trade or Arbitrators recognised by the Timber Trade Federation or by the Finnish Sawmill Owners Association or by the Swedish Wood Exporters Association.

'Where the reference is to two Arbitrators and they fail to agree upon an Award they shall appoint an Umpire. Should they fail to agree as to such appointment, then each Arbitrator shall select one name from a list of 10 persons. In the case of Finnish goods the list shall comprise 5 persons designated by the Finnish Sawmill Owners' Association and the other 5 by the Timber Trade Federation. In the case of Swedish goods the list shall comprise 5 persons designated by the Swedish Wood Exporters' Association and the other 5 by the Timber Trade Federation. The person to act as Umpire shall be the name drawn by lot from the two so selected by the Arbitrators. Should the person so chosen by lot be prevented from acting the Arbitrator who selected that name may thereupon appoint another person from the relevant list who shall act as Umpire. The lists in question may be revised on May 1st each year but vacancies occurring during a year shall be filled by the Association concerned.

'Disputes in respect of goods sold for delivery in Scotland to a buyer whose registered office or principal place of business is in Scotland shall be governed by the Arbitration (Scotland) Act, 1894. However, it shall not be competent to an arbiter to state a case for the opinion of any Court notwithstanding Section 3(1) of the Administration of Justice (Scotland) Act, 1972 or any modification or re-enactment thereof. For the avoidance of doubt it is hereby declared that such arbiter(s) shall have power to award damages and interest thereon.

'Inspection by the Arbitrators or the Umpire, as the case may be, of the goods claimed upon shall take place within fourteen days after their appointment, unless they consider inspection unnecessary, and the award shall be made within two months of the appointment of Arbitrators.

'An award shall be final and binding upon both parties. The costs of such arbitration shall be left to the discretion of the Arbitrator(s) or Umpire. In deciding as to costs the Arbitrator(s) or Umpire shall take into consideration the correspondence between the parties relating to the dispute and their respective efforts to arrive at a fair settlement.

'Any other dispute and/or claim whatsoever arising out of this contract which cannot be settled amicably shall be referred to arbitration. Such arbitration shall be held in England and conducted in accordance with the English Arbitration Acts, 1950, 1975 and 1979 or any subsisting statutory modification thereof or substitution therefor. Such Arbitrators and their Umpire need not be members of the Timber Trade. In all other respects the provisions of this clause shall apply.

'This clause applies to contracts for shipments to the United Kingdom and the Republic of Ireland only.'

As the question of arbitration is dealt with fully in Chapter 11, it is not proposed to comment further at this stage.

Notice: Clause 21

This clause is unchanged in the new Albion (1980) Contract Form and reads:

'Where under the contract Buyers are given an option or it is provided that Buyers may or are required to give notice to Sellers, notice by the Buyers to the Agents named in the contract (a) of the exercise of the option or (b) of any other matter, shall be deemed to be good notice to Sellers of the matter covered by such notice. Similarly, notice by Agents to Buyers shall be deemed to be good notice by Sellers. Wherever the word telegram appears in the Contract or in these General Conditions it shall be deemed to include "telex".'

No comment is really necessary on this clause, except that it should be noted that wherever the word 'telegram' appears in the contract it shall be deemed to include 'telex'.

LINER PARCEL AMENDMENTS TO ALBION 1980 CONTRACT FORM GENERAL TERMS, CONDITIONS AND WARRANTIES

It will be seen from the face of the Albion 1980 contract form that shipments shall not be made by liner without specific authorisation by buyers, and if this is agreed, then the general conditions must be altered in accordance with the following amendments:

Ends: Clause 2. Delete first paragraph and substitute:

'Other than as regards items for which a separate price for ends 1.8 m to 2.4 m is specified in the contract (in which case notwithstanding any provision of this Clause all ends on such items shall be at that specified price) Sellers to have the right to supply up to 3% of ends on each item at full price i.e. the full c.i.f. price for 2.7 m and up appropriate for the goods concerned. If the percentage of 3% is exceeded on any item(s) all ends (including the first 3%) on such item(s) shall be at two-thirds of the f.o.b. value (i.e. the contract price per cubic metre less the freight rate) plus one-third of the freight rate and one-third of the insurance cost appropriate to the item(s).'

Chartering, Delay and Cancelling: Clause 4. In the marginal heading delete 'Chartering' and substitute 'Shiproom'. Delete whole clause and substitute:

'Shiproom to be secured in due time by Sellers with liberty to substitute. Sellers shall promptly advise Buyers by telegram or airmail that shiproom is secured with approximate expected loading date. Sellers shall also both as regards the original vessel and any substitute vessel, promptly advise Buyers by telegram or airmail of the name of the vessel when known.

'If Owners give notice that the vessel whether original or substituted cannot be ready to load within 6 weeks after the stipulated time of shipment or if without such notice the vessel has not been ready so to load, Sellers shall instantly advise Buyers by telegram stating the exact time of the receipt of Owners' notice, if any, and Buyers shall have the right, to be exercised promptly, to cancel the contract to a corresponding extent save that if Sellers have not advised Buyers as stipulated above Buyers' right of cancellation is subject only to prompt advice after the delay has come to Buyers' notice. Sellers' obligation to give notice in respect of the original vessel shall not arise if they have substituted or have the intention to substitute another vessel.

'Should any vessel in which space has been booked under the contract be lost after being named to Buyers and previous to loading Sellers have the option of booking space in another vessel in substitution for loading within the stipulated time or six weeks thereafter or of cancelling the contract to a corresponding extent upon giving prompt notice to Buyers leaving however Buyers the right to take the goods at the stipulated c.i.f. price less cost of insurance and the rate of freight whereat tonnage lost has been secured, and on the conditions and terms of the current "Uniform" contract form, adopted by the respective Associations, the drawing date of approximate payment unless goods have been removed earlier than two months from the date of such right being exercised.

'Sellers shall not be liable for any loss suffered by Buyers from delay in shipment caused by circumstances beyond Sellers' control.

'The Bills of Lading shall be customary liner terms.'

Margin for Chartering: *Clause 6*. Delete clause.

Insurance: Clause 8. Delete first paragraph and substitute:

'Sellers shall insure the cargo for the c.i.f. value plus 10 per cent, with, at Sellers' option, a first-class Company registered in Buyers' country or with Underwriters carrying on business in the United Kingdom or with a first-class company registered outside the United Kingdom as named in the contract as per Lloyd's form of policy together with current Timber Trade Federation Clauses and in the case of policies issued in Sellers' country including Additional Clauses, as per Clause 9 hereof, losses payable in London and, subject to the sub-clauses hereunder against the risks covered by the Institute War Clauses (Timber Trade) and Institute Strikes Riots and Civil Commotions Clauses (Timber Trade) in force at the time of attachment of the insurance.'

Payment and Freight: Clause 10. Delete first paragraph and substitute:

'Buyers shall pay any unpaid freight according to Bill of Lading and shall pay to Sellers or their authorised Agents the balance of the invoice value after deducting total freight, in London, on receipt of and in exchange for shipping documents including policies of insurance as per Clause 8.'

Second paragraph, first line: delete 'any freight advance' and substitute 'any pre-paid freight'; delete 'Charter party' and substitute 'Bill of Lading'.

Third paragraph, second line: delete 'Charter party' and substitute 'Bill of Lading'.

Demurrage: Clause 16. Delete clause.

8.3 Uniform 1980

General

The Uniform Softwood (F.A.S.) contract form is adopted by the Timber Trade Federation of the United Kingdom, the Finnish Sawmill Owners Association and the Swedish Wood Exporters Association. The term 'F.A.S.' is included in the title for the first time (see earlier comments in this Chapter, page 131). Many of the form's general terms and conditions have been changed and it is now more in line with the new Albion form, covered in the first half of this Chapter.

The preamble on the face of the contract is now more explicit than hitherto; the changes are as follows:

Shipment

'To be loaded at . . . . . and to be ready for shipment on the . . . . .' (ready date).

The name of the port of loading is a part of the description of the goods, and if they are shipped from any other port, the buyers have the right to maintain that these are not the goods which they purchased unless there has been mutual agreement.

Ends

'Ends of slatings and boards 25 mm and thinner x 75 mm (see Clause 2c of the General Conditions) maximum . . . . . per cent per item/part item.'

The percentage of such ends has to be mutually agreed and inserted on the face of the contract.

Payment

At the time of writing, this clause is the same as in the previous contract. It should be borne in mind that there may be an amendment in due course in order to bring it more in line with the Albion contract.

Seller's time for completing contract

This provides space for insertion of the agreed date, but if it is not filled in, it is six weeks from the ready date mentioned above.

Claims – unseasoned goods

'Claims for condition of unseasoned goods (see Clause 18, last paragraph of General Conditions) . . . . .'.
    This has to be inserted after mutual agreement.

Liner Shipment

'Shipment shall not be made by liner unless specifically authorised by Sellers but if so authorised and so shipped the Contract and the General Conditions shall be amended by the "Liner Parcel Amendments to Uniform 1980 Contract Form" adopted by the above mentioned Associations and known to both parties.'
    The wording of this clause is the same as in the previous contract form, except for the date.

GENERAL TERMS, CONDITIONS AND WARRANTIES UNIFORM 1980

Price Basis: Clause 1

'The prices are per cubic metre (if planed goods in nominal measure) delivered free alongside the vessel.'
    This wording is the same as that of the 1969 amendments, except that British sterling is not specified. It is also the same as that of the Albion contract.

Ends: Clause 2

'Other than as regards items for which a separate price for ends 1.8 m to 2.4 m is specified in the contract (in which case notwithstanding any provision of this Clause all ends on such items shall be at that specified price) Sellers have the right to supply up to 3% of ends on each item at the full price for 2.7 m and up appropriate for the goods concerned. If the percentage of 3% is exceeded on any item(s) all ends (including the first 3%) on such item(s) shall be at two-thirds of the appropriate contract price per cubic metre.
    'Notwithstanding the foregoing, however, unless otherwise provided in the contract, ends shall not exceed the undermentioned percentages on each and every item or part item:

    a) of V1th quality – 10 per cent
    b) of boards 25 mm and thinner x 115 mm and under, all qualities – 15 per cent (unless otherwise agreed)
    c) of slatings and boards 25 mm and thinner x 75 mm – the percentage of ends as mutually agreed and inserted in the contract

d) of all other specified goods except those defined in paragraphs a), b) and c) of this Clause — 7½ per cent.

'Buyer's right to compensation in respect of ends in excess of these maximum percentages or the maximum percentages shown in the contract, if appropriate, shall not be limited to the reduction in price referred to in this Clause. Ends to be regarded as included in the contract quantity but to be disregarded in the calculation of average length.'

This clarifies the ends situation in clearer terms than hitherto. The shipment of ends is often of assistance for the safe and economical stowage of the cargo to the ship's full capacity, although this does not have the same significance as it had in the days before packaging and truck-bundling.

Seasoning, Bracking and Loading: Clause 3

'The goods are to be properly seasoned for shipment to the United Kingdom and the Republic of Ireland. Each item to be of Shippers' usual bracking, average length and fair specification for such description of goods and delivered alongside the ship in accordance with the custom of the port, the Sellers not being responsible for any deterioration occasioned by circumstances beyond their control after the goods have left Sellers' Wharf properly protected.

'Unless otherwise specifically agreed, every package shall be marked and identified with serial number as per specification.

'All bundled and packaged goods shall be adequately and securely bound.

'Except where otherwise specified, packaged goods shall mean goods which have a single length and size in each package provided that Sellers shall have the right to combine lengths where the residue is insufficient for a complete package. Truck-bundled goods shall mean goods bundled in mixed lengths of one size, the dimensions of each bundle to be mutually agreed.'

The wording of this clause has been slightly changed but it is basically the same as the previous contract. It is also the same as the Albion Clause 3; at the end of that clause there are comments on certain significant aspects and these should be referred to, as they are also associated with the Uniform terms.

An additional requirement specifies that every package shall be marked and identified with serial numbers as per specification in both contracts.

Chartering, etc: Clause 4

'Shiproom to be provided in due time by Buyers. Buyers undertake that at least 9 working days (relevant excepted days as per Clause 2 of the "Nubaltwood" charter party 1973 excluded) notice shall be given to Sellers direct before arrival of any vessel to load stating vessel's and Charterer's name. Buyers undertake that full loading orders and Charter party, which shall be on the form of "Nubaltwood" last accepted by the respective Associations as being the document on which chartering has been effected, shall be in the Seller's hands not later than 15 working days (Saturdays excluded) before the notified due date of vessel's arrival.

'If it is apparent from the Bills of Lading that the Master has failed to load the vessel in accordance with Buyer's loading instructions, Sellers shall forthwith advise Buyers of all variations therefrom and make protest to the Master, sending a copy thereof to Buyers. If due care has not been exercised by Master in giving notice of the probable date of vessel's arrival, Buyers are responsible for all charges due to non-arrival of the vessel on the date stated in the said notice.

'Buyers are bound to get inserted in the Charter party a clause that on arrival at port of loading Master has to give written notice of the approximate quantity of cargo required in Shippers ordinary office hours only.'

This clause varies slightly from the previous contract form, as it qualifies the number of days as 'working' and not 'consecutive' and states that the Master has to give written notice of the cargo required to shippers during ordinary office hours only. The buyer's undertaking to give at least nine working days notice to sellers before arrival of the vessel to load, and buyer's responsibility for demurrage due to non-arrival of the vessel, are covered in the Nubaltwood charter under Clause 2. By this clause, charterers or buyers are indemnified against any claims from sellers who may have brought goods down to the quay for loading and are faced with demurrage claims on the wagons or lighters due to the late arrival of the vessel. The written notice of quantity of cargo required is covered in Clause 6 of the Nubaltwood charter.

The buyer arranges freight through a shipbroker or shipping agent, who will require full details of the amount and type of goods to be shipped, the names of the loading and discharging ports and the dates when shipping space is required. With this information, they will endeavour to offer the buyer various freights to cover the parcel in question. The quantity being shipped is a very important factor in the chartering of shipping space. If the shipping agent offers a vessel of rather more carrying capacity than is required for the contract, the buyer may charter the whole vessel, relying on being able to purchase an additional quantity to fill it; otherwise he must realise the possibility of the shipping agent filling the remainder of the vessel's space with another buyer's goods.

The buyer must beware of very cheap freight rates, particularly from obscure foreign shipowners. In chartering a vessel of this nature, the buyer is wise to make certain that insurance cover is accepted before he completes his freight contract. There have been instances where a foreign ship chartered at a very cheap rate has been found to be in such a bad condition that no insurance company would cover the goods being carried.

Margins in Sellers' Option: Clause 5

'Sellers shall have the option to vary by 10% more or less on any or every item but not exceeding 100 cubic metres on any one item and to vary items of 10 cubic metres to 50 cubic metres to the extent of 5 cubic metres, always provided that the total quantity is not varied except under the provisions of Clause 6. Such option shall apply also to overlying goods.'

This clause is of great importance from the seller's point of view. When he receives a large consignment of logs into the mill, it is by no means certain what outfall of each size and quality the logs will produce. Therefore it is essential that the producer has some latitude in the quantities of each size and quality he supplies against a contract.

The wording of this clause is similar to that of the previous contract, except that the quantities have been revised.

Margin for Chartering: Clause 6

'A margin of 10% more or less of the total contract quantity, but not exceeding 200 cubic metres, is to be allowed to Buyers for convenience of chartering only, but when two or more shipments are made under the same contract such margin shall only apply to the quantity by the last vessel. This margin does not apply to overlying goods unchartered for or to over-wintering goods. Should Buyers under this clause demand an increase of total contract quantity, Sellers to give such increase in contract sizes, though not more than 25% increase or 25 cubic metres, whichever may be greater, on any item over 50 cubic metres or 50% increase on any item of 50 cubic metres or under.

Where a "minimum/maximum" quantity is stipulated in the contract, chartering shall be on a "minimum/maximum" basis and this Clause shall not apply.'

The wording of this clause is similar to that of the previous contract, except that the quantities have been revised. It varies only slightly from the Albion terms, the difference being that the latter provides the margin for sellers who are the charterers. Subject to these clauses, the total quantity of timber delivered must agree substantially with the quantity purchased.

Quantity, Over-shipment and Under-shipment: Clause 7

'In the event of over-shipment of any item(s) of the contract (subject to Clause 6 hereof) Buyers shall not be entitled to reject the entire shipment but shall have the option to be exercised without delay of taking up the Bills of Lading and paying from the whole quantity shipped or of taking up the Bills of Lading and paying only for the contract quantity rejecting the balance. The same conditions shall apply if the excess is not apparent from the Bills of Lading but is discovered only on arrival of the goods at their ultimate destination. If Buyers elect to take the contract quantity only, Sellers shall pay all extra expenses whatsoever incurred by Buyers in consequence of the over-shipment.

'In the event of under-shipment of any item(s) of the contract (subject to Clause 6 hereof) Buyers are to pay for the quantity shipped, but have the right to claim compensation for such under-shipment.'

It will be seen that if the total quantity shipped is less than the quantity purchased, the buyer must accept and pay for the goods shipped at the contract price but may claim compensation for such undershipment. This clause excludes the provisions of the Sale of Goods Act, which are mentioned later.

Where the overshipment is obvious from the bills of lading, the course for the buyer to adopt, if the overshipment is not to his advantage, is immediately to notify the seller's agents that he rejects the overshipment. Simultaneously, he may offer to take the excess quantity at a reduced price, being in a strong position to obtain such a concession from the seller. The clause quoted is quite clear, but in some other types of contracts this position is not covered in the same detail. In these circumstances, an undershipment or overshipment is covered by the Sale of Goods Act, Section 30.

Risk: Clause 8

'The risk of loss or destruction of any of the goods or of damage to any of the goods so extensive as to render it impossible to ship the damaged goods in the form intended on the carrying vessel shall be upon Sellers until the goods are delivered alongside the vessel. In all other respects notwithstanding that this sale is made on f.a.s. terms the goods shall be at the risk of Buyers from the commencement of the transit as defined in Clause 1 of the Timber Trade Federation Clauses and Institute Strikes Riots and Civil Commotions Clauses (Timber Trade).'

The wording of this clause is slightly different from that of the clause in the previous contract. The main difference is that the risk lies with sellers until the goods are alongside the vessel, whereas previously it was until the goods were loaded into lighters. The only other change is that 'f.a.s.' replaces 'f.o.b.'.

Insurance: Clause 9

'Marine insurance of cargo and freight advance to be covered by Buyers as per Lloyd's Form of Policy together with current Timber Trade Federation Clauses and Institute Strikes Riots and Civil Commotions Clauses (Timber Trade). Such insurance to attach as and when the goods are delivered alongside the vessel.

'The obligation to insure against War Risks shall be on the Buyers, who shall, if required by Sellers or Agents, deposit with them before the goods are put on board a cover note or policy of insurance effected with Lloyd's or a first-class British Company covering the cargo and freight advance against such risks. If these risks are not coverable or for any reason Buyers do not cover against these risks they shall provide before goods are put on board such security for payment as may be required by Sellers or Agents and, goods lost or not lost, shall pay against presentation of documents the value of the goods shipped at contract prices plus freight advance, if any, payable under the Charter party.

'Buyers shall, if requested, at any time after their obligations to insure as above have arisen, furnish Agents with sufficient proof of such insurance having been effected.'

The wording is the same as in the previous contract, except that the insurance commences when the goods are delivered alongside the vessel, whereas the previous contract specifies when the goods are loaded into lighters. The property clause states that the property in the goods (which includes all risks) passes to the buyer when the goods have been put 'on board'. The insurance of the goods, however, commences when the goods are loaded at the mill to road or rail, the buyer being covered during the period of pre-loading while the goods are between the wharf and the ocean going vessel (TTF Clauses 1 and 2; see Chapter 6).

By this clause buyers have the responsibility for arranging insurance to cover both goods and freight advance, and must be prepared to furnish proof of this insurance if required. This clause also visualises that war risk may again become vital and possibly uninsurable, in which case sellers must have some security for payment.

In the case of liner shipments of the goods, the liner shipment amendment to the contract form substitutes for 'freight advance' references to 'freight that has been pre-paid or is payable ship and/or cargo lost or not lost'.

Exceptions: Clause 10

'In case the manufacture and/or shipment and/or sea transport of any of the goods specified in the contract should be delayed or hindered by reason of fire or through an accident to mill and/or timber yard and/or yard at port of loading or through drought, ice, flood, strike or lock-out, mobilisation, or through any other cause beyond Sellers control (causes mentioned in Clause 11 excepted), Sellers, provided they give prompt notice to Buyers by telegram of the delay or hindrance, shall not be responsible for any damages resulting to Buyers therefrom. In such event only, Sellers have the right, during the time limit stated in the contract, of completing the contract. Should Sellers, however, be unable to deliver within such extended time they shall declare their inability to do so and on receipt of Seller's declaration Buyers shall have the option, to be promptly declared, of cancelling the contract or postponing the same to such date of delivery as may be mutually agreed upon, but in any event, not later than the following 15th May.

'If, however, the manufacture and/or shipment of the goods specified in the contract be prevented by destruction of the mill and/or timber yard and/or yard of port of loading, Sellers have the option, to be promptly declared by telegram, to cancel the contract without responsibility for any damages arising therefrom.'

There have been only slight variations in this clause as compared with the previous contract. Like the revised Albion contract, it now extends the cover to yard of port of loading. As described in Clause 11 of the Albion contract, this is significant, since many mills are inland and the goods are often stored in a yard at the port of loading and could suffer loss or damage at this point. The other difference is the fact that, unlike the Albion contract, a specific date, 15 May, is stipulated, whereas it was formally f.o.w.

War, etc.: Clause 11

'Should prohibition of export or import (other than export or import conditional only upon licence), war or blockade at any time before the drawing date, original or postponed according to Clause 12, or as otherwise mutually agreed upon, prevent Sellers from manufacturing and/or shipping or Buyers from lifting the goods, the contract shall be cancelled for any unpaid goods.'

The wording of this clause is the same as in the previous contract. It carries equal rights for both buyers and sellers. It is quite important to note that it does not affect goods already paid for by buyers and overlying in the seller's yard, in which case the property has already passed to buyers.

Overlying Goods: Clause 12

'Should any of the goods not be removed by the date (hereinafter called the "drawing date") six weeks from the ready date payment to be made in the manner provided in the contract but against approximate invoice of the drawing date and, provided not less than seven days notice prior to the drawing date has been given to Sellers or their authorised Agents, Buyers shall be entitled in exchange for such payment to receive a guarantee by approved Bankers of the country of shipment that if the goods or any portion thereof are not delivered free alongside if applied for by 1st August of the following year the contract value of any quantity unshipped will be refunded to the Buyers. The cost of the said guarantee shall be borne by Buyers up to a maximum of 1½%. Fire insurance on any such goods to be covered by Sellers.

'Buyers' liability to pay for the goods under this Clause shall, however, be suspended if the failure to remove the goods is due to any of the contingencies covered by Clause 10 and the drawing date shall be postponed for a period equivalent to the duration of the delay provided that ice hindrance shall not be a cause for suspension of payment unless shipment of the goods has already been delayed by any other contingency specified in Clause 10.

'If the goods or part thereof are not removed before the drawing date, rent to be paid from the said date at the rate of 0.75 per cent of the contract value of the goods per month or part of a month.

'If, however, a cause beyond Buyers' control other than ice prevents the lifting of the goods at any time after the rent has become payable Buyers shall pay rent at half of the above rate until such cause ceases to operate.

'In case goods sold ready for shipment per 15th November or later in the season and chartered for loading within a week after the ready date cannot be shipped on account of ice hindrance the rent provision in the third paragraph of this Clause shall not apply until the port concerned be declared open for the size of vessel required to lift the goods under the contract.

'Unless over-wintered goods are specified in the contract Sellers may, when executing delivery of goods after the drawing date, deliver goods of later production and/or overlying goods ready for shipment at the drawing date (hereinafter referred to as "overlying goods").

'When delivering overlying goods Sellers shall not be responsible for any deterioration of the goods caused by the postponement of delivery unless such deterioration exceeds what would be normal deterioration between the drawing date and the date of delivery of goods protected as customary.'

This clause has been revised, and the following are the significant differences.

Compared with the previous contract, Clause 14 is now Clause 12 and Clause 12 is now Clause 10. The rent to be paid if the goods are not lifted by the drawing date is at the rate of 0.75 per cent of the contract value of the goods per month or part of a month. This compares with £0.10 per cubic metre in the previous contract.

The case for goods sold ready for shipment per 15 November or later in the season and chartered for loading within a month after the ready date and which cannot be shipped on account of ice hindrance is revised in that it now states '. . . until the port concerned be declared open for the size of vessel required to lift the goods under the contract'. Hitherto it stated that rent should not be in force until f.o.w.

The buyer has a clear obligation in an f.a.s. contract to lift the goods within a specified time, described as 'in due time'. If he does not do so, even if the reason is that he has been unable to charter suitable freight (unless it is due to war, blockade, etc., as detailed in the war clause), the sellers are then entitled to receive payment for the goods, in return for which they will provide if required, at buyer's expense, a bank guarantee (if requested in time) to the effect that if the goods are not ultimately delivered to the buyers, their money will be refunded.

The drawing date is entered on the face of the contract. The bank guarantee sets out the particulars of the contract, with the quantity and value of the goods prepared for shipment, for which buyers are to pay prior to the shipment thereof, on presentation of the documents specified in the contract including the guarantee. The usual form of bank guarantee is as follows:

'The Bank Guarantee if the said goods or any part thereof, payment for which has been made to Sellers by Buyers, are not delivered free alongside or free on board the vessel as may be called for by the said contract for any reason other than fire, flood, earthquake or aerial or naval bombardment upon request being made to the Sellers so to do, the payment to the Buyers by the Sellers on demand of the contract value free alongside or free on board as the case may be, of any quantity short delivered. This guarantee is to remain in force until . . . . . with the option of the extension within the contract terms, subject to the settlement of all claims made hereunder upon or prior to the said date of termination and subject also to due allowance in respect of the shipment as a whole or any part of the said goods subsequent to any notification of claim hereunder.'

The guarantee excludes destruction of the goods by fire, but fire insurance on the goods has to be covered by sellers on behalf of buyers. To have this done under the seller's own stock fire policy is obviously better than to have buyers taking out their own insurance on the goods. There are possible difficulties in such circumstances in proving the buyer's insurable interest. The setting in of ice at the end of the year preventing buyers from lifting their goods is one of the risks accepted when buying f.a.s. With modern ice-breakers and ice-strengthened vessels, this risk is not nearly so serious as it used to be, but if it does happen, the goods must be paid for and overwintered.

Regarding the payment of rent for goods overlying, this is something which many importers resent, but seller's storage facilities are not unlimited, and if kiln-dried packaged goods are not stored properly under cover, they will inevitably deteriorate over the winter period; such goods do cause considerable expense and inconvenience to a shipper.

Under this clause a shipper is not bound to supply the same goods that he would have supplied had shipment been made at the due date. This is important, as it takes wood goods out of the category to which a legal decision some years ago applied — namely 'vintage goods'. Buyers by that decision in an English court were entitled by law to goods of the vintage of the year in which they would normally be produced for the date of readiness named in the contract. This, in fact, has not applied for many years, as sellers, having arranged to have 'sold goods' ready at a certain time, delivered more or less in rotation as the goods became ready for shipment. In doing this they assumed that buyers would be only too pleased to have goods fairly recently seasoned rather than overwintered goods which would probably be a bit weathered. Some buyers, on the other hand, wanted their overwintering goods to have the benefit of the extra seasoning, so there was room for dispute.

The increasingly common change from seasoning and storing timber in open yards to kiln-drying and storing in covered magazines or sheds makes it often physically impossible for sellers to store goods that are not fetched 'in due time' by buyers. There are difficulties under Swedish and Finnish law, for instance, since the only way to identify the goods as those belonging to the buyer in question would be to segregate the goods completely. There should never be any question of a seller supplying goods that are not properly seasoned, as he must still supply goods of the description contained in the contract. If a buyer particularly wishes to have overwintered goods, these must be described as such in the contract.

The Uniform contract Clause 5 states that the variations permitted to sellers (10 per cent more or less) apply also to overlying goods, while Clause 6 stipulates that the margin for convenience of chartering does not apply to overlying goods unchartered for or to overwintered goods.

Passing of Property: Clause 13

'Property in goods to be deemed for all purposes, except retention of Vendor's lien for unpaid purchase price, to have passed to Buyers when the goods have been put on board the vessel.'

The wording of this clause is unchanged and is the same as that of Albion Clause 13. At the end of that clause there are comments which are quite significant and are also associated with the Uniform contract.

Bills of Lading: Clause 14

'The number of Bills of Lading shall not exceed 10 per 500 cubic metres unless otherwise agreed prior to issue of loading orders, the additional cost of which to be mutually agreed at the same time. If Master calls for margin, Buyers authorise Sellers to load such margin on separate Bills of Lading.

'The cargo shall be sent alongside in such a manner as to enable Master to keep separate the cargo under each Bill of Lading. Quantities of 250 cubic metres or less for which a separate Bill of Lading is required shall be delivered to the vessel at one and the same time so as to enable Master to make one stowage of that Bill of Lading in the vessel unless part is stowed on deck.

'If it should come to Seller's notice that packaged goods have been broken open during loading they shall forthwith advise Buyers and make a written protest to the Master sending a copy to Buyers.'

The wording of this clause has been changed to a considerable extent. It is the same as the wording of Albion Clause 14. At the end of that clause there are comments which are quite significant and are also associated with the Uniform contract.

Dead Freight: Clause 15

'Sellers guarantee to pay all dead-freight admitted or proved to have been caused at the loading port by their default. If there is any such claim made against Buyers or Bill of Lading holders, Buyers shall give prompt notice thereof in writing to Sellers or their Agents. Sellers shall, within ten days after receipt of such notice, either pay the claim or give to Buyers an approved guarantee to indemnify them for any amount and costs which may be awarded to the Shipowners in respect of such claim and for interest at 2 per cent above the Bank of England's Minimum Lending Rate for the time being in force on any deposit in respect of such claim made to release the goods. In case of arbitration or lawsuit on such claim Buyers to follow the reasonable instructions of Sellers with regard to the defence and Sellers shall supply all necessary evidence and documents in support thereof.' The wording of this clause is the same as that of Albion Clause 15. The former reference to the bank rate no longer applies in the UK, since there is now the minimum lending rate, and the lowest at which banks will lend is 2 per cent above this rate. In practice, many shippers are reluctant to give the required guarantee on dead-freight claims, but buyers should not fail to press agents to obtain it on their behalf. It is not unusual for some agents to give such guarantee on behalf of their shippers.

Demurrage: Clause 16

'Sellers undertake to bring the cargo alongside the vessel in the customary manner as fast as the vessel can receive and stow during the ordinary working hours of the port, in Sweden one shift only and in Finland one or two shifts as specified below (Saturday afternoons, Sundays, general and local holidays excepted unless used in which case actual time used to count), but shall not be bound to bring alongside more per weather working day than the appropriate quantities set out in the Schedule agreed between the United Kingdom Timber Trade Shipowners' Mutual Association Limited, the Finnish Sawmill Owners' Association and the Swedish Wood Exporters' Association and current at the date of the charter party. "Weather working day" shall mean a calendar day of 24 consecutive hours when work would normally be undertaken weather permitting. If weather interrupts loading the period of such interruption shall not count as laytime.

'Subject to the provisions of Clauses 3(b) and 8(e) of the charter party laytime shall commence when the vessel is ready to load and written Notice of Readiness has been given to the Sellers or their Agents, whether in berth or not.

'If, when the harbour is working in one shift only, the notice is given before 10.00 time shall commence at 14.00 and if notice is given after 10.00 time shall commence at the commencement of the next working day. If, when the harbour is working two shifts the notice is given before 10.00 time shall commence at the commencement of the second shift and if notice is given after 10.00 time shall commence at the commencement of the first shift next working day.

'Notice may only be given in ordinary office hours. If the vessel arrives at the loading port earlier than the date notified, Sellers are not compelled to have the cargo brought alongside before 14.00 when the harbour is working one shift or before the commencement of the second shift on the notified day of arrival, if not otherwise agreed upon between Sellers and the Master of the vessel.

'Laytime shall not run during the period of any delay in loading due to shortage of stevedores or to the vessel's inability to receive and stow at the rate at which Sellers are bound to bring the cargo alongside in accordance with the first paragraph of this Clause, or to any cause whatsoever beyond Sellers' control. If the laytime is exceeded demurrage shall be paid by Sellers at the rate set out in the Schedule previously referred to in this Clause.

'Buyers shall pay or cause to be paid the demurrage contribution payable under Clause 19(b) of the "Nubaltwood" charter party.'

The terms of this clause are very similar to those of the previous contract but the wording has been slightly changed to make the provisions more explicit. The clause is the same as Albion Clause 16.

Licences: Clause 17

'The obligation to make application for and the cost of obtaining any export or import licence and to pay any export or import duty, charges or taxes, which may be payable in respect of the export or import of the goods shall be upon Sellers and Buyers respectively.

'If either party having made application has failed to obtain the requisite licence by the date stated in the contract, he shall have the right to cancel the contract provided prompt notice is given to the other party.

'If a party has not notified the other party by the above date that the requisite licence has been granted, the last-mentioned party has the right of cancelling the contract subject to prompt notice being given.

'If any requisite licence has been refused to a party or if a licence although granted is subsequently cancelled prior to shipment, such party shall forthwith advise the other party by telegram and either party shall have the right of cancelling the contract provided that notice of cancellation is given, in the case of the first-mentioned party, in the said telegram and, in the case of the other party, promptly on receipt thereof.'

The date mentioned in the second sentence is filled in on the face of the contract. The amplification of a clause covering the granting and cancelling of export or import licences has been brought about by the 'licence-ridden' conditions in which all world trades work today. Provision is made for cancelling or postponement for a number of reasons in addition to the normal war and *force majeure* clauses. The wording of this clause is the same as that of Albion Clause 17.

Claims: Clause 18

'No claim for quality and/or condition will be recognised by Sellers unless reasonable particulars are given to Agents within three months from date of vessel's final discharge. The onus shall be upon Buyers to show that proper care has been taken of the goods during this period. No other claim will be recognised by Sellers on any goods shipped under this contract unless reasonable particulars are given to Agents within six months of vessel's final discharge.

'No claim for quality shall be recognised on any item or part item shipped which has been broken into, but otherwise Buyers shall be at liberty to deal with any item or part item on which there is no such claim without prejudice to their right to claim on any intact item or part item under the arbitration clause. An item or part item shall be considered to be intact if it can be produced to the Arbitrator(s) and Umpire in its entirety as discharged.

'An item shall mean all goods of the same dimension, quality and description. Where an item is split up on different Bills of Lading the part of the item shipped on each Bill of Lading is referred to as a part item.

'On any claim for condition including discoloration Buyers are at liberty to deal with any portion of the goods on which there is no claim, the claim for condition including discoloration being confined to the quantities which the Buyers can produce to the Arbitrator(s) and Umpire.

'Reasonable particulars shall mean a statement as to whether the claim is for quality and/or condition together with a statement of the sizes complained of and an estimate of percentages and of the amount claimed. All such statements are without prejudice and conditional on the facilities for inspecting the goods.

'Sellers shall be liable in damages to Buyers in respect of all loss, damage and expense suffered by Buyers as a consequence of non-delivery for which Sellers are liable, provided that, in any case where Sellers can establish that such non-delivery did not result from a deliberate act on their part, then such damages shall be deemed to be equal to 10% of the contract price of the goods the subject-matter of the claim.

'Where the claim is in respect of the non-delivery of any complete item or items of the contract the mean quantity shall be taken for the basis of a claim without regard to margins.

'Claims for condition on unseasoned goods shall be as specified in the contract.'

This clause differs very considerably from the previous contract and requires detailed comment on many of its provisions. However, its wording is the same as that of Albion Clause 18, in the case of which such comment was provided (see page 151).

Rejection: Clause 19

'Buyers' right of rejection shall not be exercised where the claim is limited to questions of dimensions and/or quality unless the shipment or Bill of Lading as a whole (if the claim is to reject such shipment or Bill of Lading) or the item or part item (if the claim is to reject such item or part item) is not in respect of such heads of claim a fair delivery under the contract from a commercial standpoint of which, in the event of dispute, the Arbitrator(s) or Umpire are to be the sole and final judges.'

Rejection of a shipment or part shipment is limited to those circumstances in which a 'condition' of the contract has been broken. In general, this means that the goods supplied are essentially different from those described in the contract. The occasions on which rejection can be carried out and the documents returned are few and far between. If there are grounds for the goods to be rejected outright, then the documents in their entirety must be returned to the shipper's agent, the reason for their rejection being stated. If, however, there is any doubt whatsoever regarding the basic facts of the rejection, it is almost inevitable that the shipper will, as is his right under the contract, refer the matter to arbitration.

Alternatively, if a buyer feels that he has a really strong ground for rejecting a parcel, although the infringement of an actual condition is not clear, there is no reason at all why he should not retain the documents, making payment in accordance with the contract terms, and then claim rejection, stating his reasons — for example, 'the goods are unmerchantable', etc. In such cases arbitration is almost inevitable, but there have been cases like this where rejection has been given.

The circumstances for outright rejection depend primarily on the details contained in the shipping documents. The buyer must inspect these carefully before accepting them. For a 'condition' to be broken there must be something blatantly wrong and it should be immediately obvious to the buyer. Examples of such circumstances are:

(1) No insurance policy or certificate of insurance (c.i.f. only).

(2) Whitewood instead of redwood.

(3) Wrong specification or dimension — for example, 63 mm x 150 mm shipped against a contract for 75 mm x 150 mm.

Any overshipment beyond the quantity specified in the contract, in excess of the margins allowed, may be rejected even if the overshipment is not apparent from the bills of lading but is only discovered when the goods have been landed. In a contract which does not contain the overshipment and undershipment clauses of the usual softwood contracts, the question is covered by the Sale of Goods Act, which permits the buyer to reject entire shipments for excess of the margins allowed.

The phrase in the rejection clause 'a fair delivery from a commercial standpoint' is wide-ranging, but it is necessarily so where commercial aspects of a claim are concerned, when each case has to be decided on its merits. It merely prevents outright rejection, acknowledging that at the same time there has probably been a breach of warranty on which a buyer will claim damages or a reduction in price.

A further right of rejection for the buyers is provided by the marine insurance of the goods If these deteriorate or are damaged during the voyage *as a result of a peril against which they are insured* to such an extent that they are so different from the goods insured as to be of no value to the buyer, he may claim rejection from the insurers. If the insurance surveyor admits the claim, and the underwriters agree his assessment, the buyer is paid the equivalent of the total loss on the goods, while the goods pass to the insurance company for their disposal.

Arbitration: Clause 20

'Any dispute and/or claim regarding shipped goods which it may be found impossible to settle amicably shall be referred to arbitration to be held in the country of destination of the goods and, except as otherwise herein provided, to be conducted according to and governed by the law of that country, and the application of the Uniform Law on the International Sale of Goods to this contract is hereby entirely excluded. Where the claim is for quality and/or condition and has not been settled amicably within ten days after receipt of claim as stated in the first paragraph of Clause 18 either party may at once proceed to arbitration.

'If agreed by the parties the reference shall be to a sole Arbitrator but failing such agreement the reference shall be to two Arbitrators one to be appointed by each party.

'If the parties fail to agree on the person who should be appointed sole Arbitrator or, if, where the reference is to two Arbitrators, either party fails to appoint their Arbitrator within seven days after being requested through the Agents under the Contract so to do, then the Arbitrator shall be appointed by the President or failing him by the Vice-President of the Timber Trade Federation on the application of either party. The said Arbitrators shall be members of the timber trade or Arbitrators recognised by the Timber Trade Federation or by the Finnish Sawmill Owners' Association or by the Swedish Wood Exporters' Association. Where the reference is to two Arbitrators and they fail to agree upon an Award they shall appoint an Umpire. Should they fail to agree as to such appointment, then each Arbitrator shall select one name from a list of 10 persons. In the case of Finnish goods the list shall comprise 5 persons designated by the Finnish Sawmill Owners' Association and the other 5 by the Timber Trade Federation. In the case of Swedish goods the list shall comprise 5 persons designated by the Swedish Woods Exporters' Association and the other 5 by the Timber Trade Federation.

'The person to act as umpire shall be the name drawn by lot from the two so selected by the Arbitrators. Should the person so chosen by lot be prevented from acting the Arbitrator who selected that name may thereupon appoint another person from the relevant list who shall act as Umpire. The lists in question may be revised on May 1st each year but vacancies occurring during a year shall be filled by the Association concerned.

'Disputes in respect of goods sold for delivery in Scotland to a Buyer whose registered office or principal place of business is in Scotland shall be governed by the Arbitration (Scotland) Act 1894. However, it shall not be competent to an Arbiter to state a case for the opinion of any Court notwithstanding Section 3(1) of the Administration of Justice (Scotland) Act 1972, or any modification or re-enactment thereof. For the avoidance of doubt it is hereby declared that such Arbiter(s) shall have power to award damages and interest thereon.

'Inspection by the Arbitrators or the Umpire, as the case may be, of the goods claimed upon shall take place within fourteen days after their appointment, unless they consider inspection unnecessary, and the award shall be made within two months of the appointment of Arbitrators.

'An award shall be final and binding upon both parties. The costs of such arbitration shall be left to the discretion of the Arbitrator(s) or Umpire. In deciding as to costs the Arbitrator(s) or Umpire shall take into consideration the correspondence between the parties relating to the dispute and their respective efforts to arrive at a fair settlement.

'Any other dispute and/or claim whatsoever arising out of this contract which cannot be settled amicably shall be referred to arbitration. Such arbitration shall be held in England and conducted in accordance with the English Arbitration Acts 1950, 1975 and 1979 or any subsisting statutory modification thereof or substitution therefor. Such Arbitrators and their Umpire need not be members of the Timber Trade. In all other respects the provisions of this Clause shall apply.

'This Clause applies to contracts for shipments to the United Kingdom and the Republic of Ireland only.'

This clause has been reworded and now removes many of the anomalies which existed in the former contract, one example being greater clarification of Scottish arbitrations. It is now in line with Albion Clause 20. As the subject of arbitration is dealt with fully in Chapter 11 it is not proposed to comment further at this stage.

Notice: Clause 21

'Where under the contract Buyers are given an option or it is provided that Buyers may or are required to give notice to Sellers, notice by the Buyers to Agents named in the contract (a) of the exercise of the option or (b) of any other matter, shall be deemed to be good notice to Sellers of the matter covered by such notice. Similarly, notice by Agents to Buyers shall be deemed to be good notice by Sellers.

'Wherever the word "telegram" appears in the Contract or in these General Conditions it shall be deemed to include "telex".'

The wording of this clause is the same as in the previous contract and is self-explanatory.

LINER PARCEL AMENDMENTS TO UNIFORM 1980 CONTRACT FORM GENERAL TERMS, CONDITIONS AND WARRANTIES

Chartering, etc.: Clause 4. Delete clause and substitute:

'Shiproom to be provided in due time by Buyers. Buyers undertake that full loading orders, copy of the Booking Note and vessel's name and line shall be in Agents' hands not later than 12 days before expected date of vessel's arrival. If it is apparent from the Bills of Lading that the Master has failed to load the vessel in accordance with the Buyers' loading orders, Sellers shall forthwith advise Buyers of all variations therefrom and shall make written protest to the Master or Owners' Agents sending a copy thereof to Buyers.

'The Bills of Lading shall be in customary liner terms.'

Margin for Chartering: Clause 6. Delete clause.

Insurance: Clause 9. In the first paragraph delete first sentence and substitute:

'Marine insurance of cargo and of such freight that has been pre-paid or is payable ship and/or cargo lost or not lost to be covered by Buyers as per Lloyd's form of policy together with current Timber Trade Federation Clauses and Institute Strikes Riots and Civil Commotions Clauses (Timber Trade).'

In the second paragraph: first sentence — delete 'covering the cargo and freight advance' and substitute 'covering cargo and such freight that has been pre-paid or is payable ship and/or cargo lost or not lost'. Second sentence — delete 'plus freight advance, if any, payable under the Charter party' at end, and substitute 'plus freight paid or payable under the Bill(s) of Lading'.

Overlying Goods: Clause 12. In the fifth paragraph delete 'chartered' and substitute 'booked'.

Demurrage: Clause 16. Delete clause.

9   Timber Contracts III

This chapter covers those contracts which are for both softwood and hardwood, and describes the essential or significant differences between them and the previous chapter on the Albion and Uniform contracts and their terms and conditions. It also covers resale and ex-ship contracts associated with them. Chapter 10 covers the panel product contracts.

The clauses which are essentially different are quoted in full, but where only small differences are concerned, these are indicated – i.e. shipment, delivery, margins, insurance, exceptions, ends, claims, arbitrations, deck load, etc.

It should be noted that where comparison is made with the Albion and Uniform contracts, now dated 1980, such changes in these contracts should be construed accordingly.

9.1 Russian 1952

This contract form is adopted by the Timber Trade Federation of the UK and by Vsesojuznoje Exportno-Importnoje Objedinenije EXPORTLES of Moscow, and all references to Charter Parties refer to the Sovietwood Charter 1961. The wording of the contract form has not been amended since the change to the metric system, but an additional clause has been added which reads as follows:

'The goods are specified in the Contract in metric dimensions and all references in the conditions to quantities of St Petersburg Standards or English cubic feet shall be read as references to the equivalent quantities of cubic metres on the basis that one standard is the equivalent of five cubic metres. Reference to "9 feet" and "5/8 feet" shall be read and construed as if there were substituted the words "2.7 metres" and "1.5/2.4 metres" respectively.'

Although it is not specifically mentioned, reference to shillings must also be converted to present-day equivalents.

Unlike most other contracts, this contains some terms and conditions in the preamble of the contract.

Margins. This provides variations in seller's option of 20 per cent more or less on any or every item but not exceeding 20 standards on any one item, and items of 2–5 standards may be varied to the extent of 1 standard, always provided that the total quantity is not varied to an extent of more than 10 per cent of the total – the latter being a chartering margin.

Over- and Under-shipment. Although the wording is slightly different, this clause is the same as the counterpart in the Albion contract.

Shipment. The port of shipment is stated and the due date, but latitude is limited to 21 days.

Loading Orders. Buyers shall undertake that full loading orders shall be in agents' hands as early as possible, but in any case not later than a definite date.

Ends: Clause 2

'The prices for sawn and planed goods, except where otherwise stated, are for lengths 9 feet and up, Sellers usual bracking, with falling ends 5 to 8 feet at two-thirds price. Where such ends are shipped in excess of 4% of the total contract quantity if shipped at White Sea, Barents Sea and Kara Sea ports or in excess of 2% of the total contract quantity if shipped at Baltic ports, such excess ends, if according to the contract, shall be taken at two-thirds f.o.b. price plus full freight as per Charter Party or Bill of Lading. Such ends to be regarded as included in the quantities named on the other side, but to be disregarded in the calculation of average length.'

It should be noted that the Russian 'falling ends' are 5–8 ft long or their metric equivalent of 1.5–2.4 m, unlike the Swedish and Finnish ends, which are 1.8–2.4 m.

Seasoning and Bracking: Clause 3

'The goods are to bear Shipper's usual marks, to be properly seasoned for shipment to the country of destination and to be of sellers usual bracking, average length and fair specification for such description of goods, and delivered to the ship in accordance with the custom of the port, the sellers not being responsible for any deterioration occasioned by circumstances beyond their control after the goods have left shippers wharf properly protected.'

In effect, this clause is identical with the Albion clause but with slightly different wording. Reference to packaging and truck-bundling is not made but the service exists, and no mention is made of identifying numbers as per specification.

Shipment: Clause 4

This clause amplifies the wording in the preamble and stipulates that shipment must be secured by sellers in due time but that they are not liable for delays caused beyond their control. The charter is the Sovietwood charter party 1961 and all discharging expenses are for the account of buyers. The sellers have the option of chartering a substitute vessel, if the named vessel is lost before loading but after being named to buyers, to load within the same period. The shipper has the alternative of cancelling that part of the contract that was to have been lifted by the lost vessel, leaving the buyers with the option to take the goods on f.o.b. terms — which is a risky and complicated proposition when considering the White Sea.

Sellers agree to pay both dead-freight and demurrage admitted or proved to have been caused by them at loading port, and demurrage at port of discharge. If the buyers under this contract observe from the bills of lading, etc., that the shipowners claim demurrage or dead-freight, etc., they should not accept the documents without a letter of indemnity from the sellers.

Margins: Clause 5

In addition to the qualifications already mentioned in the preamble to this contract, this clause states that where more than one shipment is made under the contract, the chartering margin will only apply to the quantity shipped by the last vessel for each period of shipment. In addition, there are clauses which absolve the seller from liability if there is any variation between the loading capacity stated in the charter and the actual intake of the vessel, provided that the 10 per cent contract margin is not exceeded. Furthermore, the seller's option to shut out goods or load additional goods (provided that these are goods which are suitable for deck load and not high-quality goods normally shipped under deck) are clearly stated — again subject to the margin on the contract quantity of 10 per cent.

Some of the phrases in this clause are no more than a declaration of the law, and others substantiate earlier clauses. Although it makes the contract form longer, it does remove any possible element of doubt or ambiguity and is therefore useful.

Regarding loading orders, which are mentioned in the preamble, this clause also provides that if loading orders are not provided in the time stipulated, sellers may ship the goods as convenient to themselves to any of the ports of destination named in the contract — buyers being obliged to take delivery if so shipped. These are therefore important dates which the buyers would normally be certain to diarise at the time the contract is signed to ensure that the loading instructions are forwarded in good time. In addition, there is an obligation on buyers to give seller's agents notice of which bills of lading of deck-load may be shut out if necessary, this notice to cover at least 10 per cent of the buyer's cargo. The provisions regarding the number of bills of lading under which buyers may require the goods to be shipped follow closely the Scandinavian contracts but with the following differences:

(1) It is subject to the qualifications '. . . providing loading orders are reasonable . . .'.
(2) Goods from one mill only to be ordered on the same bill of lading.
(3) Goods ordered on one bill of lading to be shipped by one vessel.

Insurance: Clause 6

'Marine Insurance of cargo and freight advance and adding 10% for Buyer's account to the f.o.b. invoice amount to be covered by Sellers in sterling before the goods leave Shipper's wharf with a first-class company or underwriters (if foreign, to be mutually agreed upon between Buyers and Sellers), as per Lloyds form of Policy, payable in London, and according to the Timber Trade Federation Clauses, and the Additional Clauses to be inserted in Policies issued outside the United Kingdom, both as printed on the back.

Notwithstanding the above, Sellers shall arrange to cover the goods against War (including Mine) Risks, also Strikes, Riots and Civil Commotion Risks, on the Institute Clauses current at the date of sailing, but any premium in excess of five shillings % current at date of sailing payable for this cover shall be for Buyers account. Should such cover be unobtainable, or if obtained be subsequently cancelled, Sellers shall give prompt telegraphic advice to Buyers and either party shall thereupon have the option of cancelling the contract.'

Freight Advance: Clause 7

This shall not exceed one-third of the total freight and is to be settled in cash in exchange for captain's receipt and policy of insurance or cover note. The amount of the advance shall be endorsed on the bill of lading in British sterling.

Clause 8

Clause 8 corresponds with the Exception clause of the Albion form and varies only slightly from the latter. The terms of the Russian 1952 contract have an addition covering 'delays of vessel chartered'. However, although the buyer is given the option of taking the goods on f.o.b. terms, there is no mention of any 'drawing date of approximate payment'. There is no provision made for overlying goods, and strikes and lockouts are not included in the exceptions. In the event of war, etc., or prohibition or export or import preventing shipment, the contract (or unfulfilled part of it) is cancelled. If war risk insurance cannot be covered, either party may cancel the contract. If, for any reason beyond seller's control, there is an increase in sea freight of 20 per cent above the basic rate of freight which is published in shipper's schedule of prices, the sellers have the option of cancelling the contract unless the buyer agrees to pay any excess freight above the 20 per cent increase on the basic rate. The agreement by buyers to pay this increase must be made to the agent in writing within 3 days of receiving notice from the sellers. The date of shipment is stated in the preamble, followed with the words '. . . or as soon thereafter as suitable tonnage is obtainable but this latitude is limited to 21 days'. On the face of it, if the goods are not shipped within 21 days of the final date stated in the preamble, the buyers appear to have the right of cancellation. Further, the clause itself does not give buyers the right of cancellation, only the right to take the goods on the equivalent f.o.b. terms (as mentioned above). This has important implications where the goods are being resold on c.i.f. resale or ex-ship terms. This clause does not extend to storage yards at port of shipment, as does the new Albion 1980 contract.

Clause 9

Clause 9 is an extension of Clause 8 but stipulates that the basic freight is to be mutually agreed upon at . . . . . .

Payment: Clause 10

This clause does provide credit terms and reads as follows:

'Buyers shall pay to Agents Freight advance, if any, in accordance with Clause 7 and the balance of the invoice value after deducting total freight on receipt of and exchange for shipping documents and goods Policy of Insurance or Cover Note as per Clause 6 in cash less $2\frac{1}{2}\%$ discount payable in London, or subject to agreement at time of presentation of documents by approved acceptance of Sellers or authorised agent's drafts payable in London at four months from date of Bill of Lading, rate of interest to be mutually agreed.

'Payment of freight, less freight advance, if any, to be made in English Pounds sterling by Buyers direct to Shipowners or their Agents in the country of destination at the rates and in the manner stipulated in the Charterparty and in accordance with freight account made out at Loading Port.

'The goods sold hereunder are pledged with the State Bank of U.S.S.R. and proceeds for the same belong to the State Bank of U.S.S.R. as security for advances, but the delivery of documents by the Agent to the Buyer against payment of the invoice amount by the latter to the Agents shall be a complete discharge of any pledge or lien of the State Bank of U.S.S.R. on either the goods or the documents.'

Claims: Clause 11

While following the general phrasing of the Albion form, this clause stipulates that 'reasonable particulars' shall be submitted within 14 days (not working days), and this applies regardless of whether the goods are packaged or loose. The goods in respect of which a claim is made must be produced ready for inspection in 21 days from the date of the ship's final discharge. Buyers are allowed an extension of these 21 days if they can show that they require this through circumstances beyond their control. Requests for an extension of time must be supported by documentary evidence, and it is not safe to assume that an extension will automatically be granted without a proper case being put forward. This clause has caused difficulties in the past, and on occasions the sellers' ideas of what comprised 'ready for inspection' have been very difficult to carry out, the sellers repudiating a claim on the grounds that the goods were not properly 'ready for inspection'. For the buyer's protection it is certainly best to anticipate these difficulties and, while scrupulously observing the periods of notification of reasonable particulars, etc., arrange that in presenting the goods for inspection all sizes are piled separately and each bill of lading kept apart. Although this may take much space and effort, it is worthwhile to assist in the satisfactory settlement of a dispute. After the buyers have given notice to the agents that the goods are ready for inspection, the sellers must take steps within 14 days to arrive at an amicable settlement. If after this period no settlement has been reached, either party may elect to go to arbitration.

Property in Goods: Clause 12

'Property in goods to be deemed for all purposes, except retention of the State Bank of U.S.S.R. lien for unpaid purchase price, to have passed to Buyers when goods have been put on board.'

Bills of Lading: Clause 13

This clause is more comprehensive than most other contract terms and, despite the fact that it has not been converted to metric as yet, is quoted in full.

'The goods to be shipped under as many Bills of Lading as may be required by Buyers, provided that loading orders are reasonable, and that the total number of Bills required shall not exceed 5 per 100 Standards (3 from the Kara Sea) and that for any Bills in excess Buyers shall pay four guineas; in addition to which Buyers shall pay at the rate of:-

(a) 20 s. per standard if, at Buyers request, any item or parcel is split up on different Bills in smaller quantities than 5 standards and/or if any item or parcel under 5 standards is split up on different Bills of Lading.

(b) 40 s. per standard if, at Buyers request, any item or parcel is split up on different Bills in smaller quantities than 2 standards and/or if any item or parcel under 2 standards is split up on different Bills.

The charges under (a) and (b) above are payable only in respect of such parts of the item or parcel as are less than the 5 standards or 2 standards respectively resulting from such splitting up of the contract item.

'Notwithstanding the stipulations in (a) and (b) any item or parcel of under 10 standards specified in the contract may be split up on two Bills without extra charge.

'From the Kara Sea, items of under 10 standards must not be sub-divided on different Bills.

Goods from different Mills		May not be
Goods from White Sea and Leningrad Bracking		combined on
Goods of different date of readiness		one Bill of
Goods for under-deck and on-deck shipment		Lading

Goods ordered on one Bill are to be shipped in one steamer. Goods may be shipped in one or more steamers together with goods for other receivers, at Shipper's option.'

Dead Freight and Demurrage: Clause 14

This clause differs from the equivalent in the Albion contract in that both circumstances are combined in one clause; it reads as follows:

'The sellers guarantee to pay all dead freight and demurrage admitted or proved to have been incurred by them at the loading port and demurrage at port(s) of discharge. If there are any such claims made against the buyer or bill of lading holders for such dead freight and demurrage, the buyers shall give prompt notice in writing to the sellers or their agents of such claims, the sellers shall, within ten days after receipt of notice of such claim, either pay the claim or indemnify buyers for any such amount and costs which may be awarded by the court to shipowners. Should provision be made in the Charter party and/or Bill of Lading that settlement of General Average shall be made elsewhere than in London then Sellers guarantee that Cargo Underwriters will authorise Buyers to sign any form of General Average Bond as may be necessary to obtain prompt delivery of the goods.'

It will be seen that the dead freight section of this clause is quite different from the current Albion clause, since it does not specifically refer to monetary rates. In regard to demurrage, there are no explicit time restrictions, beyond the fact that sellers have ten days in which to pay or indemnify buyers for the costs awarded.

Arbitration: Clause 15

This clause follows closely the Albion clause, with one very important exception. There is an amendment which has been added to the terms and conditions which reads as follows:

'It is hereby understood and agreed that any disputes which cannot be settled amicably, except such as refer to the quality, condition, measurement, or manufacture of, or correctness of documents for goods shipped, shall be referred to the U.S.S.R. Chamber of Commerce Foreign Trade Arbitration Commission in Moscow, whose decision shall be final and binding upon both parties. Claims under any other of the above excepted headings shall if not amicably settled be dealt with in accordance with the provisions of Clause 15 of the printed conditions. It is understood and agreed that any amendments

or additions to the printed Conditions of Contract, which may be agreed
between V/O Exportles and the Timber Trade Federation of the U.K., will
apply to this Contract, except in respect of quantities which may have been
shipped before such agreement has been reached.'

In effect, this is 'arbitration in Moscow for unshipped goods'. Arbitrations
on the exceptions detailed in the clause, amounting to 'shipped goods', is
controlled by Clause 15 of the contract, which, in general terms, follows the
usual TTF Contract Terms with arbitration subject to the English Arbitration
Act of 1950 as amended by the Arbitration Act of 1979.

This 'arbitration in Moscow' clause has in the past led to much argument
between importers and shippers where disputes have arisen which the Russians
maintain should be dealt with in Moscow, whereas the buyers consider the
matter could well be classified as one capable of being dealt with by an arbitration in the United Kingdom.

Additional Clauses applicable to Kara Sea Contracts only

'It is understood that owing to the difficulties attaching to shipments from
the Kara Sea, some specification variations and/or omissions may occur in
shipment, and some variations in the executions of Buyers Loading Orders,
for which Shippers do not accept any liability, although they will endeavour
to fulfil both specification and Loading Orders as accurately as possible.'

Weather Conditions: Clause 19

'Conditions of loading in the Kara Sea differ from the conditions obtaining in
the White Sea, in that, owing to the restricted period of loading in the Kara
Sea, loading has to be continuous, irrespective of weather conditions.'

This contract is subject to the sellers making the necessary chartering
arrangements for the expedition.

9.2 Trancif 1971

This contract form is one agreed between the Swedish Wood Exporters Association and the Timber Trade Federation of the UK to cover goods up to the
point where they are loaded on to buyer's transport at port of destination.

Shipment and delivery

The contract price covers the basic cost of the goods, freight, insurance and
all discharging costs right up to the time when the goods are placed on to

buyer's transport at the port of discharge. It is incumbent on sellers to see that buyers are advised in ample time as to when the goods are available for collection, to enable them to have transport to lift them, and they are also responsible for seeing that buyers are in possession of the necessary authority for collection. Sellers are also responsible for customs clearance, or ensuring that buyers are in possession of all necessary documents to clear customs in sufficient time for the collection of the goods on arrival. Sellers are responsible for any costs incurred or demurrage on transport which may arise unless caused by any default of the buyer.

Ends: Clause 2

'Other than as regards items for which a separate price for ends 1.8 m to 2.4 m is specified in the contract (in which case notwithstanding any provision of this clause all ends on such items shall be at that specified price) Sellers to have the right to supply up to 3% of ends on each item at full price (the full c.i.f. value for 2.7 m and up appropriate for the goods concerned) save that if this percentage is exceeded on any item(s) all ends (including the first 3%) on such item(s) shall be at two thirds price, which latter price means two thirds of the f.o.b. value (i.e. the contract price per m^3 less the freight rate per m^3 for 2.7 m and up appropriate for the goods concerned) plus full freight. Ends to be regarded as included in the contract quantity but to be disregarded in the calculation of average lengths. Buyers may reject any ends in excess of $7\frac{1}{2}\%$ on any item except as regards slatings, boards 115 mm and under and VIth quality and quantity of which shall be as falling.'

Insurance

Basically this clause follows the Albion contract, with certain extensions necessary to cover loading to buyer's transport. Buyers must pay any premium for war risks in excess of £0.15 per £100 instead of £0.125 in the Albion contract.

Exceptions: Clause 9

'In case the manufacture and/or shipment and/or transport of any of the goods specified in the contract be delayed or hindered by floods, droughts, ice, damage to mill and/or timber yard or shipping yard, strike, lockout, mobilisation or any other cause beyond Seller's control, clauses mentioned in clause 10 excepted, they shall not be responsible for any damages arising therefrom, provided immediate notice by telegram be given to Buyers. In such event only, Sellers have the right to complete the contract within six weeks of the expiry of the time for shipment stipulated in the contract. Should

Sellers, however, be unable to deliver within such extended time they shall declare their inability to do so and on receipt of Seller's declaration Buyers shall have the option, to be promptly declared, of cancelling the contract, or postponing the same to such date of delivery as may be mutually agreed upon, but in any event not later than the following f.o.w. If, however, the manufacture and/or shipment of the goods specified in the contract be prevented by destruction of the mill and/or timber yard or shipping yard Sellers have the option, to be promptly declared by telegram to cancel the contract without responsibility for any damages arising therefrom. This clause shall take effect subject to the provisions concerning delivery contained in the contract.'

War, etc.: Clause 10

The amount by which the freight must not increase is £0.65 per m³ instead of above 10 per cent in the Albion contract.

Claims: Clause 13

Basically this follows the Albion contract form with one or two alterations or additions, as follows:

(1) In the opening paragraph the clause states when referring to condition: 'Notwithstanding the foregoing, no claim for condition will be recognised by Sellers on goods specified as unseasoned.' In the Albion contract, it is not stated so specifically.

(2) When defining an item, the clause states: 'An item shall mean all goods of the same dimension quality and description. Where an item is split up into different shipments, or where Buyers require delivery to different destinations each such shipment or delivery is referred to as a part item.'

(3) In the last paragraph of the clause, referring to non-delivery, a sum equal to 10 per cent of the contract price is mentioned, in line with the Albion 1980 contract.

(4) On the face of the contract there is space for the insertion of the time limit allowed for claims on packaged and truck-bundled goods. This is negotiable, unlike the Albion terms, which specify three months.

Arbitration: Clause 15

Basically this follows the Albion contract with one exception. Whereas the Albion contract includes a provision to include Finnish arbitrators approved by the Finnish Sawmill Owner's Association, the Trancif contract only mentions the Swedish Wood Exporters Association, since the contract was intended for Swedish goods.

9.3 Ligcon 1961 (revised 1967)

This contract form is adopted by the Timber Trade Federation of the United Kingdom and the Ligna Foreign Trade Corporation in Prague. This Corporation is the sole exporter of timber and wood products produced in Czechoslovakia. Sales of Czechoslovakian softwood and wood products are made against the shipper's price lists which are issued at regular intervals and contain, in addition to the basic price, extras for various thicknesses, special lengths, etc. The following points should be noted in addition to the clauses in the general terms and conditions.

(1) Shipper's prices are all c. & f. and buyers are responsible for their own insurance.

(2) Goods are normally supplied truck-bundled at no extra cost, but can be packaged to length at an extra cost. Shippers normally reserve the right to supply some packages containing three adjacent lengths.

(3) Shippers usually include a seasoning clause covering goods produced during the winter months. This clause normally guarantees that the goods will reach their destination in a bright condition but does not permit any claim for sticking costs.

(4) The carriage of goods from Czechoslovakia to the UK involves a long journey to the shipping ports and the goods are largely carried in open rail trucks. Shippers find it virtually impossible to ensure that all goods are sheeted throughout the journey, owing to losses of protecting sheets en route.

In the preamble on the face of the contract the shipment terms are identical with the Albion terms. These are further qualified in the general terms and conditions. Loading orders state, in addition to the appropriate clause: 'Fair proportion of contract quantity may be loaded on deck. If there is more than one destination the date for declaring detailed specifications for such destinations to be mutually agreed at the date of the contract. Loading Orders for Bills of Lading containing item(s) of less than six standards to be given within seven days of date of contract. Otherwise Loading Orders to be in Sellers hands six weeks before commencement of Shipping Period or seven days after date of contract if commencement of Shipping Period less than six weeks from date of contract.'

Ends: Clause 2

'Sellers to have the right to supply up to $7\frac{1}{2}\%$ of ends 6 to 8 feet (1.8 m to 2.4 m), in reasonable contract specification whether required for broken stowage or not. Such ends to be regarded as included in the contract quantity but to be disregarded in the calculation of average lengths. The price for ends to be two-thirds of the f.o.b. price, i.e. the contract price less the freight rate stated in the Charter party or Bill of Lading appropriate for the goods concerned, plus freight according to such Charter party or Bill of Lading.'

This clause is quite unlike the Albion terms, which have been amended but is similar to the Eucon terms. It should be noted that shippers sometimes alter this percentage.

Seasoning and Bracking: Clause 3

Although the wording of this clause is slightly different, its meaning is the same as that of the Albion terms, except that it makes no reference to the definition of packaged and truck-bundled goods. It should also be related to the statement mentioned in the preamble.

Chartering, Delay and Cancelling: Clause 4

Although the wording of this clause is slightly different from the Albion terms, its meaning is similar, with the following exceptions:

(1) Buyer's option to take the goods on f.o.b. terms is two months instead of six weeks.

(2) There is an additional clause: 'If the vessel fails to load all the goods sent down to the port of loading for shipment with the result that part is shut out, Sellers shall advise Buyers by telegram thereof and shall be entitled to ship the balance shut out provided they can do so within the Shipping Period or as extended by Clause 10. Should there be any delay on Railways in delivering goods sent forward for shipment resulting in a part being left behind, then provisions set out above shall apply. In either of the above events Sellers shall pay to Buyers any additional expense incurred by Buyers in consequence thereof. Where shipment is made on non-chartered vessels Bills of Lading shall be in customary liner terms.'

Margins in Sellers Option: Clause 5

'Sellers shall have the option to vary by 10% more or less any or every item but not exceeding 20 standards on any one item and to vary items of 2 to 10 standards to the extent of 1 standard, always provided that the total quantity is not varied by more than 10% or 50 standards whichever is the less.'

Unlike the Albion terms, there is no mention of overlying goods or chartering margins, nor has the clause been metricated.

Quantity, Over- and Under-shipment: Clause 6

This clause is identical with the Albion terms.

Risk: Clause 7

'The risk of loss or destruction of any of the goods or of damage to any of the goods so extensive as to render it impossible to ship the damaged goods in the form intended on the carrying vessel shall be upon Sellers until such goods are loaded into lighters for shipment after the receipt of notice of the vessel of her expected arrival or in the case of goods so loaded prior to the receipt of such notice until notice is received or if not loaded into lighters until the goods are delivered alongside the vessel. In all other respects notwithstanding that this sale is made on c. & f. terms the goods shall be at the risk of Buyers from the commencement of the transit as defined in Clause 1 of the Timber Trade Federation Clauses and Institute Strikes Riots and Civil Commotions Clauses (Timber Trade).'

The reason for this somewhat unusual clause is that, like the Fobra terms, the goods usually travel some distance to the port of shipment, but the reference to the TTF transit clause should cover the buyer should damage occur.

Insurance: Clause 8

'Marine insurance of cargo for not less than the f.o.b. value plus freight advance, if any, and freight that has been prepaid or is payable ship and/or cargo lost or not lost to be covered by Buyers. Such insurance to attach as and when the risk passes to Buyers in accordance with Clause 7 hereof. The obligation to insure against War Risks shall be upon Buyers who shall, if required by Sellers or their Agents, deposit with them before the goods are put on board a cover note or policy of insurance effected with Lloyds or a first class British Company covering the goods against such risks. If these risks are not coverable or for any reason Buyers do not cover against these risks they shall provide before goods are put on board such security for payment as may be required by Sellers or their Agents and, goods lost or not lost, shall pay against presentation of documents in accordance with Clause 9.

'Any extra insurance premium payable by Buyers on account of vessel's age and/or flag and/or classification and/or ownership shall be for Seller's account.

'Buyers shall, if requested at any time after their obligations to insure as above have arisen, furnish Seller's Agents with sufficient proof of such insurance having been effected.'

Buyers have the responsibility of arranging the insurance and the clauses in the contract form are then amended to follow more closely the Fobra terms. That is to say, whereas the property in the goods passes to the buyers only when the goods are placed upon the ocean-going vessel, they are stated in the contract to be at the risk of the buyers from the moment they are put on lighters for transport to the ship — and this may be a journey of some length.

Payment and Freight: Clause 9

'Sellers shall pay not exceeding 90% of the freight on commencement of discharge and the balance of 10% shall be payable as to 5% by Sellers on receipt of freight account and final discharge and as to 5% by Buyers on final outturn being ascertained.

'Buyers shall pay to Agents the invoice value of the goods after deducting total freight on receipt of and in exchange for shipping documents. Buyers shall also pay to Agents in cash 90% of the freight of the vessel commencing discharge and a further 5% of the freight to Agents in cash on completion of discharge free of all liens.

' "Total freight" as referred to in the second paragraph of this Clause shall mean a basis of freight covering discharge of cargo by the Owners of the vessel at the ship's rail if discharged by hand or within reach of the ship's tackle or shore crane tackle if thereby discharged and the deduction of freight in the invoice shall be the full freight as above defined and no other charges.

'Sellers undertake that Buyers shall be supplied with copy shipping documents to enable Buyers to handle the consignment on arrival in the absence of the original shipping documents. If the original shipping documents are not presented to Buyers prior to the arrival of the vessel carrying the goods and Sellers have failed to furnish copy documents as above provided, Sellers shall be liable for and pay to Buyers any extra expense which they may incur in consequence.'

This clause provides that not more than 90% of the freight will be advanced or prepaid. The reason for this is to allow the buyer some margin available for adjustment in this country in respect of claims for loss or damage against shipowners.

Exceptions: Clause 10

Basically this follows the Albion terms, with two exceptions. It gives a definition of f.o.b. terms of payment, as there is no equivalent f.o.b. contract for it, and gives a period of 2 months' option, whereas the Albion only gives 6 weeks.

War, etc.: Clause 11

This clause differs from the Albion 1980 terms in one respect. It states: '. . . a rise in the rate of sea freight should occur exceeding three guineas per standard', whereas the Albion terms have been amended to '. . . a rise in the rate of sea freight exceeding 10% as compared with the rates ruling, etc.'.

Bills of Lading, Loading Orders: Clause 12

Loading orders are covered in the preamble on the face of the contract. The requirements for bills of lading state that as many as may be required by buyers but if the total exceeds 5 per 100 standards, buyers shall pay 4 guineas for each bill in excess. The Albion contract stipulates 10 per 500 m³, and provides for additional payment to be mutually agreed.

Dead Freight: Clause 13

This clause differs from the Albion 1980 contract in one respect. It stipulates 'interest at five per cent per annum or bank rate if higher', whereas the Albion contract has been amended to 'interest at 2 per cent above the Bank of England's Minimum Lending Rate for the time being in force'.

Demurrage: Clause 14

The wording of this clause is similar to the Albion terms, the essential omission being any reference to the Swedish and Finnish Associations.

Licences: Clause 15

This clause is identical with the Albion terms.

Claims: Clause 16

Compared with the Albion terms, there are two essential differences in this clause. There is only one claiming period for all types of goods — namely 14 working days from date of vessel's discharge — and as this period is so short, no mention is made of buyer's responsibility for the care of the goods. Like the Russians, Ligna insist on absolute observance of all the conditions of the claim clause; otherwise no claim will be accepted.

Rejection: Clause 17

This clause is identical with the Albion terms.

Arbitration: Clause 18

Although the wording is slightly different, this clause is essentially the same as the Albion terms. There is one exception: it does not differentiate between 'shipped' and 'unshipped' goods, but it does refer to the Arbitration (Scotland) Act 1894. Needless to say, there is no reference to Swedish and Finnish Associations.

Notice: Clause 19

This clause is identical with the Albion terms.

9.4 Eucon 1964

This contract form is adopted by the Timber Trade Federation of the UK and is headed 'Central European (C.I.F./C. & F.) Contract'. The contract gives option of c.i.f. or c. & f. terms, and when the latter are used, the necessary amendments are given at the end of this section under an appropriate heading. In the preamble, the shipment details are identical with the Albion terms but payment -- subject to Clause 8 of the general conditions – leaves the rate of interest open for insertion in respect of payment for cash, whereas the Albion contract stipulates 2½ per cent discount. Under the heading of insurance, option is given as to whether the contract is c.i.f. or c. & f., one or the other being deleted. Freight rate, loading orders and licences are also mentioned, but are covered in the general conditions.

Ends: Clause 2

'Sellers have the right to supply up to 7½% of ends 6 to 8 feet (1.8 m to 2.4 m) in reasonable contract specification whether required for broken stowage or not. Such ends to be regarded as included in the contract quantity but to be disregarded in the calculation of average lengths. The price for ends to be two-thirds of the f.o.b. price, i.e. the contract price less the freight rate stated in the charter party or Bill of Lading appropriate for the goods concerned, plus freight according to such charter party or Bill of Lading.'

This clause is quite unlike the Albion clause, which has been completely amended.

Seasoning and Bracking: Clause 3

Although the wording is slightly different, the meaning of the clause is the same as that of the Albion clause, except that it makes no reference to the definition of packaged and truck-bundled goods.

Chartering, Delay and Cancelling: Clause 4

Although the wording of this clause is different, its meaning is basically the same as that of the Albion clause. It has an additional item, which reads as follows: 'Where shipment is made on non-chartered vessels Bills of Lading shall be in customary liner terms.'

Margins in Sellers Option: Clause 5

'Sellers shall have the option to vary by 10% more or less any or every item but not exceeding 20 standards on any one item and to vary items of 2 to 10 standards to the extent of 1 standard, always provided that the total quantity is not varied by more than 10% or 50 standards whichever is the less.'

Unlike the Albion terms, there is no mention of over-lying goods or chartering margins, nor has the clause been metricated.

Quantity, Over- and Under-shipment: Clause 6

This clause is identical with the Albion terms, except that it does not refer to chartering margins.

Insurance: Clause 7

This clause follows the wording of the Albion terms closely, except that sellers are not given the option of insuring with a company registered in their own country.

Payment and Freight: Clause 8

'Buyers shall pay freight, less any advances and prepaid freight, according to charter party or Bill of Lading and shall pay to Sellers or their authorised Agents the balance of the invoice value after deducting total freight, in London, on receipt of and in exchange for shipping documents including policies of insurance as per Clause 7. Prepaid freight and advances, if any, in accordance with the charter party which shall in the aggregate not exceed 90% of the full freight payable to be paid to Sellers or their authorised Agents in net cash against Master's receipt endorsed upon the Bill(s) of Lading in Sterling.

' "Total freight" as referred to in the first paragraph of this Clause shall mean a basis of freight covering discharge of cargo by the Owners of the Vessel at the ship's rail if discharged by hand or within reach of the ship's tackle or shore crane tackle if thereby discharged and the deduction of freight in the invoice shall be the full freight as above defined and no other charges.

'Sellers undertake to send from the loading port direct to Buyers copy shipping documents to enable Buyers to handle the consignment in the absence of the original shipping documents. If the original shipping documents are not presented to Buyers prior to the arrival of the vessel carrying the goods and Sellers have failed to furnish copy documents as above provided, Sellers shall be liable for and pay to Buyers any extra expense which they may incur in consequence.'

This clause provides that not more than 90 per cent of the freight will be advanced or prepaid. The reason for this is to allow the buyer some margin available for the adjustment in this country in respect of claims for loss or damage against shipowners. Many shippers insist that 100 per cent of the freight must be prepaid, as this is often necessary for them to obtain freight space.

Exceptions: Clause 9

The wording of this clause is the same as that of the Albion clause, except that the drawing date for the goods on f.o.b. terms is 2 months, whereas it is 6 weeks in the Albion contract.

War, etc.: Clause 10

This clause follows the wording of the Albion terms, except that the cancellation declaration must be submitted within 7 working days whereas the Albion contract stipulates 3 working days.

Passing of Property: Clause 11

This clause is identical with the Albion terms.

Bills of Lading, Loading Orders: Clause 12

Compared with the Albion terms, there are some slight variations in this clause. These are as follows:

(1) *Loading orders.* These shall be in agent's hands by the date stipulated in the contract, whereas the Albion contract stipulates not more than 15 working days before the time of shipment.

(2) *Bills of lading.* As many as required by buyers, but if the total exceeds 5 per 100 standards, buyers shall pay 4 guineas for each bill in excess. The Albion contract stipulates 10 per 500 m^3 and provides for additional payment to be mutually agreed.

Dead Freight: Clause 13

This clause is identical with the Albion terms, except for the interest rate.

Demurrage: Clause 14

'Where the contract goods are shipped under a Charterparty providing that they shall be loaded at an agreed rate per weather working day then Sellers undertake that the goods shall be loaded at the agreed rate or, where no rate is stipulated, they shall be loaded in a reasonable time and if the goods are not so loaded Sellers shall pay and discharge any demurrage due to the Shipowners before the vessel leaves the port of loading. If a demurrage claim is not so settled and the Master endorses the Bills of Lading or otherwise gives notice to Receivers of a demurrage claim at port of loading then Sellers shall deduct from the invoice the amount of any such demurrage claim and will furnish to Buyers a certified copy of the time sheet at loading port endorsed by Sellers with the amount of demurrage admitted if any.

'If a shipment is made under the "Nubaltwood" form of charter party then Sellers undertake to bring the cargo alongside the vessel in the customary manner as fast as the vessel can receive and stow during the ordinary working hours of the port (Saturday afternoons, Sundays, general and local holidays excepted unless used in which case actual time used to count) but Sellers shall not be bound to bring alongside more per hatch per weather working day than the appropriate quantities set out in the Schedule agreed between the United Kingdom Timber Trade Shipowners Demurrage Association Limited (now United Kingdom Timber Trade Shipowners Mutual Association Limited) and the shipper's organisation of the country of the port of shipment recognised by the Timber Trade Federation of the United Kingdom or failing such agreement the appropriate quantities set out in the schedule of the U.K.T.T.S.D.A. In all cases the Schedule shall be that current at the date of the Charterparty and the quantities shall be 20% less for boards 1 inch and under, slatings and other small sizes and unedged birch. "Hatch" means a hatch, not being a bunker hatch of normal dimensions with at least one workable winch. A large hatch with not less than two workable winches and capable of being worked by two gangs simultaneously shall be counted as two hatches provided labour is permitted and willing to load in such manner. "Weather working day" shall mean a calendar day of 24 consecutive hours when work would normally be undertaken weather permitting. If weather interrupts loading the period of such interruption shall not count as laytime.

'Subject to the provisions of Clauses 3(b) and 8(e) of the charter party laytime shall commence when the vessel is ready to load and written notice of readiness has to be given to the Sellers or their Agents, whether in berth or not. If the notice is given before 10 a.m. time shall commence at 2 p.m. If the notice is given after 10 a.m. time shall commence at the commencement of the next working day. Notice may only be given in ordinary office hours. If the vessel arrives at the loading port earlier than the date named, Sellers are not compelled to have the cargo brought alongside before 2 p.m. of the notified day of arrival if not otherwise agreed between Sellers and the Master of the vessel.

'Laytime shall not run during the period of any delay in loading due to shortage of stevedores or to the vessel's inability to receive and stow at the rate at which Sellers are bound to bring the cargo alongside in accordance with the second paragraph of this Clause, or to any cause whatsoever beyond Sellers control. If the laytime is exceeded demurrage shall be paid by Sellers at the rate set out in the applicable Schedule previously referred to in this Clause.

'Buyers shall pay or cause to be paid the demurrage contributions payable under Clause 20 of the "Nubaltwood" charter party.'

In many respects this clause is similar to the Albion terms, the main omissions being reference to Swedish and Finnish Associations.

Licences: Clause 15

The wording of this clause is identical with that of the Albion terms.

Claims: Clause 16

There are two essential differences in this clause compared with the Albion clause. Reasonable particulars must be given to the agents within 21 days (not working days) of any claim. If, by reason of circumstances beyond their control, buyers are not able to provide such particulars, then, on notification to agents, they are entitled to an extension of the time limit.

Inspection: Clause 17

This clause is an additional one and is also found in the Pacif and Fobra contracts. It really does no more than confirm the terms found under the headings of Claims and Arbitration.

Rejection: Clause 18

The wording of this clause is identical with that of the Albion terms.

Arbitration: Clause 19

Although the wording is slightly different, this clause is essentially the same as that in the Albion contract. There is one exception: it does not differentiate between 'shipped' and 'unshipped' goods, but it does refer to arbitrations subject to the Arbitration (Scotland) Act, 1894. Needless to say, there is no reference to Swedish or Finnish Associations.

Notice: Clause 20

The wording of this clause is identical with that of the Albion terms.

AMENDMENTS OF THE GENERAL CONDITIONS FOR USE IN THE CASE OF C. & F. SHIPMENTS

Price Basis. Clause 1. Delete the words 'cost, freight and insurance' and substitute therefor 'cost and freight'.

Risk. Clause 6A. Add as a new clause the following:

'6A. The risk of loss or destruction of any of the goods or of damage to any of the goods so extensive as to render it impossible to ship the damaged goods in the form intended on the carrying vessel shall be upon Sellers until such goods are loaded into lighters for shipment after receipt of notice from the vessel of her expected arrival or in the case of goods so loaded prior to the receipt of such notice until notice is received or if not loaded into lighters until the goods are delivered alongside the vessel. In all other respects notwithstanding that this sale is made on c. & f. terms the goods shall be at the risk of Buyers from the commencement of the transit as defined in Clause 1 of the Timber Trade Federation Clauses and Institute Strikes Riots and Civil Commotions Clauses (Timber Trade).'

Insurance. Clause 7. Delete Clause 7 and substitute therefor new clause as follows:

'7. Marine insurance of cargo for not less than the f.o.b. value plus freight advance, if any, and freight that has been prepaid or is payable ship and/or cargo lost or not lost to be covered by Buyers. Such insurance to attach as and when the risk passes to Buyers in accordance with Clause 6A hereof. The obligation to insure against War Risks shall be on Buyers who shall, if required by Sellers or their Agents, deposit with them before the goods are put on board a cover note or policy of insurance effected with Lloyds or a first-class British Company covering the goods against such risks. If these risks are not coverable or for any reason Buyers do not cover against these risks they shall provide before goods are put on board such security for payment as may be required by Sellers or their Agents and, goods lost or not lost, shall pay against presentation of documents the value of the goods shipped at contract prices plus freight advance, if any, payable under the charter party and/or Bill of Lading.

'Buyers shall, if requested at any time after their obligations to insure as above has arisen, furnish Seller's Agents with sufficient proof of such insurance having been effected.'

Payment and freight. Clause 8. Delete the words 'including policies of insurance as per Clause 7'.

9.5 Pacif 1958

This contract form is adopted by the Timber Trade Federation of the UK and is headed 'Pacific Coast (C.I.F.) Softwood Contract'. In the preamble there are some items which are worthy of mention.

(1) *Grading.* 'The goods to be graded in accordance with the current . . . . . List of the West Coast Lumber Inspection Bureau and British Columbia Lumber Manufacturers Association.'

The appropriate grading list for the particular class of timber covered by the individual contract therefore is inserted in the space (e.g. NLGA). This grading certificate forms one of the shipping documents of the contract in accordance with Clause 7. It is not, however, binding upon buyers, so there is a claim against shippers if it can be established that the goods received were not graded in accordance with the specified rules.

(2) *Shipment.* 'The goods are to be shipped in the usual and customary manner from the Pacific Coast per steamship(s) or full powered motor vessel(s) expected by Owners, disponents or time charterers ready to load . . . . . to . . . . . or as near thereto as the vessel can safely get and discharge, always afloat, lighterage, if any, to be at the risk and expense of Buyers except insofar as lighterage is due to the unsuitability of the carrying vessel to discharge in accordance with the custom of the port of destination. On deck shipment permitted except as to . . . . .'.

The point concerning lighterage is important. If the goods are to be lightered at the port of destination, this is at buyer's risk and expense. On the other hand, if the vessel is chartered to a specific dock in the port, but owing to the size or draught of the vessel she is unable to proceed to the port or dock named and has to lighten in order to reach the declared destination, the buyers have a claim against shipowners or shippers for the cost of the lighterage, and this claim should be made at once. Alternatively, if the inability of the vessel to reach the stipulated destination is due to some casualty or defect and not to the size or draught of the vessel, then there can be no claim normally, because the charter will usually include the phrase 'To . . . . . or as near thereto as she may safely get.'

The reference to shipment on deck is also of some significance. Clause 11 defines this as follows: 'Goods stowed in a covered shelter deck in the vessel shall be considered as shipped under deck whether or not such space is included in the vessel's registered tonnage, provided the Policy of Insurance specifically accepts such goods as shipped under deck and provided Buyers at time of purchase do not specifically exclude such method of stowage.'

(3) *Payment.* 'Payment to be made in accordance with Clause 7 of the general conditions in cash less 2½% discount within 30 days from date of first presentation of documents in accordance with Clause 7 or within 30 days from ship's final sailing date from British Columbia (or in the case of goods shipped from American ports from the State in which the goods originated) whichever is earlier or by approved acceptances payable in London at 120 days after 30 days from the first presentation of the documents or after 30 days from the ship's final sailing date as defined above whichever is earlier.'

In the case of Pacific coast goods, where a particularly long voyage is involved, 30 days' credit is given from the date of presentation of the documents or date of sailing, whichever is the earlier. The normal terms of 2½ per cent discount for cash or a 4 months bill on net terms apply after this 30 days' credit. In other words, the buyer electing to take a bill in effect pays for the goods 5 months from the date of shipment or presentation of documents. The additional credit compensates him for the additional length of the voyage. The convenience and advantage of credit terms such as this is something which has to be paid for, which is why buyers will usually elect to pay cash if they are able.

Shiproom: Clause 2

'Shiproom to be secured by Sellers with liberty to substitute. Sellers shall promptly advise Buyers by telegram or airmail when shiproom is secured with approximate expected loading date. Sellers shall also both as regards the original vessel(s) and any substituted vessel(s) promptly advise Buyers by telegram or airmail of the name of the vessel(s) when known. Sellers further to advise Buyers by telegram or airmail of date of vessel(s) departure. Should any vessel, or substitute, provided for the contract and already named to Buyers be lost or delayed more than four weeks beyond the expiry of the shipment period as stated in the contract for the goods affected, Sellers shall have the option of substituting vessel or vessels loading within nine weeks of the expiry of the shipment period as stated in the contract, or of cancelling the contract or any unfulfilled portion thereof.'

The significant point in this clause is that in the event of the vessel named to lift the goods being lost or delayed for more than 4 weeks beyond the expiry of the shipment period, the sellers have the option of substituting another vessel loading within 9 weeks on expiry of the shipment period – as compared with 6 weeks in the Albion contract.

Margins in Sellers Option: Clause 3

'Sellers shall have the option to vary any or every item of up to 200 standards by 10% more or less, any or every item of more than 200 standards but not exceeding 500 standards by 7% more or less, and any or every item of more than 500 standards by 5% more or less.'

This is an unusual stipulation, since it provides variations of margin which differ according to the total quantity of the contract.

Over- and Under-shipment: Clause 4

The wording of this clause is identical with that of the Albion terms, except that the latter includes a reference to the clause on margins.

Insurance: Clause 5

This clause closely follows the Albion terms, with a few exceptions. The first paragraph states that the cargo is to be insured by sellers for the 'c.i.f. value plus 10% in sterling, whereas the Albion contract stipulates 'c.i.f. value plus 10%'. The clause goes on to state that buyer's option of cancelling the contract can only be exercised if war risk insurance can only be covered for a premium of not less than 25 per cent. The Albion contract provides the same option in the event of the premium being not less than 10 per cent.

Policies issued outside the UK: Clause 6

This clause is identical with that in the Albion contract and provides sellers with the option of insuring in their own country; the name of the insurers is inserted in the relevant place on the face of the contract.

Payment and Freight: Clause 7

'Buyers shall pay freight on foreign measure according to Bill of Lading and shall pay to Sellers or Agents the balance of the invoice value after deducting freight, in London, in accordance with the contract. Documents shall include a policy of insurance as per Clause 5, Pacific Lumber Inspection Bureau and/or Western Wood Products Association and/or West Coat Lumber Inspection Bureau, and/or MacDonald Inspection certificate unless otherwise stated in the MacDonald Inspection certificate unless otherwise stated in the Contract and Certificates of Origin as required.

'In lieu of a policy of insurance as above provided Sellers may tender and Buyers shall accept a Certificate of Insurance issued outside the United Kingdom provided such certificate complies in all respects with a policy issued under the terms of Clause 5 hereof and can be stamped as a policy in the United Kingdom and that such certificate makes express provision that losses shall be payable in the United Kingdom against production thereof.

'The deduction of freight in the invoice shall be at the net rate only and shall not include the charges, if any, which may be payable under the Bill(s) of Lading for delivery beyond the ship's rail or tackle, unless otherwise provided for in the contract.'

This clause merely amplifies the payment terms shown in the preamble already quoted and Clause 5: Insurance.

Exceptions: Clause 8

'In case the manufacture and/or shipment and/or sea transport of any of the goods specified in the contract should be delayed or hindered by reason of fire or through an accident to the sawmills, or through drought, ice, flood, strike or lock-out, mobilisation, acts of God, King's enemies, restraint of Princes, rulers and people, labour disturbances, inability of vessel or vessels on which space has been booked for the goods under the contract to proceed via the Panama Canal, or through any other cause whatsoever beyond Seller's control, Sellers, provided they give prompt notice to Buyers by telegram of the delay or hindrance, shall not be responsible for any damages resulting to Buyers therefrom.

'If shipment of the whole or part is thereby effectively rendered impossible within nine weeks of the expiry of the shipment period as stated in the contract, Sellers shall give prompt telegraphic notice thereof to Buyers and unless otherwise mutually agreed by Buyers and Sellers within fourteen days thereof the contract shall be cancelled to the extent of any unshipped portion.'

This clause is more comprehensive than most contracts, and it should be noted that there is a period of 9 weeks of the shipment date and buyers are not given the option of taking the goods on f.o.b. terms. The reference to the Panama Canal is obviously specific to this contract.

War, etc.: Clause 9

The wording of this clause is the same as in other c.i.f. contracts and is allied to the appropriate clauses covering Shiproom and Exceptions.

Passing of Property: Clause 10

This is identical with the Albion terms.

Loading Orders, Bills of Lading: Clause 11

'Loading orders unless otherwise mutually agreed shall be given at the time of signing the contract. The goods to be shipped under as many Bills of Lading as may be required by Buyers, but not exceeding 8 per 100 standards. The cargo shall be sent alongside in such manner as to enable Master to keep separate the cargo under each Bill of Lading. Quantities of 50 standards or less for which a separate Bill of Lading is required shall be delivered to the vessel at one and the same time so as to enable Master to make one stowage of that Bill of Lading in the vessel unless part is stowed on deck.

'Goods stowed in a covered shelter deck in the vessel shall be considered as shipped under deck whether or not such space is included in the vessel's registered tonnage, provided the Policy of Insurance specifically accepts such goods as shipped under deck and provided Buyers at time of purchase do not specifically exclude such method of stowage.'

This clause is associated with the preamble statement regarding shipment.

Licences: Clause 12

The wording of this clause is identical with that of the Albion terms.

Claims: Clause 13

There are two essential differences in this clause compared with the Albion terms. Reasonable particulars must be given to the agents within 21 days (not working days) of any claim. There is no mention of liquidated damages being paid by sellers in the event of non-delivery.

Inspection: Clause 14

This clause is an additional one and really does no more than confirm the terms found under the headings of Claims and Arbitration. It is also identical with the Fobra clause.

Rejection: Clause 15

The wording of this clause is identical with that of the Albion terms.

Arbitration: Clause 16

Although the wording is slightly different, this clause is essentially the same as that in the Albion contract. There are two exceptions: it does not differentiate between 'shipped' and 'unshipped' goods but it does refer to arbitrations subject to the Arbitration (Scotland) Act, 1894. Needless to say, there is no reference to Swedish or Finnish Associations.

Notice: Clause 17

The wording of this clause is identical with that of the Albion terms.

9.6 Ecancif 1958

This contract is adopted by the Timber Trade Federation of the United Kingdom, Canadian Lumbermen's Association and Maritime Lumber Bureau. It is headed 'Eastern Canadian (C.I.F.) Softwood Contract'. Although it covers Canadian timber, it varies quite considerably from the Pacif contract. In the preamble, certain items should be mentioned.

(1) *Ends.* There is no clear definition of ends beyond the fact that the length commences at 5 ft. This should be determined by the buyer at the time the sale is closed. Accordingly, it is necessary to complete the blank space on the face of the contract by the insertion of limit of lengths for ends appropriate to the specification being purchased.

(2) *Shipment.* This item is identical with the Pacif terms, except that it does not mention 'goods from the Pacific Coast'.

(3) *Payment.* This reads as follows: 'To be made in accordance with Clause 9 of the General Conditions in cash less 2½% discount or at Buyers option by approved acceptances payable in London at 120 days from sight of documents.' This clause is less informative than the equivalents in the Albion and Pacif contracts but is more closely allied with the latter.

(4) The preamble also mentions insurers, loading orders and licences, and these are described in the general terms and conditions.

Ends: Clause 2

'Sellers to have the right to supply up to 7½% of ends in reasonable contract specification whether required for broken stowage or not at two-thirds f.o.b. price plus freight as per Charter party or Bill of Lading. Such ends to be regarded as included in the quantities named in the contract, but to be disregarded in the calculation of average lengths.'

At one time, the phrase 'as falling' was used in respect of ends but this was replaced by 'in reasonable contract specification', giving considerably greater protection to the buyer.

Grading and Condition: Clause 3

'The goods shall be of Shippers usual grading (or in accordance with current Maritime Lumber Bureau Grading Rules if called for) and fair specification for such description of goods. Sellers not being responsible for any deterioration occasioned by circumstances beyond their control after the goods have been delivered alongside the vessel. All bundled goods shall be adequately and securely bound.'

The wording of this clause is overdue for amendment, as it implies that the grading can be 'shipper's usual' or to recognised rules. At the present time, most goods exported from the East Coast are in accordance with the NLGA Rules.

Chartering, Delay, Cancelling: Clause 4

The wording of this clause is very similar to that of the Albion terms, with a few exceptions. The clause gives the buyer the right to take the goods on f.o.b.

terms in the event of the loss of the vessel named to load, or delay beyond 6 weeks of shipment due to causes named in the contract. There is no f.o.b. contract to match the Ecancif contract, so a clause defines the f.o.b. price as 'c.i.f. price less cost of insurance and freight at the rate stated in the contract . . .' and the 'drawing date' as being 2 months from the date in which the buyer elected to take the goods on f.o.b. terms, unless they are removed earlier. There is a following paragraph which reads:

'Where goods have been specifically sold for shipment by liner where such liner space is not available within six weeks beyond the expiry of the shipment period as stated in the contract for the goods affected, Sellers shall then give prompt telegraphic notice thereof to Buyers, and Buyers shall have the option of taking the goods unshipped on the basis set out in the preceding paragraph or of cancelling the contract or any unfulfilled part thereof provided that Buyers exercise their option by notice in writing to the Agents named in the contract within 14 days of receipt of Sellers telegraphic advice that liner space is not available.'

Margins in Sellers Option: Clause 5

'Sellers shall have the option to vary by 10% more or less any or every item but not exceeding 20 standards on any one item and to vary items of 2 to 10 standards to the extent of 1 standard, always provided that the total quantity is not varied by more than 10%.'

Unlike the Albion terms, there is no mention of over-lying goods or reference to chartering margins.

Over- and Under-shipment: Clause 6

The wording of this clause is identical with that of the Albion terms, except that the latter includes a reference to the clause on margins.

Insurance: Clause 7

Although the wording varies slightly, this clause closely follows the Albion terms, and, like the Pacif contract, states that buyer's option of cancelling the contract can only be exercised if war risk insurance can only be covered for a premium of not less than 25 per cent, whereas the Albion contract stipulates not less than 10 per cent. The Ecancif contract is phrased to cover shipments by both chartered vessels and liners, and the insurance clause goes on to state that 'freight is payable ship lost and/or cargo lost or not lost . . .', then the sellers shall insure for the full c.i.f. value plus 10 per cent.

Policies issued outside the UK: Clause 8

This clause is identical with the Albion terms, and provides sellers with the option of insuring in their own countries. The name of the insurers is inserted in the relevant place on the face of the contract.

Payment and Freight: Clause 9

'Buyers shall pay freight less advances, if any, according to charter party or Bill of Lading and shall pay to Sellers or Agents the balance of the invoice value, after deducting freight, in London, on receipt of and in exchange for shipping documents including policies of insurance as per Clause 7 and Certificate(s) of Origin.

'In lieu of a policy of insurance as above provided Sellers may tender and Buyers shall accept a Certificate of Insurance issued outside the United Kingdom provided such certificate complies in all respects with a policy issued under the terms of Clause 7 hereof and can be stamped as a policy in the United Kingdom and that such certificate makes express provision that losses shall be payable in the United Kingdom against production thereof.

'Any freight advance which shall not exceed the Master's requirements permitted by the "Benacon" charter party to be paid to Sellers or Agents in net cash against Master's receipt endorsed upon the Bill(s) of Lading in sterling.'

This clause merely amplifies the payment terms shown in the preamble already quoted and Clause 7: Insurance.

Exceptions: Clause 10

This clause varies in wording from both the Albion and Pacif terms and is quoted in full.

'In case the manufacture and/or shipment and/or sea transport of any of the goods specified in the contract should be delayed or hindered by reason of fire or through an accident to the sawmills, or drought, ice, flood, strike or lock-out, mobilisation, acts of God, King's enemies, restraint of Princes, rulers and people, labour disturbances, or through any other cause or causes whatsoever beyond Seller's control, Sellers, provided they give prompt notice to Buyers by telegram of the delay or hindrance, shall not be responsible for any damages resulting to Buyers therefrom.

'If shipment of the whole or part is thereby effectively rendered impossible within six weeks of the expiry of the shipment period stated in the contract, Sellers shall give prompt notice to Buyers and the contract shall be cancelled to the extent of any unshipped portion, but if within fourteen days of the receipt of such notice Buyers so elect they shall have the right to take the goods that are available at the stipulated c.i.f. price less cost of insurance and freight at the rate stated in the contract, on f.o.b. terms and conditions, the drawing date of approximate payment, unless goods have been removed earlier, being two months from the date such election is exercised.'

The first paragraph of this clause is identical to the equivalent in the Pacif contract but more comprehensive than in the Albion contract. It should be noted that there is a period of 6 weeks of the shipment period — unlike the Pacif contract, which stipulates 9 weeks — and buyers are given the option of taking the goods on f.o.b. terms after 2 months.

War, etc.: Clause 11

This clause is the same as the equivalent in other c.i.f. contracts and is allied to the appropriate clauses covering shiproom and exceptions.

Passing of Property: Clause 12

This is identical with the Albion terms.

Bills of Lading: Clause 13

'The goods to be shipped under as many Bills of Lading as may be required by Buyers, but no Bill of Lading shall be for less than 20 standards, except in the case of liner shipments where the minimum Bill of Lading shall be 7 standards.

'If it is apparent from the Bills of Lading or other evidence that the Master has failed to load the vessel in accordance with Buyers loading instructions Sellers shall forthwith advise Buyers of all variations therefrom and make protest to the Master or Owner's Agent, sending copy thereof to Buyers.'

This clause is quite unlike other contract clauses, but is self-explanatory.

Dead Freight and Demurrage: Clause 14

The wording of this clause is identical with that of the Albion terms, except for the interest rate.

Licences: Clause 15

The wording of this clause is identical with that of the Albion terms.

Claims: Clause 16

There are two essential differences in this clause, compared with the Albion terms. Reasonable particulars must be given to the agents within 21 days (not working days) of any claim. If, by reason of circumstances beyond their control, buyers are not able to provide such particulars, then, on notification to agents, they are entitled to an extension of the time limit. There is no non-fulfilment of contract mentioned in the contract which provides buyers with a claim for damages.

Inspection: Clause 17

This clause is an additional one and really does no more than confirm the terms found under the terms of the Pacif and Fobra contracts.

Rejection: Clause 18

The wording of this clause is identical with that of the Albion terms.

Arbitration: Clause 19

Although the wording is slightly different from that of the Albion contract there are two exceptions, as in the Pacif contract. The clause does not differentiate between 'shipped' and 'unshipped' goods, but it does refer to arbitrations subject to the Arbitration (Scotland) Act, 1894. Needless to say, there is no mention of Swedish or Finnish Associations.

Notice: Clause 20

The wording of this clause is identical with that of the Albion and Pacif contracts.

9.7 Fobra 1957

This contract form is adopted by the Timber Trade Federation of the UK and is headed 'Brazilian Softwood (F.O.B.)'. In the preamble it states: 'Payment to be made in cash in London to Agents on receipt of and in exchange for shipping documents.' No credit terms are mentioned and Brazilian exchange regulations do not permit discount for cash. However, as mentioned elsewhere, for other such contract terms, it is quite normal for buyers to obtain credit through seller's agents. The general terms and conditions are not as comprehensive as those in the Uniform contract but some are identical. Those clauses which are significantly different are as follows.

Grading and Seasoning: Clause 2

'The goods are to be free from wormholes but otherwise to be at least equal to the Official Brazilian Grading Classification set out in Decree Law No. 30325 dated 21st. December 1951, and are to be properly seasoned for shipment to the United Kingdom and are to be delivered on board the vessel in accordance with the custom of the port. All bundled goods shall be adequately and securely bound.'

The reference to proper seasoning is an important provision because the goods are shipped under deck and, during the long sea voyage, insufficiently seasoned goods could suffer severe deterioration.

Shiproom: Clause 3

'Sellers to arrange space under deck for Buyer's account to the port of destination under the contract at not exceeding Conference rate ruling at time of loading.'

This is unusual, because although described as an f.o.b. contract, sellers are responsible for arranging the freight contract, and delivering the goods 'all free on board the vessel'. It should also be noted that all goods are loaded under deck. The clause goes on as follows:

'If shipping space to lift the goods is not available by the ready date or by such later date permitted by Clause 7 (Exceptions), Sellers shall have the right of completing the contract within four weeks from such date. If at the expiration of such further period such space is not available Sellers shall at once give notice to Buyers to this effect and so far as possible give the earliest date(s) and the name of the vessel(s) by which shipment of the whole or part of the goods can be effected. On receipt of such notice Buyers shall have the option, to be promptly declared, of cancelling the contract or of postponing the date of shipment for such period as may be mutually agreed upon or of taking the goods by the vessel(s) named (if any) and cancelling the balance (if any). Should Sellers fail to give notice as above provided within seven days from the expiration of the further four weeks period then Buyers shall thereafter have the option of cancelling the contract provided such notice of cancellation is received by Sellers before the goods are shipped. All such notices shall be by telegram except that Buyers may give notice in writing by letter addressed to Agents who shall telegraph such notice to Sellers.'

It will be seen that the buyer is given the option of either cancelling or postponing shipment in the event of delay beyond 4 weeks, if shipping space is not available, or 6 weeks in the case of delay and hindrance beyond seller's control — Clause 7.

Quantity, Over- and Under-shipment: Clause 4

This clause is identical with both the Uniform and Albion forms except that it does not refer to margins. There is no margin clause in the Fobra contract, as for some considerable time shippers have been accustomed to ship almost exact quantities.

Risk: Clause 5

'The goods shall be at the risk of Sellers until they are loaded into lighters for shipment after receipt of notice from the vessel of her expected arrival or in the case of goods so loaded prior to the receipt of such notice until such notice is received or if not loaded into lighters until the goods are loaded on board the ocean-going vessel but in all such cases only as regards any loss of the goods not resulting from damage. Otherwise notwithstanding that this sale is made on f.o.b. terms the goods shall be at the risk of Buyers and shall be insured by them on the conditions of the Timber Trade Federation Insurance Clauses and Institute Strike Clauses (Timber Trade) (Extended Cover), from the commencement of transit as provided for in Clause 1 of the said clauses.'

The reason for this divergence from the normal accepted practice of an f.o.b. contract is that in the case of shipments from Brazil the goods are often loaded into lighters and travel some distance before being placed on board the vessel. Cases have occurred in the past where damage has taken place before the goods were shipped and in such cases the buyers would have no claim under an insurance policy taken out to cover an ordinary f.o.b. shipment, since they have no 'insurable interest' in the goods at the time the damage occurred. The only remedy then is to seek to recover their damages from the shippers.

By providing in the contract that the goods are at risk for buyers from the time they leave the mill for transit to the ocean-going vessel, the insurable interest of the buyer is established. The TTF insurance clauses as stipulated in their 'warehouse to warehouse' cover provide a complete protection for the buyers. Shipments from Brazil are made on liner terms, with the usual provision of the liner bill of lading that freight is payable 'lost or not lost'. It is important that buyers insure the full rate of freight. Also, it is important to remember that whereas the property in the goods passes to buyers only when the goods are placed on board the ocean-going vessel, they are stated in the contract to be at risk from the moment they are put on lighters for transport to the vessel.

Insurance: Clause 6

This clause is similar in wording to the Uniform clause but has to be associated with the unusual provisions of the preceding Clause 5: Risks.

Exceptions: Clause 7

The wording of this clause is similar to that of the Albion clause. As mentioned in Clause 3, there is a 6 week period which gives buyers the option of cancellation for the reasons stated.

War, etc.: Clause 8

The wording of this clause is similar to that of both the Uniform and the Albion terms.

Passing of Property: Clause 9

This clause is identical with Uniform Clause 15.

Bills of Lading: Clause 10

'The goods to be shipped under as many Bills of Lading as may be required by Buyers but unless otherwise mutually agreed, not exceeding 5 per 100 Standards. Loading orders unless otherwise mutually agreed shall be given at the time of signing the contract.

'The cargo shall be sent alongside in such a manner as to enable the Master to keep separate the cargo under each Bill of Lading. Quantities of 50 Standards or less for which a separate Bill of Lading is required shall be delivered to the vessel in such a manner as to enable Master to make one stowage of that Bill of Lading in the vessel.'

This clause is self-explanatory.

Dead Freight and Demurrage: Clause 11

'Sellers guarantee to pay all dead freight and demurrage admitted or proved to have been caused at the loading port by their default. If there is any such claim made against Buyers or Bill of Lading holders, Buyers shall give prompt notice thereof in writing to Sellers. In the case of arbitration or lawsuit on such claim Buyers to follow the reasonable instructions of Sellers with regard to defence and the Sellers shall supply all necessary evidence and documents in support thereof.'

This clause is self-explanatory.

Licences: Clause 12

Although the wording of this clause is slightly different, the meaning is the same as in the Uniform and Albion terms.

Claims: Clause 13

There are three essential differences in this clause, compared with the Uniform and Albion terms. Reasonable particulars of a claim must be given to agents within 21 days (not working days). There is provision for this period to be extended if buyers are unable to comply through circumstances beyond their control. There is no mention of liquidated damages being paid by sellers in the event of non-delivery.

Inspection: Clause 14

'The goods upon which a claim is made shall, within twenty-one days from the date of ship's final discharge at the port of destination of such goods be made available for inspection and notice of such availability shall be given by Buyers to Agents. If by reason of circumstances shown by Buyers to be beyond their control the goods cannot be made available for inspection within the said twenty-one days then Buyers shall, on giving notice to Agents, be entitled to an extension of time for the period covered by such delay. If at the expiry of twenty-eight days from receipt by Agents of Buyer's notice of availability an amicable settlement of the claim has not been reached then unless otherwise agreed between the parties the claim shall forthwith be submitted to arbitration in accordance with the provisions of Clause 16 hereof. If at the expiry of fourteen days from the appointment of the later appointed of the two Arbitrators no award has been made then unless otherwise agreed between the parties the dispute shall forthwith be submitted to an Umpire who unless he considers inspection unnecessary shall inspect the goods within fourteen days of his appointment.'

This clause is an additional one and really does no more than confirm the terms found the under the headings of Claim and Arbitration.

Rejection: Clause 15

The wording of this clause is similar to that of both the Uniform and the Albion terms.

Arbitration: Clause 16

Although the wording is different, this clause is essentially the same as in the Uniform and the Albion terms, with two exceptions. It does not differentiate between 'shipped' and 'unshipped' goods and it does refer to arbitrations subject to the Arbitration (Scotland) Act, 1894. Needless to say, there is no reference to the Swedish and Finnish Associations.

Notice: Clause 17

The wording of this clause is identical with that of both the Uniform and Albion terms.

9.8 Poland—Albion 1933 (revised 1938)

This contract is used for the sale of Polish softwood and is suitably amended. It is adopted by the Timber Trade Federation of the United Kingdom and the sole shippers Paged Centrala Handlu Zagranicznego of Warsaw and their agents Polish Timber Products Limited of London; it is a c. & f. contract. The preamble on the face of the contract contains a number of terms and conditions and specifies which clauses in the general terms and conditions are cancelled by agreement. There is a separate sheet attached to the form giving additional clauses. The following terms are on the face of the contract.

(1) 'The wood goods hereinafter specified, subject to a variation in seller's option of 10% more or less on any or every item, but not exceeding 20 standards on any one item, and items of 2 to 10 standards may be varied to the extent of one standard, always provided that the total quantity is not varied except under the provisions of Clause 5. In the event of over-shipment of any item of the contract or of the total contract quantity buyers shall not be entitled to reject the entire shipment but shall have the option to be exercised without delay of taking up the bills of lading and paying for the whole quantity shipped or of taking up the bills of lading and paying only for the contract quantity rejecting the balance. The same conditions shall apply if the excess is not apparent from the bills of lading but is discovered only on arrival of the goods at their ultimate destination in the United Kingdom or other country of destination. If buyers elect to take the contract quantity only the sellers shall pay all extra expenses whatsoever incurred by buyers in consequence of the over-shipment. In the event of under-shipment of any item, buyers are to accept or pay for the quantity shipped, but have the right to claim compensation for such short shipment. Each item of this contract to be a separate interest.'

(2) 'The goods are to be shipped at . . . . .by steamer or full powered motorship, calculated by owners ready to load during . . . . . shiproom to be secured in due time by the sellers who shall promptly advise buyers; in the event, however, of vessel chartered under this contract not being ready to load within six weeks after stipulated time of shipment, sellers shall notify buyers that the ship named cannot load within that time, and the buyers shall have the right of cancelling the contract to a corresponding extent, subject to giving notice to that effect to sellers to enable them to cancel the charter party within the time stipulated in same provided that the sellers notice states the time for cancellation and has been given instantly on receipt of the shipowners notice under clause 3(c) of the "Baltwood" charter.'

(3) 'It is understood and agreed that Clauses 2, 6, 7 and 10 on the reverse side shall not apply to this Contract.'

These refer to Ends, Insurance, Freight Advance and Payment and Freight, respectively.

(4) 'Notwithstanding anything to the contrary contained in the Insurance Clause in the Additional Clauses relating to this Contract, this Contract is on Cost and Freight Terms. Insurance is Buyers responsibility.'

ADDITIONAL CLAUSES TO CONTRACT

(1) 'The dimensions stated in this Contract are in metric measure and all references to St. Petersburg Standards are to be read as being cubic metres on the basis that one standard equals five cubic metres. The reference to "9 feet" and "6/8 feet" shall be substituted by "2.7 metres" and "1.8/2.4 metres" respectively.

'The prices for Sawn and Planed goods are for lengths 2.7 m and up other than as regards items for which a separate price for ends 1.8 m to 2.4 m is specified in the Contract (in which case notwithstanding any provision of this Clause all ends on such items shall be at that specified price). Sellers have the right to supply up to 3% of ends on each item at full price (the full c. & f. value for 2.7 m and up appropriate for the goods concerned) save that if this percentage is exceeded on any item(s) all ends (including the first 3%) on such item(s) shall be at two-thirds price, which latter price means two-thirds of the F.O.B. value (i.e. the Contract price per cubic metre less the freight rate per cubic metre for 2.7 m and up appropriate for the goods concerned) plus full freight.

'Ends to be regarded as included in the Contract quantity but to be disregarded in the calculation of average lengths. Buyers may reject any ends in excess of 7½% on any item except as regards slatings, boards 115 mm and under and V1th quality, the quantity of which shall be as falling.'

(2) *Insurance.* 'To be effected by Buyers or their Agents for Buyer's account.'

(3) *Payment.* 'Cash in exchange for shipping documents less 2½% discount on the F.O.B. value of the goods. Freight to be prepaid by the Shippers but such prepayment not to be for more than 90%. The balance to be deducted from Shipper's invoice(s) and the amount(s) in Pounds Sterling so deducted to be settled directly by Buyers with the ship.'

(4) *Chartering.* 'It is mutually agreed that "Nubaltwood" charter party 1973 − Polish Terms (Clause 15a) known to all parties, shall be substituted for "Baltwood" wherever appearing in this Contract.'

(5) *Bills of Lading.* 'Notwithstanding anything to the contrary contained in Clause 12, minimum quantity of any item or part item on a Bill of Lading to be 25 m³.'

(6) *Claims.* 'Notwithstanding anything to the contrary contained in Clause 14, no claims for quality and/or condition will be recognised by Sellers

in respect of packaged goods unless reasonable particulars are in Agent's hands
within thirty days from date of ship's final discharge.'

(7) *Licence.* 'Subject to export licence.'

The difference between the terms of the revised 1938 Albion contract and
the present revised 1964 contract is of no great significance, although it is not
clear why the Polish contract is not based on the latter. However, the additional clauses appear to cover all circumstances satisfactorily. It should be
noted that the contract form quotes the Timber Trade Federation Insurance
Clauses 1938 in full, whereas the current Clauses are 1979.

9.9 Unicif 1952

This contract has been adopted by the National Hardwood Importers Section
(Importers Division) and the Hardwood Agents and Brokers Section (Agents
Division) of the Timber Trade Federation of the United Kingdom. It is headed
'U.K. Hardwood C.I.F. Contract' and is the principal contract in use for the
sale of hardwoods. It is in a more simple form than most others, and the
general terms and conditions are less comprehensive, even though they provide
the basic information concerning the terms of the contract. On the face of
the form, it is stated: 'The undermentioned wood goods at the prices and on
the terms, conditions and warranties stated hereunder and at the back hereof.'
This makes provision for the insertion of additional terms agreed between the
parties concerned, and since this contract form is in world-wide use, it follows
that shippers, in particular, may require special terms and conditions to suit
their respective needs. As the printed terms and conditions are unlike those of
the softwood contracts, they are given in full.

Shipment: Clause 1

'(a) Unless otherwise stated, shipment means placing the goods on board
ocean going vessel at original shipping port. Goods for prompt shipment must
be shipped within 45 days of the date of the Contract, subject to freight space
being available, Sellers, provided prompt notice be given to the Buyers, shall
not be liable for damages for delay in delivery or non-delivery if arising from
any cause or causes whatsoever beyond their control but should the shipment
be delayed beyond the time stipulated the Buyers shall have the right to
cancel the Contract, or any part unshipped, if they give due notice before the
goods are shipped.

'(b) Subject to sub-clause (a) above, should shipment not be made within
the time stipulated Buyers shall have the right to cancel that part of the Contract which has not been shipped within the time stipulated provided they
give due notice before the goods are shipped and without prejudice to any
claim for damages for non-shipment.

'(c) Sellers to give prompt . . . . . advice of any shipment made under this Contract giving the quantity loaded, the name of the vessel and approximate sailing date. "Airmail" or "telegraphic" to be inserted.

'(d) Unless otherwise agreed all goods shall be shipped under deck.'

Clause (a) deals with delays in shipment through causes beyond seller's control, whereas Clause (b) deals with delay in shipment *not* beyond seller's control. In each case, buyers are given the right of cancellation, provided that their cancellation is received by sellers before the goods are shipped. In the first clause the sellers are not liable for damages, provided that they advise buyers promptly. In the second clause the buyer's cancellation does not prejudice any claim for damages which he may have. If this latter clause were not inserted, buyers would be entitled to reject the documents in the event of late shipment, as these would not be in respect of goods of the contract description and there would be obligation upon the buyer to give notice of cancellation.

It should be noted that, unless otherwise agreed, all goods shall be shipped under deck.

Insurance: Clause 2

'Marine insurance, including current Timber Trade Federation Clauses, Institute War Clauses (Timber Trade) and Institute Strikes Riots and Civil Commotions Clauses (Timber Trade), to be effected with Lloyds or first-class British Companies. Claims to be payable in sterling in the United Kingdom. Insurances to cover c.i.f. value plus 10% for Buyer's benefit. Should the cost of insuring against War Risks exceed 25p % such excess over 25p % to be payable by Buyers.'

It should be noted that no option is given for insuring with a foreign company.

Property: Clause 3

'Property in goods to be deemed for all purposes, except retention of Vendor's lien for unpaid purchase price, to have passed to Buyers when goods have been shipped.'

In this contract a definition of 'shipment' is given as 'placing the goods on board ocean going vessel at original shipping port'. A clear unambiguous point of passing of property from buyer to seller is important when insurable interest is considered. While the TTF insurance clauses include a 'warehouse to warehouse' clause, the cover of insurable risk is not as nicely tied up as one would wish.

There are two distinct legal rights in considering these aspects of contracts:

(1) Right of property or ownership of goods. As will be seen above, this

passes to the buyer on shipment, subjecting him to the risk of any accident that may befall the goods – against which risks he is, of course, insured.

(2) Right of possession of the goods. This normally follows the right of property, but it can be defeated if the buyer does not carry out his part of the contract by making payment to the seller in exchange for the shipping documents.

Licences and Duty: Clause 4

'The obligation to make application for and the cost of obtaining any export or import licence and to pay any export or import duty, charges or taxes which may be payable in respect of the export or import of the goods shall be upon Sellers and Buyers respectively.

'If either party having made application has failed to obtain the requisite licence by . . . . . he shall have the right to cancel the Contract provided prompt notice is given to the other party. If a party has not notified the other party by the above date that the requisite licence has been granted, the last mentioned party has the right of cancelling the Contract subject to prompt notice being given.

'If any requisite licence has been refused to a party or if a licence although granted is subsequently cancelled prior to shipment, such party shall forthwith advise the other party by telegram and either party shall have the right of cancelling the Contract, provided that notice of cancellation is given, in the case of the first mentioned party, in the said telegram and, in the case of the other party, promptly on receipt thereof.'

The wording of this clause is identical with that of the Albion and most other contract terms. The one slight difference is that the specified date is not inserted on the face of the contract.

Payment: Clause 5

'Payment of the invoice amount to be made in cash to the Agents named in this Contract on first presentation of and in exchange for shipping documents consisting of on board Bill of Lading, Insurance Policy or Certificate, and Certificate of origin where necessary, together with Specifications and Invoice both in triplicate. Where goods are sold subject to out-turn weight or measurement, payment to be based on pro forma invoice, final settlement for or against being made on landing and weighing or measuring of the goods at the port of discharge, or place of first storage.

'Freight, unless already paid, to be deducted from invoice and paid by Buyers in terms of usual Liner Bill of Lading. Freight to include free discharge to Receiver at port of destination.'

It should be noted that no credit terms are written into the contract but, as mentioned before, it is still possible to obtain credit directly from the agent in the form of a 4 month bill.

Claims: Clause 6

'(a) No claim (except for measurement) shall be allowed unless same be made and formulated in writing within 21 days from the final discharge of the goods at Dock, Wharf, Yard or any other premises for first storage.

'(b) Claims for measurement must be made and formulated in writing within 30 days from final discharge of the goods at Dock, Wharf, Yard or any other premises for first storage except where there are delays beyond the control of the Buyers of which notice must be given within the said period of 30 days.

'(c) Pending settlement of claims, bulk shall not be broken without the written permission of Sellers or their Agents.

'(d) No claim for rejection shall be allowed on goods taken away from the area of the ports of c.i.f. destination and forwarded to an inland point and in the event of any claim for damages on such goods, the basis of settlement shall be as if the goods were still at the port.'

These terms are rather more stringent than those of softwood contracts. It should be noted that the claim period is not for 'reasonable particulars' but for the claim itself 'in writing'. For example, the Uniform and Albion contracts give no time limit for submission of the claim itself, provided that reasonable particulars are given within time.

Pending the settlement of a claim, the goods must be retained intact and 'bulk shall not be broken'. The question of dealing with items on which there is no claim is not clearly covered. From this it would appear safer to retain the entire parcel intact until the claim is settled, to avoid any misunderstanding or possibility of the claim being upset. If the goods are moved from the area of the port through which they were imported, they cannot be rejected, although they may be the subject of a substantial claim. In any case the basis of the claim would be as if they were still at the port. In other words, the buyer cannot claim from the seller any charges, etc., incurred in moving the goods from the port to the inland yard.

Quantity: Clause 7

'When used the term "about" shall mean within 10% in proportion of the specification under or over the quantity specified or 500 cubic feet, whichever is the less, except in the case of dimension stock when the term "about" shall mean within 5% of the number of pieces in proportion of the specification under or over the quantity specified or 250 cubic feet, whichever is the less. In the case of logs the term "about" shall mean within 10% of the quantity specified or 20 tons, whichever is the less.'

It will be seen that there is no mention of overshipment or undershipment, since such circumstances are comparatively infrequent in the hardwood trade and margins do not present the same importance as they do in the softwood trade. Overshipment and undershipment are covered by the Sale of Goods Act, 1893, Section 30.

Arbitration: Clause 8

'Should any dispute arise with respect to any matter connected with this Contract the Buyers shall nevertheless accept custody of the goods if and as shipped and make due payment, but such acceptance and payment shall be without prejudice. All disputes (including claims for non-shipment), except as provided below, shall be settled by friendly arrangement if possible, failing which they shall be referred to the decision of an Arbitrator to be mutually agreed upon. In default of such agreement one Arbitrator shall be appointed by each party. In the event of either party failing to appoint his Arbitrator within seven days after being requested through the Agents under this Contract so to do, the Arbitrator thus required shall be appointed by the Chairman, or failing him the Deputy Chairman, for the time being, of the Hardwood Agents and Brokers Section, Agent's Division, or the National Hardwood Importers Section, Importers Division, of the Timber Trade Federation. The Arbitrators shall, before entering upon the arbitration, appoint an Umpire, but if within 21 days after appointment they fail to agree as to the Umpire then the Chairman, or failing him the Deputy Chairman, for the time being, of either the aforesaid Sections, on the application of either party or his Arbitrator, shall appoint an Umpire. In the case of any claim not exceeding £100, one Arbitrator shall be appointed by mutual agreement, or failing such agreement by the Chairman, or failing him the Deputy Chairman, for the time being, of either the aforesaid Sections. All Arbitrators and Umpires shall be selected from the Panel of Arbitrators for Hardwood approved by the Timber Trade Federation, and all Arbitrations shall be held in the United Kingdom.

'The award of the Arbitrators or Umpire shall be final and binding on all parties under this Contract.

'The allocation of the costs of the Arbitration shall be left to the discretion of the Arbitrators or Umpire, but, in this connection any offers of settlement made by either parties to the dispute shall be taken into consideration.

'In other respects the said Arbitration shall be subject to the English Arbitration Act, 1950, or any statutory modification thereof or substitution therefor except in the case of goods sold to Scottish buyers for shipment to a Scottish port when the said Arbitration shall be in Scotland subject to the Arbitration (Scotland) Act, 1894, or any statutory modification thereof or substitution therefor and Arbitrators shall have power to assess and award damages.'

This clause is somewhat unusual, since it stipulates that the buyer shall accept custody of any goods shipped and make payment for them 'without prejudice', before proceeding to arbitration. It goes rather further in limitation of buyer's right of rejection than the rejection clause inserted in most softwood contracts, which usually limit buyer's right of rejection to disputes concerning dimensions and/or quality unless the whole shipment is involved. While this clause does not prevent the buyer from claiming 'rejection' at arbitration, it may place him in a weaker position, because he has paid for the goods and may feel that he is worse off than if he had not paid. Legally he is no worse off, and, in fact, his correct execution of his contract liabilities should assist him in the impression he gives to the arbitrators or umpire. However, if the settlement of the dispute is prolonged, he may suffer by having some part of his working capital tied up.

Non-Compliance: Clause 9

'In the case of non-compliance by the Buyers with any of the terms of Clause 5 of this Contract the Sellers shall have the right of immediate re-sale for Buyer's account.'

This clause does not appear in any of the softwood contracts. Its effect is to override the normal property clause and permit an unpaid seller to resell the goods without having first obtained a court order. It is an unusual feature and is confined to the hardwood contracts and certain panel products contracts.

9.10 American Hardwood Lumber 1960

This contract form is adopted by the National Hardwood Importers Section of the Timber Trade Federation of the United Kingdom and the National Lumber Exporters Association (USA). In many respects it is unlike the Unicif contract, and is quoted in full. It bears no code name, and although the fact is not mentioned, it is usually regarded as a c.i.f. contract. On the face of the form it is stated: 'The undermentioned wood goods at the prices and on the terms, conditions and warranties stated hereunder and at the back hereof.' Like the Unicif contract, this makes provision for the insertion of additional terms agreed between the parties concerned. On the face of the contract is the heading 'Payment', which is a question of negotiation; there is no reference to this in the general terms and conditions.

Shipment: Clause 1

'Unless otherwise stated the term "shipment" means dispatch from the mill or interior shipping point.

'(a) Goods for prompt shipment must be shipped within 45 days of the date of the contract.

'(b) Sellers are not liable for failure to ship or delay in shipment if arising from any cause over which they have no control, provided that when the cause arises immediate (airmail) notice is given to Buyers.

'(c) Subject to the preceding clause should shipment not be made within the time stipulated Buyers shall have the right to cancel that part of the contract which has not been shipped within the time stipulated provided they give due notice before the goods are en route or the car number declared without prejudice to any claim for damages for non-shipment.

'(d) Sellers or their fowarding agents to give immediate (airmail) advice when stock is loaded at the mill of any shipment made under this contract giving the quantity loaded, the name of the declared steamer/vessel and approximate sailing date. In the event of the name of the steamer/vessel being changed immediate cable advice must be given.

'(e) Unless otherwise agreed all goods shall be shipped under deck.'

This contract contains no property clause at all and the word 'shipment' is used in its American sense and defined as 'despatch from the mill or interior shipping point'. Therefore, it is essential to consider the question of passing of property and insurable interest. Fortunately, the insurance clause includes the TTF Clauses and there is 'warehouse to warehouse' cover.

Quality: Clause 2

'Unless otherwise specified all lumber to be graded according to the grading rules of the National Hardwood Lumber Association in force at the date of this contract.'

Claims: Clause 3

'(a) No claim (except for Measurement and/or non-shipment) shall be allowed unless same be made and formulated in writing within 10 days excluding Saturday, Sunday and Holidays from the final discharge of the goods at Dock, Wharf, Yard or any other premises for first storage.

'(b) Claims for measurement must be made within 30 days from final discharge of the goods at Dock, Wharf, Yard, or any other premises for first storage, except where there are delays beyond the control of the Buyers.

'(c) No claim for rejection shall be allowed on goods taken away from the area of the port of c.i.f. destination and forwarded to an inland point and in the event of any claim for damages on such goods the basis of settlement shall be as if the goods were still at the port.

'(d) All goods claimed to be below grade should be laid aside in a separate and distinct pile at the time they are received. In any case where this has not been done the Sellers through their Agents may demand, and Arbitrators are empowered (if they so desire) to order such separation to be made within a period fixed by Arbitrators. The Arbitrators are empowered to allocate the expenses involved in such separation.'

This clause is very similar to the Unicif terms, except that it allows only 10 days for the claim to be formulated in writing instead of 21 days. It contains the same restrictions on breaking bulk and rejection.

Insurance: Clause 4

'On goods sold c.i.f. Marine Insurance, including current Timber Trade Federation Clauses, Institute War Clauses (Timber Trade) and Institute Strikes Riots and Civil Commotions Clauses (Timber Trade), to be effected with Lloyds or other first class Company. Claims to be payable in the United Kingdom. Insurances to cover c.i.f. value plus 10% for Buyer's benefit. Should the cost of insuring against War Risks exceed 5 shillings (£0.25)%, such excess over 5 shillings to be payable by Buyers. The Buyers shall accept the usual certificate of Marine Insurance in lieu of the actual policy.'

This clause is very similar to the Unicif terms, with the exception that the words 'to be effected with Lloyds or other first class company' are used, rather than the words 'Lloyds or first class British companies'. Furthermore, it states that claims will be 'payable in the United Kingdom', whereas the Unicif contract states 'payable in sterling in the United Kingdom'. In both cases the goods are to be insured for the c.i.f. value plus 10 %.

Measurement: Clause 5

'In accordance with the rules of the National Hardwood Lumber Association in force at the date of this contract and to be
 (a) tallied on a width and length basis
 (b) tallied on the Board Rule content basis.
 (Delete (a) or (b) as applicable)'

Quantity: Clause 6

'Unless this contract states a specific quantity of either cubic or superficial feet a carload shall be considered to contain the equivalent of about 15 000 superficial feet B.M. of 1 inch. When used, the term "about" shall, unless otherwise specified, mean within 7½% in proportion of the specification under or over the quantity specified except in the case of dimension stock when the term "about" shall mean within 2½% of the number of pieces in proportion of the specification under or over the quantity specified.'

It will be seen that there is no mention of overshipment and undershipment since such circumstances are comparatively infrequent in the hardwood trade and margins do not present the same importance as they do in the softwood trade. Overshipment and undershipment are covered by the Sale of Goods Act, 1893, Section 30. This clause is similar in most respects to the Unicif terms.

Arbitration: Clause 7

'Should any dispute arise with respect to any matter connected with this contract the buyers shall nevertheless accept custody of the goods and make due payment, but such acceptance and payment shall be without prejudice. All disputes (including claims for non-shipment) except as provided below, shall be settled by friendly arrangement if possible, failing which they shall be referred to the decision of an Arbitrator to be mutually agreed upon. In default of such agreement one Arbitrator shall be appointed by each party. In the event of either party failing to appoint his Arbitrator within seven days after being requested through the Agents so to do the Arbitrator thus required shall be appointed by the Chairman, or failing him the Deputy Chairman, for the time being, of the National Hardwood Importers Section of the Timber Trade Federation of the United Kingdom or The Hardwood Agents and Brokers Association Limited. The Arbitrators shall, before entering upon the Arbitration, appoint an Umpire, but if within seven days after appointment they fail to agree as to the Umpire then the Chairman, or failing him the Deputy Chairman, for the time being, of the National Hardwood Importers Section of the Timber Trade Federation of the United Kingdom, on application of either party or his Arbitrator, shall appoint an Umpire. In the case of any claim not exceeding 15 % of the c.i.f. value, or £100, whichever is the less, one Arbitrator shall be appointed by mutual agreement, or failing such agreement by the Chairman, or failing him the Deputy Chairman, of the National Hardwood Importers Section of the Timber Trade Federation of the United Kingdom. All Arbitrators and Umpires shall be selected from the Panel of Arbitrators for Hardwood agreed by the Timber Trade Federation of the United Kingdom and by the National Lumber Exporters Association and all Arbitrations shall be held in the United Kingdom.

'The Award of the Arbitrators or Umpire shall be final and binding on all parties under this contract.

'The allocation of the costs of the Arbitration shall be left to the discretion of the Arbitrators or Umpire, but, in this connection, any offers of settlement made by either party to the dispute shall be taken into consideration.

In other respects the said Arbitration shall be subject to the English Arbitration Act, 1950, or any statutory modification thereof or substitution therefor except in the case of goods sold to Scottish buyers for shipment to a Scottish port when the said Arbitration shall be in Scotland subject to the Arbitration (Scotland) Act, 1894, or any statutory modification thereof or substitution therefor and Arbitrators shall have power to assess and award damages.'

This clause is similar to the Unicif arbitration clause, but there are a few exceptions. The time for appointing an umpire is 7 days instead of 21 days; there is provision for a claim not to exceed 15 % or £100, whichever is the less; and the National Lumber Exporters Association is mentioned in respect of the selection of arbitrators and umpires. In all other respects the comments given on the Unicif contract clause apply.

Licences and Duty: Clause 8

'The obligation to make application for and the cost of obtaining any export or import licence and to pay any export or import duty, charges or taxes which may be payable in respect of the export or import of the goods shall be upon Sellers and Buyers respectively.

'If a licence although granted to a party is subsequently cancelled prior to shipment, such party shall forthwith advise the other party by cable and either party shall have the right of cancelling the contract provided that notice of cancellation is given, in the case of the first mentioned party, in the said cable and, in the case of the other party, promptly on receipt thereof.'

This clause is self-explanatory and only differs because it does not specify any time limit.

Non-Compliance: Clause 9

'In the case of non-compliance by the Buyers with the payment terms stated on the face of this contract the Sellers shall have the right of immediate resale for Buyers account.'

This clause does not appear in any of the softwood contracts. Its effect is to override the normal property clause and permit an unpaid seller to resell the goods without having first obtained a court order. It is an unusual feature and is confined to the hardwood contracts and certain panel products contracts.

It should be noted that there is no property clause but there is an additional measurement clause.

9.11 C.I.F. Reselling Contracts

GENERAL

C.I.F. reselling contracts are for sales where goods are purchased f.o.b. or c.i.f. by an importer and resold to another importer on c.i.f. terms.

TABLE 9.1 RESELLING CONTRACTS

Code Name	Date	Revised	Type	Original	Countries
Scanref	1964	1965 1970	c.i.f resale	(Uniform) (Albion)	Sweden and Finland
Scanrex	1964	1965 1970	ex ship	(Uniform) (Albion)	Sweden and Finland
Pacref	1959	–	c.i.f resale	Pacif	Pacific Coast
Pacrex	1959	–	ex ship	Pacif	Pacific Coast
Ecanref	1959	–	c.i.f. resale	Ecancif	East Canada
Ecanrex	1959	–	ex ship	Ecancif	East Canada
Rebraf	1957	–	c.i.f resale	Fobra	Brazil
Rebrax	1957	–	ex ship	Fobra	Brazil
Reruf	1955	1966	c.i.f resale	Russian	USSR
Rerux	1955	–	ex ship	Russian	USSR

It should be noted that certain of these contract terms may be amended in due course to bring them in line with the new Uniform and Albion 1980 contracts.

The principal c.i.f. reselling contracts are listed in table 9.1 and have been negotiated between the National Softwood Importer's Section and the Merchant's Section of the TTF.

The essential feature in a c.i.f. reselling contract form is that the sellers obligations in his own f.o.b. or c.i.f. purchase contract must be covered, and that all exceptions and rights of cancellation granted to the original seller are incorporated in the contract, this time for the benefit of the reseller.

SELLER'S RESPONSIBILITIES

These are the same as in a normal c.i.f. contract — that is to say, to supply goods of the description contained in the contract, delivered to the destination named in the contract and fully insured on the basis of Lloyd's or Institute Standard Form of Policy with the current TTF clauses.

BUYERS' RESPONSIBILITIES

These, again, are primarily limited to paying for the goods against presentation of the correct documents.

DESCRIPTION

The description contained in the contract is particularly important, since the quality and specification of the goods shipped will be quite beyond the immediate control of the seller. He must beware of committing himself in his c.i.f. resale contract to a description which is more exacting than the description contained in his original contract with the shipper. If the goods are not up to standard or specification and he has a claim made against him by the c.i.f. resale buyer, he must be in a position to sustain a claim successfully against the shipper.

FREIGHT

The rate of discharge and other conditions are to be in accordance with the charterparty, freight booking note and/or bills of lading under the terms of which the goods are shipped 'which buyers hereby agree to adopt'. This places a most important obligation on buyers, since under the contract the sellers have no obligation to provide a copy of the charter party or freight booking note. It means that the buyers must attempt to obtain a copy of the charter party or freight booking note to make quite certain whether or not there are any unusual provisions or obligations falling on holders of bills of lading (which the buyers become, after accepting and paying for the shipping documents).

If, for instance, goods are freighted under Nubaltwood terms, they must ensure that they make claims for shortages on under-deck bills of lading (in pieces) against shipowners *within 8 days* of final discharge. The responsibility for this notification and claim rests entirely on the buyers as bills of lading holders; it does not concern the sellers, who by then have parted with the goods. The right of the vessel to carry part of the goods on deck is clearly stated. This right, of course, has already been conceded by sellers in the charter.

INSURANCE

Insurance is to include the current TTF clauses and a policy or certificate of insurance must be included with the shipping documents 'or an undertaking by Sellers to hold Buyers covered for the c.i.f. value hereunder, less freight plus freight advance or pre-paid freight'.

If the original goods are purchased on c.i.f. terms, they will normally have been insured for the c.i.f. value plus 10 per cent. The reseller must first be satisfied that this insured value in his purchase contract is adequate to cover the value at which he is reselling the goods. It may be necessary for the seller on the resale contract to cover a further amount of insurance.

There is no obligation for the c.i.f. reseller to cover his buyer's profit, which is a point that the buyer on a c.i.f. resale contract should always consider. If he wishes his purchase to be insured for c.i.f. value plus his profit, he must arrange the additional insurance himself.

The insurance policy taken out by the shipper on the original c.i.f. contract is passed to the first c.i.f. buyer, with all the benefits attached to it, who, in turn, as the c.i.f. reseller can pass this policy (suitably endorsed) on to the c.i.f. resale buyer. This is in most cases difficult to achieve in practice unless a whole shipment is being resold.

Certificates of insurance rather than policies are much more likely to form part of the shipping documents, particularly where the c.i.f. reseller has actually arranged the insurance. Alternatively, the undertaking described above applies, where in place of a policy or certificate of insurance the resellers are in effect insuring the buyers against loss.

The inclusion of this wording in the contract form establishes the c.i.f. reseller's 'insurable interest' in the goods, although the property in the goods may at that time have passed to the resale buyer.

MARGINS

These are wide enough normally to permit the possibility of the maximum deviation of shippers and/or shipowners in loading. The standard overshipment and undershipment clauses also apply.

Care must be observed particularly with small quantities, as the overall percentage margin on the resale contract may not be sufficient to cover the specific margin in standards permitted on small quantities in the purchase contract.

A further difficulty is sometimes encountered when the shippers, under certain purchase contracts, are authorised 'to load margins on separate bills of lading'.

This clause in purchase contracts *allows* shippers to load margins on separate bills of lading; it does not *oblige* them to load margins on separate bills of lading.

Margins are applicable to items, and if an item comprises a number of bills of lading, it is quite conceivable that the margin could be loaded on one bill of lading only, with a result that this comprises a quantity greater than the resale buyer is obliged to accept, notwithstanding the fact that the original importer, now as reseller, is given a margin of 20 per cent. For example, imagine an item of 200 m^3 which has been ordered to be loaded on four bills of lading each of 50 m^3. The shipper exercises his chartering margin of 10 per cent on the item. In most cases the shipper will endeavour to spread the margin more or less equally over the four bills of lading concerned, but he has no specific obligation to do so and the position could arise where one of the four bills of lading comprises either 30 m^3 or 70 m^3, depending on which way the shipper exercises his margin. In reselling this one bill of lading the original importer as a reseller will therefore not be covered by the 20 per cent margin allowed him in his resale contract, being either 10 m^3 over or 10 m^3 under the quantity permitted. The potential reseller therefore can only protect himself fully by seeing that on his purchase contract he makes certain that further provision is added to ensure that the shipper spreads the margin evenly as far as possible.

EXCEPTIONS

These are extensive and, in general, favour the seller. If a vessel fixed for the contract is lost before commencing to load, or if the charter party is cancelled, or should it be impossible to find suitable or convenient freight, *sellers* have the option of substituting another vessel or cancelling the contract. Incidentally, at no place in the contract is the vessel named, nor are the sellers required to notify the buyers the name of the vessel when fixed. The usual exceptions and *force majeure* clauses are included giving *sellers* the option of cancelling, provided that they give notice in writing within 6 weeks of the latest date of shipment named in the contract.

Sellers are also usually given the option of cancelling if it is found impossible to arrange war risk insurance.

Most of the c.i.f. purchase contract forms envisage conditions where the sellers give the buyers the option either of cancelling their contract or of taking the goods on the equivalent f.o.b. terms. It is clearly not possible to translate these into suitable terms for buyers under a c.i.f. resale contract, and so usually these develop into right of cancellation for the c.i.f. reseller.

Most c.i.f. resale contracts give the buyers a right of cancellation if the goods are not shipped within 6 weeks of the shipment date named in the contract. This usually follows the right of cancellation that the original importer has in his purchase contract but there is one extremely important exception.

The Russian 1952 c.i.f. contract permits the buyer no right of cancellation if the goods are not shipped within the stated period. On the other hand, the Reruf 1955 c.i.f. resale contract (and also the Rerux 1955 ex-ship contract) relating to Russian goods give the buyers under those contracts the right of cancellation if the goods are not shipped within 6 weeks of a date named in the contract. This leaves an important gap in which the importer reselling on c.i.f. terms is not covered.

It has been suggested that the importers have in fact some right of cancellation, but it would have been happier and safer if the reselling contracts and the original purchase contracts were more closely in agreement.

PROPERTY

There is no specific clause stating where the property passes to the second buyer. In such a case it would normally be at the time of shipment, since this is the first moment that the goods are clearly ascertained (this still being a contract for the sale of future goods by description). However, in all these contracts there is a non-compliance clause giving the sellers the right of resale if the buyers fail to comply with any of the terms of the contract. This refers principally to the payment clause, so it may be taken that the property passes when the bills of lading are transferred.

The normal clause in reselling contracts states: 'Property in goods to be deemed for all purposes, except retention of Vendor's lien for unpaid purchase price, to have passed to Buyers when goods have been put on board the vessel, or if sold "afloat", at the date of the contract.'

CLAIMS AND REJECTION

The claims and rejection clauses follow closely the purchase contract clauses with the exception of the period for notification of 'reasonable particulars' and the period for producing the goods for inspection is smaller than in the original purchase contract. This must be done to ensure that the sellers can in their turn submit reasonable particulars of their claim against the original shippers within the period stated in their purchase contract.

9.12 Ex-ship Reselling Contracts

GENERAL

These are contract forms for sales where goods purchased f.o.b. or c.i.f. by an importer are resold ex ship to other importers or merchants. Negotiated between the National Softwood Importer's Section and the Merchant's Section of the TTF. As in the c.i.f. reselling contract form, the seller is covered in this contract form for all obligations, risks, right of cancellation, etc., undertaken and accepted by him in his original purchase contract.

SELLERS' RESPONSIBILITIES

These are different from the responsibilities undertaken by the seller in any form of c.i.f. contract. They are clearly defined in a special clause headed 'Ex ship definition'.

(1) To deliver the goods described in the contract to the buyer from the ship which has arrived at the port of delivery named in the contract, at the ship's rail (if the goods are discharged by hand), or within reach of the ship's tackle shore-crane (if so discharged).

(2) To pay the sea freight, and any demurrage or dead freight charges so that the shipowners' lien on the goods is released.

(3) To furnish the buyer with a delivery order or released bill of lading, effectual to give delivery of the contract goods to the buyer.

BUYERS' RESPONSIBILITIES

These are as follows.

(1) To provide craft or lighters for overside delivery, and to pay any landing charges, etc., incurred through absence of craft or lighters.

(2) To pay any charges incurred by the sellers relating to work done by the ship *beyond* the limit of the ship's rail.

(3) To pay for the goods in the terms set out in the contract.

DESCRIPTION

As in the c.i.f. reselling contract, the description of the goods will follow closely the description of the original purchase contract. The prices are ex ship, so that all charges up to the ship's rail, including freight, demurrage contributions, etc., port charges (other than quay charges) and import duty (if any) are payable by sellers. Goods sold ex ship have in fact been imported, so import duty is paid by sellers. Sometimes such a price basis is termed 'ex-ship duty paid'.

FREIGHT

The rate of discharge and other conditions are to be in accordance with a charter party, freight booking note or bills of lading. There is no obligation on sellers to supply a copy of the charter or booking note. The buyers, therefore, must take it upon themselves to learn the terms of the charter. As in the c.i.f. reselling contract, where goods have been freighted on Nubaltwood terms, they must make claims against shipowners for shortages on underdeck bills of lading *within 8 days* of final discharge.

A clause stipulates that the vessel is to have the privilege of taking part of the cargo on deck, and buyers are obliged to accept *all* or *part* of the contract goods carried on deck. When a sale is negotiated after loading orders have been issued by the original importer, it is important that the resellers ensure that the terms of sale as to whether the goods are to be on deck or under deck, are in accordance with the loading orders that they have issued to the shipper.

INSURANCE

The insurance of the goods does not concern the buyer, except in relation to war risk insurance. The prices are stated to be based upon a declared rate of war risk insurance, any increase or decrease for buyers account. If it is not possible to cover against war risks, sellers have the option of cancelling the contract. The marine insurance policy of the goods lapses as the goods leave the ship. The TTF 'warehouse to warehouse' clause which covers the goods during the period of discharge, and during transit to their ultimate destination, is not therefore available for the benefit of the buyers. It is extremely important, therefore, that the ex-ship buyer should obtain full protection against these risks (which go beyond the normal risks of fire against which he insures his stock), and normally this is done by means of a separate open cover.

MARGINS, EXCEPTIONS, PROPERTY, CLAIMS AND REJECTION

In general, all these items follow the similar provision of the c.i.f. resale contract. The property in the goods passes on discharge from the ship, but as in the c.i.f. resale contract, is qualified by a non-compliance clause giving the sellers the right of resale in the event of the buyers not complying with any of the terms of the contract.

It will be seen from table 9.1 that the Scanref and Scanrex contracts have been revised and they are now more in line with their related Uniform and Albion contract terms. The details of their revision are given below.

9.13 Scanref 1964 (revised 1970)

In the preamble on the face of the contract the clause 'Price for ends' is deleted and is now covered by the revised Clause 2.

TTF Warranty Clause: Clause 1

'Goods are not tested or sold as fit for any particular purpose. Any term warranty or condition expressed implied or statutory to the contrary is excluded.'

This clause only appears in resale or ex-ship contracts.

Prices: Clause 2

'The prices are in British Sterling or foreign measure per cubic metre (if planed goods in nominal measure) and include first cost, freight (discharging expenses and demurrage contribution, if any, for Buyer's account) and insurance to the port of destination.

'Sellers to have the right to supply at full price up to 3 per cent of ends 1.8 m to 2.4 m on each item except those for which a separate price for ends is stated in the contract.

'If any contract(s) made by Sellers to produce the goods provides for variation of price(s) or for the cancellation of such contract(s) in the event of alteration in rate(s) of exchange and if by virtue of such provision either the price of any of the goods to be paid by Sellers, or the Sterling equivalent thereof, is varied or the contract(s) is cancelled then the price(s) of such goods under this contract shall be varied by the same amount or Sellers at their option shall have the right to cancel this contract by notifying Buyers in respect of any goods not delivered to Buyers at that date.

'Any variation in the cost to Sellers of effecting delivery of the goods to Buyers or in charges directly or indirectly affecting the goods which occurs after the date of the contract and prior to delivery of the goods to Buyers shall be for Buyer's account save that any variation in sea freight other than by reason of devaluation shall be for Seller's account.'

This change not only changes the contract to metric terms but also makes the 'ends' more in accord with the original contracts.

Seasoning and Bracking: Clause 3

The second paragraph has been deleted and now reads: 'Packaged and truck bundled goods shall not be supplied unless specified in the contract.' An additional paragraph has been added, as follows:

'Except where otherwise specified packaged goods shall mean goods which have a single length and size in each package provided that Sellers shall have the right to combine lengths where the residue is insufficient for a complete package. Truck bundled goods shall mean goods bundled in mixed lengths of one size the dimensions of each bundle to be mutually agreed.'

This change is in accord with the original contracts, which differentiate between packages and truck bundles.

Margins in Seller's Option: Clause 5

This merely converts to metric and reads as follows:
    Delete '5 stds.' and substitute '25 cubic metre' in each case.
    Delete '1 std.' and substitute '5 cubic metre'

Insurance: Clause 7

This also converts to metric and reads as follows:
    Delete '2/6 per £100' and substitute '£0.125 per £100.00'.

Exceptions: Clause 8

This also converts to metric and reads as follows:
    Delete 'three guineas per standard' and substitute '£0.63 per cubic metre'.

Loading Orders and Bills of Lading: Clause 10

This also converts to metric and reads as follows: Delete 'five per 100 standards' and substitute '7 per 500 cubic metre'.

Claims: Clause 15

The first sentence of the first paragraph is deleted and replaced by the following:

'No claim for quality and/or condition will be recognised by Sellers unless reasonable particulars are given to Agents within 10 working days from date of vessel's final discharge in the case of loose goods and within 80 days from date of vessel's final discharge in the case of packaged and truck bundled goods. In the latter case the onus shall be upon Buyers to show that proper care has been taken of the goods during this period. No other claim will be recognised by Sellers on any goods shipped under this contract unless reasonable particulars are given to Agents within 160 days of vessel's final discharge.'

The main difference between these terms and those of the original contract is the time factor: 10 working days instead of 14 working days is stipulated for loose goods and 80 days instead of 3 months for packaged or truck-bundled goods. No other claim will be recognised within 160 days as opposed to 6 months.

Arbitration: Clause 16

This merely deletes '£100' and substitutes '£200.00'.

Scanrex 1964 (revised 1970)

This differs slightly from the preceding contract revisions as follows:

There is no provision for the price of ends, although the TTF Warranty Clause is included.

Prices: Clause 2

'The prices are in British Sterling or foreign measure per cubic metre (if planed goods in nominal measure) ex-ship at the port of destination; lighterage, if any, to be at the risk and expense of Buyers.'

The following third and fourth paragraphs are identical with the Scanref terms.

Seasoning and Bracking: Clause 4

This clause is identical with the SCANREF terms.

Margins in Seller's Option: Clause 6

This clause is identical with the SCANREF terms.

Insurance: Clause 8

This clause is identical with the SCANREF terms.

Exceptions: Clause 9

This clause is identical with the SCANREF terms.

Claims: Clause 13

This clause is identical with the SCANREF terms.

Arbitration: Clause 16

This clause is identical with the SCANREF terms.

The remaining contracts covering reselling and ex ship have not yet been revised at the time of writing and are not metricated, but follow quite closely the terms of the original contracts to which they are associated. Obviously, in the course of time, revision will take place, but since so many documents are involved, it will take some time. It must be left to those parties who negotiate such contracts to ensure that they are familiar with current terms.

10   Timber Contracts IV

This chapter covers the official Contract Forms for Panel Products. With the exception of the Britfibre contract, all are adopted by the Timber Trade Federation of the UK. These are as follows:

(1) Plycif 1957: c.i.f. contract for plywood and allied products
(2) Plycif 1957: amendments for Canadian plywood
(3) Plycif 1957: amendments for Russian plywood
(4) Plydef 1972: delivered contract for plywood and allied products
(5) Parcif 1963: c.i.f. contract for particle board
(6) Pardel 1973: delivered contract for particle board
(7) Britfibre 1978: c.i.f. contract for fibre building board

Contracts (2), (3) and (4) above are closely related to the Plycif contract, and any variations in terms and conditions are mentioned. The remaining contracts do bear a resemblance in terms and conditions but, because the variations are greater, they are mostly quoted in full.

10.1 Plycif 1957

This contract form is adopted by the Timber Trade Federation of the UK and was amended in 1976 and 1979. It is a c.i.f. contract and it is used for the sale and purchase of blockboard, laminboard or battenboard and the description 'plywood' wherever used in this form shall be deemed to mean the particular materials the subject matter of the contract. Since the terms and conditions are so different from timber contracts, most of the clauses have to be quoted in full.

Quality: Clause 2

'Sellers guarantee that the goods shipped under this contract will be of their average quality and manufacture as at present supplied to the UK'
   In effect, this is the same as the term 'shipper's usual'.

Sizes: Clause 3

'The term "press" may include, in addition to the stated size, (a) sizes larger in width and/or length than the stated size, and (b) sizes within 100mm in width and/or length smaller than the stated size, provided always that not more than one size smaller than the stated size is included in each item which combines the same thickness, quality and press in each shipment.'

Quantity Variations: Clause 4

'Except in the case of boards cut to special sizes, when the exact quantity must be shipped as called for in the contract, Sellers, at their option, may ship 2½% in footage more or less than the contract quantity of each item of the specification. In the event of over-shipment of any item of the contract or the total contract quantity Buyers shall not be entitled to reject the entire shipment but shall have the option, to be exercised within 3 clear days of receipt of the specification, of taking up the Bills of Lading and paying for the whole quantity shipped or of taking up the Bills of Lading and paying only for the contract quantity, rejecting the balance. If the excess is not apparent from the shipping documents Buyers shall exercise their option within 3 clear days of the final outturn of the goods at their ultimate destination. If Buyers elect to take the contract quantity only Sellers shall pay all extra expenses whatsoever incurred by Buyers in consequence of the over-shipment.

'In the event of under-shipment of any item of the contract or of the total contract quantity, Buyers are to pay for the quantity shipped but have the right to claim damages for such under-shipment.'

This clause corresponds to the margin clauses in most other contracts and is explicit in limiting variations to 2½ per cent more or less than the contract quantity. However, it should be noted that in the case of special sizes, no variation is permitted.

Packing: Clause 5

'The goods shall be despatched from the mill in undamaged condition and shall be adequately packed. Each package shall contain only one size, one thickness and one quality and there shall be uniformity as regards the number of boards in packages containing the same size, thickness and quality. Cross-grained boards shall be packed separately. The number of boards per package of special sizes shall be left to the discretion of Sellers unless otherwise arranged.'

Marking: Clause 6

'Every package shipped under this contract to be legibly marked on two adjacent edges with size, quality, thickness and number of boards, and on one edge with package number and Buyers mark. Where packages or boards bear a

trade mark the country of origin must be legibly marked thereon.' The
reference to buyers' mark does not mean that its presence is mandatory, since
not all buyers stipulate such a requirement.

Insurance: Clause 7

'Unless otherwise agreed Marine, War and Strike Risks Insurance to be
covered by Sellers or their Agents in the joint names of Sellers and Buyers for
the contract price plus 10% with Lloyds or a first class British Company
under policies payable in sterling in Great Britain including the current
Timber Trade Federation Insurance Clauses, Institute Strikes Riots and Civil
Commotions (Timber Trade), and Institute War Clauses (Timber Trade). The
cost of War and Strike Risks (as defined in the Institute War and Strikes
Clauses in force at the time the risk attaches) up to £0.125 per £100.00 to be
borne by Sellers, any excess over such rate to be at Buyers expense. If the
rate for War and Strike Risks exceeds the said rate of £0.125 per £100.00,
Sellers shall cable to the Agents the rate quoted and Buyers shall promptly
advise the Agents of their acceptance or otherwise. If not accepted Buyers
shall have the right of effecting cover against such risks themselves (in which
event Buyers shall provide the Agents with proof of insurance against such
risks for not less than the c.i.f. value before shipment) or of calling upon
Sellers to ship goods uninsured as to War and Strike Risks. In the latter event
Buyers shall if required open a confirmed Letter of Credit in the U.K. in
favour of Sellers' Agents available against shipping documents or provide such
other security as may be acceptable to Sellers.

'If War and Strike Risks cannot be covered by Sellers or their Agents or by
Buyers within one month after the Agents have advised Buyers that the goods
are ready for shipment, Buyers shall have the option of cancelling such part
of the contract as cannot be so insured or of calling upon Seller to ship
goods uninsured as to War and Strike Risks on the terms referred to above.'

This clause is very similar in content to the Albion insurance clause but is
differently worded. The additional rates are identical and any excess is for
Buyer's account. It also gives the buyer the right to cancel the portion of the
contract which cannot be insured but, unlike the Albion, it gives a time limit
of one month.

Policies issued outside the UK: Clause 8

The wording of this clause is the same as that of Clause 9 of the Albion contract.

Shipping: Clause 9

'Shipment means placing goods on board ocean-going vessel at original ship-

ping port unless otherwise stated herein. All goods to be stowed under deck.'
Unlike some other contract terms, this clause leaves no doubt as to when shipment begins and gives no option as to where the goods must be stowed.

Property in Goods: Clause 10

'Property in goods to be deemed for all purposes (except retention of vendor's
lien for unpaid purchase price) to have passed to Buyers when goods have
been shipped.' This clause is identical with the Albion property clause 13 except that it states 'when goods have been shipped', whereas the Albion clause
states 'when goods have been put on board'. In effect, there is no significance
between the two, because they both cover vendor's lien and, in any event, are
covered by the 'warehouse to warehouse' clause. It is recommended that the
explanations given in Clause 13 of the Albion contract be carefully considered
in respect of this contract.

Payment: Clause 11

'Payment for invoice amount to be made to the Agents by cash without discount on presentation of and in exchange for shipping documents, invoice to
be finally adjusted on proved contents of packages.' This is one of several contracts in which no credit terms are included but it does not mean that these
are not available. As mentioned earlier, if no credit terms are written into the
contract, it is still possible for the buyer to obtain credit directly from the
agent in the form of a bill and to all intents and purposes it is the same as if
the seller were granting the credit.

Presentation of Documents: Clause 12

'If the documents are not presented to Buyers prior to the arrival of the
steamer, Buyers shall nevertheless take up the documents on presentation, but
any charges incurred through delay in presentation of documents unless due
to causes beyond Sellers control shall be payable by Sellers unless previous
sufficient particulars of shipment have been supplied to enable the consignment to be handled without delay or extra expense. Unless prepaid the freight
to be deducted from the invoice and paid by Buyers in terms of customary
Bill of Lading. Where Buyers cover War and Strike Risk Insurance under the
provisions of Clause 7 hereof, Sellers portion of the premium shall be deducted
from the invoice.

'Shipping documents shall consist of clean on board bill(s) of lading specification, invoice, certificate of origin where required, and policy or certificate
of insurance, provided the latter certifies all risks in the contract to be covered.
The bill(s) of lading shall not be rejected on the ground that a number of

packages (not exceeding two packages or 10%, whichever is the greater) be signed for in dispute but shall be taken up on a satisfactory indemnity.'

This clause does not really require any explanation beyond the fact that it is associated with the payment clause 11, but it does qualify the number of packages or volume which can be rejected if in dispute.

Licences and Duties: Clause 13

'The obligation to make application for and the cost of obtaining any export or import licence and to pay any export or import duty, charges or taxes which may be payable in respect of the export or import of the goods shall be upon Sellers and Buyers respectively.' In the main, this clause refers to goods imported from those countries which are now predominant outside the EEC.

Cancellation: Clause 14

'Should shipment be delayed beyond the time stipulated, Buyers shall have the right (without prejudice to their rights under this contract) to cancel such part of the contract goods as are not shipped by the stipulated date, provided they give notice to the Agents who shall immediately cable Shippers accordingly. If the goods have already been despatched from the mill at the time of receipt by Sellers of such notice of cancellation, then they shall, within three clear days of such time, notify Buyers through the Agents by cable accordingly and documentary proof of such despatch shall be sent by registered airmail within four days thereafter if required. In such event time for shipment of press sizes shall be extended for a period of 17 days from the date the goods left the mill. Special sizes which have been manufactured before receipt by Sellers of notice of cancellation must be accepted by Buyers provided Sellers supply promptly the specification of such goods as are manufactured and the goods are shipped within twenty-one days from the date of the receipt of notice of cancellation. Where special sizes are sold in sets Buyers shall only be required to accept complete sets. Should Sellers fail to comply with these provisions, either in respect of press sizes or special sizes, Buyers original notice of cancellation shall be deemed to be effective unless failure to ship within the extended period is due to causes beyond Sellers control. Sellers shall not be liable in damages for non-delivery or delay in shipment if such non-delivery or delay arises from causes beyond their control. If Sellers claim that by reason of any such cause beyond their control, they will be unable to ship within the time stipulated herein they shall give immediate telegraphic notice of such claim to Buyers through the Agents.

'Subject to Sellers proving that delay in shipment resulted from a cause beyond their control to the satisfaction of Buyers or the Arbitrators appointed hereunder, Buyers shall not cancel this contract unless such delay in shipment will exceed four weeks from the shipment date stipulated in the contract, and Sellers shall not be held liable for delivery under this contract beyond a period of three months.

'When the contract calls for declaration(s) and/or destination(s) and Buyers fail to give same in accordance with contract provisions, Sellers shall have the option of cancelling that part of the contract to which the missing declaration(s) relate. Alternatively, in the case of press sizes, Shippers may ship an average specification and, in the case of special sizes, have the option of shipping an equivalent quantity of press sizes as may suit Seller in the grades and thicknesses contracted for, at prices in force for press sizes at the time the contract was made. Such shipments shall be made to the port of Buyers address as stated in the contract, or the nearest suitable port available thereto and accepted and paid for by Buyers as provided by this contract. Should Sellers decide to exercise either of these options they shall notify Buyers through the Agents accordingly. Failure by Sellers to avail themselves of the options herein granted shall not affect in any way their rights under this contract.'

This contract term does not appear in other contracts but is self-explanatory.

Claims: Clause 15

'(1) (a) Subject to the provisions of Clause 15 (1) (b), (c) and (d) no claims for defective quality, manufacture and/or packing shall be made in respect of goods shipped under this contract unless written notice of claim together with reasonable particulars is given to the Agents within twenty-one days from the date of final landing return or delivery to private premises within the territorial limits covered by the Marine Insurance Policy. The reasonable particulars shall state whether the claim is in respect of quality, manufacture and/or packing, together with such information as Buyers can furnish at the time. Any statement shall be without prejudice and conditional upon the facilities for inspecting the goods. Buyers shall have the right to deal with any package on which there is no claim. When notifying a claim Buyers shall not have opened packages in excess of 10% of the quantity upon which a claim is made or 10 packages, whichever is the greater.

'(b) Claims for faulty adhesion must be made within nine months from the date of final landing return or delivery to private premises within the territorial limits covered by the Marine Insurance Policy but the identity of the goods must be established.

'(c) Where the standard of adhesion is specified in the contract, Buyers may reject in whole or in part during the period of nine months from the date of the final landing return or delivery to private premises within the territorial limits covered by the Marine Insurance Policy any goods that do not comply with such standard.

'(d) Buyers may reject in whole or in part during a period of twelve months from the date of final landing return or delivery to private premises within the territorial limits covered by the Marine Insurance Policy any goods containing any of the defects enumerated below:

(i) Plywood in which manufacture damp is present.

(ii) Plywood containing clips, wire or other metal fastenings in any form.

(iii) Where the packing or the plywood contains live worm providing Buyers can prove that such attack did not result from contamination after shipment.

The identity of the goods must be established.

'(e) Claims under this sub-clause (1) shall not exceed the total c.i.f. value of the goods under dispute, together with import duty and all proved expenses paid by Buyers in taking delivery from the vessel to warehouse and/or effecting delivery to customer's premises in the United Kingdom including any such expenses incurred in the handling, storage and insurance of the goods. In no event shall Sellers be liable for consequential loss.

'(2) Goods upon which there is a claim for rejection are to be stored by Buyers under cover and insured against usual risks but for the account and expense of Sellers in the event of the claim for rejection being upheld.'

The extension of the period in which buyers may make a claim or even reject the goods covered by the contract in the event of defects in manufacture is the most important difference from other claim clauses. It will be appreciated that proving that the goods on which there is a claim where purchased under a certain contract may be a difficult matter nine months later. Similarly, the proving that the packing for the plywood itself was not infected after shipment is also difficult, since species of *Lyctus* and furniture beetle are active in many parts of the UK.

Arbitration: Clause 16

'Any dispute and/or claim which it may be found impossible to settle amicably, shall in the case of claims of £200.00 or less be referred to a sole arbitrator to be mutually agreed upon between the parties. Claims of more than £200.00 shall be referred to two arbitrators, one to be appointed by each party, with power in such arbitrators, should they fail to agree, to appoint an umpire.

'If the reference is to a sole arbitrator and the parties fail to agree upon the appointment of such arbitrator or where the reference is to two arbitrators, in the event of either party failing to appoint their arbitrator within seven days of being requested through the Agent under this contract so to do or in the event of the arbitrators failing to agree upon the appointment of an umpire, then the arbitrator or umpire required shall, on the application of either party, be appointed by the President, or failing him, the Vice-President, for the time being of the Timber Trade Federation, whose appointment shall be binding upon the parties. Unless otherwise mutually agreed, every arbitrator and/or umpire shall be selected from the approved list of plywood arbitrators issued by the Timber Trade Federation or shall be directly engaged in the plywood trade.

'Any arbitrator and/or umpire shall be domiciled in the United Kingdom and the arbitration shall be held in the United Kingdom. Any award shall be final and binding upon both parties. The costs of such arbitration shall be at the discretion of the arbitrators or umpire who, in deciding as to costs, shall take into consideration the correspondence between the parties relating to the dispute and their respective efforts to arrive at a fair settlement.

'In other respects the said arbitration shall be subject to the English Arbitration Acts 1950, 1975 and 1979 or any subsisting statutory modification thereof or substitution therefor, except in the case of goods sold for delivery in Scotland to a buyer whose registered office or principal place of business is in Scotland when the said arbitration shall be held in Scotland and subject to the Arbitration (Scotland) Act 1894 or any subsisting statutory modification thereof or substitution therefor. However, it shall not be competent to an arbiter to state a case for the opinion of any Court notwithstanding Section 3 (1) of the Administration of Justice (Scotland) Act 1972, or any modification or re-enactment thereof. For the avoidance of doubt it is hereby declared that such arbiter shall have power to award damages and interest thereon.

'This clause shall not apply to any parcel shipped to countries other than the United Kingdom and Republic of Ireland.'

There is no essential difference between this arbitration clause and those in other contracts but it should be noted that reference to Scottish law is made.

N.B. It is intended that this type of Scottish provision will be included in all contract forms as and when they are reprinted.

Non-compliance: Clause 17

'In the case of non-compliance by Buyers with the provisions of Clause 11 (Payment) of this contract Sellers shall have immediate power of resale for Buyers' account after seven days notice in writing has been given.'

This clause does not appear in any of the softwood contracts but with slight variations of wording it is included in hardwood and fibre board building contracts. The effect of this clause is to override the normal property clause and permit an unpaid seller to resell the goods without having first obtained a court order. It is an unusual feature that over the years this non-compliance clause has regularly been written into hardwood contracts, a point albeit a minor one given away by buyers, while it does not even appear in the Russian softwood contract, which is not noted for any remarkable generosity of terms for buyers.

SCHEDULE OF AMENDMENTS TO PLYCIF 1957 FOR USE IN RESPECT OF PURCHASES OF PLYWOOD FROM CANADA

On face of contract, insert following as new line beneath 'include Cost, Freight and Insurance to . . .':

'Last date for obtaining Licences (see Clause 13). . . .'

Clause 7: Insurance

Delete existing clause and substitute therefor:

'Unless otherwise agreed Marine, War and Strike Risks Insurance to be covered by Sellers or their Agents for c.i.f. value plus 10% with Lloyds or a first class British Company under policies payable in sterling in Great Britain including Timber Trade Federation of the United Kingdom Insurance Clauses, Institute Strikes Riots and Civil Commotions Clauses (Timber Trade) and Institute War Clauses (Timber Trade). The cost of War and Strike Risks (as defined by the Institute War and Strike Clauses in force at the time the risk attaches) up to £0.125 per £100.00 to be borne by Sellers, any excess over such rate to be at Buyers expense. If Sellers are unable to effect War and Strike Risks Insurance on the goods for a premium not exceeding 2% or at all, they shall, at least seven working days before the vessel is expected to commence loading the contract goods advise Buyers through the Agents by cable of the expected loading date and either of their inability to insure or the rate quoted, whereupon Buyers shall promptly advise the Agents that they accept the rate quoted or that they will endeavour to effect such insurance themselves. In the latter event Buyers must either provide the Agents with proof that they have effected insurance against such risks for not less than the contract c.i.f. value or call upon the Sellers to ship the goods uninsured as to War and Strike Risks in which latter case Buyers shall if required open a confirmed Letter of Credit in the United Kingdom in favour of the Agents available against shipping documents or provide such other security as may be acceptable to Sellers and goods lost or not lost shall pay against presentation of shipping documents. Proof of Insurance or the provision of a Letter of Credit or other security shall be provided at least four working days before the expected loading date.

'Unless notice of Buyer's option has been received by Agents at least three working days prior to the expected loading date, Sellers shall ship the goods at the premium quoted provided such rate of premium is 10% or less, in which event the premium in excess of £0.125 per £100.00 shall be for Buyer's account but if the rate is more than 10% or War and Strike Risks Insurance is not obtainable then the contract in whole or in part as is affected shall be cancelled.

'Working days referred to in this Clause shall mean Monday to Friday inclusive, Saturdays Sundays Bank or Public Holidays being excluded.'

Clause 13: Licences and Duties

Delete existing clause and substitute therefor:

'The obligation to make application for and the cost of obtaining any export or import licence and to pay any export or import duty, charges or taxes which may be payable in respect of the export or import of the goods shall be upon Sellers and Buyers respectively.

'If either party having made application has failed to obtain any requisite licence within the time stated in the contract he shall have the right to cancel the contract provided prompt notice is given to the other party. If either party being obligated to obtain any requisite licence has not notified the other party by the day following the last date for obtaining licences that the requisite licence has been obtained the other party shall have the right of cancelling the contract subject to prompt notice being given. If any requisite licence is refused to a party or having been granted is subsequently cancelled prior to shipment such party shall forthwith advise the other party by telegram and either party shall have the right of cancelling the contract provided that notice of cancellation is given either in the said telegram or promptly on receipt thereof.'

Clause 14: Cancellation

Delete existing clause and substitute therefor:

'Should shipment be delayed beyond the time stipulated, Buyers shall have the right (without prejudice to their rights under the contract) to cancel the contract in whole or in part as is not shipped by the stipulated date, provided Buyers give notice in writing to the Agents who shall immediately cable Sellers accordingly. If 96" x 48" panels have already been despatched from the mill at the time of receipt by Sellers of such notice of cancellation, then Sellers shall, within three clear days of such time, notify Buyers through the Agents by cable accordingly and documentary proof of such despatch shall be sent by registered airmail within four days thereafter if required. In such event time for shipment of 96" x 48" panels shall be extended for a period of seventeen days from the date the goods left the mill. Sizes other than 96" x 48" which have been manufactured before receipt by Sellers of notice of cancellation must be accepted by Buyers provided Sellers supply promptly the specification of such goods as are manufactured and the goods are shipped within twenty-one days from the date of the receipt of notice of cancellation. Where sizes other than 96" x 48" are sold in sets Buyers shall only be required to accept complete sets. Should Sellers fail to comply with these provisions, either in respect of 96" x 48" panels or sizes other than 96" x 48" Buyers original notice of cancellation shall be deemed to be effective unless failure to ship within the extended period is due to force majeure.

'Sellers shall not be liable in damages for non-delivery or delay in shipment if such non-delivery or delay is due to force majeure. Should any vessel, or substitute, booked to lift goods under the contract and already named to Buyers be lost or delayed more than four weeks beyond the expiry of the shipment period as stated in the contract for the goods affected, this shall constitute force majeure. Without limitation the expression force majeure shall include Strikes, Lock-outs and any other causes whatsoever, beyond Sellers control affecting the manufacture and/or transportation and/or shipment of the goods.

'If Sellers claim that by reason of force majeure, they will be unable to ship within the time stipulated herein they shall give immediate telegraphic notice of such claim to Buyers through the Agents. Subject to Sellers proving force majeure to the satisfaction of the Buyers or the Arbitrators appointed hereunder Buyers shall not cancel the contract unless the delay in shipment will exceed nine weeks from the expiry of the shipment period stated in the contract, but should shipment not be possible within nine weeks of the expiry of the shipment period stated in the contract, then the contract in whole or in part as cannot be so shipped shall be cancelled.

'When the contract calls for declaration(s) and/or destination(s) and Buyers fail to give same in accordance with contract provisions, Sellers shall have the option of cancelling the contract in whole or in part to which the missing declaration(s) and/or destination(s) relate. Alternatively, in the case of 96" x 48" panels Sellers may ship such specification of grades and thicknesses contracted for as may be suitable to Sellers and in the case of sizes other than 96" x 48" have the option of shipping an equivalent quantity of 96" x 48" panels in the grades and thicknesses contracted for at prices in force for 96" x 48" at the time the contract was made. Such shipments shall be made to the port of Buyer's address, as stated in the contract, or the nearest suitable port available thereto and accepted and paid for by Buyers as provided by the contract. Should Sellers decide to exercise either of these options they shall notify Buyers through the Agents accordingly. Failure by Sellers to avail themselves of the options herein granted shall not affect in any way their right under the contract.

'In the event of war, whether declared or not, or national emergency, resulting in prevention of export or import (except by reason of licence) shipment of all or part of the contract should be rendered impossible within the time stipulated or within such extended time as is provided elsewhere in the contract, Sellers shall have the right of cancellation in whole or in part as shall be affected, effective immediately upon giving notice of such cancellation to Buyers through the Agents.'

SCHEDULE OF AMENDMENTS TO PLYCIF 1957 FOR USE IN RESPECT OF PURCHASES OF PLYWOOD FROM THE U.S.S.R: AMENDED 1976

Clause 3: Sizes

Delete existing clause and substitute therefor:

'The term "press" may include, in addition to the stated size, (a) sizes larger in width and/or length than the stated size, and (b) sizes within 4" in width and/or length smaller than the stated size.'

Clause 4: Quantity Variations

Delete existing clause and substitute therefor:

'Except in the case of boards cut to special sizes, Sellers at their option may ship 15% in footage more or less of each item of the specification, provided that the total quantity shipped against the contract be not varied by more or less than 7½%. In the case of boards to be cut to special sizes the exact quantity must be shipped as called for in the contract unless otherwise agreed between buyers and sellers.

'In the event of over-shipment of any item of the contract or of the total contract quantity Buyers shall not be entitled to reject the entire shipment but shall have the option, to be exercised within 3 clear days of receipt of the specification, of taking up the bills of lading and paying for the whole quantity shipped or of taking up the bills of lading and paying only for the contract quantity, rejecting the balance. If the excess is not apparent from the shipping documents Buyers shall exercise their option within 3 clear days of the final outturn of the goods at their ultimate destination. If Buyers elect to take the contract quantity only Sellers shall pay all extra expenses whatsoever incurred by Buyers in consequence of the over-shipment. In the event of under-shipment of any item of the contract or of the total contract quantity Buyers are to pay for the quantity shipped, but have the right to claim damages for such under-shipment.'

Clause 6: Marking

Delete existing clause and substitute therefor:

'Every package shipped under this contract to be legibly marked on two edges with size, quality, thickness and number of boards, and on one edge with Buyer's mark. Where packages or boards bear a trade mark the country of origin must be legibly marked thereon.'

Clause 7: Insurance

Delete existing clause and substitute therefor:

'Unless otherwise agreed maritime insurance to be covered by Sellers for c.i.f. value plus 10% under policies payable in sterling in Great Britain including the current Timber Trade Federation Insurance Clauses, Institute Strikes Riots and Civil Commotions Clauses (Timber Trade) and Institute War Clauses (Timber Trade).

'Notwithstanding the above, Sellers shall arrange to cover the goods against war (including mine) risks, also strikes, riots and civil commotions risks, on the Institute Clauses current at the date of sailing, but any premium in excess of £0.125 per £100.00 current at date of sailing payable for this cover shall be for Buyer's account. Should such cover be unobtainable, or if obtained be subsequently cancelled, Sellers shall give prompt telegraphic advice to Buyers, who shall have the right of effecting cover against such risks themselves (in which event the Buyers shall provide the Agents with proof of insurance against such risks for not less than the c.i.f. value before shipment) or of calling upon the Sellers to ship the goods uninsured as to war and strike risks. In the latter event Buyers shall, if required, open a confirmed Letter of Credit in the United Kingdom in favour of Seller's Agents available against shipping documents, or provide such other security as may be acceptable to Sellers.

'If war and strike risks cannot be covered by Sellers, or their Agents, or by Buyers within one month after the Agents have advised Buyers that the goods are ready for shipment, such part of the contract shall be deemed to be cancelled unless Buyers within 10 days give notice to Seller's Agents calling upon Sellers to ship the goods uninsured as to war and strike risks on the terms referred to above.'

Clause 8: Policies issued outside the UK

This clause to be deleted.

Clause 11: Payment

Delete existing clause and substitute therefor:
'Payment of the invoice amount shall be made by the Buyers to the Agents hereunder in cash in sterling without discount upon first presentation of and in exchange for shipping documents. Freight, unless prepaid, is to be deducted from the invoice and paid by the Buyers in terms of Bill of Lading. The goods sold hereunder are pledged with the State Bank of the U.S.S.R. and proceeds for the same belong to the State Bank of the U.S.S.R. as security for advances but the delivery of the documents by the Agents to the Buyers against payment of the invoice amount by the latter shall be a complete discharge of any pledge to or lien of the State Bank of the U.S.S.R., on either the goods or the documents. Invoice to be finally adjusted on proved contents of packages.'

Clause 12: Presentation of Documents

Delete existing clause and substitute therefor:
'If the documents are not presented to Buyers prior to the arrival of the steamer, Buyers shall nevertheless take up the documents on presentation, but any charges incurred through delay in presentation of documents unless due to causes beyond Seller's control shall be payable by Sellers unless previous sufficient particulars of shipment have been supplied to enable the consignment to be handled without delay or extra expense. Unless prepaid the freight

to be deducted from the invoice and paid by Buyers in terms of customary bill of lading.

'Shipping documents shall consist of clean on board bill(s) of lading, specification, invoice, certificate of origin where required, and policy or certificate of insurance, provided the latter certifies all risks in the contract to be covered. The bill(s) of lading shall not be rejected on the grounds that a number of packages (not exceeding two packages or 10%, whichever is the greater) be signed for in dispute but shall be taken up on a satisfactory indemnity.'

Clause 14: Cancellation

Delete existing clause and substitute therefor:

'Should shipment be delayed beyond the time stipulated, Buyers shall have the right (without prejudice to their rights under the contract) to cancel such part of the contract goods as are not shipped by the stipulated date, provided they give notice in writing to the Agents who shall immediately cable Sellers accordingly. If the goods concerned have already been despatched from the mill at the time of receipt by Sellers of such notice of cancellation then they shall, within three clear days of such time, notify Buyers through the Agents by cable accordingly and documentary proof of such despatch shall be sent by registered airmail within seven days thereafter if required. In such event time for shipment of press sizes shall be extended for a period of twenty-one days from the date the goods left the mill. Special sizes which have been manufactured before receipt by Sellers of notice of cancellation must be accepted by Buyers provided Sellers supply promptly the specification of such goods as are manufactured and the goods are shipped within twenty-one days from the date of the receipt of notice of cancellation. Where special sizes are sold in sets Buyers shall only be required to accept complete sets. Should Sellers fail to comply with these provisions, either in respect of press sizes or special sizes, Buyers original notice of cancellation shall be deemed to be effective unless failure to ship within the extended period is due to causes beyond the Seller's control.

'Sellers shall not be liable in damages for non-delivery or delay in shipment if such non-delivery or delay arises from causes beyond their control. If Sellers claim that by reason of any such cause beyond their control they will be unable to ship within the time stipulated herein they shall give telegraphic notice of such claim to Buyers through the Agents within a period of five days.

'Subject to Sellers proving that delay in shipment resulted from a cause beyond their control to the satisfaction of Buyers or the Arbitrators appointed hereunder, Buyers shall not cancel the contract unless such delay in shipment will exceed four weeks from the shipment date stipulated in the contract, and Sellers shall not be held liable for delivery under this contract beyond a period of three months.

'When the contract calls for declaration(s) and/or destination(s) and Buyers fail to give same in accordance with the contract provisions, Sellers shall have the option of cancelling that part of the contract to which the missing declaration(s) and/or destination(s) relate. Alternatively, in the case of press sizes, Sellers may ship an average specification and, in the case of special sizes, have the option of shipping an equivalent number of cubic metres of press sizes as may suit Sellers in the grades and thicknesses contracted for, at prices in force for press sizes at the time the contract was made. Such shipment shall be made to the port of Buyer's address, as stated in the contract, or the nearest suitable port available thereto and accepted and paid for by Buyers as provided by this contract. Should Sellers decide to exercise either of these options they shall notify Buyers through the Agents accordingly. Failure by Sellers to avail themselves of the options herein granted shall not affect in any way their rights under this contract.'

Clause 15: Claims

Delete existing sub-clauses (1) (b) and (1) (d) and substitute therefor:
    '(1) (b) Claims for faulty adhesion must be made within six months from the date of final landing return or delivery to private premises within the territorial limits covered by the Marine Insurance Policy but the identity of the goods must be established.
    '(1) (d) Buyers may reject in whole or in part during a period of nine months from the date of final landing return or delivery to private premises within the territorial limits covered by the Marine Insurance Policy any goods containing any of the defects enumerated below:

    (i) Plywood in which manufacture damp is present.
    (ii) Plywood containing clips, wire or other metal fastenings in any form.

The identity of the goods must be established.'

10.2 Plydef 1972 (amended 1976)

This contract form is adopted by the Timber Trade Federation of the UK and is headed 'Plywood Delivered Contract Form.' It is a c.i.f. contract and includes cost, all charges under the contract of affreightment, insurance and the cost of delivery of goods on road or rail transport to the destination named on the face of the form. Any differences between it and the terms of the Plycif contract are given below.

Definition: Clause 1

This clause is identical with the Plycif terms.

Quality: Clause 2

This clause is identical with the Plycif terms.

Declarations: Clause 3

'Where required, Buyers undertake to provide declarations in due time to enable despatch to take place. All declarations are to be confirmed by Sellers promptly upon receipt thereof.'
    This clause is an additional one and does not appear in the Plycif contract.

Quantity Variations: Clause 4

Although the wording of this clause is slightly different from the Plycif terms, its meaning is the same.

Packing: Clause 5

'The goods shall be despatched from the mill in undamaged condition, adequately protected, and shall be loaded to facilitate fork-lift discharge in lift loads not exceeding 1000 kilograms, comprising only one size, one thickness and one quality and there shall so far as possible be uniformity as regards the number of boards in lift loads containing the same size, thickness and quality. Cross-grained boards shall be stacked separately.'
    This clause is more explicit than the Plycif terms since it specifies the limit of the lift load weight.

Marking: Clause 6

'Every lift load shipped under this contract to be legibly marked on two adjacent edges with size, quality, bonding standard, thickness and number of boards, and on one edge with lift load number and Buyer's mark.'
    This clause refers to lift loads instead of packages and has an additional reference to bonding standard.

Insurance: Clause 7

When compared with the Plycif terms, this clause has one essential difference. The cost of war and strike risk insurance to be paid by sellers is £0.15 per £100.00, whereas in the Plycif contract it is £0.125.

Policies issued outside the UK: Clause 8

This clause is identical to the Plycif terms.

Property in Goods: Clause 9

'Property in goods to be deemed for all purposes (except retention of Vendor's lien for unpaid purchase price) to have passed to Buyers when goods have arrived at United Kingdom Ferry Terminal.'

This differs from the terms of the Plycif contract which states that property passes when goods are shipped. As this contract is on delivered terms, the difference is self-explanatory.

Delivery: Clause 10

'When the goods are despatched from the mill, Sellers shall notify the Agents promptly, by cable or Telex, and shall send by airmail complete original documents, one complete set only of documents comprising invoice, specification, insurance certificate, certificate of origin where applicable and delivery order or carrier's receipt shall accompany the goods; the invoice accompanying the goods shall be clearly marked "For customs purposes only – to be retained by Forwarding Agents at port of entry". Sellers or Carriers Forwarding Agents at the port of loading shall notify the Agents promptly by cable or Telex the date of loading on board vessel, stating vessel's name, contract reference and Carriers Forwarding Agents at the port of discharge who shall be responsible for clearance of the goods through Customs on behalf of Buyers. Buyers undertake to make prompt repayment of any Import Duty, charges or taxes for which they be liable, to enable clearance of Customs to be effected without delay. Buyers shall be responsible for unloading the vehicle without delay during normal working hours, between 0900 and 1630, Mondays to Fridays, on arrival at the final destination stated in the contract, unless otherwise agreed. Upon failure to do so (or if Sellers exercise their right to withold delivery until the purchase price is paid in accordance with the contract) any rent, insurance or other charges or expenses thereafter incurred in connection with the goods shall be for Buyer's account.'

This clause does not appear in the Plycif contract for obvious reasons since this contract is on delivered terms. The clause is self-explanatory.

Payment: Clause 11

Although the wording of this clause is slightly different from the Plycif terms, its only difference is reference to delivery order signed on behalf of the port terminal or other person having custody of the goods or carrier's receipt, whereas the Plycif terms stipulate cash without discount on presentation of and in exchange for shipping documents.

Licences and Duties: Clause 12

This clause is identical with the Plycif terms.

Cancellation: Clause 13

'Should delivery be delayed beyond the time stipulated, Buyers shall have the right (without prejudice to their rights under this contract) to cancel such part of the contract goods as are not delivered by the stipulated date, provided they give notice in writing to the Agents who shall immediately cable Sellers accordingly. If the goods concerned have already been despatched from the mill at the time of receipt by Sellers of such notice of cancellation, Sellers shall, within 3 clear days of such time, notify Buyers through Agents by cable accordingly and documentary proof of such despatch shall be sent by registered airmail within 4 days thereafter if required, in which case Buyers shall accept the delivery of the goods. Special sizes which have been manufactured before receipt by Sellers of notice of cancellation must be accepted by Buyers provided Sellers supply promptly the specification of such goods as are manufactured and the goods are despatched within twenty-one days from the date of the receipt of notice of cancellation. Where special sizes are sold in sets Buyers shall only be required to accept complete sets. Should Sellers fail to comply with these provisions, either in respect of standard sizes or special sizes, Buyer's original notice of cancellation shall be deemed to be effective unless failure to deliver or despatch as the case may be within the extended period is due to causes beyond Seller's control.

'Sellers shall not be liable in damages for non-delivery or delay in delivery if such non-delivery or delay arises from causes beyond their control. If Sellers claim that by reason of any such cause beyond their control they will be unable to deliver within the time stipulated herein they shall give immediate telegraphic notice of such claim to Buyers through the Agents.

'Subject to Sellers proving the delay in delivery resulted from a cause beyond their control to the satisfaction of Buyers or the Arbitrators appointed hereunder, Buyers shall not cancel the contract unless such delay will exceed four weeks, and Sellers shall not be held liable for delivery under this contract beyond a period of three months from the date stipulated.

'When the contract calls for declarations and/or destinations and Buyers fail to give same in accordance with the contract provisions, Sellers shall have the option of cancelling that part of the contract to which the missing declarations and/or destinations relate. Alternatively, in the case of standard sizes, Sellers may ship an average specification and, in the case of special sizes have the option of shipping an equivalent quantity of standard sizes as may suit Sellers in the grades and thicknesses contracted for, at prices in force for standard sizes at the time the contract was made. Such goods shall be delivered to the destination as stated in the contract, or the nearest suitable port available thereto. Should Sellers decide to exercise either of these options they shall notify Buyers through the Agents accordingly. Failure by Sellers to avail themselves of the options herein granted shall not affect in any way their rights under this contract.'

Although the wording of this clause is slightly different from the Plycif terms, its meaning is much the same. To suit the terms of a delivered contract, the word 'delivery' is used instead of 'shipment' but otherwise the periods are the same in respect of notification, etc. It should be noted that unlike the Plycif contract, which refers to press sizes, this contract only mentions special sizes.

Claims: Clause 14

There is no essential difference between this clause and the Plycif terms, except that delivery is mentioned instead of shipment, but periods are the same in respect of notification, etc.

Arbitration: Clause 15

This clause is identical with the Plycif terms.

Non-Compliance: Clause 16

This clause is identical with the Plycif terms.

10.3 Parcif 1963 (amended 1976 and 1979)

This contract form is adopted by the Timber Trade Federation of the UK and is headed 'Particle Board C.I.F. Contract Form'. It is very similar in terms to the Plycif contract — apart from the different characteristics of the product — so the essential differences are shown hereunder.

Quality: Clause 1

This clause refers to standard quality, whereas the Plycif refers to average quality.

Quality Variations: Clause 2

This clause is identical with the Plycif terms.

Packing: Clause 3

'The goods shall be despatched from the mill in undamaged condition and shall be adequately packed. Each package/pallet shall contain only one size, one thickness and one density and there shall be uniformity as regards the number of boards in packages/pallets containing the same size, thickness and density. The number of boards per package/pallet of special sizes shall be left to the discretion of Sellers unless otherwise arranged.'

This is self-explanatory, the only difference being reference to density.

Marking: Clause 4

'Every package/pallet shipped under this contract to be legibly marked on two edges, where possible two adjacent edges, with size, thickness, density and number of boards, and on one edge with package/pallet number and Buyer's mark. Where packages/pallets or boards bear a trade mark the country of origin must be legibly marked thereon.'

Here, again, the question of density is mentioned.

Insurance: Clause 5

This clause is identical with the Plycif terms.

Policies issued outside the UK: Clause 6

This clause is identical with the Plycif terms.

Shipping: Clause 7

This clause is identical with the Plycif terms.

Property in Goods: Clause 8

This clause is identical with the Plycif terms.

Payment: Clause 9

This clause is identical with the Plycif terms, except that pallets are mentioned in addition to packages.

Presentation of Documents: Clause 10

The wording of this clause is slightly different from the Plycif terms but it is a minor question of reference to pallets in addition to packages.

Licences: Clause 11

This clause is identical with the Plycif terms.

Cancellation: Clause 12

This clause is identical with the Plycif terms, except that only special sizes and not press sizes are mentioned. Otherwise the periods for cancellation and delivery are the same.

Claims: Clause 13

'(1) (a) Subject to the provisions of Clause 13 (1) (b) no claims for defective quality, manufacture and/or packing shall be made in respect of goods shipped under this contract unless written notice of claim together with reasonable particulars is given to the Agents within thirty days from the date of final landing return of delivery to private premises within the territorial limits covered by the Marine Insurance Policy. The reasonable particulars shall state whether the claim is in respect of quality, manufacture and/or packing, together with such other information as Buyers can furnish at the time. Any statement shall be without prejudice and conditional upon the facilities for inspecting the goods. Buyers shall have the right to deal with any package/ pallet on which there is no claim. When notifying a claim Buyers shall not have opened packages/pallets in excess of 10% of the quantity upon which a claim is made or 10 packages/pallets, whichever is the greater.

(b) Buyers may reject in whole or in part during a period of twelve months from the date of final landing return or delivery to private premises within the territorial limits covered by the Marine Insurance Policy any goods containing any of the defects enumerated below:—

(i) Particle Board in which the bonding is defective.

(ii) Particle Board which, when despatched from the factory, contains foreign matter in any form which might damage tools or machinery.

The identity of the goods must be established.

'(c) Claims under this sub-clause (1) shall not exceed the total c.i.f. value of the goods under dispute, together with import duty and all proved expenses paid by Buyers in taking delivery from the vessel to warehouse and/or effecting delivery to customer's premises in the United Kingdom, including any such expenses incurred in the handling, storage and insurance of the goods. In no event shall Sellers be liable for consequential loss.

'(2) Goods upon which there is a claim for rejection are to be stored by Buyers under cover and insured against usual risks but for the expense of Sellers in the event of the claim for rejection being upheld.'

This varies from the Plycif terms because thirty days are allowed for submission of reasonable particulars for a claim instead of twenty-one days and the defects from which the product may suffer are different from plywood. In other respects, there is little difference.

Arbitration: Clause 14

The wording of this clause is the same as in the Plycif contract, except that claims of £100.00 or less shall be referred to one arbitrator, whereas the Plycif has been amended to £200.00. This is a mere formality, since all contracts are slowly being amended to conform.

Non-Compliance: Clause 15

This clause is identical with the Plycif terms.

10.4 Pardel 1973 (amended 1976)

This contract form is adopted by the Timber Trade Federation of the UK and is headed 'Particle Board C.I.F. and Delivered Contract Form'. On the face of the form it states that all prices include cost, all charges due under the contract of affreightment, insurance and the cost of delivery of goods on road or rail transport to the destination named. Any differences from the terms of Parcif contract are given below.

Quality: Clause 1

'Sellers guarantee that the goods delivered under this contract will be of their usual quality and manufacture as at present supplied to the United Kingdom.'

The only difference in this clause is 'usual quality' instead of 'standard quality'.

Quantity Variations: Clause 2

Although the wording of this clause is slightly different from the Parcif terms, its meaning is the same. It contains one additional stipulation: 'Goods over-delivered to be stored by Buyers under cover and insured against usual risks but for account and expense of Sellers.'

Declarations: Clause 3

'Goods are only to be shipped against Declarations and Buyers undertake to provide Declarations in due time to enable despatch to take place. All Declarations are to be confirmed by Sellers promptly on receipt thereof.'

This is an additional clause and does not appear in the Parcif contract.

Packing: Clause 4

'The goods shall be despatched from the mill in undamaged condition, adequately protected to withstand the normal risks of transit to the contractural destination and shall be loaded to facilitate fork lift discharge in loads not exceeding 1000 kilograms, unless otherwise agreed, comprising only one size, one thickness and one quality and there shall so far as possible be uniformity as regards the number of boards in lift loads containing the same size, thickness and quality. Where, by mutual agreement, boards are loaded on edge, they shall be properly secured.'

This clause is more explicit than the Parcif terms since it specifies the limit of the lift load weight.

Marking: Clause 5

'Every lift load shipped under this contract to be legibly marked, where practicable on two adjacent edges or otherwise on two long edges, with size, thickness, density, number of boards and such other marks as may be necessary to identify the goods.'

This clause differs from the Parcif terms, since it refers to lift loads and not packages/pallets and it does not mention trade marks and country of origin.

Insurance: Clause 6

When compared with the Parcif terms, this clause has one essential difference.

The cost of war and strike risk insurance to be paid by sellers is £0.15 per £100.00 instead of £0.125.

Policies issued outside the UK: Clause 7

This clause is identical with the Parcif terms.

Property in Goods: Clause 8

'Property in goods to be deemed for all purposes (except retention of Vendor's lien for unpaid purchase price) to have passed to Buyers on presentation of and in exchange for Delivery Order signed on behalf of the United Kingdom Ferry Terminal or by another person having custody of the goods, or Carriers receipt, whichever shall be the earliest.'

This differs from the Parcif terms, which state that property passes when the goods are shipped. As this contract is on delivered terms, the difference is self-explanatory.

Documentation and advice of Shipment: Clause 9

'When the goods are despatched from the mill Sellers shall ensure that Buyers are notified promptly, by cable or telex, and shall send by airmail complete original documents, one complete set only of documents comprising invoice, specification, insurance certificate, certificate of origin where applicable and delivery order or carriers receipt shall accompany the goods; the invoice accompanying the goods shall be clearly marked "for Customs purposes only – to be retained by forwarding agents at port of entry". Sellers shall ensure that Buyers are notified promptly, by cable or telex, the date of loading on board vessel, stating vessel's name, contract reference and name of carriers forwarding agents at the port of discharge.'

This clause does not appear in the Parcif contract for obvious reasons, since this contract is on delivered terms. The clause is self-explanatory.

Clearance of Customs: Clause 10

'(a) Unless otherwise agreed Sellers to be responsible for U.K. Customs clearance.

'(b) Buyers undertake to make prompt payment of any import duty, charges or taxes for which they may be liable, to enable clearance of Customs to be effected without delay.'

Delivery: Clause 11

'(a) Sellers, their hauliers, or their forwarding agents to be responsible for giving Buyers during normal working hours, a minimum of 24 hours, or one clear working day, notice of intended delivery to final destination.

'(b) Buyers shall be responsible for unloading the vehicle without unreasonable delay during normal working hours, on arrival at the final destination stated in the contract unless otherwise agreed. Upon failure to do so any rent, insurance or other charges or expenses thereafter incurred in connection with the goods shall be for Buyer's account.

'(c) Should Buyers defer or amend delivery, any agreed additional expenses to be for Buyer's account.'

Payment: Clause 12

Although the wording of this clause is slightly different from the Parcif terms, its only difference is reference to Delivery Order signed on behalf of the port terminal or other person having custody of the goods or Carriers receipt. The Parcif terms stipulate cash without discount on presentation of and in exchange for shipping documents.

Licences and Duties: Clause 13

This clause is identical with the Parcif terms.

Cancellation: Clause 14

This clause is identical with the Parcif terms.

Claims: Clause 15

This clause is identical to the Parcif terms.

Arbitration: Clause 16

The wording of this clause is the same as in the Parcif contract except that it states that claims of £200 or less be referred to a sole arbitrator and those of more than £200 to two arbitrators instead of £100.

Non-Compliance: Clause 17

'(a) In the case of non-compliance by Buyers with the provisions of Clause

12 of this contract Sellers shall have immediate power to re-sell for Buyer's account after seven days notice in writing has been given.

'(b) If Sellers exercise their right to withhold delivery until the purchase price is paid in accordance with the contract, any rent, insurance or other charges or expenses thereafter incurred in connection with the goods shall be for Buyer's account.'

This clause is slightly different from the Parcif terms but is self-explanatory.

10.5 Britfibre 1978

This contract form is adopted by the Fibre Building Board Federation and is headed 'Fibre Building Board C.I.F. Contract Form'. It is the only contract form which is outside the jurisdiction of the Timber Trade Federation of the UK. While its terms and conditions are similar in many respects to those in other panel product contracts, the wording is quite different and is mostly quoted in full. In the preamble on the face of the contract there is provision for the insertion of the company with which the goods are insured at Seller's option.

Quality: Clause 1

'The goods shall be of merchantable quality and shall in any event be of quality at least equal to the Sellers usual quality in respect of board presently being imported into the country of destination.' In effect, this is the same as the term 'shipper's usual'.

Sizes: Clause 2

'When used the term "Full Press Size" signifies the maximum size produced by the factory. It is understood that unless otherwise agreed Buyer's specification will comprise complementary sizes which will leave no waste.'

Quantities: Clause 3

'When used the term "about" shall mean that Sellers at their option may ship in respect of any bill of lading a margin of 2½ per cent in quantity more or less on any or every item of the specification.' This percentage is the same as in other contract terms but does not specify any time limit for notification nor does it mention over- and under-shipment.

Packing: Clause 4

'Packing shall be as specified in the Contract and, save where otherwise provided, shall be properly packed for export to the country of destination to be despatched in undamaged condition from Seller's warehouse or quay, properly protected. There shall be uniformity in number of boards per package as regards both size and thickness of contents. Each package to contain only one size and thickness. The number of boards per package shall be in accordance with Sellers usual packing unless otherwise agreed.'

Marking: Clause 5

'Every package shipped under this contract to be legibly marked with trademark, country of origin, size, thickness, number of boards and weight, in addition to any other marks specified.'

This clause is different in wording from the other panel product clauses but, in effect, is much the same in meaning.

Insurance: Clause 6

'(a) Marine Insurance to be covered by Sellers or their Brokers on their behalf in Sellers or Buyers country for c.i.f. value plus 10 per cent with a first class Insurance Company registered in Sellers or Buyers country. The insurance to be subject to Institute Cargo Clauses (All Risks) and Institute Cargo Clauses (Extended Cover).

'(b) War and Strike Risks (as defined by the Institute War and Strike Clauses including Extended Cover Clauses in force at the time the contract of insurance is entered into) shall be covered by Sellers, if possible, any premium in excess of 25p per £100 to be borne by Buyers. If these risks be covered by Buyers, proof of insurance must be lodged before shipment with Seller's Representatives.

'If Sellers are unable to effect war risk insurance on the goods for a premium of maximum £2 per £100 they shall give Buyers immediate telegraphic advice and Buyers shall thereupon have the option of endeavouring to effect war risk insurance themselves or accepting the increased premium or of calling upon Sellers to ship the goods uninsured. In every event Buyers to give Sellers Representatives prompt notice after receipt of advice of Seller's inability to insure at the aforesaid rate of the option they intend to exercise.

'(c) Should it not be possible to cover such insurance or should insurance whether effected by Sellers or Buyers be cancelled by insurers, Sellers or Buyers as the case may be shall give prompt telegraphic advice to the other party, and Buyers shall thereupon have the option of cancelling the contract or of calling upon Sellers to ship the goods uninsured.

'If Buyers call upon Sellers to ship the goods uninsured they shall provide, before the goods are put on board, such security for payment as may be required by Sellers or their Representatives and shall pay goods lost or not lost, against presentation of documents the value of the goods shipped at contract prices.

'(d) Any additional cover requested by Buyers to be effected by Sellers if possible but for Buyer's Account.

'(e) If insurance is effected by Sellers other than with Lloyds or a British Insurance Company, Sellers shall ensure that the insurance will include the following provisions:

(i) Any question as to the interpretation of the Insurance Policy to be decided according to English Law, the jurisdiction of the English Courts being admitted by the Insurers.

(ii) Settlement to be made in London and names of paying brokers and/or Agents, to whom notice of claim is to be sent and who shall be authorised to accept service of writ for and on behalf of the insurers, to be stated on Policy.

(iii) Where the insured amount is expressed both in sterling and in another currency, claims shall be adjusted at the rate of exchange thereby indicated. If the insured amount is expressed in a currency other than sterling, the settlement shall be effected at the rate in force for sight bills in London on the date of the Policy.'

This clause does give the seller the option of insuring outside the UK provided that the TTF clauses are included.

Shipment: Clause 7

'Shipment means placing goods on board at original shipping port or at other port at Shipper's option unless otherwise agreed. All goods to be stowed under deck.'

Unlike some other contract terms, this clause leaves no doubt as to when shipment begins and gives no option as to where the goods must be stowed.

Shipping Documents and Payment: Clause 8

'(a) Shipping documents shall consist of a complete set of original on board Bills of Lading, Invoices with Specifications, Certificate of Origin if required and Policy or Certificate of Insurance provided that the latter specifies the risks covered. Documents shall not be rejected on the grounds that a number of packages totalling up to and including 10% of the total Shipment or 50 packages whichever is the less be signed for in dispute but shall be taken up on a satisfactory indemnity.

'(b) Payment for invoice amount less any freight payable at destination to be made by nett cash on first presentation of and in exchange for shipping documents. If the contract is signed by Seller's Representatives such payment is to be made to the said Representatives.

'(c) In cases of shortage or overage and/or wrong dimensions and/or wrong descriptions, Invoice to be finally adjusted on proved contents of packages.

'(d) If the documents are not presented to Buyer prior to the arrival of the vessel, Buyers shall nevertheless take up the documents on presentation. Any charges incurred through delay in presentation of the documents shall be payable by Sellers unless previous sufficient particulars of shipment have been supplied to enable the consignment to be handled without delay or extra expense.'

This is one of the few contracts which do not mention credit terms but, as mentioned before, it is still possible for the buyer to obtain credit directly from the agent in the form of a Bill, and to all intents and purposes it is the same as if the seller were granting the credit.

Exceptions: Clause 9

'(a) In case the manufacture and/or shipment of any of the goods be delayed or prevented by Act of God, war, mobilisation, blockade, strikes, lockouts, prohibition of export or import, drought, floods, ice, accident to mill, fire, shortage of fuel or power or any other cause beyond Seller's control, they shall not be responsible for any damages arising therefrom provided immediate notice be given to Buyers.

'(b) In case the manufacture and/or shipment be delayed or prevented by any cause beyond Seller's control, except war, prohibition of export or import or blockade, Sellers to have the right to extend the stipulated time of delivery by six weeks. Should Sellers be unable to deliver within such extended time, Buyers and Sellers shall have the option of cancelling the contract or postponing the shipment to such date as may be mutually agreed upon. In the case of Buyers cancelling the Contract such cancellation to be subject to the stipulation in paragraph (d) below. Sellers may exercise their right to extend the original shipping date by six weeks only provided that they, if requested, submit to Buyers proof of the reason which has caused the delay.

'(c) Should prohibition of export or import (other than export or import conditional only upon licence) war or blockade at any time before the shipping date, original or postponed according to above, prevent Sellers from manufacturing and/or shipping or Buyers from receiving the goods, the contract shall be cancelled.

'(d) Should for any other reason than those set out in paragraph (a) above shipment be delayed beyond the time stipulated Buyers shall have the right (without prejudice to their rights under the contract) to cancel such part of the contract as does not comply with the stipulated shipment dates, but only if they give notice in writing to Seller's Representatives in time to enable them to notify Sellers by cable before the goods are despatched from the Mill. Should Buyers cancellation instructions be received by Sellers after the goods have left the Mill, Sellers to notify their Representatives by cable to this effect within six days from the receipt of Buyer's cancellation instructions to the said Representatives, in which case Buyers shall accept the goods.

'(e) If the contract calls for specifications and/or destinations, Buyers to declare these in writing not later than six weeks before the earliest time of shipment or of each instalment. Failing such advice, Sellers shall have the option of cancelling the contract quantity to the extent of the undeclared specification(s) and/or destination(s) or (in the case of an undeclared specification) shipping an average specification pro rata to the total specification remaining for shipment under the contract and (in the case of an undeclared destination) shipping to the Port of Buyers domicile or nearest available thereto. Any shipments made by Sellers under the said option shall be accepted and paid for by Buyers as provided in the contract. Sellers shall notify Buyers by telegram which options hereunder they propose to exercise. Failure by Sellers to exercise such options shall not affect in any way their rights under the contract.'

This clause is more comprehensive than most and is divided into five parts. Part (a) relieves the sellers of liability for damages due to prevention or delay of shipment beyond seller's control, provided that prompt notice is given to buyers. Part (b) virtually automatically extends the delivery time by six weeks for 'any . . . cause beyond Seller's control'. It is important for the buyer to realise that the period of shipment is extended by this six weeks period, since the buyer is bound to accept delivery if made in this extended period – always provided, of course, that the sellers have submitted proof of the reason for delay. If the sellers cannot deliver the goods within the additional six weeks, the date of shipment may be extended by mutual agreement or either party can cancel. If buyers decide to cancel the contract they must do this in accordance with part (d). Part (c) provides for automatic cancellation if manufacture or shipment is prevented by war, etc., or prohibition of import or export, etc. Part (d) gives the buyer a right of cancellation if shipment is delayed beyond the stipulated date (it does not include the extra six weeks) for any reason – other than those beyond seller's control. In general, it must be assumed that any delay will normally be claimed by sellers to be caused by circumstances beyond their control. This clause also sets out the procedure to be adopted by buyers if they elect to cancel – the important point being that the sellers must receive notice of the buyer's cancellation before the goods are despatched from their mill. It is essential, therefore, for the buyers to notify the sellers immediately they cancel the contract. Part (e) concerns large contracts for shipment in instalments over a period of time where the specification and port of destination are left open, to be notified by buyers to sellers before each shipment. If such notifications are not received by sellers by six weeks before the date of shipment, the sellers have the option of cancelling (to that extent) or of shipping a specification pro rata to the specification remaining to be shipped – to the nearest port to the buyer's domicile.

Claims: Clause 10

'(a) In the event of any claim for quality, quantity, condition or packing the Buyer shall not reject any of the goods but shall accept and pay for them as provided above. Goods upon which there is a claim for rejection must be stored under cover by the Buyer and insured against all risks but for the account and expense of the Seller in the event and to the extent that the claim of the Buyer for rejection is upheld.

'Reasonable particulars of claim, as above, must be sent in writing to the Seller's representative within a reasonable time and in any event not more than thirty days from final delivery of goods into a public warehouse or wharf or private premises within the limits covered by the Marine Insurance Policy. Reasonable particulars shall mean a statement as to whether the claim is for quality, quantity, condition or packing together with such other information as the Buyers can furnish at the time. Any such statement shall be without prejudice to the Buyer's right to amend the same in any way and shall also be conditional upon facilities being available for inspection of the goods.

'(b) The Buyers have the right to deal with any package on which there is no claim without prejudice to their right to claim on any intact package. Packages opened by Buyers shall not exceed 10% of the number of packages in the total consignment or 10 packages whichever is the greater. No claim shall exceed the total C.I.F. value of the goods under dispute together with proved costs paid by the buyers taking delivery from the vessel to the final destination as specified overleaf including import duty, storage and insurance.'

Although this clause limits the buyer's right of rejection by stating '. . . the Buyer shall not reject any of the goods but shall accept and pay for them', this does not mean to prevent them from rejecting goods which are materially different from those described in the contract. In the case of shortages or overages, wrong dimension or description, this is covered in clause 8 (c) which states: 'Invoice to be finally adjusted on proved contents of packages.' This is declaratory of the law, since a buyer is not obliged to pay for goods which he has not received.

Property in Goods: Clause 11

'Property in goods to be deemed for all purposes (except retention of vendors lien for unpaid purchase price and the right of stoppage in transit) to have passed to Buyers when the goods have been put on board at original shipping port.'

Each Shipment a Separate Contract: Clause 12

'Each shipment under the Contract shall be considered as a separate contract and default on one or more shipments shall not invalidate the balance.'

This clause does not appear in any of the other contract forms and it should be associated with clause 9 (e).

Non-Compliance and Late Payment: Clause 13

'(a) in the case of non-compliance by Buyers with payment under Clause 8 (b) Sellers have the right to suspend further shipments until payment for the goods shipped has been received and shall have the power of re-sale for Buyer's account after seven days' notice in writing has been given.

'(b) The Buyer shall be liable to pay interest on any sums which have not been paid on the due date at the rate of 1½% per month calculated on a day to day basis.'

This clause does not appear in any of the softwood contracts, but part (a), covering the resale in case of non-compliance, is found in hardwood and panel products contracts, even though the wording varies. Part (b) is an unusual stipulation and is not found in any other contracts.

Import and Export Licences and Duties: Clause 14

'The Contract is subject to Import and Export Licences if required. Export Duty and/or Export Taxes (if any) to be paid by Sellers. Import Duty and Import Licence (if any) to be paid by Buyers.'

This clause is unusual since it stipulates who is responsible for the payment, whereas other contracts stipulate payment on a shared basis.

Arbitration: Clause 15

'Should any dispute and/or claim arise between the parties hereto out of or in connection with the contract which the parties fail to settle amicably, the same shall forthwith be referred to a sole Arbitrator to be mutually agreed between the parties, or, failing such agreement, to two Arbitrators one to be appointed by the Sellers and one by the Buyers. Such Arbitrators to appoint their Umpire.

'The Arbitrators and Umpire shall be engaged in or conversant with the Fibre Building Board Trade.

'In the event of a party failing to nominate an Arbitrator within fourteen days of the receipt of a notice from the other party calling upon them to do so or the Arbitrators fail to appoint an Umpire within fourteen days of the latest date of their appointment then the appointment of such Arbitrator or Umpire, as the case may be, shall be made by the President for the time being of the Fibre Building Board Federation upon the request of either party.

'Any notice required under this clause shall be given to Seller's Representative by registered letter and shall constitute effective notice to the Seller. Should there be no Representative of Sellers named in the contract, then notice shall be given direct to Sellers by cable.

'Any award shall be final and binding upon the parties and the obtaining of an Award shall be a condition precedent to any right of action here-under.

'The costs of such Arbitrations shall be in the discretion of the Arbitrators or Umpire who, in reaching their decision thereon, shall have agreed to the efforts of the respective parties to reach an amicable settlement.

'The Arbitration shall be held in the United Kingdom and in all other respects than mentioned above the said arbitration shall be subject to the English Arbitration Act, 1950, or any statutory modification thereof or substitution therefor except in the case of goods sold to Scottish buyers for shipment to a Scottish port when the said arbitration shall be in Scotland subject to the Arbitration (Scotland) Act, 1894, The Administration of Justice (Scotland) Act, 1972, or any statutory modification thereof or substitution therefor and arbitrators shall have the power to assess and award damages and interest thereon.'

Although the wording of this clause is different from other contract terms, its meaning is substantially the same. There are a few exceptions. Reference to a sole arbitrator is not limited by the amount of the claim, and in the event of a party failing to appoint an arbitrator within fourteen days, the appointment is made by the President of the Fibre Building Board Federation and not the TTF. The clause also covers arbitrations held in Scotland and, in addition to the Arbitration (Scotland) Act, 1894, mentions the Administration of Justice (Scotland) Act, 1972.

Severability: Clause 16

'In the event of any clause or part of a clause in these Terms and Conditions being declared invalid then that shall not affect the rest of the Terms and Conditions hereof.'

This clause is not found in any other contract forms but is self-explanatory.

Waiver: Clause 17

'No waiver by either party whether express or implied of any term hereof or any breach or default by either party shall constitute a continuing waiver nor should a waiver in respect of any one term or breach prevent either party from enforcing all or any of its rights in respect of any other term or breach hereof.'

There is no doubt a good reason for including this unusual clause but it is rather obscure.

Applicable Law: Clause 18

'These terms and conditions and any contract incorporating them shall be governed by and interpreted in accordance with the provisions of English Law.'

The need for this clause is doubtful, since all contracts are subject to the Sale of Goods Act and, in any event, the arbitration clause refers to Scotland and Scottish law.

11　Arbitration

11.1 General

The arbitration clause in a contract is the ultimate safeguard for the buyer, that if in his opinion the seller has failed to fulfil the contract in all respects, he can demand arbitration, and if it is decided that he has good cause for complaint, he will be awarded compensation. This applies not only to goods shipped but also to non-shipment; in fact, *any* dispute under the contract, if not settled amicably, has to be dealt with under the arbitration procedure.

It should not be overlooked that arbitration is something which, if invoked, must be paid for, by one side or both, and may possibly be a costly business, whereas 'amicable settlement' costs the buyer nothing. In such a trade as timber, complaints and claims are inevitable, yet some of the largest firms in the trade in the UK do not have one arbitration in years. Shippers' agents ask no fee for putting their experience at the service of the parties to effect 'amicable settlement'. There are, however, cases where there is so fundamental a difference of honest opinion between buyer and seller that arbitration is the best course to adopt.

It is important to both seller and buyer, under the TTF contracts, in view of the ultimate allocation of costs according to the efforts of either party to reach amicable settlement, that they should make promptly a serious effort to settle the dispute and to commit those efforts to writing as evidence. The custom is for the seller's agent to supply the shipper with detailed particulars of the buyer's complaint and also an unbiased inspection report on the goods complained of, to enable him to estimate the justice of the buyer's complaint and claim.

While a seller's agent is not legally responsible either for the carrying out of the contract or the payment of an arbitration award, his reputation is involved, and it is extremely seldom that ultimate failure to pay a properly executed award has been recorded. Arbitrators and umpires are at liberty to award more than the sum claimed or less than the sum offered, which may, in the case of a claim judged to be unfounded, be nothing at all.

In the eyes of the law an arbitration is an adjudication and the powers and position of an arbitrator or umpire are very similar to those of a judge; in fact, he is sometimes referred to as a lay judge.

The Arbitration Acts, 1950, 1979, in general, govern arbitrations in England, give arbitrators and umpires their power, and enable the courts to enforce their awards. The provisions of these Acts may be varied by the terms of the submission to arbitration, as is frequently the case with arbitration clauses in TTF contract forms. Several of these variations are examined in this chapter.

Up to the time of the passing of the Arbitration Act, 1979, where the matter in dispute involved a point of law rather than one of commercial practice, the arbitrators or their umpire, could, either at the request of one or both of the parties or of their own volition, submit the question for the decision of the court. This process, known as 'stating a case', has been altered under the new Arbitration Act, which received the Royal Assent on 4 April 1979, by abolishing the present 'case stated' procedure, which had come to be used by certain interests as a means of postponing the implementation of an award and thus tending to discourage adoption of 'London arbitration' for settlement of disputes. In place of the 'case stated' procedure, the Act introduces a more limited right of appeal on points of law only, but the parties in many arbitration agreements can exclude this right should they wish to do so.

11.2 The Reference Note

Before there can be any arbitration, the parties (that is, the buyer and the seller) must have agreed to submit disputes between them to arbitration; in practice, in the timber trade the buyer and the seller do this by virtue of the existence of an arbitration clause in the printed forms of contract used in the trade. The arbitration clause amounts to an agreement to submit future disputes to arbitration. The arbitration clauses do not, however, name the arbitrators themselves nor do they give them their jurisdiction. The buyer and the seller do this usually by means of a 'reference note' (sometimes known as a 'submission note') which sets out the terms of reference for the arbitrators in a particular arbitration, limits the disputes to be settled by the arbitrators and also names the parties concerned, describes the matter in dispute, and names the arbitrators. It is not essential that there should be a reference note; sometimes, when one of the parties is unco-operative, it might be necessary for a buyer, for example, to act in default of the seller's willingness to arbitrate by applying the default procedure contained in the arbitration clauses, or where this does not exist in the clauses, in the Arbitration Act itself. In any event, provided that both parties appoint their arbitrators in writing (e.g. by letter) and in doing so they give the arbitrators their jurisdiction and set out the matter to be resolved by arbitration, then this is sufficient.

The reference note usually takes the following form:

A DISPUTE HAVING ARISEN between . . . . the Buyer,
and . . . . the Seller, with regard to the (quality)
(condition) of . . . . pieces . . . . about
. . . . m^3, shipped per m.s. . . . .
at . . . . to . . . . , under Bill of Lading dated
. . . . against Contract dated London the . . . .
IT IS HEREBY AGREED to leave the matter to the arbitration of Mr. . . . .
of . . . . acting for the Buyers, and Mr. . . . .
of . . . . acting for the Sellers, who are hereby empowered to appoint
an Umpire, thoroughly conversant with the class of goods from the port of shipment
named; the decision of the Arbitrators, or of their Umpire, to be final and binding on
both parties in the terms of the above-named Contract.

In the event of SOLE ARBITRATION, then: –
IT IS HEREBY AGREED to leave the matter to the Sole Arbitration of Mr . . . .
. . . . of . . . . whose decision shall be final and binding
on both parties in the terms of the above named Contract.

11.3 The Rules of Arbitration

GENERAL

Arbitration is governed by the Arbitration Act, 1950. The rules and
regulations laid down in this Act are modified by the arbitration clauses in
various TTF contracts.

The Uniform and Albion contracts state:

'Any dispute and/or claim regarding *shipped goods* which it may be found
impossible to settle amicably shall be referred to arbitration to be held in the
country of destination of the goods and, except as otherwise herein provided,
to be conducted according to the Law of that country and in the case of
Scotland the arbitrators shall have the power to assess and award damages.

'Any other dispute and/or claim whatsoever arising out of this contract
which cannot be settled amicably shall be referred to arbitration. Such
arbitration shall be held in England and conducted in accordance with the
English Arbitration Act, 1950, or any subsisting statutory modification
thereof or substitution therefor. Such Arbitrators and their Umpire need not
be members of the Timber Trade. In all other respects the provisions of this
clause shall apply.'

In most other contract forms there is not the same differentiation between
shipped and unshipped goods, the wording generally being as follows:

'In other respects the said arbitration shall be subject to the English
Arbitration Act 1950 or any subsisting statutory modification thereof or
substitution therefor except in the case of goods sold for delivery in Scotland
to a Buyer whose registered office or principal place of business is in Scotland
when the said arbitration shall be subject to the Arbitration (Scotland) Act
1894 or any subsisting statutory modification thereof or substitution therefor

but Arbitrators acting under the provisions of such Arbitration (Scotland) Act 1894 shall have power to assess and award damages.

'All such arbitrations shall be held in the United Kingdom.

'This clause to apply to shipments to the United Kingdom and the Republic of Ireland only.'

There may be minor differences in the arbitration clauses between the various TTF contract forms and, in the event of a claim having to be referred to arbitration, it is always advisable to check the clause of the relevant contract. The Russian contract is a major exception to these terms and contains an amendment to the printed clause 15 which reads as follows:

Russian Contract (1952) — Arbitration Clause

'It is hereby understood and agreed that any disputes under this contract which cannot be settled amicably, except such as refer to the quality, condition, measurement, or manufacture of, or correctness of documents for goods shipped, shall be referred to the U.S.S.R. Chamber of Commerce Foreign Trade Arbitration Commission in Moscow, whose decision shall be final and binding upon both parties. Claims under any of the above excepted headings shall, if not amicably settled, be dealt with in accordance with the provisions of Clause 15 of the printed conditions.

'It is understood and agreed that any amendments or additions to the printed Conditions of Contract, which may be agreed between V/O Exportles and the Timber Trade Federation of the U.K., will apply to this Contract, except in respect of quantities which may have been shipped before such agreement is reached.'

This is in effect 'arbitration in Moscow for unshipped goods'.

Arbitration on the exceptions detailed in the clause, amounting to 'shipped' goods, is controlled by clause 15 of the contract, which, in general terms, follows the usual TTF contract forms with arbitration subject to the English Arbitration Act, 1950, etc. The question of Scottish arbitration is discussed at the end of this chapter.

The Unicif and American hardwood contract forms stipulate that the buyers shall accept custody of any goods shipped, and make payment for them 'without prejudice', before proceeding to arbitration.

Unicif and American Hardwood — Arbitration Clause

'Should any dispute arise with respect to any matter connected with this Contract the Buyers shall nevertheless accept custody of the goods if and as shipped and make due payment, but such acceptance and payment shall be without prejudice'.

This goes rather further in limitation of buyers' right of rejection than the "Rejection" clause inserted in many softwood contracts, which limits buyers' right of rejection to disputes concerning dimensions and/or quality, unless the whole shipment is involved (see page 291).

APPOINTMENT OF ARBITRATORS

The appointment of arbitrators and the appointment of umpire are the points usually covered in most detail in the arbitration clauses in timber contracts.

Uniform, Albion

'The reference shall be to a sole Arbitrator mutually agreed upon. In default of such agreement claims of more than £200 shall be referred to two Arbitrators, one to be appointed by each party, and claims of smaller amounts to a sole Arbitrator to be appointed as stipulated in the next paragraph.

'If either party fails to appoint their Arbitrator within seven days after being requested through the Agents under the contract so to do, or if the claim is for not more than £200, then the Arbitrator thus required shall be appointed by the President or failing him by the Vice-President of the Timber Trade Federation of the United Kingdom on the application of either party. The said Arbitrators shall be members of the timber trade or Arbitrators recognised by the Timber Trade Federation of the United Kingdom or by the Swedish Wood Exporters' Association and the Finnish Sawmill Owners' Association.'

The agent will have acted as intermediary between the buyer and the seller in attempting to arrive at amicable settlement.

A panel of names of experienced members of the trade is maintained by the TTF, from which arbitrators can be appointed when required, but selection is by no means limited to any list, and usually each side selects some person in whom they have confidence to understand their view of the dispute. The panel of names maintained by the TTF is listed in the TTF *Annual Handbook*, with the individual's special experience, and these are members of the Timber Arbitrators Association of the UK.

The arbitration clause in these 1964 contracts was amended in 1969, and paragraph 7, regarding 'unshipped goods', now reads as follows:

'Any other dispute and/or claim whatsoever arising out of this contract which cannot be settled amicably shall be referred to arbitration. Such Arbitration shall be held in England and conducted in accordance with the English Arbitration Act, 1950, or any subsisting statutory modification thereof or substitution therefor. Such Arbitrators or their Umpires need not be members of the timber trade. In all other respects the provisions of this clause shall apply.'

This clause applies for shipments to the UK and the Republic of Ireland only.

A dispute concerning unshipped goods will rarely be a matter in which the commercial experience of a timber trade arbitrator will be of much avail. It is much more likely to revolve around fine points of law and evidence from the seller's country to support either the *force majeure* or war clause. For this reason the arbitration clause in the Uniform contract is worded to permit the arbitrators', if necessary, being legal arbitrators.

While for small claims there is only one arbitrator, it is far better if these small claims are settled without going to arbitration. In general, it is unwise to take extreme measures for minor differences.

The Nubaltwood charter incorporates an arbitration clause providing for reference to arbitration in accordance with the Arbitration Act, 1950, or the Scottish Arbitration Act of 1894.

The Arbitrators and umpires shall be 'commercial men', and unless the parties agree to the contrary, the arbitration is to be held in London or, in the case of charterers or receivers who are resident in Scotland, at a place in Scotland to be named in the charter.

The claimant's arbitrator *must* be appointed, and notice of the appointment given to the other side, within 12 months of the date of the final discharge of the vessel; otherwise the claim is barred.

The Sovietwood charter also incorporates an arbitration clause, but in somewhat simpler terms. No distinction is made between Scottish and English buyers. The arbitrators do not have to be 'commercial men' and, provided that a claim has been lodged within 12 months, there is no time limit within which the claimant must appoint his arbitrator.

It is often assumed that arbitrators are entitled to act as advocates for the party appointing them, or that they have power to negotiate a settlement of the dispute on behalf of the party appointing them setting out the terms of such settlement in the form of an award. This is not so; when the arbitrators are appointed, they constitute the tribunal by whom the dispute is to be settled. Until the matter is submitted to an umpire, the arbitrators must remain impartial, and act judicially, as though they were both jointly the umpire in all their dealings in relation to the arbitration until they find themselves in a position in which they must disagree as to the award. The arbitrators are not bound to disagree. If one arbitrator considers that the case of the party appointing him is wrong, he is perfectly at liberty to agree the form of the award with the other arbitrator so that the matter need never be referred to an umpire. It is only when the arbitrators are unable to agree as to the form the award should take that the umpire, in effect, then takes over. At that stage it is generally recognised that, in a sense, the individual arbitrators may then act as advocates for the party appointing them, in that they submit to the umpire their own point of view of their party's case and, if necessary, their party's own contentions. The arbitrators have no power to negotiate a settlement as such; they, or the umpire, should adjudicate on the case as it is presented to them and make their award only on the basis of the merits of the case, and not on the basis of what the arbitrators would regard as a fair settlement, in disregard of the merits.

A sole arbitrator, or an umpire, remains throughout absolutely impartial; in the event of the arbitrators being unable to agree, and referring the matter to the decision of the umpire, they will each then represent to him their view of the case, and the umpire may thus find a considerable measure of agreement which he does not need to review in detail, and he then merely has to settle the outstanding differences. On the other hand, the umpire may decide that he should consider the whole matter from the start as if he had originally been appointed sole arbitrator: those are matters which are left to his discretion.

APPOINTMENT OF UMPIRE

If the two arbitrators cannot agree on an award in the case, the final result must be decided by the umpire, who is selected as below:

Uniform, Albion

'Should the Arbitrators fail to agree upon an award they shall appoint an Umpire. Should they fail to agree as to such appointment, then each Arbitrator shall select one name from a list of 10 persons. In the case of Finnish goods the list shall comprise 5 persons designated by the Finnish Sawmill Owners' Association and the other 5 by the Timber Trade Federation of the United Kingdom. In the case of Swedish goods the list shall comprise 5 persons designated by the Swedish Wood Exporters' Association and the other 5 by the Timber Trade Federation of the United Kingdom. The person to act as Umpire shall be the name drawn by lot from the two so selected by the Arbitrators. Should the person so chosen by lot be prevented from acting the Arbitrator who selected that name may thereupon appoint another person from the relevant list who shall act as Umpire. The lists in question may be revised on May 1st each year but vacancies occurring during a year shall be filled by the Association concerned.

'Inspection by the Arbitrator(s) or the Umpire, as the case may be, of the goods claimed upon shall take place within fourteen days after their appointment, unless they consider inspection unnecessary.

'An award shall be final and binding upon both parties. The costs of such arbitration shall be left to the discretion of the Arbitrator(s) or Umpire. In deciding as to costs the Arbitrator(s) or Umpire shall take into consideration the correspondence between the parties relating to the dispute and their respective efforts to arrive at a fair settlement.

'This clause applies to contracts for shipments to the United Kingdom and the Republic of Ireland only.'

The umpire must be appointed strictly as above. Unless it is specifically set out in the reference note, the arbitrators may *not* delegate their duties in the selection of the umpire. The arbitrators are under no obligation to obtain the approval of the buyers or sellers to their selection of umpire. Although it is not necessary to have the appointment of the umpire in writing, it should be endorsed upon the reference note.

In the case of softwood contract forms other than the Uniform and Albion, and in the case of hardwood and plywood contract forms: the nomination of the umpire, if the arbitrators are unable to agree as to his appointment, is made by the President or Vice-President of the TTF or the Chairman or Deputy Chairman of the relevant section of the TTF.

AWARD BY ARBITRATORS

By the Arbitration Act an arbitrator or umpire shall have power to make an award at any time, but the High Court may, on application of any party to a reference, remove an arbitrator or umpire who fails to use all reasonable dispatch in entering on and proceeding with the reference and making an award.

RELEGATION TO UMPIRE

If the arbitrators allow the time for making the award (that is, the three months period or the extended period) to expire without having made an award, or if they cannot agree on an award, then the umpire may enter the arbitration in place of the arbitrators.

AWARD BY UMPIRE – TIME LIMIT

If the case is relegated to an umpire, he must make his award within one month after the original or extended time for the arbitrators to make their award has expired. Within this time he may in writing extend the time for making his award.

EVIDENCE, WITNESSES, EXAMINATION

Subject to any legal objections, the arbitrators or umpire may subject either of the parties to examination upon oath or affirmation. The parties must produce, if required, all books, letters or documents in their possession.

If any witnesses are called, the arbitrators or umpire may examine them under oath or affirmation.

Most official contract forms state a time limit for the appointment, inspection and making the award. These vary quite considerably, and the relevant terms should be carefully checked.

AWARD

An award by arbitrators or umpire is final and binding on the parties concerned. Only one final award can be made, but there is power for an interim award, if the necessity for this arises and provided that the power is not excluded by the terms of the reference note.

The award must be: (1) in writing (a usual form of award is appended); (2) within the required or extended time; (3) certain, final and explicit as to how effect is to be given to it; (4) not bad on the face of it (in the same way that a judge's decision must be legally correct); (5) to cover the matters submitted for arbitration, no more and no less; (6) signed by both arbitrators in each other's presence.

Award

A DISPUTE having arisen between . . . . .the Sellers and . . . . the Buyers, in regard to the quality (condition) (manufacture) of about . . . . m^3 of . . . . marked . . . . , shipped per m.s. . . . . at . . . . under Bill of Lading dated . . . . against Contract dated . . . . , and the same having been referred to the undersigned as Arbitrator(s) by Submission dated . . . . I(WE) having carefully surveyed the goods above referred to where stored at . . . . on . . . . and having considered the documents and correspondence relative to this dispute submitted to me(us)
DECIDE AND AWARD that the Sellers pay to the Buyers the sum of £. . . . . in full and final settlement of all claims under this submission.
I(WE) ALSO AWARD that the expense of this Arbitration and award shall be paid (as to . . . . per cent.) by the Sellers (Buyers).
                              (Signed)

Expenses of this Arbitration
                    Fees   . . . .
                    Expenses   . . . .

                    Total   . . . .
                                              (Initialled)

COSTS

The TTF clause leaves the matter of costs entirely in the hands of the arbitrators and umpire.

'An award shall be final and binding upon both parties. The costs of such arbitration shall be left to the discretion of the Arbitrator(s) or Umpire. In deciding as to costs, the Arbitrator(s) or Umpire shall take into consideration the correspondence between the parties relating to the dispute and their respective efforts to arrive at a fair settlement.'

Although the costs are left to the discretion of the arbitrators or umpire, this is a discretion which should be exercised 'judicially' — that is, the arbitrators should follow the usual rule of making the losing party pay all the costs (even where the award is in the form of a special case), unless there are strong reasons to the contrary, such as the consideration of the efforts to arrive at a fair settlement as mentioned above.

11.4 The Award

AMOUNT OF AWARD AND DAMAGES

When a warranty in a contract has been broken, the buyer may claim either or both of the following:

(1) *A reduction of price*. This might even be a claim for the full amount. If the claim is for the quality of the goods, it is based upon the difference in value between the goods delivered and those contracted for.

(2) *Damages* — being the estimated loss to the buyer directly and naturally caused in the ordinary course of events by the breach of warranty by the seller.

TAKING UP THE AWARD

When the award has been made by the arbitrators or umpire, signed with a statement of the costs, it is put in a sealed envelope and the parties to the arbitration are informed that the award is ready and will be delivered on payment of costs amounting to so much. It is usually the buyer who 'takes up' the award by paying the costs and thereafter proceeds to put it into effect. If the arbitration awards a sum about half-way between what the buyer claimed and what the seller was willing to pay, the arbitrators may decide that the costs shall be equally divided between them, and it may then seem to the parties that it was a pity they did not come to 'amicable agreement' to split the difference and save the costs. Extreme cases are not unknown where, for instance, the buyer has had to pay costs exceeding the amount awarded to him, leaving him finally out of pocket, or, on the other hand, the seller has had to pay all the costs in addition to an award of the full amount claimed.

If the arbitration awards a sum to be paid by the seller to the buyer, the latter sends the award for collection to the seller's agent, who, in turn, obtains the seller's authority to pay it.

Although there is no obligation on the arbitrators to do so, it is possible, if requested, for the arbitrators to communicate to the party appointing them how the award was arrived at, but it is repeated that no arbitrator can be forced to do so. This will only take place after the award has been 'taken up'. It will readily be understood that such information, which may be, and often is, verbal and confidential, may be of considerable service by way of guidance in handling any future similar dispute.

Any reasons for an award should, as a matter of practice, be kept off the face of the award itself, which should simply state the decision. If reasons are given, this should be done only unofficially.

ENFORCING THE AWARD

The Arbitration Act, 1950, states in Section 26:

'An award on an arbitration agreement may, by leave of the High Court or a judge thereof, be enforced in the same manner as a judgment or order to the same effect.'

For the purposes of enforcement, an award has the same status as a judgment, and by taking out the appropriate form of writ, the applicant may seize such property as the defaulting party may have within the jurisdiction of the court. This method of enforcement is quite simple, but is limited by the jurisdiction of the court, which does not extend to foreign countries.

When one of the parties is in a foreign country outside the jurisdiction of the court, as is the shipper of timber, the enforcement can only be effected by a legal action on the award. This can be a costly and lengthy process, and its success depends to a great deal on the law of the foreign country concerned.

SETTING THE AWARD ASIDE

There is no appeal, as such, from the award of arbitrators or an umpire, to the courts. Thus, if one party feels that the umpire has come to a wrong decision, he nonetheless has to accept the award. However, the courts have a general jurisdiction over arbitrators and umpires, but this jurisdiction is exercised only within certain limits. Thus, if there is an error of law which appears on the face of the award (e.g. if an umpire gives reasons for his decision in the award itself, and these reasons are wrong in law), then either party may apply to the court for the award to be set aside. Further, Section 23, Arbitration Act, 1950, states:

'(2) where an arbitrator or umpire has misconducted himself, or an arbitration or award has been improperly procured, the High Court may set the award aside.'

Misconduct is thus a further ground for setting aside.

Misconduct refers to legal as well as personal misconduct. A sole arbitrator or umpire must not do anything which is not in itself fair and impartial. It is deemed misconduct in an arbitration for him to receive relevant information from one party which is not disclosed to the other. If he receives such a communication from one party, he should immediately inform the other. In the same manner he should not grant a private interview to one party without the other being represented.

The improper appointment of the umpire by the arbitrators constitutes misconduct — for example, relegating the selection of the umpire to another person.

Finally, there are the more obvious items of misconduct, fraudulent concealment of matters that should be disclosed, wilful deception of arbitration or umpire, bribery of the arbitrators, etc.

11.5 Scottish Arbitrations

Whereas the Sale of Goods Act, 1893, makes special provision for those parts of the act affected by the law of Scotland, there are other Acts which do not do so. Among the latter is the English Arbitration Act, 1950, arbitration in Scotland being governed by Scottish law and the Arbitration (Scotland) Act, 1894.

Under Scottish law arbitrators are only able to judge a dispute commercially, leaving the successful party to take the award to court to get damages assessed and valued. This has been overcome by the inclusion in contracts of the following clause:

'Any dispute arising under this agreement shall be governed by the Arbitration (Scotland) Act, 1894. However, it shall not be competent to an Arbiter to state a case for the opinion of any Court notwithstanding Section 3 (1) of the Administration of Justice (Scotland) Act, 1972, or any modification or re-enactment thereof. For the avoidance of doubt it is hereby declared that such arbiter shall have power to award damages and interest thereon.

'In other respects the said arbitration shall be subject to the English Arbitration Act, 1950, or any statutory modification thereof or substitution therefor except in the case of goods sold to Scottish buyers for shipment to a Scottish port when the said arbitration shall be in Scotland subject to the Arbitration (Scotland) Act, 1894, or any statutory modification thereof or substitution therefor *and arbitrators shall have power to assess and award damages*.'

12 Importing Wood Goods — Customs and Dock Procedure — Claims

12.1 Importing Wood goods

GENERAL

The importer of any goods into the UK is required by law to deliver a written declaration to Customs in respect of them. Under Section 28 of the Customs and Excise Act, 1952, the 'entry' (— that is, Customs declaration) must be in such form and manner and contain such particulars as the Commissioners may direct.

The main purposes of Customs entries are: to enable any duty, levy, value added tax or other charges payable on the goods to be assessed and collected, to control the grant of reliefs from duty, etc., and to provide information from which trade statistics are compiled. Penalties, including forfeiture of the goods, may be imposed for failure to supply full and accurate particulars. It follows that accuracy and care is required in the completion of the various documents involved.

In recent years, and particularly since the UK became a member of the European Economic Community (EEC), the procedure and its accompanying tariffs have changed considerably and continue to change each year. Therefore, because of its complexity and constant changes, it is impossible to give all the accurate details in one chapter. The information which is given is based on the annual TTF document (sixteenth edition), which is effective from January 1978 and is issued by the Federation's Statistician, Charles Norman. Because it is so complex, only the most significant aspects can be quoted, and it must be left to those involved to obtain current information from the appropriate authorities. This can be obtained from any Collector of Customs and Excise or from HM Customs and Excise, Kings Beam House, Mark Lane, London, EC3R 7HE. VAT Notices can be obtained at any local VAT office.

IMPORT DUTIES

Both the pre-accession United Kingdom Tariff and the EEC Common

Customs Tariff are based on the internationally agreed system of classification known as the Customs Co-operation Council Nomenclature (formerly Brussels Nomenclature). Certain minor changes in the wording of the published international text have been made for legal reasons, but these do not affect the practical scope of the headings. The Nomenclature provides a systematic classification for all the goods of international commerce, designed to ensure, with the aid of general Interpretation Rules and Notes to the sections and chapters, that each article falls in one place only within the Customs Tariff.

The Tariff and procedure is described in detail in the following publications, obtainable from HM Stationery Office.

Nomenclature for the Classification of Goods in Customs Tariffs 1976.

Explanatory Notes to the Customs Co-operation Council Nomenclature (These *Notes* describe the goods falling in each heading, often giving details of their physical characteristics, method of production and uses. In addition, they include a commentary on Interpretative Rules and an explanation of the practical effects of the various section and chapter notes.)

Alphabetical Index to the Explanatory Notes and Customs Co-operation Council Nomenclature

Customs Co-operation Council Nomenclature Classification Opinions (including amending supplements)

DEFINITIONS

Excise duties apply to beer, hydrocarbon oils, matches, mechanical lighters, spirits, perfumed spirits, tobacco products, wine, made-wine, cider and perry whether imported or produced in the UK. In the case of imported goods, the excise duties are chargeable in addition to any customs duties which may be payable.

Revenue duty on imported tobacco is mainly a fiscal duty, but the full rate incorporates a protective element equal to the customs duty of the EEC Common Customs Tariff.

Customs duties. In this Tariff duties other than excise, revenue and anti-dumping duties are referred to as customs duties.

Tariff quotas. Certain imported goods may be chargeable at a reduced rate or a nil rate of duty and/or levy within the limits of a tariff quota. When a quota has been exhausted, further imports will be chargeable with the standard rate of duty or levy.

Meaning of per cent. Except where the context otherwise provides, per cent or the symbol % means percentage of value.

Value. The value to be declared on import entries for goods subject to duty *ad valorem* is the value set out in EEC Regulations and applied by Section 258 of the Customs and Excise Act, 1952, as amended by the European Communities Act, 1972. Briefly stated, this value is the price the goods would fetch, at the time the Customs accept the entry for home use, on a sale in the open market between a buyer and a seller independent of each other, giving delivery to the buyer at the place of introduction into the customs territory of the Community. The seller bears the freight, insurance, commission and all other costs, charges and expenses incidental to the sale and delivery. The exception is duty or tax chargeable in the customs territory of the Community. However, in the case of goods imported in the course of trade within the Community the value is to be declared on the basis of a delivery to the buyer at the port or place of importation into the UK.

When goods are imported under a contract of sale, their value is normally based on the contract price, provided that the price corresponds to that of an open market sale and is adjusted as necessary to take account of any circumstances of the sale which differ from those covered in the preceding paragraph, and provided that the goods are entered within a reasonable time of the date of the contract.

For converting to sterling an amount expressed in foreign currency, the most recent selling rate published on the date of presentation of the entry should be used.

The value as above must be the value at the time the goods were entered for customs duty payment. When warehoused goods are entered for customs duty payment, the value may be different from the time of entry for warehousing at importation.

Value added tax. All goods imported from abroad are liable to VAT either at a positive or the zero rate, whether or not they are imported on purchase. VAT on imported goods is chargeable and payable as if it were a duty of customs, and the rate that is in force at the time of entry for home use is delivered to the Customs. VAT is chargeable at importation, but if the importer is a registered taxable person importing goods in the course of a business carried on by him, he may remove the goods without payment, provided that he accounts for the tax due in his VAT account.

The value for VAT is defined in Section 11 of the Finance Act, 1972, and is the value of the goods as defined for *ad valorem* duty purposes (whether or not the goods are actually liable to *ad valorem* duty) plus any customs duty or levy payable on importation into the customs territory of the Community together with any excise duty payable on importation of the goods into the UK.

GSP. The UK operates the Generalised System of Preferences of the EEC, for which quota levels and ceilings have been fixed for the year January to December. Goods covered by certain Tariff headings are granted G.S.P. treatment within the ceilings established for the EEC as a whole. Within each ceiling there is an inner ceiling, being the maximum amount of any particular item which may be imported into the community from any one particular beneficiary country. When a ceiling or maximum amount is reached, the Commission may bring a regulation into force reimposing the full rate of duty. Information is given monthly in the TTF Bulletin and other circulars about current position of the ceilings.

CUSTOMS DUTIES AND OVERSEAS TRADE DESCRIPTIONS   44.05   Section IX

Tariff heading and Trade description	Special Provisions	Tariff/Trade Code Number	Unit(s) of Quantity	Full Rate of Duty
44.05 WOOD SAWN LENGTHWISE, SLICED OR PEELED, BUT NOT FURTHER PREPARED, OF A THICKNESS EXCEEDING 5 MM:				
A. Small boards for the manufacture of pencils	¶¶	4405 1000	1.kg 2.cub.m	Free
B. Coniferous wood of a length of 125 cm or less and of a thickness of less than 12.5 mm:				5%
European redwood (*Pinus sylvestris*)		4405 2010	1.kg 2.cub.m	
European whitewood (*Abies alba/Picea abies*)		4405 2020	1.kg 2.cub.m	
Douglas fir (*Pseudotsuga taxifolia*)		4405 2030	1.kg 2.cub.m	
Western hemlock (*Tsuga heterophylla*)		4405 2040	1.kg 2.cub.m	
Western red cedar (*Thuja plicata*)		4405 2050	1.kg 2.cub.m	
Other– Mixed consignments of European redwood and whitewood .		4405 2081	1.kg 2.cub.m	
Mixed consignments of douglas fir and western hemlock . . .		4405 2082	1.kg 2.cub.m	
Mixed consignments of western hemlock and balsam (hembal)		4405 2083	1.kg 2.cub.m	
Other		4405 2099	1.tonne 2.cub.m	
C. Other:				Free
Tropical hardwood– Limba (afara)		4405 3100	1.kg 2.cub.m	
Utile		4405 3300	1.kg 2.cub.m	
Other– Keruing		4405 3910	1.kg 2.cub.m	
Mahogany		4405 3920	1.kg 2.cub.m	
Obeche (wawa)		4405 3930	1.kg 2.cub.m	
Ramin		4405 3940	1.kg 2.cub.m	
Teak (*Tectona grandis*)		4405 3950	1.kg 2.cub.m	
Meranti		4405 3960	1.kg 2.cub.m	
Sapele		4405 3970	1.kg 2.cub.m	
Afrormosia		4405 3980	1.kg 2.cub.m	
Iroko		4405 3990	1.kg 2.cub.m	
Other		4405 3999	1.kg 2.cub.m	
Other– Coniferous wood– European redwood (*Pinus sylvestris*)		4405 4010	1.kg 2.cub.m	
European whitewood (*Abies alba/Picea abies*)		4405 4020	1.kg 2.cub.m	
Douglas fir (*Pseudotsuga taxifolia*)		4405 4030	1.kg 2.cub.m	
Western hemlock (*Tsuga heterophylla*)		4405 4040	1.kg 2.cub.m	
Western red cedar (*Thuja plicata*)		4405 4050	1.kg 2.cub.m	

Continued on next page

¶¶ Goods entered under this subheading are subject to Customs end-use control–see

Notice No. 770.
1 January 1978

Tariff heading and Trade description	Special Provisions	Tariff/Trade Code Number	Unit(s) of Quantity	Full Rate of Duty
44.05 C. – *continued*				Free
Other–				
Mixed consignments of European redwood and whitewood		4405 4060	1.kg 2.cub.m	
Mixed consignments of douglas fir and western hemlock ..		4405 4070	1.kg 2.cub.m	
Mixed consignments of western hemlock and balsam (hembal)		4405 4080	1.kg 2.cub.m	
Other		4405 4099	1.kg 2.cub.m	
Other–				
Oak		4405 7100	1.kg 2.cub.m	
Beech (*Fagus silvatica*)		4405 7300	1.kg 2.cub.m	
Poplar		4405 7400	1.kg 2.cub.m	
Walnut...........................		4405 7500	1.kg 2.cub.m	
Other–				
Birch (*Betula*)......................		4405 7910	1.kg 2.cub.m	
Other		4405 7999	1.kg 2.cub.m	
[44.06] –				
44.07 RAILWAY OR TRAMWAY SLEEPERS OF WOOD:				
A. Injected or otherwise impregnated to any degree		4407 1000	1.kg 2.cub.m	5%
B. Other		4407 9000	1.kg 2.cub.m	3%
[44.08] –				
44.09 HOOPWOOD; SPLIT POLES; PILES, PICKETS AND STAKES OF WOOD, POINTED BUT NOT SAWN LENGTHWISE; CHIP-WOOD; DRAWN WOOD; PULPWOOD IN CHIPS OR PARTICLES; WOOD SHAVINGS OF A KIND SUITABLE FOR USE IN THE MANUFACTURE OF VINEGAR OR FOR THE CLARIFICATION OF LIQUIDS; WOODEN STICKS, ROUGHLY TRIMMED BUT NOT TURNED, BENT OR OTHERWISE WORKED, SUITABLE FOR THE MANUFACTURE OF WALKING-STICKS, UMBRELLA HANDLES, TOOL HANDLES OR THE LIKE:				
A. Drawn Wood		4409 0100	kg	6%
B. Pulpwood in chips or particles		4409 1000	kg	Free
C. Wooden sticks, roughly trimmed but not turned, bent, or otherwise worked, suitable for the manufacture of walking-sticks, umbrella handles, tool handles or the like		4409 5000	kg	3%
D. Other		4409 9000	kg	4%
[44.10] –				
44.11 FIBRE BUILDING BOARD OF WOOD OR OTHER VEG-ETABLE MATERIAL, WHETHER OR NOT BONDED WITH NATURAL OR ARTIFICIAL RESINS OR WITH OTHER ORGANIC BINDERS:				11%
Hardboard–				
Unworked.............................		4411 1000	1.kg 2.sq.m	
Worked		4411 2000	1.kg 2.sq.m	
Other–				
Unworked......................		4411 3000	1.kg 2.sq.m	
Worked		4411 9000	1.kg 2.sq.m	

1 January 1978

DUTIES ON TIMBER AND WOOD PRODUCTS

These are set out in Section IX, Chapter 44, of the Tariff. A reproduction of one part of this is given in table 12.1. It will be seen that while the Tariff headings and trade descriptions are broadly the same as in earlier years, there are other columns which provide for special provisions, tariff/trade code number, unit(s) of quantity and full rate of duty. The first column indicates whether the item is subject to, say, tariff quotas (TQ) or anti-dumping duties (AD). The second column indicates the code number which is appropriate for every item imported, and this is prefixed by the section number of the Tariff heading — in this case 44.05. The third column indicates the standard units of quantity and the final column, the full rate of duty. As mentioned earlier, it must be noted that the latter item is subject to revision and could well have changed since this was written. Reference should always be made to a current copy of the Customs and Excise Tariff before documents are completed.

12.2 Import Entry Procedure

GENERAL

It is of the utmost importance that great accuracy is used in completing the necessary forms to effect entry of the goods, especially since the revised system is more complex than hitherto. Under the 1952 Act, penalties are prescribed for failing to supply the necessary particulars. A general outline only can be given of this procedure, which is liable to amendment from time to time and may even differ slightly in different ports.

In 1977 a revised Form C.10 was introduced, known as the General Import Entry. This form is designed for use for most types of importation and replaces the following earlier forms:

C.10	(Home use — 1976 and earlier)	C.275	(Process inwards)
C.12	(Bill of Sight)	C.275S	(Process inwards)
C.26	(Exhibitions)	C.277	(Temp. importation)
C.111	(T.I. Samples)	C.294	(T.I. Magnetic tapes, etc.)
C.188	(M.O.D.)	C.599	(Adjustment)
C.217	(Repair or re-exportation)	GW 10	(Warehousing)

The following Customs notices also deal with importation:

Notice No.	Title
37	Coding lists used in completion of documents
101	Deferment of duty
252	Valuation of imported goods
461	General information for importers
702	VAT — Imports

A list of all notices published by HM Customs and Excise is given in Notice
No. 1000. All are free of charge.

THE GENERAL IMPORT ENTRY — FORM C. 10

The completion of this form is appropriate in the majority of importations
and a copy in reduced size is given in figure 12.1. Importers and agents are

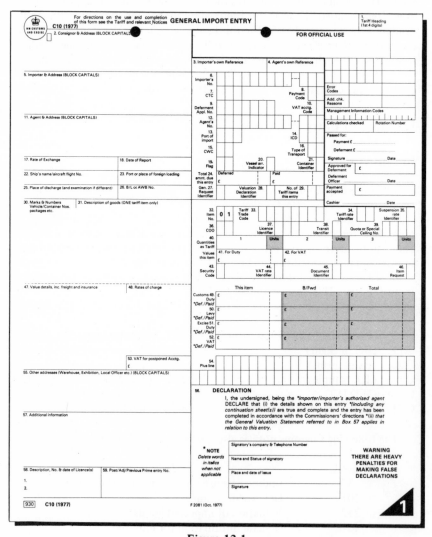

Figure 12.1

CHECK LIST

A. COMLETENESS OF ENTRY

Check that:

(1) no space on the entry which should be completed has been left blank and, where appropriate:

    (a)   the duty deferment approval number(s), Box 9 (Box 54, where applicable),

    (b)   the Importer's unique reference number, Box 6,

    (c)   the agent's reference number, Box 12,

    (d)   the Customs Transaction Code (CTC). Box 7. and

    (e)   the General Valuation Statement (GVS) reference number (Box 57) are correctly shown;

(2) the declaration (Box 56) has been properly completed, signed and dated:

(3) the proper number of copies of the entry has been prepared (additional copies are required for Exchange Control and goods entered for warehousing);

(4) all copies are legible and any corrections have been made clearly and initialled on all copies; and

(5) any special declaration, claim or request has been made in the correct terms.

B. SUPPORTING DOCUMENTS

Check that all the relevant supporting documents (including necessary copies) are attached and correctly completed, e.g.:

(1) import licence or other licences or certificates;

(2) invoice, or other evidence of value, packing list, specification and, where necessary, translations;

(3) Form C.105 where coding "D" appears in Box 28;

(4) evidence of freight charges;

(5) Form VAT 905 where relief from VAT is claimed at the time of importation in respect of antiques, works of art and scientific collections;

(6) additional copies of the invoice:

    (a)   if evidence of duty payment is required;

    (b)   for VAT (where goods are consigned to more than one Importer, i.e. "balked" entries);

    (c)   if some of the goods on the invoice are to be entered on a separate entry;

    (d)   if the importer is a person established in a Member state of the EEC other than the United Kingdom;

    (e)   if an undertaking to produce Form C.105 subsequently has been given (coding "E" or "G" in Box 28);

(7) evidence of entitlement to preferential tariff treatment;

(8) importer's authority when required for agent to give an undertaking or to make a special request, claim or declaration;

(9) work sheet when:

    (a)   there are several invoices;

    (b)   entry comprises more than one tariff item;

    (c)   goods are subject to CAP charges and calculations cannot be shown on face of entry, due to insufficient space;

(10) Form C. & E.578 where a specific undertaking to produce Form C.105 subsequently has been given (coding "G" in Box 28).

C. TARIFF, STATISTICAL AND VAT CLASSIFICATION

Check that:

(1) description of goods, Tariff/Trade code number and rate of duty are consistent; and

(2) for goods chargeable with VAT the correct value for VAT and rate are indicated.

D. QUANTITY AND VALUE

Check that:

(1) the net quantity is expressed in the unit(s) shown in the quantity column(s) of the Tariff in figures only and in the correct order;

(2) all the goods and the full value on each invoice page are included in the entry;

(3) the proper rate of exchange has been used;

(4) appropriate adjustments to the invoice value have been made according to the terms of the invoice and Form C.105 where applicable; and

(5) any special basis of value which has been notified by Customs to the importer has been applied correctly.

E. CALCULATIONS

Apply a mental check to each calculation on the entry to detect any obvious error, such as misplaced decimal points and/or transposed figures, in:

(1) currency conversions;

(2) entered quantity;

(3) value, and

(4) amount of duty or other charge.

Also check that any amounts on continuation sheets are correctly carried forward.

required to complete certain of the 'boxes' on the form, which are divided into plain language and code. There are 59 in all. The form provides for a single tariff code, and continuation sheets — C. 10A — are required if a mixed consignment includes goods classified under more than one tariff/trade heading.

Form C. 10 uses a Customs Transaction Code (C.T.C.) to identify precisely the type of importation, and for the timber trade the codes are as follows:

General entries	Code No.
Duty free goods	804
Dutiable goods	804
Goods subject to quota	804
Bill of sight	710
End-use relief	544
Exhibition goods	244
Low value goods (£50)	950
Packings returnable	252
Reimported in same state	404
Warehousing goods entered for customs duty purposes only	943

It is essential that the correct C.T.C. be used, because its selection is a declaration and legally binds the signatory to the entry. At this point it should be mentioned that the person completing the declaration must show the capacity in which he signs, the name of his company, its telephone number and the place where the declaration is being made and the date. Letters of authority to sign entries on behalf of an importer should be sent to the Collector of Customs and Excise for the places at which the entries are to be presented.

There are a number of other items which should be clarified, and these are as follows:

Bill of sight. When an importer or his authorised agent is unable for want of full information to make a perfect entry, he may make an entry on Form C. 10 under the bill of sight procedure. When such an entry has been made, Customs may allow the importer to examine the goods, under official supervision, with a view to making a perfect entry. The date of the presentation of the bill of sight entry determines the date of entry for duty and valuation purposes.

Valuation declaration identifier. This box must be completed if the entered value for duty exceeds £500 and *ad valorem* duty or VAT is being paid outright or deferred at importation or the goods are for warehousing. There is a general valuation statement — Form C. 109 — which covers this, and should accompany the entry together with the other appropriate documents.

Form C. 105. A declaration on this form must also be completed when goods exceeding £500 in value, which are not chargeable with *ad valorem* duty, are chargeable with VAT at a positive rate and the importer is not registered for VAT purposes.

Import Licences. In the case of goods which require a specific import licence or other certificate for their importation, the appropriate licence or certificate (other than an open individual licence issued by the Department of Trade) must be attached to the entry.

Country of Origin. All countries have a code number, and this must be inserted on the entry. In cases where goods are not wholly produced in one country, or where they are not accompanied by a certificate of origin, the country of origin should be taken to be that in which the final substantial processing or working took place, resulting in the manufacture of a new product or representing an important stage in its manufacture. For example, when goods are transhipped through entrepôt ports such as Rotterdam or Antwerp, the country whence consigned is the original country of despatch and not the Netherlands or Belgium, unless the goods were subject to a further commercial transaction — for example, a change in ownership — in one of those countries.

COMPLETENESS OF ENTRY

As a guide to completing an accurate entry, a check list is given on page 285. This indicates the information which is required, and refers to most of the essential boxes on Form C. 10 which have to be completed in order to avoid queries and delays.

REFUND OF DUTY

If it transpires that duty has been overpaid for any reason, such as shortage of measure, allowances for quality, condition or damage to the goods, a refund of the overpayment of duty may be claimed. Over a period when substantial quantities of goods are involved, the recovery of overpaid duty may be substantial.

DOCK AND LABOUR CHARGES

Obviously, these will vary within the areas concerned and it is not possible to quote accurate details. Before an importer can obtain delivery of his goods from the ship, he must pay certain charges to the Port Authority. These are known as dock or town dues, and cover the administration and maintenance cost of the docks. After the goods have come out of the ship, if they are left on the quay for a certain period, rent is payable for the period they remain there. These rates are all set out in the schedule of charges for the port concerned and may be obtained from the Port Authority.

Labour in a port may be divided into three sections: stevedores, master porters and forwarding agents. Stevedores are responsible for handling the

TABLE 12.2 PORT OF LONDON AUTHORITY TABLE OF CHARGES EFFECTIVE 1 JANUARY 1979

Description	Softwood per cubic metre	Hardwood per cubic metre	Plywood, veneers, hardboard, liner-board, waste paper and wood pulp per tonne (100 kg)
	£	£	£
Transit charge	2.95	4.95	4.80
Reduced transit charge	—	4.35	—
Daily rent per working day or part thereof	1.50	1.50	1.50
Storage rent per week or part thereof (minimum charge as for 4 weeks)	0.50	1.00	1.00
Late application charge	3.50	3.50	3.50
Additional charge for delivery to water conveyance	0.32	1.02	0.65
Sheeting charge	0.97	1.29	1.45
Late documentation charge	*	*	*
Minimum charge	£11.91 per consignment		

* The application of the late documentation charge is suspended until further notice.

goods from the hold of the ship, with or without the use of the ship's tackle, depending upon port facilities, and delivering the goods to the rail of the ship. Master porters or cargo superintendents are responsible for taking the goods from the stevedores at the ship's rail and delivering them to the quay alongside the receiver's transport. Forwarding agents are responsible for taking the goods from the quay and putting them on the transport carrying them away.

In some ports all three classes of labour will be found working independently, each group working for a self-contained firm. However, more often a firm will combine two or possibly three functions.

Ports which are controlled by a single authority, such as the Port of London Authority at Tilbury No. 34 Berth, undertake to do all the necessary work. As a general guide, their Table of Charges is as given in table 12.2.

12.3 Examination of Shipment – Claims, etc.

GENERAL

When one considers the vast quantity of wood goods which change hands throughout the world together with the many qualities and dimensions and the number of hazards in transit, it must be conceded that it is inevitable that occasional difficulties will arise and that disputes will require settlement. Both exporters and importers would be optimistic if they did not recognise these possibilities, and for this reason all contracts contain a clause outlining the procedure for formulating claims. Added to the variations of quality and manufacture are the many circumstances which can affect the condition of the goods before and during their journey to this country.

The most common form of claim is formulated by the importer or receiver of the goods, and this can be directed towards three different parties, depending on the cause of the complaint: (1) the shipper or seller, (2) the insurance company or (3) the ship owner.

The shipper or seller is responsible for claims involving quality, condition (when shipped) and quantity supplied against contract stipulation and measurement. He may also be responsible for any breach of contract warranty involving damages.

The insurance company (usually referred to as underwriters) is responsible for loss of and damage to a cargo during the voyage – excluding deck cargo damage by, say, sea-water. They may be responsible for loss of deck cargo caused by rough weather.

The ship owner is responsible for shortages – that is, the difference between bill of lading quantity of pieces and those ultimately delivered. The ship's master signs the bill of lading for number of pieces only, and today it is common for bills to say 'so many packages or truck bundles said to contain so many pieces'. The master does not take responsibility for the exact contents of packages.

It should be noted that in every instance responsibility has to be proved and the negotiation for the settlement of claims is normally effected by the agent on behalf of the parties concerned. It is very seldom that amicable settlement cannot be arranged, but when it does fail, the matter is referred to arbitration – see section on Arbitration.

Without exception, all contracts contain clauses which clearly define the conditions for dealing with these matters. It should be noted that these conditions do vary and should be fully studied by the parties concerned. The importing of wood goods, particularly timber, from overseas is fraught with hazards; it is a natural product and its grading is often a matter of experience and judgement only. Considering the millions of pieces involved, each one being different, it is obvious that errors will occur – sometimes to the advantage of the seller and sometimes to the advantage of the receiver. The quality of the logs going into a mill may vary considerably. A poor run of logs may result in an unusually high proportion of low-quality sawn timber being produced or an abnormally low 'average length'. On other occasions average quality and length may be better than usual. Shipments should be assessed as a whole, since it is unrealistic to complain about a very small percentage of errors – particularly in grading. One can often find unsorted pieces in fifths and also fifths in sixths.

12.4 Examination of Documents

The shipping documents should arrive some time before the ship reaches the port of destination. The first stage in the examination of a timber shipment consists in the close check and examination of the documents. It is first necessary to see that required documents are there and that they are in order and agree with each other and also with the contract conditions (as detailed in chapters 7–10). If the documents are not in order or are incomplete, the matter should be taken up at once with the seller's agents, and, if necessary, returned to them in their entirety. If in order, the following checks should be carried out on the specification of quantities:

(1) Arithmetical check of accuracy.

(2) Check quantities against contract conditions. In the case of the last or only shipment against a contract, this will show any undershipment or overshipment. If there is a considerable overshipment above the marginal quantities allowed, the amount overshipped may be rejected (see pages 140 and 162).

(3) Check average length and width and compare these with contract description. If the contract states a specific average length or width and the specification reveals that the average shipped is less, the buyer has grounds for a claim and, in certain cases, rejection. However, short average length or width is usually treated as a breach of warranty only, to be met by a suitable reduction in price.

(4) Check deck cargo conditions. The bills of lading will show which items

have been shipped on deck, and these should be compared with the contract and loading orders. It frequently happens that the master of the vessel decides that, from a safety point of view, he cannot comply fully with the buyer's loading orders. If, under these circumstances, the deckload becomes sea-water damaged, it is extremely difficult for an importer to pursue a claim against either the shipper or the owners.

(5) Comparison of insurance policy or certificate of insurance with invoice and other documents, to ensure that the full value of the goods shipped has been covered in accordance with the contract – that is, f.a.s. value plus 10 per cent plus freight advance, or c.i.f. value plus 10 per cent.

(6) Check invoice prices (from contract), quantities (from specification), deductions for freight advance (from bills of lading – where these are endorsed).

It is important to note that the only time that an importer can reject goods out of hand is when he receives the documents, and rejection in this way can only be carried out when there is a straightforward and obvious infringement of a *condition* as opposed to a *warranty* of the contract. As an example as to when rejection could be made and the documents returned to the agent, the position might arise where the contract calls for redwood and all the documents show that whitewood has been shipped; or a contract might call for a shipment of 38 x 225 mm goods and the documents show that 25 x 225 mm goods have actually been shipped. In other words, there must be some basic *condition* of the contract not complied with, which can be seen from the documents; otherwise a rejection is usually only possible by taking up the documents, in the correct way, and submitting a claim for rejection on the shipper, through the agent, in the usual way. These cases nearly always result in an arbitration, as few shippers will accept rejection on an infringement of a warranty without a fight. It will be seen from this how important a thorough examination of the documents and comparison with the contract really is.

12.5 Examination of Goods and Ship

By the time the ship arrives, the shipping documents will have been checked and the goods probably paid for. The importer will have followed the progress of the ship, and should have notice of its arrival from the shipping agents. The examination of the goods is, of course, best done on the quayside, but of recent years more and more shipments are arriving at ports situated far from the actual importer's yard. Many of these ports are small, run in some cases by wharfingers, whose one aim is to get the vessel discharged and away again with as little delay as possible. Under these circumstances, it will be seen that it may well be impossible for anyone from the importing firm to see the goods before they are discharged and the vessel has sailed. Indeed, more often than not, it is some days before the wharfingers advise the importer that the goods are ready for delivery on their quayside.

In the past, when the general rule was for cargo quantities to be shipped to the larger ports, it was possible for a responsible person from the importing firm to see the goods actually being discharged, and if there were signs of deckload damage, the ship's officers could be questioned and the ship's log examined. This is still to be strongly recommended whenever conditions permit, but, if through likely delays due to having to transport the goods a long distance, it is always advisable to request an extension of time for presenting claims. Shippers are quite aware of the difficulties faced by buyers in this respect and will usually agree to a reasonable extension of time.

When inspecting a cargo at the quayside, the first thing to look at is the ship itself — signs of a rough voyage can usually be seen easily. If signs of a rough passage are seen on boarding the ship, or if news reports have told of bad weather, it may be necessary to either inspect the ship's log or obtain extracts from it. The log will indicate what has happened during the voyage. There may be references, very slight perhaps, to shifting of the deck cargo or 're-battening down deck cargo'. These indicate that some of the deck cargo *may* have gone overboard. If really rough weather has been encountered, the log may state that part of the deck cargo has been jettisoned, but in such circumstances the master will enter a protest on reaching port. The ship's agent will tell the importer if this has been done, but in any case it is always as well to ask. Now that almost all timber is packaged, the likelihood of cargo being washed overboard is very much reduced. The log may tell of flooding of the holds. This might well cause damage to the timber and could give rise to a claim against the insurance company. The log, therefore, is a most vital document; extracts from it will provide the evidence for claims for shortages in deck cargo, or possibly damage to cargo in the hold.

The examination of the timber itself must cover the following factors:

Dimension

A check of the various items for dimension — that is, width and thickness. Some sellers have a reputation for 'scant' or under measure; others for 'full measure', which gains for the latter considerable sales advantages over the former. Pieces in several packages must be inspected and measurements made, and the variation must be general and not just in isolated pieces in order to justify a claim being made.

Packages, Pieces and Measurement

The master of the ship signs the bill of lading for number of pieces only and is only responsible for delivering that number of pieces to the importer.

With packaged and truck-bundled goods it is realised that it is quite impossible for the master of the vessel to check the number of pieces in each package or truck-bundle and it has therefore become customary for the bills of lading for goods shipped in this way to be made out: '*x* packages said to contain *y* pieces'. The captain is then only responsible for delivering the correct number of packages and not the exact number of pieces. If the tally on discharge discloses that there is a deficiency in the number of pieces, in the case of loose cargoes, or number of packages, in packaged or truck-bundled cargoes, the insurance company is responsible if it is deck cargo lost overboard or jettisoned, or the shipowner is responsible if it is hold cargo. Great care should be taken by the stevedores in handling the packaged and truck-bundled goods out of the hold of the vessel. When packaged goods were first shipped, almost as many packages were broken during discharge as arrived on the quayside intact. It was quickly realised that although much of this damage could be accounted for by careless handling during loading and discharge, the way that the packages were made up at the mill had a lot to do with the condition of their ultimate arrival. Much experimental work was done by shippers, and nowadays most packages arrive in good condition. The factors chiefly affecting the stability of packaged timber are adequate number of 'cross tie laths' at regular levels in the pack together with the strapping of the packages under pressure. The pre-slinging of the packages in the hold and on the deck of the vessel has also contributed to the landing of packages in good condition.

Quality

The quality of a particular parcel can only be assessed by someone with experience. Grading rules can be obtained for American and Canadian timber, and in lesser detail for practically all timber-exporting countries. These rules, even in the hands of an experienced man, are really of no practical use, and ultimately the accurate assessment of a cargo of timber rests entirely on the experience of the importer and his knowledge of the shipper concerned. The hardwood and plywood grading rules are rather more clear, but still cannot replace sheer judgement in assessing the quality of goods on the quayside.

Scandinavian softwoods are graded at the producing mills, generally with little reference to any grading rules but solely on the experience of the particular mill's brackers, and for this reason the basis of grading is generally stated in the contract as 'sellers' usual', which requires special knowledge and experience of the mill to judge.

Condition

The condition of timber is quite different from graded quality. A high-grade timber can be ruined by being shipped in bad condition, such as an insufficiently seasoned state. The quality of timber is judged by the presence of inherent defects, such as knots, wane, rate of growth, checks, etc. Condition refers to the state of the timber, such as freshness, weathering and discoloration. Deterioration of this nature may have been present when the timber was in the shipper's yard, or it may have occurred during shipment.

If the voyage was normal, bad condition of timber may be shown to be due to insufficient seasoning or kilning for the voyage to the particular port of destination, and for this the importer must claim against the seller. On the other hand, if through the 'perils of the sea' the length of the voyage is increased much beyond normal, resulting in 'sweating' of the timber in the hold and fungal mould forming, it is unlikely that a claim against the shipper would succeed. Condition in such cases may possibly be grounds for an insurance claim, but there are certain difficulties in such claims, which are dealt with later in this chapter. In any case, it is always advisable to notify both the shipper and the underwriters in such condition claims, inviting both of them to arrange for inspection of the goods.

Damage by water may be freshwater or sea-water. It is fairly easy to ascertain whether the timber has been damaged by sea-water by applying the following chemical test. If a 5 per cent solution of silver nitrate, made up in distilled water, is applied to the wet surface of the timber, a white precipitate will form almost immediately if there is salt present. Even after the timber has dried, the same result may be obtained but it may take a little longer before the whiteness appears. There is no known test to distinguish sap water from rain-water or snow-water.

Where a claim is made for anything other than measurement, there are two essentials to be observed, and these are the subjects of the next two sub-sections.

INSPECTION

For claims against sellers, inspection is by the seller's agents or their own UK selling organisation. For claims against the insurance company, inspection is by the insurance company's surveyor. These are experienced men trained in specialised damage surveying.

This inspection must be done quickly: if at all possible, on the same day the importer himself has seen the parcel. Timber that has developed fungal growth in the hold of the ship may appear awful when it first comes out of the ship, but given a spell of fine dry weather and the packages opened up and the goods open-piled, much of the fungal growth may disappear. In such cases, if the inspection is left for two or three days, the timber might appear superficially to be in perfect condition and the importer's chance of a successful claim for breaking open packages and sticking would be small, although it would appear to be absolutely necessary at the time of discharge.

RETENTION OF BULK

If the claim is for 'quality', the buyer must not 'break bulk'. By this is meant that the parcel or item of a parcel complained of (which may be only a single dimension of one bill of lading) must be kept so intact that, in the case of arbitration, it can be produced to the arbitrators in its entirety as discharged. It is usually accepted by arbitrators that a claim for quality is based on the interpretation of quality as expressed in both the Swedish and the Finnish grading rules, which read as follows:

'Defects in quality.
(i) Structure (knots etc.).
(ii) Manufacture.
(iii) Shakes, checks and splits.
(iv) Deformities.'

Many people argue that shakes should be a defect of condition and not.of quality, and there are arguments to support this view; however, both the Swedish and the Finnish rules show this defect as one of quality, and an importer would be very unwise to break bulk when a claim for shake is being pursued.

Seller's agents are frequently asked to authorise the breaking of bulk, but normally they have no authority to give this, and in any case the contract is so worded that there is really no hardship in letting matters follow the prescribed course. Indeed, if a buyer relies on 'permission to break bulk', he may find himself in a less favourable position if the matter eventually goes to arbitration, and in any event arbitrators would not take into consideration any goods that had been disposed of.

If the claim is for condition, the buyer can dispose of any part of the item he is not claiming on, without detriment to his claim on the rest. It is here worth recording the official definition of 'condition' − again as given in the Swedish and the Finnish grading rules:

'Defects in condition.
(i) Moisture.
(ii) Blue.
(iii) Other discoloration.'

In either case there is no obligation to hold the goods at any particular place, or even all in one place, so long as the whole item in the case of a quality claim, and the quantity complained of in the case of condition, is available for inspection as discharged.

12.6 Claims

If it appears that a claim will have to be made on a shipment against an Albion or Uniform contract, the seller's agents must be advised, reasonable particulars being given, within 14 working days if the cargo is loose or 3 months if the goods are packaged or truck-bundled: both periods to be worked from the date of the vessel's final discharge. According to the contract, reasonable particulars shall mean a statement as to whether the claim is for quality and/or condition, together with a statement of the sizes complained of and an estimate of percentages and of the amount claimed. All such statements are without prejudice and conditional on the facilities for inspecting the goods. Other contract forms give slightly different time limits, but this is dealt with in the chapters on contracts. Many importers are in the habit of giving 'notice of claim' on every shipment they receive, and it has been known, in fact, for an agent to receive notice of claim on goods while the vessel is still at sea. Such notice of claim has really no value whatsoever and in no way frees a buyer from the obligation of giving full particulars within the stipulated time shown in the contract. If a delay in receiving the goods is likely, an importer should at once ask the shipper's agent to obtain an extension of time for presenting claims, which is rarely refused by any reputable shipper. An importer should not rely on the fact that he has given the agent notice of claim; this means nothing.

DIMENSION CLAIMS

These are simply claims for the difference in measure between the goods supplied and those contracted for. The claim may be for scantness in thickness, width or length, and may be for part or all of the item.

If boards contracted for and invoiced as 25 mm do not hold up to 25 mm in thickness, the claim against the seller would probably be to reduce them to the next recognised size down – that is, 22 mm.

It is possible in certain circumstances to claim also that the smaller dimension is not worth so much per cubic metre as the original dimension. In these cases the claim is made up in two parts: the shortage in measurement and the reduction in price per cubic metre.

QUANTITY CLAIMS

Quantity claims against the ship or insurance company for shortage of pieces are based upon the difference between the number of pieces as per seller's specification or bill of lading and the number of pieces received on discharge. It is important that the importer obtain the original master porter's or cargo superintendent's tally if there is any dispute over a claim made in this manner.

When the number of pieces short has been established and agreed by the other party, the importer's claim may then be compiled, the average cost per piece over the bill of lading in question being taken – for example,

$$645 \text{ pieces } 75 \times 225 \text{ mm} = 47.93 \text{ m}^3 \text{ at £75.00 per m}^3$$
$$= £3594.75$$

shortage 23 pieces

shortage claim = £128.18

It is assumed in this method of calculation that any shortage is of the same average specification as the whole bill of lading. If the shortage comprises all long lengths, the importer will be out of pocket; if the shortage is all of short lengths, the importer will obviously gain.

The only accurate method of establishing a shortage is on *independent measure*, but unfortunately it will not be accepted by all shipowners and insurance companies. The measurement, piece by piece, is carried out by trained timber men, and where especially accurate measurement is required, the importer may employ the services of the Customs Fund Measurers, who can be found in all the major ports. A claim submitted in this manner is compiled simply from the difference between seller's and third party's measurements. A copy of the specification compiled by the third party will have to be produced to support the importer's claim.

However, claims for shortages against shipowners under the Nubaltwood charter of 1973 must be made within eight days of final discharge. Not only does this make it practically impossible to rely on out-turn details from a Port Authority, owing to the length of time these take to be prepared, but also the importer, to be certain of being able to formulate the claim within this very short period, may have to arrange for a special tally to be taken at the ship's rail.

QUALITY AND CONDITION CLAIMS

There is no set form for compiling claims for quality or condition; the claim depends upon the circumstances and detail of each case. In a claim against a seller for quality it might be argued that a parcel of U/S redwood was of such poor quality as to be only saleable as V redwood and the claim would be made for the difference between the two prices. However, it is rarely possible to establish that the whole quantity is sufficiently bad to be so downgraded, and it is more normal for a certain percentage in each size to be the basis of a claim.

A claim for condition, such as discoloration, might be based upon the estimated cost per cubic metre to bring the timber to a saleable condition: say the estimated cost of brushing off mould and sticking the timber to dry out, or if the discoloration has penetrated and become deep-seated, the goods might have to be reduced in price to a lower grade.

Where only part of the parcel has been damaged or broken by handling or attacked by insects, the claim is generally based upon the difference between the amount invoiced and the amount of good timber that can be cut out of the parcel. If the good timber so obtained is much smaller in dimension, then the claim can also include the difference in price between wide and narrow goods, the latter invariably being cheaper.

MARINE INSURANCE CLAIMS

Brief mention has been made elsewhere in the text of circumstances giving rise to claims against insurers, and the chapter on Marine Insurance gives details of the cover afforded by the Timber Trade Federation Clauses. It may, however, be helpful in this chapter to summarise the more usual situations with which timber importers may be faced and the procedure to be followed in making insurance claims.

Casualty to the vessel

This can include total loss, collision and/or jettison of deck cargo and washing overboard, and may necessitate salvage services and/or putting in to a port of refuge.

It is essential that prompt advice be given to the marine insurers, who may instruct the Salvage Association or other surveyors, and in some cases solicitors, to protect cargo interests.

General Average and/or Salvage Services

Some of the contingencies mentioned above will lead to a declaration of general average by the shipowner, and he will stipulate what security he requires before the cargo is released to consignees. He will certainly require a general average bond, which is signed by the cargo owner, and may require a general average guarantee from the marine insurers. In some cases the shipowner may demand the payment of a cash deposit from consignees, in exchange for which a general average deposit receipt is issued. These formalities are arranged by the average adjusters appointed by the shipowners, and it is those adjusters who will subsequently draw up a general average statement, listing the contributions to be made by the respective interests.

When the marine insurers issue a guarantee, they establish direct contact with the average adjusters, and make direct settlement of the contribution in respect of the cargo they have insured.

If a cargo receiver pays a general average deposit, he should send the original receipt to his insurers, who will usually reimburse the cargo receiver, and again deal direct with the average adjuster, in respect of the cash adjustment ultimately found to be necessary.

While the agreement of a general average statement is a matter for the insurers' technical experts, it will be appreciated that in the case of serious casualties there may be considerable delay before the general average can be adjusted. In the first place, it is the aim of both the cargo owner and the marine insurers to deal with any claim of the cargo owner under his policy of insurance. To that end he must work closely with surveyors appointed by the insurers and provide the shipping documents, extracts from the vessel's log and out-turns of cargo received, together with his statement of claim. When the cargo claim has been settled by the insurers, the documents will be sent by the insurers to the general average adjusters, in order that they can take account of any general average loss or damage in their statement, and compute the contributory value of the cargo delivered.

When a vessel receives salvage services, it may be that security is given to the salvor by the shipowner in respect of both ship and cargo, the shipowner in turn taking general average security from cargo interests as above. It is by no means unusual, however, for shipowners to leave cargo owners to give their own separate security to salvors. In that case the matter should be referred to the cargo insurers, who will usually give a guarantee and thereafter negotiate a settlement direct with the salvor.

Not all loss or damage of cargo sustained as a result of a casualty necessitating a declaration of general average is a general average loss. As only one example, partial loss by fire is particular average, whereas damage by water used to extinguish fire in other cargo is a general average loss. Such niceties need not concern the cargo owner unduly, as both causes of damage are covered by the TTF clauses, and are mentioned only to emphasise the need to establish all the facts with the insurers and their surveyors, so that the proper allowances may be given in the general average statement.

Before leaving the subject of casualties, it should be mentioned that damage proximately caused by delay is not allowed in general average, nor is it covered by the TTF clauses, even though the delay is caused by an insured peril. This exclusion sometimes confuses claimants who are aware that the extended cover clause provides that the insurance shall remain in force during delay beyond the control of the assured. The position is that, subject to the TTF clauses, the goods are covered *during* such delay against insured perils, but not against loss or damage *caused* by delay.

Particular Average

Particular average means partial loss or damage from fortuitous causes and is borne by the owner of the goods, and if the cause of the loss or damage is an insured peril, by his insurers.

Claims arise from non-delivery, shortage of pieces and damage, and the consignee should remember that the initial responsibility may lie with the shipowner or carrier.

Written notice of claim must therefore be given to the shipowner or carrier within any time stipulated in the contract of carriage, by either the consignee or his agent. Failure to comply with the carrier's conditions prejudices the right to recover from the carrier, and in those circumstances the insurer may subsequently decline to pay the claim under the policy in full, taking account of the extent to which recovery has been prejudiced.

In addition, the consignee should give prompt notice of claim to the marine insurers, who may instruct surveyors in the case of damage claims or loss adjusters to investigate claims for shortage or non-delivery.

Provided that due notice of claim has been given to the carrier by the consignee, it is customary for the insurer to settle the claim under the policy and then pursue the recovery from the carrier under subrogation.

A shipowner is normally discharged from all liability in respect of loss or damage unless suit is brought within twelve months from the date of discharge from the ship, or twelve months from the date when the goods should have been delivered. That time limit operates even though the shipowner has been given full details of the claim in good time. If necessary, therefore, the consignee must obtain an extension of the time limit in writing from the shipowner or issue a writ to preserve his rights. Until such time as the insurers have settled a claim, they cannot acquire any rights under subrogation and it is for that reason that the owner of the goods must preserve the position.

Minimising the loss

It is the duty of the assured, and in fact a legal requirement, to take such measures as may be reasonable to avert or minimise a loss, and the 'sue and labour' clause in a marine policy makes it clear that the insurers will pay for such measures, provided that the expenses are reasonably incurred and also provided that they are incurred to avert or minimise a loss which is covered by the policy. It is this duty which gives rise to the expression that an assured 'must act as if uninsured'. An importer should bear this in mind when considering the cost of opening up packages for sticking when the goods have been loaded on deck, as insurers will be most unlikely to meet the cost of this operation.

The function of Marine Surveyors

It is not always appreciated that the function of a marine surveyor is limited to inspecting damaged goods and reporting as to the cause and extent of the damage. The surveyor is not concerned, at least in theory, with the question as to whether or not the loss or damage is recoverable under the policy, and the fact that the extent of loss or damage may be agreed between an assured and the surveyor cannot always be taken as an indication that the marine insurers are liable.

Submission of claims to Insurers

Claims should be presented to insurers as soon as possible, accompanied by the original policy or certificate of insurance, if issued, bills of lading, shipper's invoice and specification, landing returns, out-turns at final destination, and the correspondence exchanged with the shipowner or carrier.

When a surveyor has been appointed by the insurers, his report will be issued to the insurers direct.

Although an assured should submit a statement of claim, it may be necessary for an adjustment to be prepared in accordance with marine insurance practice and the conditions of the policy concerned, and the adjustment will be made up by the assured's insurance brokers or by the insurers themselves, or, in unusually complicated cases, by average adjusters.

THE TIME ELEMENT AND QUESTION OF FACT

In prosecuting a claim successfully against shipowners, marine insurance companies or, indeed, shippers themselves, many timber importers fail in their efforts by neglecting to observe certain simple precautions.

Time

The time element is all-important in claims against shippers and shipowners. It is surprising how many importers fail to recognise this point and do not make their claim within the time limits set out in their contract or charter. Their claims are then 'out of time' and can be debarred. In many cases, by the time it is known to the importer that he is likely to have a claim, the period in which he must make a claim has already passed. There are comparatively few importers who diarise closely the dates from the berthing and discharging of the ship to make certain that they are fully aware of the last date on which they can make a claim without it being 'out of time'.

In the case of claims against shipowners, under most charters, if the charterer and the shipowner cannot agree, provision is made for reference to arbitration, but a time limit of twelve months is normally set. Cases have been known where the shipowners' agents have prevaricated, with correspondence which indicated that the matter was 'under review' or 'being referred to their principals', and all too quickly the twelve months had passed. In these cases, although a claim has been submitted, the importers suddenly find that they have lost their right of arbitration.

Determination of Fact

A high proportion of claims on shipowners and insurance companies, and to some degree on shippers, depend in the end upon the ability of the importer to prove *question of fact*. No clear rules can be given for this, except that the importer must always have in mind at all stages of a transaction that if difficulties arise he must be able to substantiate his claim in a court of law. Claims are much more easily resolved successfully if it is appreciated that claims are likely to occur.

The proving of fact is often not easy. Claims for dead freight from shipowners will arise if the goods are heavier than 'properly seasoned' as described in the charter. It then falls to the importer to prove the degree of seasoning of the goods at the time of loading. By the time he knows there is a claim for dead freight, the goods are probably already loaded.

The problem then becomes one of how far the goods differ, on the one hand, from the degree of seasoning demanded by the charter, and on the other, from the degree of seasoning implied in the f.a.s. contract.

The condition of goods on discharge to the quay also presents problems where claims on shippers or marine insurance policies are concerned. Where the goods have deteriorated in the ship through contamination with other cargo, it is of paramount importance that the importer arrange for the goods to be surveyed immediately they come out of the ship. Delay on the quay may favour the superficial appearance of the goods.

Possibly the most contentious question of fact that must be faced is in the matter of 'out-turn figures' from both ship and port in cases of claims for shortage.

The usual explanation from the shipowner is that they delivered all the goods they had to the quay. The port authorities say that they delivered all the goods they received from the ship. The matter can then be further complicated by perhaps having several receivers of the same mark of goods. In such circumstances, all too often the importer is left unable to prove either that the ship did not deliver the goods that the master signed for on bills of lading or that the port authority have mixed up the bills of lading and delivered the wrong goods.

The basic principle is the same all the way through. If the importer can prove the facts of the case, then his claim will succeed. If he cannot or is uncertain in any way, then immediately the successful basis of his claim is undermined. In cases of ship's out-turn, without doubt, the best solution is for the importer to face the expense of paying for his own or independent tallymen at the ship's rail.

13 Transport, Handling, Storage and Office Routine

13.1 Transport

There have been many developments during the past 10–15 years in connection with the transport of timber from the mill to the ultimate end user's yard.

At one time it was the practice of importers to satisfy their requirements by contracting for several cargo loads from a few selected shippers from whom, by experience, they had learned exactly what they could expect to receive by way of quality and specification, etc. Most of such purchases would be made on f.a.s. terms, the chartering being carried out by the importer himself.

As the years have gone by, the systems of production have changed and most importers have also gradually changed their pattern of purchasing and now buy more from 'hand to mouth' in smaller, more regular shipments. Now that the majority of mills in Scandinavia kiln-dry most, if not all, of their production and modern ice-breakers are able to keep ports open for most of the winter months, it is not so necessary any more to look so far ahead. Timber buyers in the UK are able to spread their import more evenly over the year, bringing in much of their timber in regular shipments by liner tonnage.

Instead of negotiating cargo quantities against stock notes issued by shippers, it is more common today for importers to pass specifications of their requirements to shippers through their agents or UK selling organisations. These sales are usually negotiated on c.i.f. terms or delivered right through to the final destination. The importer is thus able more easily to finance his imports and obtain more the specification which he requires. As the shipments are made on regular liner sailings, he can arrange for them to come forward at regular weekly, monthly or longer intervals.

There are regular liner sailings from all the main Finnish ports and the majority of southern Swedish ports, including Lake Vänern, to the east coast of the UK from Scotland to Shoreham, and all these arrival ports are well equipped through the vessel's agents to handle the shipment on arrival, pass customs on the goods and arrange their onward transmission by road or other means. Importers do, of course, still buy considerable quantities in cargo shipments, and this applies particularly to purchases from the USSR, Czechoslovakia and Poland, and bulk purchases from Canada. The USSR ship mostly in their own vessels on c.i.f. terms, sales being made against fixed schedules of prices issued at appropriate times. Bulk shipments are also still made from Sweden and Finland, particularly from the larger and better-known mills.

Transport from the quay of discharge to final destination has changed considerably of recent years, the railways being used less and less in favour of road transport. The network of motorways makes road transport a much quicker and more satisfactory way of carrying timber, and when brought in to an east coast port, can be conveyed to almost anywhere in the country very rapidly and comparatively economically.

RAIL

At one time much of the imported timber coming through the docks was handled by rail, and this applied also to the carriage of timber between importer and merchant or consumer.

At the present time little, if any, timber is carried by rail, with the exception of a limited number of containerised shipments through certain ports. No docks are now controlled by British Rail. The only other timber carried by rail is a certain amount for pulping, which is carried on specially adapted wagons, but this is nearly entirely confined to Scotland.

ROAD

Operators' licensing was introduced in 1970 under Section 60 Transport Act, 1968. This section states that no person shall use a goods vehicle on the road for the carriage of goods for hire or reward or in connection with any trade or business carried on by him except under an operator's licence (O licence).

An O licence, when granted, gives complete freedom to the holder to carry whatever goods he wishes for any person or firm and over any distance and to any area of the UK without restriction.

The sole criterion for obtaining a licence to operate rests on the ability of the operator to ensure that the requirements of all the appropriate regulations are met. These are:

(1) Appropriate vehicle parking.
(2) Adequate maintenance facilities to ensure that all vehicles are maintained to a satisfactory standard.
(3) Financial resources.
(4) From January 1978 an applicant will have to identify the licensed transport manager, whose name will appear on the O licence.

Great importance is placed by the Licensing Authority on the word 'user', and in general terms the person who pays the drivers' wages is the 'user'.

Application for an O licence must be made to the Licensing Authority for each traffic area in which the vehicles are based. This base will be the operating centre for the vehicles, and one O licence will be sufficient to cover any number of vehicles operating at one centre and any number of centres in any one traffic area. If operating centres are in different areas, then separate O licences will be required for each traffic area.

No person may drive a heavy goods vehicle of any class on the road unless he has an appropriate heavy goods vehicle licence to do so, and he must not be employed by another person to do so either. The heavy goods vehicle licence is required in addition to an ordinary current Group A driving licence for drivers (including part-time drivers such as fitters) of any rigid goods vehicle which has a permissible maximum weight of 7.15 metric tons (7.38 tons) gross and any articulated vehicle.

Each individual haulage contractor will have his own terms and conditions; British Road Services publish their own terms and conditions, which are available from any BRS area office.

In any case it is prudent to ascertain beforehand the period within which claims must be notified and made.

Road haulage is a competitive business: advantage should be taken of obtaining quotations from more than one contractor so that the best may be obtained. Haulage contractors operate much the same way as merchant ship freighters or 'tramps'. If a haulage contractor can be provided with a return load where otherwise his vehicle would be empty, it is usually possible to obtain a very economical rate.

Private haulage contractors operate 'clearing houses', where they go for return loads. The addresses of these clearing houses may be found in nearly all classified telephone directories. A trader advises the clearing house of the load he has at the same time as obtaining rates from local contractors.

13.2 Handling

When the last edition of this book was published, the bulk of the timber imports coming into the UK were shipped loose. This meant that when the goods left the mill, each piece had to be loaded on to rail trucks or into barges by hand, then stowed piece by piece in the hold of the ship. On arrival in the UK the pieces were made up into 'sets' in the hold of the ship and then by the same laborious process loaded onto transport for conveyance to the buyer's yard for unloading and stacking away.

Length packaging and truck-bundling has certainly cut down the time of loading and unloading and led to a considerable saving of labour and freight, but it has called for a very heavy outlay for both shippers and buyers in handling equipment. The size and weight of packages is all-important, as this is governed by the handling capacity of the smallest piece of equipment in the journey from the mill to the buyer's yard. It is no use making up packages at the mill so large that the fork-lift trucks on the quayside in the UK cannot handle them. Therefore, packages have evolved of such a size that they can be dealt with quite easily at all stages of the journey.

The most usual handling equipment is the fork-lift truck in one of its many forms. There are types for use under almost any conditions. Some yards have only narrow alleyways between the stacks and require one type — the side-loader; in other yards it may be found that a truck which clamps the packages by their ends and lifts them end-on is more satisfactory.

Motorised wheeled cranes are also used in many importer's yards, with very satisfactory results, but the use of slings is necessary with these cranes, which involves delay in inserting the slings under the packages and adjusting the balance before lifting can commence.

Straddle wagons are widely used in shippers' yards, and these have proved themselves very satisfactory for conveying packages at a fairly high speed for considerable distances. For this reason they can convey goods from storage sheds to the ship's side very rapidly and economically.

Even felling and extraction of logs in most timber-producing countries has been almost completely mechanised, equipment having been designed to fell, lop off branches, cut logs to length, de-bark and finally extract the logs from the felling area.

The whole question of mechanical handling has been covered in an extremely well produced supplement to the *Timber Trades Journal* of 23 September 1978, and copies of this are obtainable from Benn Publications Ltd, 25 New Street Square, London EC4A 3AJ.

13.3 Storage

At the beginning of the line of transportation, storage commences at the overseas shipper's yard. In those countries where seasoning by kiln-drying takes place, it is now customary for the goods in packaged form to be stored under cover in large sheds or 'magazines', as they are called in Scandinavia. Obviously, it is quite wrong to reduce the moisture content of the timber to a low level and then to expose it to adverse weather conditions by storage in the open. The only exception to this rule is where the packages are adequately protected by a wrapping of waterproof paper or plastics. This latter practice is becoming quite common, since it protects the goods throughout transit and even aids the UK receiver to store, if necessary, in the open. Many shippers regard this as a worthwhile investment, especially since the time limit for claims was increased to three months.

In the UK the storage of packaged goods depends entirely upon the receiver's facilities. Ideally, under-cover storage is essential, but such facilities depend upon the financial means of the receiver. Where it is limited, the better-quality goods such as unsorted or joinery quality are stored under cover and the lower qualities have to be stored in the open. It is not possible to say with any accuracy what percentages are involved, but it is well known that a vast quantity of the UK import is stored in the open.

UK storage yards can be divided into two types — public and private.

Public storage yards are not as numerous or even essential to the same extent as in past years. In earlier times, when handling and transportation methods were so different, it was customary for a considerable percentage of our imported goods to be stored for a rental and, in the case of loose goods, even tallied. Public storage yards also provided an essential service to the importer who lacked space in his own yard. With the changes which have already been mentioned, these facilities are not so significant today. On arrival, goods are often loaded direct on to road transport and delivered to the importer's customer or the ultimate consumer. Thus, the importer is relieved of the need to provide storage space in his own yard. In addition, the trend towards arrivals being smaller in quantity and at regular intervals has also contributed to less need for large storage areas.

Private storage yards — both importer's and consumer's — are more common today. There was a time when such yards were sited on a canal or river and transportation by barge was commonplace. Many had direct railway sidings to their yard from the docks, but this facility has also declined, since private sidings are very expensive to build and, in any event, such methods do not lend themselves to the handling of packaged units. There is no doubt that the move towards road transport has become universal.

Today the majority of private storage yards have only road access and there is no likelihood that the position will change, since the system lends itself to unitisation and mechanical handling. Not only is it more efficient, but also it is more economical.

13.4 Office Routine

The importing of timber and its allied products and its subsequent sale in this country depends upon an efficient office routine. Long experience by buyers in firms of importers and high-pressure salesmanship by the firm's representatives on the road can be set at naught by an inefficient office. The method or system used matters little; it is the results that count. If an office is to be started or reorganised, the system or routine that is introduced must be such that accurate information, data and records can be produced easily. Therefore, before the system is put into effect, it is essential to make certain exactly what information, etc., is required, and then base the system on these definite requirements.

In the timber trade an office system may be divided into three main divisions: (1) telex messages and cables (in and out), correspondence and filing; (2) finance and accounts; (3) stock control and costing. It is not proposed here to discuss the question of labour costing.

The first two of these divisions apply to any business, and many changes have taken place since the publication of the last edition of this book as far as they are concerned. Any importer or agent will tell you that the number of letters, in or out, going through his office compared with 10—15 years ago is very small indeed. The cost of producing a letter at the present time, bearing in mind the high salaries of typists, the ever-increasing cost of postage and the ever-decreasing efficiency of the postal services, has led to all but the smallest timber firms installing telex machines. In addition, the introduction of the telephone STD system enables an individual sitting at his desk to connect himself in a matter of a few seconds to almost any buyer or supplier. The use of telex and the more efficient telephone service has meant a virtual abandonment of the letter post except for the passing of shipping documents and for personal or private and confidential matters. As a result of these changes, negotiations are conducted very much more quickly, and by confirming important details by telex a written copy of the negotiation is obtained instantly by both parties.

A good and efficient filing system is still essential, as the number of telex messages is considerable. Here it is worth mentioning that the numbering of such messages with a master file of every one received or sent is a great help, as with most telex paper rolls many more copies are produced than are required for general distribution.

Accounting, too, has undergone many changes, computers and other systems of like nature having replaced in most large firms the old systems of book-keeping. However, details of such systems are quite beyond the scope of this book, and, for that matter, are not really related to timber as such.

It is the division, stock control, which is really the keystone of the timber office. Outside experts in office management and book-keeping methods can help a timber merchant in planning the correspondence and book-keeping side of his office, since many trades are fundamentally the same in this respect, but in planning a stock control system the timber merchant must not rely on any outside help. Only he knows what he wants, and outsiders tend to complicate matters. Stock control of timber is centred around the stock book or stock sheets which are still in use in many offices or else the computer records for firms which have gone over to this system of stock records.

THE STOCK BOOK

The ruling and design of the stock book governs the system. This is the information that is wanted:

(1) Details of the particular stock, including details of contract, seller, name of ship, etc.

(2) Date received into stock, date placed in stick (if necessary), date of final discharge of ship and date of possible claim on the goods.

(3) Cost — c.i.f. price (or equivalent) together with all other charges such as dock and labour charges, transport or storage charges that have accumulated on the parcel, to give actual net cost at any time to the firm.

(4) Full specification, to enable out-turn (amount received from the ship) to be checked against seller's invoice and specification and claim for shortage

(if any) against the ship. The number of packages and pieces per package must be recorded, with details of lengths in truck-bundled shipments. The majority of Scandinavian mills nowadays supply details of lengths in a truck-bundle.

(5) Full specification of goods in stock at any one time by quality, size, length and packages. As each sale is made, the quantity is marked off the opening stock figure. It should be possible to check stock physically at any particular time, and for this stock to agree, with very small variations, with the stock book figure.

(6) Balance of stock remaining to be sold. This, of course, is not necessarily the same as (5), as some goods may have been sold but not removed from stock by the purchaser. To avoid overselling any parcel, it is necessary to know at all times how much remains to be sold, although this figure does not have to be exact. The stock lists or sales lists, showing what the merchant or importer has available for sale, are made up from these figures on the stock book.

The stock book may be a simple ledger ruled up by an office clerk or it may be an expensive loose-leaf book with highly complicated, specially printed sheets. Whatever form it takes, it fails in its purpose if it does not produce the information set out above quickly and easily.

STOCK CONTROL BY COMPUTER

The stock control of timber and allied products, certainly as far as large importers are concerned, is now largely controlled by computer in some form or other.

Whereas in the past details of the particular stock, including details of contract, seller, name of ship, date received into stock and date of final discharge, were essential items of information required for stock records, nowadays, for all but the better joinery stocks, etc., it is quite usual to store timber more by qualities, sizes and lengths, regardless of the source of supply. This is particularly so in the case of terminals handling bulk shipments of Canadian lumber, where stocks may be held for a considerable time at the port of entry.

With the use of computers it is now possible to supply stock balances for any particular item together with the history of that size (i.e. sales, orders not delivered, etc.).

With computerised stock-keeping it is possible to obtain at any given time a price per cubic metre or standard taking into consideration all landing and storage costs, differences in price, up or down, of fresh shipments arriving so that an overall price can be given for the total holding at any time. The computer can give full specifications of packages, lengths, number of pieces per package held in each size and quality without delay. It is also possible to record whether a pack contains more than one width and the quantity of each width in the pack.

14　Inland Sales, Charges and Costs

14.1 Inland Sales

Timber may be bought and sold in this country at several stages varying from the purchase of it while it is still in transit to this country to the purchase of it delivered to the ultimate user's factory or yard.

The timber is cheaper at the earlier stages, but must be purchased in quantity, with possibly the inclusion of less popular sizes or specifications. In the later stages the timber is dearer by virtue of labour, services, etc., performed on the timber, but, on the other hand, the buyer has the power to select just what is required, inspect the stock beforehand and purchase only very small quantities.

C.I.F. RESALE

An importer buying timber f.a.s. or c.i.f. may resell it on the same terms, but it is seldom resold f.a.s., almost always c.i.f. This is achieved by endorsement and transfer of the relevant bills of lading and insurance policies, the property thus being transferred in the bills of lading to the new purchaser. The new purchaser is protected in the same manner as the original importer was; all the terms and conditions applying to a c.i.f. contract protecting the original buyer also protect the buyer in a c.i.f. resale contract.

For all practical purposes the buyer in a c.i.f. resale contract is in the same position as a buyer in an original c.i.f. contract, except that the c.i.f. resale price is usually higher, since it includes the working profit, etc., of the original importer. A sale on these terms must be in complete bills of lading to enable the transfer of the property in the goods to be carried out.

The TTF c.i.f. reselling contract forms are discussed in Chapter 9.

EX SHIP

Timber may be sold by the importer at the point where it crosses the ship's rail. In these 'ex ship' sales the importer pays the import duty (if any), dock and town dues, tolls, etc., and a small proportion only of the labour charges. The buyer pays the porterage charges and also quay rent, etc., if the timber is taken on to the quay.

The importer is responsible for all charges to the ship, such as demurrage or dead freight, in addition to the normal freight charges, and must provide the ex ship buyer with a clear delivery order to obtain the goods from the ship.

The TTF ex ship contract forms are discussed on page 226.

An ex ship sale will enable the new buyer to take the timber overside direct into railway wagon, lighter or road transport to his own yard, which gives him the advantage of a considerable saving in labour charges. Again the sale must be of complete bills of lading, as this is the minimum quantity for which separate disposal instructions can be given to the stevedores unloading the ship.

EX QUAY (LANDED)

When the importer has taken his bills of lading on to the quay, paying the full labour charges, etc., he may sell either complete bills of lading or else parts of bills of lading for delivery to the customer's vehicle at the quay. The sale of a part of a bill of lading from the quay largely depends upon the labour services available. In some cases it is possible to arrange for the master porters to lay the bill of lading out and to deliver specific widths or lengths from a mixed parcel.

The term 'landed' is primarily used to distinguish a sale from an 'overside' or 'ex ship' sale, but it may be used in reference to goods that have been moved from the quay to a storage ground. There is no hard and fast definition of 'landed', and it must be interpreted by its relation to all other factors of the sale that are disclosed.

EX PUBLIC STORAGE YARD

Some ports in the UK have open or covered public storage yards either at the quayside or with direct rail, road or water connection with the quays. It is possible in some ports for the importer to take his goods 'overside' either into railway wagon or lighter, straight into the storage ground. These storage grounds are very useful to the importer, as they provide an overflow for his own yard. The charges made are usually in two parts — (1) receipt, handling and redelivery to vehicle, (2) rental charge per week, as for most warehousing — and the importer knows exactly what his handling has cost him.

The rates for handling and storing in public storage yards are generally very competitive, and with the saving obtained by taking the goods 'overside' it is possible for timber sold ex public storage yard to be cheaper than the same goods sold ex private yard.

EX PRIVATE STORAGE YARD

The last stage is the sale from a private storage yard. Here the timber will have accumulated all the labour charges from ship to yard and therefore the ultimate cost of the timber is greater, although some saving can be made where the yard has direct rail, road or water connection with the quay. In addition to labour charges there is also the cost of carriage of the goods from the quay to the yard, and in the case of yards well inland from the port these carriage charges can be considerable. The bulk of the timber stocks in the country are carried in private yards, since there are only a limited number of public storage yards anyway and most of these are around the ports.

Sales from a private yard offer the consumer the greatest service he can get. Here he can pick and choose, inspect the timber before he buys it, specify lengths, widths and qualities, and buy whatever quantity he wants from a tenth to a hundred cubic metre. Frequently the yard is part and parcel of a sawmill, so that the consumer may purchase his own particular requirements of sawn or machined timber; in fact if he urgently requires one particular size that is not in stock, it can usually be sawn for him from larger dimensions. A comparison can be made here with a sale of timber from a public storage yard, since if the purchaser wishes to have his timber sawn or machined, it must be carried from the public storage yard to a sawmill, handled in and out, sawn, machined, etc., and in the end may cost more than the same timber purchased from the private yard attached to the sawmill.

The ex quay, ex public storage yard and ex private yard sales have been considered in relation to relative costs delivered on to the transport that will convey the timber to the purchaser's yard or factory. The importer may deliver the timber on his own vehicles from any of the stages shown above, in which case the price is a 'delivered' price.

An inland sale is far less liable to difficulties or disputes as to quality or measurement, since when sales are made of 'landed' goods from quay or storage yard, the buyer can inspect them before placing his order. For these sales nothing more than a written order is required. The onus is entirely upon the buyer; *caveat emptor*, which means 'let the buyer beware', expresses the legal attitude.

Where a sale is made ex ship, ex quay or ex public storage yard, it is necessary for the seller to forward a 'delivery order' either direct to the master porters or storage yard or to the buyers who can present it to the master porters or storage yard. A 'delivery order' takes no set form but is merely an authorisation from the seller for the release of the timber being sold to the buyer.

An inland sale is much simpler than a sale between a foreign seller and an importer in this country. In the latter delivery is effected by transfer of documents; in the former by the transfer of the goods themselves. It is usual to send with the goods a consignment note or delivery note giving details at any rate of the number of pieces sent. This is signed by the buyers as they take delivery, and the signed note is returned to the seller. Sometimes a full specification of the goods is sent either with or on the delivery note, but usually it is only practicable for the number of pieces received to be signed for, without an actual measurement check of each piece as it is received.

The invoice will certainly be accompanied by a full specification of the goods, if the specification has not already been sent.

It is important to remember that all the correspondence and documents relating to an inland sale are as important as the contract form in a c.i.f. or f.a.s. sale from the legal point of view. In case of dispute all the letters, memoranda, etc., relating to the sale constitute the terms and conditions of the sale. There is no necessity for any document relating to the sale of goods to be stamped, or for any special set form to be used; many firms use 'sale notes' to confirm the terms of a sale but this is not necessary if the terms are already contained in other documents, such as an order from the customer, memoranda offering the goods, etc. Taken together, all these documents give sufficient detail usually to give written form as a legal contract. That is to say, names of parties, description of goods, price and signature of buyer.

14.2 Conversion and Machining Charges and Costs

Conversion and machining charges show immense variation between individual firms and different parts of the country. Most sawmills have their own local trade association from which a 'sawing and planing list' is issued setting out the rates to be charged for various operations. These lists can only be a guide, and each firm will have its own scale of charges. The great variations that exist in sawmill charges arise principally through lack of adequate information upon which a rational scale of charges could be drawn up. As a result, guesswork and rule of thumb methods coupled with copying or following sawing lists issued in other areas have been the basis for many of the rates used to-day.

If a sawmill is to be operated economically, it is essential to have accurate data as to the cost of various operations, quite apart from an overall financial costing of the trading of a sawmill over a given period of time. In a sawmill that is producing the same articles day in and day out, this is comparatively easy. A sawmill or machine shop attached to a joinery factory or furniture factory can be costed fairly easily; the difficulties occur in the all-purpose sawmill.

First of all, the units on which sawmill charges are based themselves vary as follows:

Log sawing   Charged per cubic metre or 100 m² of sawing.
Deep cutting   Softwoods, per cubic metre.
               Hardwoods, per 100 m² of sawing.
Flat cutting   Softwoods, per cubic metre or 100 m² of sawing.
               Hardwoods, per 100 lineal metres.

Cross-cutting	Softwoods, per cubic metre or per cut.
Machining	Softwoods, per cubic metre.
	Hardwoods, per 100 m² or per 100 lineal metres.

This variation complicates any costing system, and much of it is unnecessary. A typical anomaly arising from the above methods of charging is seen with the deep cutting charges. These are either per cubic metre, with varying rates for the number of deep cuts in battens or deals of varying thickness, or per 100 square metre of sawing. If the charge is for one deep cut in 50 mm x 225 mm and it is based on square metre, then the total lineal metre will be half that of 50 mm x 150 mm. The modern band re-saw will cut both just as fast with no noticeably increased effort. With modern equipment it would appear to be more rational to base costs and charges on a lineal or metre run basis. This certainly simplifies the costing system. It is not suggested that 50 mm x 100 mm and 50 mm x 300 mm should be both charged at the same rate per 100 metre run; some graduation is necessary and separate rates for up to 100 mm, 100–150 mm and 150–225 mm.

If more rational rates for sawing charges are adopted, costing becomes easier. All that is required is the metre run, under, say, four different headings of depth, produced by a particular sawbench per hour, day or week. The first stage in costing has then been reached. This information can be taken out week by week, and provides an accurate basis for comparison of the production of the mill.

The next stage is to calculate as accurately as possible the cost of that amount of sawing. Certain items are directly chargeable, such as labour (sawyer, etc.), holiday pay and national insurance. In the assessment of the labour item it must not be forgotten that a sawyer is paid for 38 hours (or whatever applies) during the week. Each hour of that time must be taken up on cost sheets. It is not sufficient merely to put down the time the sawyer was actually cutting timber. Setting up, changing saws, breakdowns, etc., all mean time that must be accounted for. In highly organised engineering works this is all listed under 'lost time', but in a sawmill it is simplest merely to include it in the time on a particular job.

The remaining items that cannot be easily or quickly calculated are as follows: factory expenses, indirect labour charges and overhead charges or on-costs. The method of assessment of these depends upon how accurately the costs are required.

Depreciation, running costs, power consumption, insurance and proportion of factory floor area occupied may all be calculated or compiled to give a value per week, month, etc., of a particular machine. This value is, in its turn, split into the various costs of work produced by the machine in a given period.

There remains at the end a hard core of 'overhead' charges, which may either be added to the costs of the job as a percentage of direct labour and materials or based upon time, capital value of machine, etc.

The more difficult items of overheads, factory expenses, etc., can only be based on, say, six months' or twelve months' trading figures, but when calculated, they remain fixed. It is only necessary then on each costing to take up the amount of direct labour, etc.

The control of materials and their place in costing is also extremely important, but does not have a direct bearing in this case on the charging rates. If an adequate stock control system is in operation, it is often much simpler to confine costing to labour only. There is always the problem of 'off-cuts' in material costing. One dimension of timber will go into a mill for sawing and machining to a particular section. During this process an off-cut may be produced which is used to produce, say, a standard moulding or slating batten, etc.

Sawmill costing can never be easy while a sawmill is flexible in the class of work that it handles, since one machine may not do the same job twice, and may have many variations in class of work in one day. However, if it is felt that a full job costing system cannot be started (whereby each job is costed separately), it is often possible to cost a mill or part of a mill as a whole, without trying to account for materials in the costing.

In this type of costing the total amount of work performed by the mill in a week is compiled − that is, total amount of deep cutting, flat cutting, machining, etc. This is then extended into a value of 'labour services' performed by the mill during the week or period. All that is now required is the cost of running the mill for a week (i.e. wage bill and an assessment of overhead charges to be carried by the whole mill for one week). This type of costing system gives a week-by-week control on the running of a mill and at the same time confirms or disproves the sawmill charging rates in force.

Costing, like office systems, should be based upon the information that is required. In installing a costing system a sawmill owner can obtain much excellent experienced technical advice, but in the end it is only he who can devise the best costing system for his works, since only he knows exactly what information he wants from his costings. Notwithstanding this, there is still much to be learned about costing in the timber trade. Many lessons could be taken from the engineering trades, which are so far advanced in these matters, and when the trade in general becomes more advanced in its outlook on costing, sawmill charging rates and price lists will become more rational.

15   Measurements, Calculations and Units of Sale

15.1 Historical

Since the last edition of this book was published, two most significant changes have taken place in the trade under the heading of this chapter. In the UK decimal currency has been introduced and, with few exceptions, which will be mentioned later, the trade has changed from Imperial to metric measure. Despite opposition from some quarters, this was a logical change, because at least 85 per cent of the world's population operates under a metric system and 75 per cent of the world's trade is transacted in metric terms. There is no doubt that world metrication will be achieved in due course.

For the reader who may not be familiar with the background leading up to the change and because a certain number of transactions are still negotiated in the old Imperial terms, a brief explanation of the system is given at the end of this chapter.

Following the decision of the British Government to support the change to metric, the construction industry was one of the first to plan the change-over. The British Standards Institution published a document in early 1967, PD 6030: '*Programme for the Change to the Metric System in the Construction Industry*', together with PD 6031: '*A Guide for the Use of the Metric System in the Construction Industry*'. A second edition of the latter was published in 1968, with certain revisions which are quoted later. Since the construction industry is the timber trade's largest and most important customer, the trade had anticipated the implications with considerable speed and had already set up an *ad hoc* TTF Metrication Committee in 1967 to consider the effect upon the timber trade. This was followed by urgent activity in the form of consultation with all sections, including the countries from which we import timber. In 1969 BS 4471: *Dimensions for Softwood*, Part 1 was published; this has been amended a number of times since then, following experience gained and representations from certain parties. This standard is possibly the most important ever published for the trade. Part 2, *Small Resawn Sections*, was published in 1971. General discussion on the implications of BS 4471 are given later in this chapter.

It is true to say that the changeover created many difficult problems for the importing trade in the UK during the earlier stages. Exporters were quick to commence shipment of metric goods, and there was a long transitional period when stocks here consisted of goods conforming to the old and the new dimensions and lengths. To a limited degree, this situation exists today, because softwood from North America and many hardwoods are still imported in Imperial measure but have to be sold in the metric equivalent, since all sectors of the construction industry design and build accordingly. The Building Regulations do not permit any other system.

Exporters or shippers had little difficulty in changing their methods of production, because they were familiar with the metric system already in use in their country. It is an interesting fact that the major exporting countries such as the USSR, Sweden and Finland had always produced Imperial dimensions for export — not only to the UK, but also to the Continent and elsewhere. Undoubtedly, this was because the UK had always been their best customer and they standardised their production accordingly. Obviously, it would not have been a viable proposition to produce different systems. Needless to say, all these other countries had to resell the goods as metric equivalents.

It must be stated that metrication was initially a national industrial decision and, as everyone knows, applies to industry as a whole. It may not be popular in all quarters, but the fact remains that the UK Government supported the change but did not in any way impose it upon the country. The length of time it will take to achieve metrication throughout industry is unknown. Our own industry has had a number of years to familiarise itself with the system and very many organisations have helped by issuing explanatory documents and conversion charts; seminars have been held and everything possible has been done to make the changeover as easy as possible. The greatest task was undertaken by the British Standards Institution which had to revise a vast number of specifications to cover metric units. This involved committees and discussions and, taking industry as a whole, thousands of Standards are still being affected. To sum up, the upheaval and work to be undertaken is formidable but in the interests of world trade — in particular, the UK commitment with the EEC, exports elsewhere and the desirability of standardisation between so many countries — it becomes clear that the ultimate result will justify the effort.

15.2 Units of Measure

The units adopted are known as the International System. This system, the Systéme Internationale d'Unités (SI), is the most advanced form of the metric system. PD 6031, already mentioned, gives guidance as to how the various units or symbols should be expressed, and it is desirable that those which affect the trade should be quoted, since one sees so many incorrect or misleading references in correspondence and documents.

The six SI base units are as follows:

Quantity	Unit	Symbol
Length	metre	m
Mass	kilogram	kg
Time	second	s
Electric current	ampere	A
Thermodynamic temperatures	kelvin	K
Luminous intensity	candela	cd

In addition, there are supplementary units which are related to these base units. In the main, these are for specialist use and are unlikely to concern our trade. We shall be using units for length, mass, area and volume as follows:

> Length: metre (m)
> Section: millimetre (mm)
> Mass (weight): kilogram (kg)
> Bulk (area): square metre (m^2)
> Bulk (volume): cubic metre (m^3)

The centimetre and decimetre are not used in the SI system for linear measurement. For length we have the metre as a base unit; a thousandth part of it, the millimetre; and 1000 metre, called a kilometre.

The following points are a guide to the use or misuse of these units or symbols in everyday documents. To give one common example, it has long been continental practice to use a comma as a decimal point, whereas in the UK it has been used to denote thousands. For instance, 12,250 is very different from 12.250.

(1) The use of the comma should be abandoned in figures up to 9999. If needed, the thousand marker in five-digit numbers should be a space thus: 12 250.

(2) The decimal marker should be a central point thus: 12·250; but since most typewriters only have a full stop, it is acceptable to write it as 12.250.

(3) There should be a zero before a decimal point if the number is less than unity — for example 0.12, not .12.

(4) No full stop is used after SI units — for example, 12 mm, not 12 m.m. or 12 mm.

(5) Where typewriters have no ^{2} or ^{3} signs, an acceptable alternative is sq and cu but not sq. or cu. — for example 12.250 sq m or 12.250 cu m.

(6) A full stop is only required after a symbol if it is at the end of a sentence.

(7) The same unit symbol is used for singular and plural — for example, 12.250 m not 12.250 ms; 12.250 km, not 12.250 kms.

(8) Always use the correct case for symbols — for example, 12 m, not 12 M, 12 kg, not 12 Kg.

(9) Whole numbers may be expressed without a decimal marker thus: 12; 120; 1200.

(10) There should be one unit of space between a figure and its symbol – for example, 12 m, not 12m.

Conformance with these simple rules is a means of gaining international understanding and avoiding possible expensive mistakes. Unfortunately, they are greatly misunderstood or ignored by many.

15.3 Methods of Calculating

In view of the time which has elapsed since the UK changed to the metric system, there cannot be many people employed in the trade who have not become fully conversant with everyday calculations. One of the strongest arguments in favour of metrication is the fact that it lends itself to mechanisation. There are few individuals in companies who do not have access to a calculating machine which is essentially designed to cope with the decimal system. With the old Imperial system, we were obliged to calculate decimally and convert back to standards, feet, inches, pounds, shillings and pence. With the adoption of the metric system, the whole process of addition, subtraction, multiplication and division has become simplified, as no conversion factors are required, since they are all of ten. All that is needed is care to ensure that the decimal point is correctly placed, and with experience this can be done visually without any further operation of the calculating machine. The same facility also applies to those who use slide rules.

First, it should be emphasised that one needs to avoid unnecessary accuracy in calculations. For instance, if we multiply length by width by thickness and price, we could easily be multiplying a five-digit number by two three-digit numbers and a four-digit number, which would give us fifteen digits in the answer – about ten more than is needed for a reasonable degree of accuracy. The way round this problem – which is beyond the capacity of the small calculators commonly used – is to approximate to the required degree of accuracy at each separate stage. The important thing to remember is that, converting from one unit to another, it is only necessary to move the decimal point. To take a simple example:

$$320.75 \text{ m of } 225 \text{ mm by } 125 \text{ mm at £75.50 per m}^3$$

Convert to metres, which is

$$320.75 \text{ m} \times 0.225 \text{ m} \times 0.125 \text{ m} \times £75.50 \text{ per m}^3$$

Multiply 320.75 m × 0.225 m, which equals 72.168 75, which is far more accurate than is needed; taking this to two decimal places, it becomes 72.17 (since 0.17 is nearer to 0.168 than 0.16). Multiply 72.17 × 0.125 to get 9.02 cubic metre (9.02 m^3). Multiply 9.02 × £75.50 and we get £681.01. Had we taken the figure 72.168 75, the answer would have been £681.092 57 – so we are talking in terms of 8p or less than 1p per m^3.

A further illustration of the simplicity of the same calculation is as follows:

Lineal (m) x width (mm) x thickness (mm) divided by 1 000 000 equals volume in m^3.

320.75 m x 225 mm x 125 mm

$$= \frac{320.75 \quad x \quad 28\ 125}{1\ 000\ 000} = \frac{9\ 021\ 094}{1\ 000\ 000} = 9.02\ m^3$$

The decimal point has merely been moved six places.

BASIC METRIC FORMULAE – VOLUME AND AREA FROM DIMENSIONS

Volume

The volume in cubic metres equals the width and thickness in millimetres multiplied by length in metres with the decimal point moved six places to the left. For example:

100 mm x 50 mm x 80 m = 100 x 50 x 80 = 400 000.0
Move decimal point six places left   = 0.400 000 = 0.4 m^3

Area

Area equals the length in metres multiplied by width in millimetres with the decimal point moved three places to the left. For example:

$$210.41\ m\ x\ 25\ mm = \frac{210.41 \times 25}{1000} = \frac{5260.25}{1000} = 5.26\ m^2$$

Linear Volume

To obtain metre run per cubic metre from a given section in square millimetres divide 1 000 000 by the section in square millimetres. For example: How many metres of 22 mm x 100 mm in 1 m^3?

$$\frac{1\ 000\ 000}{22 \times 100} = \frac{1\ 000\ 000}{2\ 200} = 454.55\ m$$

Area Volume

To obtain square metre per cubic metre divide 1000 by thickness in millimetres. For example:

$$\text{For thickness 19 mm area volume} \quad = \quad \frac{1000}{19} \quad = \quad 52.63 \text{ m}^2$$

Linear Area

To obtain linear metre per square metre divide 1000 by width in millimetres. For example:

$$\text{For width 125 mm linear area} \quad = \quad \frac{1000}{125} \quad = \quad 8.0 \text{ m per m}^2.$$

ROUND WOOD OR LOGS

In so far as home-grown logs are concerned, the Forestry Commission changed to the metric system in 1971 and is now fully metricated. The changeover in the private sector was slower but, except for some small isolated areas, the same system has been adopted. The main variation from the sawn goods trade is that the centimetre is used rather than the millimetre. This unit was chosen as it involves less use of unnecessary digits.

Broadly speaking, three systems are used to measure the volume of home-grown logs, although all trees and logs are expressed as diameters in centimetre and lengths in metre. In one system the top diameter of a felled saw log is measured and the volume in cubic metres against length. A second system is the measurement in diameter at mid-point and the volume in cubic metres against length. Finally, in the case of standing trees, it is customary to measure diameter at breast height standardised at 1.30 m, which replaces the former Imperial height of 4 ft 3 in. The Forestry Commission has published conversion tables which give the volume in cubic metres against diameter and length. Adjustment for over-bark and under-bark difference in volume is taken into consideration.

In regard to imported hardwood logs, which are considerably larger, the old long-standing system of measurement is still widely used. In recent years this has become a declining trade but it still thrives from certain sources. These systems are described in the section entitled 'Imperial measure'.

15.4 Standard Sizes

The change from Imperial to metric measure could not have been made by merely converting the old common sizes of feet (ft) and inches (in) to millimetres and metres. This can be illustrated by the fact that 1 in equals 25.4 mm and 1 ft equals 304.8 mm or 0.30 m. The standard sizes selected were based on reality and approved by the Conference of European Exporters and Importers and, in fact, are very close to formerly used sized but rounded off to the nearest whole number. After considerable discussion with the International Standards Organisation (ISO), a British Standard was produced in 1969 — BS 4471: *Dimensions for Softwood*. This has been amended a number of times, the latest revision being in 1978 and affecting, among other things, the sizes of sawn and planed timber.

Table 15.1 shows the basic sizes (cross-sectional), all in millimetres.

TABLE 15.1

Thickness	Width								
	75	100	125	150	175	200	225	250	300
16	x	x	x	x					
19	x	x	x	x					
22	x	x	x	x					
25	x	x	x	x	x	x	x	x	x
32	x	x	x	x	x	x	x	x	x
36	x	x	x	x					
38	x	x	x	x	x	x	x		
44	x	x	x	x	x	x	x	x	x
47*	x	x	x	x	x	x	x	x	x
50	x	x	x	x	x	x	x	x	x
63		x	x	x	x	x	x		
75		x	x	x	x	x	x	x	x
100		x		x		x		x	x
150				x		x			x
200						x			
250								x	
300									x

* This range of widths for 47 mm thickness will usually be found to be available in constructional quality only.
NOTE. The smaller sizes contained within the broken lines are normally but not exclusively of European origin. The larger sizes outside the dotted lines are normally but not exclusively of North and South American origin.

Table 15.2 shows the basic lengths of sawn timber, all in metres.

TABLE 15.2

1.80	2.10	3.00	4.20	5.10	6.00	7.20
	2.40	3.30	4.50	5.40	6.30	
	2.70	3.60	4.80	5.70	6.60	
		3.90			6.90	

NOTE. Lengths of 6.00 m and over will generally only be available from North American species and may have to be recut from larger sizes.

SIZES AND PERMISSIBLE DEVIATIONS OF SAWN GOODS

(1) *Resawing allowance.* When smaller sizes are produced by resawing from larger, not more than 2 mm reduction of size of each piece so produced shall be allowed; this reduction is not additional to those given in table 15.3 showing planing tolerances. Sellers offering or supplying such timber shall describe it as 'resawn ex larger'.

(2) Permissible deviations on sizes as originally produced. *Cross-section*: Minus deviations in cross-section are permissible on not exceeding 10 per cent of the pieces in any parcel of softwood.

(3) *Thickness and widths*. In thickness and widths not exceeding 100 mm the permissible deviation is minus 1 mm and plus 3 mm.

In thicknesses and widths over 100 mm the permissible deviation is minus 2 mm and plus 6 mm.

(4) *Lengths*. On lengths no minus deviation is permissible, but overlength is unlimited.

(5) *Actual sizes*. The actual sizes of any piece of timber will vary with its moisture content at the time of measurement. The sizes in table 15.1 are to be measured as at 20 per cent moisture content. For any higher moisture content up to 30 per cent, the size shall be greater by 1 per cent for every 5 per cent of moisture content in excess of 20 per cent; and for any lower moisture content, the size may be smaller by 1 per cent for every 5 per cent of moisture content below 20 per cent. For any higher moisture content than 30 per cent, no larger size will be required than at 30 per cent.

Table 15.3 shows the reductions from basic size to finished size by planing of two opposed faces, and is in millimetres.

TABLE 15.3

Class	Figures to subtract from basic sizes			
	15 to and including 35	Over 35 to and including 100	Over 100 to and including 150	Over 150
(a) Constructional timber	3	3	5	6
(b) Matching*; interlocking boards	4	4	6	6
(c) Wood trim not specified in BS 584	5	7	7	9
(d) Joinery and cabinet work	7	9	11	13

*The reduction of width is overall the extreme size and is exclusive of any reduction of the face by the machining of a tongue or lap joint.

Floorings and wood trim are covered by separate British Standards: flooring, BS 1297; wood trim, BS 584.

Permissible deviations. For all finished sizes after planing a manufacturing deviation of plus or minus 0.5 mm shall be allowed.

Regularising. The following reductions will apply to timber to be regularised: 3 mm off the width only for timber up to and including 150 mm width and 5 mm off the width for timber over 150 mm width. These reductions are not additional to those shown in table 15.3. For all finished sizes after regularising, a manufacturing deviation of plus or minus 0.5 mm shall be allowed.

The revision of BS 4471 includes an Appendix to cover timber imported from Canada. It reads as follows:

General. Producers in Canada supply sizes and stress grades of timber for their domestic constructional markets in accordance with their own national standards. These standard sizes and stress grades do not necessarily accord with all the clauses of this standard or with BS 4978 'Timber Grades for Structural Use'. In order to facilitate their application for structural purposes in the UK, CP 112. Part 2. 1971 'The Structural Use of Timber' and its amendment slips 1 and 2 recognise their use in the UK by providing tables of geometrical properties for certain sizes and grade stresses for a limited number of grades.

'Timber produced to this standard has rounded arrises, not exceeding 3 mm.

'It is desirable that details of all the standard sizes referred to in CP 112 should be found in the same document, and it is the purpose of this appendix to give the relevant information for timber planed in accordance with Canadian Standards Association Standard 0141 – 1970 'Softwood Lumber'. Canadian timber planed all round (P.A.R.) as described in this standard refers to timber surfaced 4 sides (S.4.S.) as described in Canadian terminology.'

Table 15.4 shows these processed sizes, which have been converted from the original Imperial sizes but rounded off to the nearest millimetre for commercial application.

Permissible deviations. No minus deviation is permissible, but oversize is unlimited.

TABLE 15.4

Thickness	Width
38	63
38	89
38	140
38	184
38	235
38	285

Actual sizes. The actual size of any piece of timber will vary with the moisture content at the time of measurement. The sizes in table 15.4 are to be measured as at 19 per cent moisture content. For any higher moisture content up to 30 per cent, the size shall be greater by 1 per cent for every 4 per cent of moisture content in excess of 19 per cent. For any lower moisture content, the size may be smaller by 1 per cent for each 4 per cent of moisture content below 19 per cent. For any higher moisture content than 30 per cent, no larger size will be required than at 30 per cent.

BS 4471 makes reference to the following British Standards and special publications: BS 584: Wood Trim (Softwood); BS 1297: Grading and Sizing of Softwood Flooring; BS 2482: Timber Scaffold Boards (38 mm x 225 mm); BS 4978: Timber Grades for Structural Use; CP 112, Part 2: The Structural Use of Timber.

Imported sawn softwoods have always had a wide variety of names, depending upon their dimensions. These are as follows:

Term	Dimension
Plank	50 mm to 100 mm x 275 mm and wider
Deal	50 mm to 100 mm x 225 mm to under 275 mm wide
Batten	50 mm to 100 mm x 125 mm to 200 mm wide
Scantling	50 mm to 100 mm x 50 mm to 100 mm wide
Board	under 50 mm x 100 mm and wider
Strip	under 50 mm x 100 mm and under
Slating	16 mm to 25 mm x 25 mm to 75 mm wide
Square	25 mm x 25 mm to 125 mm x 125 mm
Baulk	100 mm x 100 mm or greater

15.5 General Observations

When metrication was introduced, it was both hoped and expected that it might mean reduction or rationalisation of the multitude of dimensions which the trade was expected to produce and stock. With few exceptions, such as ½ in widths of boards, this has not been achieved. If anything, there has been a proliferation of sizes, which, although understandable, is regrettable. The main reason for this is that certain dimensions and lengths may be suitable for, say, joinery Unsorted, while others may only be suitable for, say, carcassing fifths. This is a problem which appears to be insoluble, since so many interests are involved in the UK and elsewhere, and there is also the dilemma of exporters, who are required to produce goods. The latter can only offer that which falls from the quality of the raw material available.

It is a fact that for many years exporters have tried to produce dimensions and lengths which importers have demanded, and it appears that they have been demanded because they have been offered. The anomaly is that neither importers nor exporters seem to realise the true situation — or if they do, there seems to be no practical solution to the problem beyond international standardisation. There are many who think that part of the fault lies with the specifiers or architects, who are inclined to demand dimensions which are non-standard. There is no doubt that in the past this has led to considerable waste and expense in remachining, but with the efforts made to introduce modular co-ordination in the construction industry, which is already taking significant effect, many of these anomalies will be eliminated.

In regard to BS 4471 and its specified basic dimensions and tolerances, these have not been produced without very considerable thought and consultation by all the parties concerned in its implementation. Perhaps it is unfortunate that many of the thicknesses are so close and virtually unidentifiable from one another when the allowable tolerances are considered. For example, the standard allows tolerances of minus 1 mm and plus 3 mm, and this is particularly significant for all the thicknesses of 32, 36, 38, 44, 47 and 50 mm. While this is confined to only 10 per cent of the pieces in any parcel, and at a moisture content of 20 per cent, it does mean that these thicknesses can overlap and become indistinguishable. For example:

$$
\begin{array}{llll}
32 \text{ mm plus} & 3 \text{ mm} & = & 35 \text{ mm} \\
36 \text{ mm minus} & 1 \text{ mm} & = & 35 \text{ mm} \\
44 \text{ mm plus} & 3 \text{ mm} & = & 47 \text{ mm} \\
47 \text{ mm plus} & 3 \text{ mm} & = & 50 \text{ mm} \\
50 \text{ mm minus} & 1 \text{ mm} & = & 49 \text{ mm}
\end{array}
$$

In terms of the practical timber man with a pocket rule, it is difficult — if not impossible — to measure a piece of sawn timber with rough edges to an accuracy of 1 mm. In regard to the tolerance of 0.50 mm allowed on regularised timber by planing, such accuracy can only be achieved by the use of a caliper gauge. The main anomaly is 47 mm and 50 mm. For decades 50 mm or its equivalent 2 in has been a standard carcassing size. Before metrication $1^7/_8$ in could be sold as 2 in because the then current standard allowed a tolerance of $^1/_8$ in. This no longer applies, since 50 mm cannot measure less than 49 mm — a 1 mm minus tolerance. To continue with this former practice could involve infringement of the Trade Description Act.

15.6 Units of Sale

The selling of timber and allied products can be classified under two headings:

(1) Bulk selling by overseas exporters to importers through an agent or direct.

(2) Selling by importers to merchants or consumers. This can be on a large or small scale, depending upon circumstances.

The selection of units upon which a sale is made is a local arrangement between the buyer and seller. It depends on the quantity being sold and upon the buyer's particular trade. Obviously, a large builder will buy in bulk, whereas a small DIY business will require a picked specification in limited quantity.

The first measurements and units of sale that affect the trade are those used in importing goods to the UK. Most of the European contract forms have been amended to read price per cubic metre, but, at the time of writing, some still stipulate: sawn goods per St Petersburg standard of 165 ft^3; planed goods per St Petersburg standard of 165 ft^3 (nominal measure). As mentioned earlier, the time will come when the universal unit of sale will be in cubic metre – at least in bulk quantities.

The three basic units for selling are cubic metre, square metre and linear metre or metre run, but the latter is usually confined to smaller quantities, particularly boards, floorings and mouldings. Panel products of all types are usually sold in square metres but bulk quantities may be sold in cubic metres and very small quantities at a price per sheet.

Now that wood goods are imported in packaged or truck-bundled form, these are stored in this form by importers, who naturally prefer to sell them as units without breakdown and selection. Packaged goods which are all of one length can be sold as a complete unit of the required length on a price per m^3 basis. Truck-bundled goods which are random lengths suit those receivers who have no specific length requirements – for example, boards and floorings. In both instances the importer will have shipping documents giving the total volume of each unit, so eliminating the need for a separate tally. This has obvious advantages over the system of former days when goods were received loose and every sale from stock had to be sorted and tallied.

AVOIDING LOSS WHEN SELLING IMPERIAL AS METRIC

As already mentioned, at the present time the trade is obliged to import certain goods in Imperial measure and to resell almost exclusively in metric measure. Because the units were rounded off in deciding upon the new counterparts – cross-section and lengths – they differ to varying degrees. For the most part, the new sizes are smaller than the old ones and the total reduction in volume can be as much as 4.88 per cent, depending upon thickness. This is illustrated by the actual equivalents:

$$1 \text{ in} = 25.4001 \text{ mm}$$
$$1 \text{ ft} = 304.8010 \text{ mm, or } 0.3048 \text{ m}^3$$
$$1 \text{ ft}^3 = 0.0283 \text{ m}^3$$
$$1 \text{ standard } (165 \text{ ft}^3) = 4.6720 \text{ m}^3$$

As the metric units have been rounded off,

$$1 \text{ in} = 25.000 \text{ mm}$$
$$1 \text{ ft} = 0.3000 \text{ m (length increment)}$$

It follows that the volume will vary from the standard of 4.6720 m³. For this reason conversion factors have to be used to compensate for the loss in measure. To give an example:

1 ft of 2 in by 6 in converted to exact metric volume would be 304.8 mm × 50.8 mm × 152.4 mm, the volume of which would be 2 359 737 mm³, or 2.360 m³.

The price would be sold in the rationalised form as 300 mm × 50 mm × 150 mm, the volume of which would be 2 250 000 mm³, or 2.250 m³.

There is a difference in volume of 2.360 m³ minus 2.250 m³ = 0.11 m³.

As 4.6720 m³ exactly equals 1 standard, the equation has to be arranged as follows:

$$4.6720 \times \frac{2.250}{2.360} = 4.4550$$

or

$$4.6720 \times \frac{300 \times 50 \times 150}{304.8 \times 50.8 \times 152.4} = 4.550$$

Therefore, 1 standard of 2 in by 6 in sold in metric measure equals 4.550 m³. It follows that all other dimensions will vary accordingly. The actual equivalents are shown in table 15.5 together with conversion factors in terms of price.

It has become customary for importers to regard the figure of 4.4550 as the average conversion factor. As shown in table 15.5, it covers all widths from 75 mm rising in 25 mm increments to 300 mm and thicknesses of 25, 50, 75 and 100 mm. Tables 15.6–15.8 provide all the other information normally required — for example, running metres in 1 m³.

SELLING BY IMPORTERS TO MERCHANTS OR CONSUMERS

As mentioned earlier, the unit of sale depends on the requirements of the purchaser and the volume involved. For sawn timber the price is quoted on a 10 m or 100 m run basis or, in the case of larger quantities, on a cubic metre basis. The same applies to planed goods, which are usually sold in smaller quantities than sawn goods used for carcassing. Panel products of all types are sold on a 10 m² basis or, in the case of very small quantities, at a price per sheet.

TABLE 15.5 METRIC CONVERSION

Widths: Metric 75, 100, 125, 150, 175, 200, 225, 250, 275 & 300 mm
Imperial 3, 4, 5, 6, 7, 8, 9, 10, 11 & 12 inch

Standards and £ per m³

Thickness (mm)	16 and 32 mm	19 and 38 mm	22 and 44 mm	63 mm	25, 50, 75 and 100 mm
Thickness (inch)	5/8 and 1¼ inch	¾ and 1½ inch	⅞ and 1¾ inch	2½ inch	1, 2, 3 & 4 inch
	0.022	0.022	0.022	0.022	0.022
	0.055	0.055	0.056	0.056	0.056
	0.110	0.111	0.112	0.111	0.112
	0.219	0.222	0.223	0.223	0.224
	0.438	0.443	0.446	0.445	0.449
	0.658	0.665	0.670	0.668	0.673
	0.877	0.886	0.893	0.891	0.898
	1.096	1.108	1.116	1.113	1.122
	1.315	1.329	1.339	1.336	1.347
	1.534	1.551	1.562	1.559	1.571
	1.754	1.772	1.786	1.781	1.796
	1.973	1.994	2.009	2.004	2.020
	2.192	2.215	2.232	2.227	2.245
	4.384	4.430	4.464	4.454	4.489
	5.480	5.538	5.580	5.567	5.612
	10.960	11.076	11.159	11.134	11.223
	16.441	16.614	16.739	16.702	16.835
	21.921	22.151	22.319	22.269	22.447
	32.881	33.227	33.478	33.403	33.670
	43.841	44.303	44.638	44.537	44.893

Metric / Imperial (centre column)

Metric	Imperial
0.100	
0.250	
0.500	
1.000	
2.000	
3.000	
4.000	
5.000	
6.000	
7.000	
8.000	
9.000	
10.000	
20.000	
25.000	
50.000	
75.000	
100.000	
150.000	
200.000	

m³ and £ per Standard

Thickness	16 and 32 mm	19 and 38 mm	22 and 44 mm	63 mm	25, 50, 75 and 100 mm
	0.456	0.451	0.448	0.449	0.446
	1.140	1.129	1.120	1.123	1.114
	2.281	2.257	2.240	2.245	2.228
	4.562	4.514	4.481	4.491	4.455
	9.124	9.029	8.961	8.981	8.910
	13.686	13.543	13.442	13.472	13.365
	18.248	18.058	17.922	17.962	17.820
	22.810	22.572	22.403	22.453	22.275
	27.371	27.086	26.883	26.944	26.730
	31.933	31.601	31.364	31.434	31.185
	36.495	36.115	35.844	35.925	35.640
	41.057	40.630	40.325	40.415	40.095
	45.619	45.144	44.805	44.906	44.550
	91.238	90.288	89.610	89.812	89.100
	114.048	112.860	112.013	112.265	111.375
	228.095	225.720	224.025	224.530	222.750
	342.143	338.580	336.038	336.795	334.125
	456.190	451.440	448.050	449.060	445.500
	684.285	677.160	672.075	673.590	668.250
	912.380	902.880	896.100	898.120	891.000
Conversion Factor	4.5619	4.5144	4.4805	4.4906	4.4550

Explanation of Table

The Standard is equal to 4.672 m³ but thickness and width will differ to a varying degree – up or down – from the true conversion from Imperial measure. To avoid loss in selling, adjustment has to be made and the table has been calculated with the appropriate conversion factor. The figure in the centre column is used to read off whichever of the following equivalents is required:

(a) Standards to m³
(b) m³ to Standards
(c) £ per Standard to £ per m³
(d) £ per m³ to £ per Std.

Example: 16 and 32 mm. Taking 50 in the centre column as the common denominator, the following is obtained:

Left Hand Column.	Right Hand Column.
50 m³ = 10.960 Stds.	50 Stds. = 228.093 m³
£50 per Std. = £10.960 per m³	£50 per m³ = £228.093 per Std.

TABLE 15.6 RUNNING METRES IN 1 m³

Thickness (mm) / Width (mm)	75	100	125	150	175	200	225	250	275	300
16	833.33	625.00	500.00	416.67	357.14	312.50	277.77	250.00	227.27	208.33
19	701.75	526.32	421.05	350.87	300.75	263.16	233.92	210.52	191.39	175.44
22	606.06	454.54	363.64	303.03	259.74	227.27	202.02	181.82	165.29	151.51
25	533.33	400.00	320.00	266.67	228.57	200.00	177.78	160.00	145.45	133.33
32	416.66	312.50	250.00	208.33	178.57	156.25	138.89	125.00	113.64	104.17
38	350.88	263.16	210.53	175.44	150.38	131.58	116.96	105.27	95.69	87.72
44	303.03	227.27	181.81	151.52	129.87	113.64	101.01	90.91	82.64	75.76
47	283.69	212.77	170.21	141.84	121.58	106.38	94.56	85.11	77.37	70.92
50	266.66	200.00	160.00	133.33	114.29	100.00	88.89	80.00	72.73	66.67
63	211.64	158.73	126.98	105.82	90.70	79.36	70.55	63.49	57.72	52.91
75	177.78	133.33	106.67	88.89	76.19	66.67	59.26	53.33	48.48	44.44
100	133.33	100.00	80.00	66.67	57.14	50.00	44.44	40.00	36.36	33.33

TABLE 15.7 BOARD FEET IN 1m³ (423.801 board feet = 1 m³)

Board Feet	0	100	200	300	400	500	600	700	800	900	1000
0	—	0.2360	0.4719	0.7079	0.9438	1.1798	1.4158	1.6517	1.8877	2.1236	2.3596
1	0.0024	0.2383	0.4743	0.7102	0.9462	1.1822	1.4181	1.6541	1.8900	2.1260	—
2	0.0047	0.2407	0.4766	0.7126	0.9486	1.1845	1.4205	1.6564	1.8924	2.1284	—
3	0.0071	0.2430	0.4790	0.7150	0.9509	1.1869	1.4228	1.6588	1.8948	2.1307	—
4	0.0094	0.2454	0.4814	0.7173	0.9533	1.1892	1.4252	1.6612	1.8971	2.1331	—
5	0.0118	0.2478	0.4837	0.7197	0.9556	1.1916	1.4276	1.6635	1.8995	2.1354	—
6	0.0142	0.2501	0.4861	0.7220	0.9580	1.1940	1.4299	1.6659	1.9018	2.1378	—
7	0.0165	0.2525	0.4884	0.7244	0.9604	1.1963	1.4323	1.6682	1.9042	2.1402	—
8	0.0189	0.2548	0.4908	0.7268	0.9627	1.1987	1.4346	1.6706	1.9066	2.1425	—
9	0.0212	0.2572	0.4932	0.7291	0.9651	1.2010	1.4370	1.6730	1.9089	2.1449	—
10	0.0236	0.2596	0.4955	0.7315	0.9674	1.2034	1.4394	1.6753	1.9113	2.1472	—
20	0.0472	0.2832	0.5191	0.7551	0.9910	1.2270	1.4630	1.6989	1.9349	2.1708	—
30	0.0708	0.3067	0.5427	0.7787	1.0146	1.2506	1.4865	1.7225	1.9585	2.1944	—
40	0.0944	0.3303	0.5663	0.8023	1.0382	1.2742	1.5101	1.7461	1.9821	2.2180	—
50	0.1180	0.3539	0.5899	0.8259	1.0618	1.2978	1.5337	1.7697	2.0057	2.2416	—
60	0.1416	0.3775	0.6135	0.8495	1.0854	1.3214	1.5573	1.7933	2.0293	2.2652	—
70	0.1652	0.4011	0.6371	0.8731	1.1090	1.3450	1.5809	1.8169	2.0529	2.2888	—
80	0.1888	0.4247	0.6607	0.8966	1.1326	1.3686	1.6045	1.8405	2.0764	2.3124	—
90	0.2124	0.4483	0.6843	0.9202	1.1562	1.3922	1.6281	1.8641	2.1000	2.3360	—

TABLE 15.8 PRECISE CONVERSION FACTORS

Acre	0.404 686	hectares
	4 046.86	square metres
Centimetre	0.393 701	inches
Centimetre diameter	0.309 212	inches quarter-girth
Chain (66 feet)	20.116 8	metres (exactly)
Cord (128 stacked cubic feet)	3.624 56	stacked cubic metres (stéres)
Cubic metre	27.736 1	hoppus feet
	35.314 7	cubic feet
	1.307 95	cubic yards
Cubic metre per hectare	11.224 4	hoppus feet per acre
Cubic yards	0.764 555	cubic metres
Foot	0.304 8	metres (exactly)
Gallon	4.546 09	litres (cubic decimetres)
Hectare	2.471 05	acres
Hoppus foot	0.036 054 0	cubic metres
Hoppus foot per acre	0.089 052 0	cubic metres per hectare
Hoppus foot per ton	0.035 485	cubic metres per tonne
Hundredweight	0.050 802 3	tonnes
Hundredweight per acre	125.535	kilogram per hectare
Inch	0.025 4	metres (exactly)
Inch quarter-girth	3.234 03	centimetres diameter
Kilogram	2.204 62	pounds
Kilometre	0.621 371	miles
Litre (cubic decimetre)	0.219 969	gallons
	1.759 76	pints
Metre	1.093 61	yards
	3.280 84	feet
Mile (statute)	1.609 34	kilometres
Pint	0.568 261	litres (cubic decimetres)
Pound	0.453 592	kilograms
Pound per acre	1.120 85	kilograms per hectare
Pound per cubic foot	16.018 5	kilograms per cubic metre
Square chain	404.686	square metres
Square foot	0.092 903 0	square metres
Square metre	1.195 99	square yards
Square yard	0.836 127	square metres
Ton (UK)	1.016 05	tonnes
Tonne	0.984 207	tons (UK)
Yard	0.914 4	metres (exactly)

NOTE. The above conversion factors are provided for reference purposes. In practice, most conversions will be made by reference to special conversion tables which will usually incorporate the appropriate rounding-off conventions. The above factors may, however, be useful for conversions using a calculating machine. Where it is not possible to give exact conversions, the above factors are expressed to six significant figures.

BASIC PRICE CONVERSIONS – VOLUME, AREA AND LINEAR

(1) Price per square metre from price per cubic metre: Multiply price per cubic metre by thickness in millimetres and move the decimal point three places to the left.

(2) Price per cubic metre from price per square metre: The price per cubic metre equals the price per square metre divided by the thickness in millimetres, with the decimal point moved three places to the right.

(3) Price per metre from price per cubic metre: The price per metre equals the price per cubic metre multiplied by the width and thickness in millimetres, with the decimal point moved six places to the left.

(4) Price per cubic metre from price per lineal metre: The price per cubic metre equals the price per metre run divided by the area in square millimetres, with the decimal point moved six places to the right.

(5) Price per metre from price per square metre: The price per metre equals the price per square metre multiplied by the width in millimetres, with the decimal point moved three places to the left.

(6) Price per square metre from price per lineal metre: The price per square metre equals the price per metre run divided by the width in millimetres, with the decimal point moved three places to the right.

15.7 Imperial Measure

Before the introduction of metrication the trade had used so-called Imperial measure for some 200 years. The units were basically feet and inches, both lineal and cubic. The cubic foot was, and still is at the present time, the unit used by the hardwood trade, whereas the softwood trade extended this to the 'standard', which consisted of 165 ft^3. This latter unit is still being used by North American exporters at the time of writing but – as mentioned earlier – is due to change in the future.

The origin of the standard is associated with Russian exports; it was known as the Petrograd Standard Hundred (PSH) and consisted of 120 pieces (a 'long hundred') measuring 1½ in by 11 in and 12 ft long. The standard quantity of any specification was arrived at by obtaining the total lineal or running feet, multiplied by the width and thickness in inches and divided by 144. This gave the total cubic feet, which, when divided by 165, gave the total standards.

In addition to this, we had a considerable number of other units of measure, the most important being:–

Gothenburg standard = 180 ft^3
Gefle standard = 100 ft^3
Christiana standard = 103$^1/_8$ ft^3
Drammen standard = 121 ft^3
Irish/London standard = 270 ft^3

Quebec standard = 229 ft³
Piled fathom = 216 ft³
Piled fathom (Russian) = 343 ft³
Lathwood = 288 ft³
Cord = 128 ft³
Load (hewn goods) = 50 ft³
Upper Gulf hewn baulks = 150 ft³
Board measure = lineal foot of 1 in by 12 in
Square (boards) = 100 ft² of any thickness
Logs
Customs Fund caliper measure = $L \times D^2 / 183$
Customs Fund string measure = 113 divisor
Hoppus system = 144 divisor
Francon and Auquart measure = metric equivalent of Hoppus
Scribner log table = 20 in diameter − 350 board feet
Spaulding log table = 20 in diameter − 345 board feet
British Columbia log table = 20 in diameter − 326 board feet
Ericson's log table = feet run of certain diameters
Liverpool string or quarter
Girth measure = 144 divisor
84 factor system = evaluation of West African logs

These units of measure were rarely used in everyday trading. They are quoted to illustrate the quite extraordinary and illogical system which was developed over the years for reasons which are no longer remembered beyond the fact that they were traditional. Even those who were originally opposed to change can hardly dispute the fact that the present system is more sensible.

15.8 Hardwoods

Hardwood units of sale and measurement are, as mentioned earlier, still Imperial, with a few exceptions. With the possible exception of North America, the unit is usually the cubic foot. Some expensive or heavy hardwoods, such as lignum vitae, boxwood, ebony, etc., are sold by weight, but they are the principal exceptions.

In North America the unit of measurement of hardwoods is the *board foot*. This is a square foot of timber 1 in thick (12 in × 12 in × 1 in) and therefore equal to one-twelfth of a cubic foot. A full definition of the measurement of a board foot is given in the N.H.L.A. (para. 16) grading rules, and is reproduced on page 369. In calculating the board measure of a parcel of timber all measurements 1 in and over are converted to square feet 1 inch thick. If the parcel is of 1 inch boards, then the board measure is simply the sum of the surface area in square feet of each piece. A piece 12 ft × 9 in × 1 in contains 9 board feet, usually written 9 ft B.M.

When boards are thicker than 1 in, the surface area (in feet) is multiplied by the thickness. Thus a board 12 ft x 9 in x 2 in contains 18 ft B.M.; one 12 ft x 9 in x 3 in contains 27 ft B.M.

For very large transactions, to avoid being too cumbersome, the measurements are taken 'per thousand board feet', 37 000 board feet is then written 37 M.ft B.M. or, more often, 37 m.b.m.

Boards under 1 in thick are sold per square foot surface measure of that particular thickness, so that M.ft B.M. of ¾ in contains only three-quarters of the quantity of M.ft B.M. of 1 in.

In importing hardwood into the UK, the quantity in the contract is often given in *carloads*. This is a term used regularly in the American hardwood trade, and simply denotes the amount of timber that can be carried in one of the long American railway covered 'cars'. In the UK it would be called a 'wagon load', although the quantity would be much smaller and the British wagons are open. The American Hardwood Lumber contract defines a carload as follows: 'Unless this contract states a specific quantity of either cubic or superficial feet a carload shall be considered to contain the equivalent of about 15,000 superficial feet B.M. of 1 inch'.

Unedged boards are usually measured at the middle, or average, width (including half the wane, calculated by taking the mean of the two sides) to the nearest lower half inch and lengths to the nearest lower half foot. Under 1½ inch thick are usually measured inside the wane.

ROUND TIMBER MEASUREMENTS

The Customs Fund Calliper Measurement

This is based upon $L \times D^2/183$, where L is length in feet and D is diameter in inches at mid-length of log.

Customs Fund String Measure, or 113 Divisor

Another measurement that may be used to calculate the actual contents of a round log is Customs Fund string measure, sometimes called 'string measure' or '¼ girth measure'. The circumference of the log is measured in the middle, or at various places in its length – and an average figure for the circumference of the log thereby obtained. From elementary geometry principles the circumference (C inches) is equal to $2\pi r$ ($\pi = 3.1416$; r = radius in inches). The mean cross-section area of the log is πr^2 (presuming it to be cylindrical). Since $C = 2\pi r$, $r = C/2\pi$.

The cross-section area is therefore:
$$\pi \times C/2\pi \times C/2\pi = C^2/4\pi \text{ in}^2 \text{ or } C^2/4\pi \times 144 \text{ ft}^2$$
which may be written $(C/4)^2 \times 1/\pi \times 36 = (C/4)^2 \times 1/113$.

The volume of timber in the log is given by the length x cross-section area and is therefore $L \times (C/4)^2 \times 1/113$, where L is the length in feet and $C/4$ is the quarter girth in inches — that is, the circumference divided by 4.

Hoppus System — 144 Divisor

Round timber may also be measured by the Hoppus system, also known as 'Hoppus quarter-girth', 'string 144 divisor', 'quarter-girth 144 divisor', etc. This is a simplified system and is based on assumptions of what can be sawn out of a particular log rather than on any attempt to calculate the true volume of the log. The circumference of the log is measured in the middle in inches by string or tape and divided by 4, which gives the 'quarter-girth'. The length is taken in feet. The calculation is then based upon $L \times (C/4)^2 \times 1/144$, the result being in 'cubic feet Hoppus measure'.

This measure may be visualised by theoretically converting the log into a square baulk of which each side is equal to the quarter-girth, the slabs on the four sides being thrown in, as it were, for good measure. Incidentally, while the baulk would give a clear measurement across any one face, of the amount of the quarter-girth, simple geometrical considerations will show that it would have a small amount of wane on each corner.

Measurement by the 144 divisor method gives about 21½ per cent less than the true contents as given by the 113 divisor. The units of measurement so obtained are sometimes called 'Hoppus feet' or simply 'cubic feet'. The latter is, of course, not correct as far as actual volume is concerned, although it represents closely the volume of usable timber that can be produced from the log. Wherever used in this connection, the words 'cubic feet' should be qualified by 'Hoppus measure'. Full sets of calculating tables are obtainable based upon the Hoppus system. (The same result in 'Hoppus feet' is obtained by taking the diameter instead of the quarter-girth and dividing by 233.)

Francon and Auquart measure is the metric equivalent of Hoppus.

There are other systems of log measurement in use in America of which complete tables are set out in *Brereton's Practical Lumberman*. The following measurements in board feet of a 20 ft log of 20 in and of 40 in diameter indicate how these differ from Hoppus and from each other:

Measurement	20 in diameter	40 in diameter
Actual measurement	524	2094
Hoppus measurement	412	1648
Scribner log table	350	1505
Spaulding log table	345	1481
British Columbia log table	326	1411

Swedish shippers have sometimes referred to 'Ericson's log measurement tables'. These are purely mathematical, showing the actual cubic contents of so many feet run of logs (as cylinders) of certain diameters. As a basis of sale one would, of course, want to know whether the diameter was being taken at the top (as customary) or at the middle.

Imported Round and Hewn Logs

These are measured by the 'Liverpool string or quarter-girth' measure, based on 144 divisor as detailed above. Length is called down to the nearest quarter-foot and quarter-girth called down to the nearest quarter-inch. If measurement of the quarter-girth is made over the bark, an allowance is made by deduction off the dimensions before calculating the quantity. For quarter-girth up to 11¾ in the deduction is ½ in; 12 in to 17¾ in deduction is 1 in; 18 in and over deduction is increased by an additional ½ in for each increase of 6 in (or part) of quarter-girth.

84 Factor System

This system is employed for the evaluation of West African logs to determine the proportion of A, B and C quality logs in a FAQ (fair average quality) shipment. The method of arriving at the amount by which the selling price has to be adjusted is as follows:

$$
\begin{array}{l}
\text{A logs } 40\% \times 100 = 40 \\
\text{B logs } 40\% \times 80 = 32 \\
\text{C logs } 20\% \times 60 = 12 \\
\hline
\phantom{\text{C logs } 20\% \times 60 = }84 \\
\hline
\end{array}
$$

To arrive at the factor for any particular parcel, the above percentages are replaced by the cubic content given in the out-turn.

Bark Allowances

Where the volume of round logs is being calculated from measurement of the circumference of the log, the presence of the bark can clearly greatly affect the measurements. By far the most satisfactory method is to strip the bark off and then measure the quarter-girth. If measurement is made over bark, usually abbreviated TOB (tape over bark), the allowance may be in the form of the 'Liverpool Conventional Allowance' off the dimension of the quarter-girth, or it may be an allowance in the form of a percentage off the total calculated quantity. The percentage allowance varies between England and Scotland and between the various species of trees.

Species	England and Wales	Scotland
Conifers	7½%	10%
Ash, sycamore, beech, birch	7½%	7½%
Poplar, elm, alder, lime	15%	15%
Oak, chestnut and others	10%	10%

16 Grading Rules for Timber

16.1 General

It will be seen from chapter 3 (section on 'Grading and Shippers Marks') and chapter 8 (section 8.2 Albion 1980) that the classification of timber into various qualities and grades is of major importance. In the early days of any timber-producing country the grading of the timber into qualities must have been purely by experience and rule of thumb. In many countries it remains that way, and up to quite recently there have been few basic changes. The most significant of these is stress grading, which is covered in chapter 21.

During the past 10–15 years many producers have been considering seriously alternative ideas on grading and have developed several innovations which will be dealt with later in this chapter. Despite these new ideas, the majority of the Scandinavian mills still maintain the old and tried system of grading their goods into:

Unsorted (first, second, third and fourth qualities as falling)
fifths and sixths

In Canada and the USA grading rules are scientifically planned on a very comprehensive scale to cover a great number of grades. Grading rules of this type are very useful in that they do establish a definite basis. In theory every piece of timber in a particular parcel should be graded individually, but it is not truly practicable to examine each piece as closely as the grading rules provide. It would simply not be possible to count and measure each knot as the pieces pass by on the conveyor belts. In many modern mills nowadays the pieces pass through so rapidly that it has been found necessary to increase the number of brackers, and usually in such mills there are three brackers sitting at a console side by side. As the pieces go by on the conveyor belt, they are automatically turned over, each piece in front of one of them. When he has decided on the grade of the piece in front of him, the bracker presses the relevant button on his console, which automatically arranges for that piece to be marked on the ends and conveyed to the appropriate storage bin for its quality and length. At the same time the tally is automatically recorded with a typed specification. By this method, as each bracker only deals with every third piece, he has longer to make an accurate decision as to quality. Since all basic grading is visual, whether in accordance with official grading rules or not, it follows that slight differences of opinion must be accepted. This aspect is not always appreciated by the receivers of wood goods, who cannot understand why it is that the odd piece of a lower grade is sometimes found in, say, Unsorted, and an Unsorted piece among the fifths. For example, there is very little difference between a low-line fourth in a parcel of Unsorted and a superior fifth. When the merits of a parcel are being assessed, it is therefore fair and reasonable to bear the foregoing in mind and to aim to gain an over-all impression.

There is in practice a very general but not invariable rule, which makes an essential distinction between the grading of softwoods and that of hardwoods.

Softwoods, such as Baltic redwood and whitewood and Canadian spruce and Douglas fir, are normally used for construction work in the sizes in which they are shipped, and the grading is based on that assumption. Consequently the practical reason for the degrading of any piece, from the basic standard grade to a lower one, is the existence of any defect or combination of defects affecting the strength of the piece in its own size. For instance, a batten with a very large (compared with the size of the piece) knot or group of knots near the middle making it unfit for use in normal construction work in its existing length must be degraded, in spite of the fact that if the knotty section were cut out, the remaining pieces might be faultless.

By the way, it is not the knot which causes the loss of strength in timber so much as the divergence of the grain surrounding the knot.

The grading is based on constructional use, not on recutting. An example of an exception to this rule is Quebec pine, which is normally used, not for construction work but for pattern making.

Hardwoods, on the other hand, are graded mainly according to the amount of wood free from defects and of reasonable size which can be cut out of the piece, so that, contrary to the case of constructional softwood, the existence of a serious defect which can easily be cut out, leaving the rest of the piece faultless, would entitle the whole to be regarded as high grade. The grading of hardwoods is based on 'cutting', not on 'construction' value.

16.2 Finland

The grading in Finland of sawn goods for export to this country is mainly confined to separating from the Unsorted quality any pieces which do not come up to the shipper's standard for that grading. Although the qualities of timber vary between one shipper and another and also between one part of the country and another, there are National grading rules, published in 1960. These are reprinted hereunder by permission of the Association of Finnish Sawmillmen. In order to update these rules, they have been converted from Imperial to metric measure.

INSTRUCTIONS FOR THE GRADING OF EXPORT TIMBER
(Association of Finnish Sawmillmen)
PREFACE
(extract)

The Foundation for Forest Products Research included in 1930, on the initiative of the Association of Finnish Sawmillmen, the grading of sawngoods in its programme. As a result of extensive research the Foundation published 'Grading Rules for Export Timber' in 1936. A second edition of this publication was issued without changes in 1947. As mentioned in the preface to this publication, its object was to further the unification and improvement of the grading of Finnish export timber and enhance its reputation on the foreign markets.

Since these grading rules were published the production and marketing of sawngoods have undergone some changes. It has therefore been found that these grading rules are somewhat out of date and do not correspond to the actual situation today. Therefore, the Association of Finnish Sawmillmen decided in 1957 to appoint a committee to revise, modernise and where necessary complete the grading rules of 1936.

The committee has been in close touch with the corresponding committee in Sweden. As a result of this co-operation, the grading instructions now issued simultaneously in Sweden and Finland are uniform in their essential parts.

These revised grading instructions are, as those of 1936, intended as a general guidance for grading of sawngoods for export and do not constitute any binding rules for the individual mills. The committee hopes that these grading instructions will contribute to the further development and unification of the grading of Finnish export timber and thus improve our competitive position on the international timber markets.

GENERAL PRINCIPLES

These grading instructions assume that the timber to be graded is edged and cut to final length, and that the goods have been cut according to general custom.

It is a general rule that the grade is decided mainly on the basis of the better face and the edges of the piece.* Nevertheless, the inferior face must also be taken into consideration when deciding the quality of a piece. The rules in these grading instructions concerning the size, number, and situation of defects permitted in the various qualities must be flexibly applied, always taking into consideration the total impression of all defects and the general appearance of the piece.

The thickness and width of a piece generally decide the size and number of the defects permitted. The defects on the edges influence in a higher degree than those on the faces the decision on the quality. Defects appearing on the edges of the piece are more serious if they reach the arris. Defects appearing in the middle part of the piece affect in a higher degree its quality, than those near the ends. When defects occur in clusters, the size and number of the

---

*Throughout this publication 'face' refers to the broad surfaces and 'edge' refers to the narrow surfaces.

defects must be less than would be otherwise allowed, also the composite effect of the cluster of defects must be taken as the basis for deciding the grade.

The usual export qualities are:– Unsorted (U/S), containing the qualities I–IV, Fifth quality (V), Sixth quality (VI), Schaalboards and 'Halvrena'.

In general, not more than one of the largest defects permissible may appear in the same piece of I–IV quality.

DEFECTS IN SAWNGOODS

The defects in sawngoods are, according to general custom, classified as follows.

A. DEFECTS IN QUALITY
(1) Structure (2) Manufacture (3) Shakes (4) Deformities

B. DEFECTS IN CONDITION
(1) Moisture (2) Blue (3) Other discoloration

A. DEFECTS IN QUALITY

(1) STRUCTURE: Defects in structure are: knots, pitch-pockets, pitch-streak, scars, ingrown bark, compression wood, cross grain, rot and damage by insects.

KNOTS are defined and measured as follows:
(*a*) *The character of the knots,*
   Sound knot: Live knot, firmly attached to the surrounding wood.
   Dead knot: A partly or entirely loosened dry knot.
   Rotten knot: A knot, partly or entirely affected by rot.
   Barkringed knot: A knot, partly or entirely surrounded by ingrown bark.
(*b*) *The form and position of knots,*
   Round and oval knot: A knot cut across its long axis, appearing on the face or on the edge.
   Arris knot: A knot situated on the arris, crosscut on the face as well as on the edge.
   Leaf knot: A knot cut lengthwise, appearing on the face and not reaching the edge.
   Splay knot: A knot cut lengthwise and reaching the edge.
   Pin knot: Size, 3 mm – 6 mm.
(*c*) *The situation of knots,*
   Scattered knots: Knots situated at random without forming groups.
   Knot cluster: Knots situated closely together forming a distinct group.
   Branch knots: A pair of opposite splay knots.

(*d*) *The measuring of knots,*

Round or oval knots: The size of these knots is determined by the average of their largest and smallest diameter.

Arris knots: The surface of an arris knot appearing on the face and the surface appearing on the edge shall both be taken into account separately. They are then measured as round and oval knots.

Splay knots: The surface appearing on the face is calculated according to the average of its length and width in its middle. This average may, depending on the character of the knot, be 1½–2 times the size permitted for round or oval knots on the face. The surface of the knot on the edge is measured as a round or oval knot.

Each surface of the knot is to be taken into account when judging the face and the edge of the piece respectively.

Leaf knots: A leaf knot is measured as a round or oval knot. Its calculated size may, depending on the depth of the knot, be 2–3 times the size permitted for a round or oval knot on the face.

Branch knots: These are measured as two splay knots.

When judging knots, excessive irregularities of the grain around the knot must also be taken into account.

Figures 16.1 and 16.2 show the numbers of knots permitted on a length of 1.5 m measured on the poorest part of the respective edge or better face of redwood. In Whitewood a larger number of smaller knots are permitted provided these are of the same colour as the surrounding wood.

The first figure for the number of knots refers to knots of the size indicated on the above charts and second figure refers to smaller knots which may be $^2/_3$ of the aforementioned. Further, some still smaller scattered knots are permitted.

The largest size of knots permitted in the grades I–V can be extracted from the graph as follows:– Take the point of intersection between the horizontal index showing the thickness of the piece and the vertical index showing its width. Follow the nearest curve to the line of the table under the graph where the permitted sizes of knots are shown.

PITCH-POCKETS Openings between the growth rings usually containing resin. They are measured according to their length. A small pitch-pocket is ≤ 50 mm, a large one is > 50 mm.

PITCH-STREAK Excessive resinocity.

SCARS AND INGROWN BARK. Scars are chinks in the wood containing resin and also, quite often, ingrown bark. They are generally caused by the overgrowing of a damage to the tree.

Ingrown bark is a chink partly or entirely filled with bark.

These defects are measured according to their length, but with large ones, the width must also be considered. Small ones are ≤ 50 mm, large ones are > 50 mm. These defects can either appear only on the surface or reach through the piece.

COMPRESSION WOOD. This is darker coloured wood of harder structure.

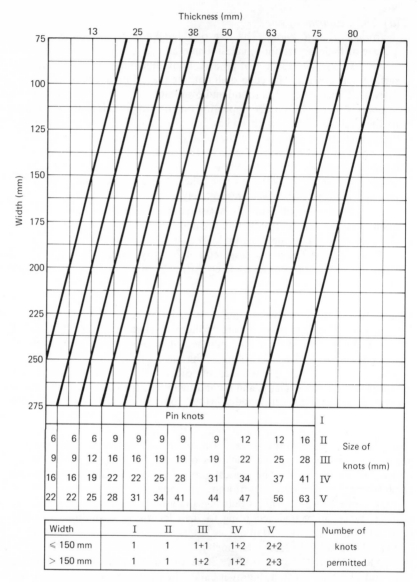

Figure 16.1 Size and number of knots permitted on the edge

Its size and importance are judged according to what extent this defect causes changes in the form of the piece.

CROSS GRAIN. This is a deviation of the grain from the direction of the main axis of the piece and it is measured according to the angle of deviation.

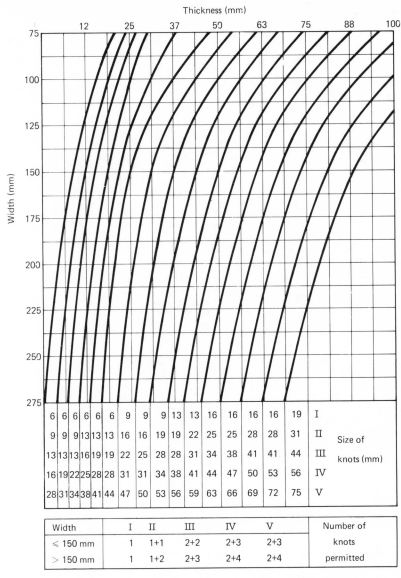

Figure 16.2 Size and number of knots permitted on the better face

ROT is a fungal decay in the wood, making it softer, weaker and often darker. There is hard and soft rot. Its extent is defined in proportion to the surface where it appears.

DAMAGE BY INSECTS. Cavities in the wood caused by insects or their

TABLE 16.1 FINNISH GRADING RULES

Other Defects

Defect	Grade 1	Grade II	Grade III	Grade IV	Grade V
Shakes on face	Combined depth of shakes must not exceed $h\%$ of the thickness of the piece and their length on one face must not exceed $l_1\%$ of the length of the piece. The combined length on both faces must not exceed $l_2\%$ of the length of the piece.				Allowed on whole length of the piece, partly right through, provided it holds well together.
	$h = 10\%$ $l_1 = 20\%$	$h = 20\%$ $l_1 = 30\%$ $l_2 = 40\%$	$h = 30\%$ $l_1 = 50\%$ $l_2 = 70\%$	$h = 40\%$ $l_1 = 65\%$ $l_2 = 90\%$	
	Other face must be free from shakes.	Combined depth of shakes is the depth appearing on both sides, opposite each other, added together.			
on edge	The length on the edge or edges must not exceed 50% of the length allowed on one face in the grade. Shakes must not run from the edge onto the face.				Not to exceed 50% of length. May run from edge to face.
oblique	Allowed as deep as shakes straight along the length but shorter than those, depending on their obliquity.				
Blue log blue	None	None	None	A few light streaks and spots permitted on pieces otherwise of a higher U/S grade.	Light log blue permitted to a small degree.
deal yard blue	None	None	None	Light superficial blue permitted to a small degree.	To limited extent, partly even some severe blue.

Rot	None	None	None	None	Narrow streaks of hard rot permitted.
Insect damage wood wasp	None	None	None	None	None
bark beetle	None	None	None	None	Light, in a few pieces per parcel.
Pitch pockets (per 1.5 m of piece)	One allowed, small, shallow and closed.	A few allowed, small, shallow and closed.	Some allowed, small and shallow.	Some allowed, small and not penetrating right through.	Reasonable amount.
Compression wood	None	Allowed, provided it does not affect shape.	None	Allowed, provided it does not seriously affect shape.	Allowed.
Scars and ingrown bark (per 1.5 m of piece)	None	One small, firm, closed chink allowed.	A few small, firm, closed chinks allowed.	Some small, firm closed chinks or a few bigger.	A few allowed: through the piece if closed.
Wane on one edge	$h = 15\%$ $l = 15\%$	$h = 20\%$ $l = 20\%$	$h = 25\%$ $l = 25\%$	$h = 30\%$ $l = 30\%$	$h = 50\%$ $l = 60\%$
on two edges	$h = 20\%$ $l = 20\%$	$h = 25\%$ $l = 25\%$	$h = 35\%$ $l = 30\%$	$h = 50\%$ $l = 40\%$	$h = 70\%$ $l = 60\%$

Gradually diminishing wane allowed up to $h\%$ of thickness and $l\%$ of length of piece.

Gradually diminishing wane allowed to combined depth up to $h\%$ of thickness and combined length up to $l\%$ of length of piece. It may not exceed on either edge what is allowed on one edge.

Wane in the middle of the piece must not exceed half the length permitted at the end of the piece.

The following further defects affect the quality and must be considered when deciding the grade of the piece: bow, spring, twist, cup, wrong measure and otherwise faulty manufacture, cross-grain and pitch streaks.

larvae. These damages are divided into two categories: 1. Damage by wood wasps (Siricidae). 2. Damage by bark beetles.

(2) MANUFACTURE: Defects in manufacture are: wane, wrong measure and otherwise faulty manufacture.

WANE is the part of the surface of the piece which has not been touched by the blade. Its size is given as a proportion of the nominal measure of the piece.

WRONG MEASURE is a deviation from the nominal measure.

OTHERWISE FAULTY MANUFACTURE. These are imperfect surfaces, marks of rollers, crookedness, etc.

(3) SHAKES: are divided according to their nature into heart shakes, ring shakes and seasoning shakes.

Heart shakes: These run mainly from the centre of the log in a radial direction. They are visible in a newly felled tree and may widen when the wood seasons.

Ring shakes: These follow the growth rings and are often visible in a newly felled tree.

Seasoning shakes: These appear during the seasoning of the timber.

All shakes are measured according to their length and depth, taking also their width into account.

(4) DEFORMITIES (figure 16.3): are:—

    Bow: A lengthwise bending of the faces.

    Spring: A lengthwise bending of the edges.

    Twist: A spiral distortion of the piece.

    Cup: A transversal convexity or concavity.

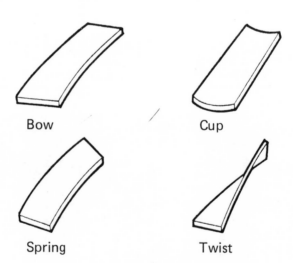

Figure 16.3 Deformities in softwood

B. DEFECTS IN CONDITION

(1) MOISTURE: The moisture content of the timber is excessive if it does not correspond to what is commonly regarded as normal for 'shipping dry' goods. The goods are 'shipping dry' when they can stand without deterioration, a normal transportation in the hold of a ship to the port of destination and storage there with usual care.

(2) BLUE: Blue is a discoloration of the timber caused by fungi. It does not impair the strength of the timber. There are two kinds of blue: log blue, which develops in the log before it is sawn, and deal yard blue, which develops after cutting and is mainly limited to the surface. It appears as light or severe discoloration. The extent of discoloration is given as a proportion of the surface on which is appears.

(3) OTHER DISCOLORATION: These are colour changes in the surface during seasoning and storing, for example, weathered, browned, etc. They do not impair the strength of the wood.

Although there is practically no export to the UK of Finnish sawngoods sorted into I–IV, which are shipped together as Unsorted quality, Continental buyers have a much stricter interpretation of 'shipper's usual bracking' and insist that when they sort the goods on arrival, the proportion of the higher qualities shall be up to standard. Importers in this country are more broad-minded and look at a shipment more as a whole. In addition, importers in this country seldom sort the goods when yarding them.

The amount of defects permitted in IV and therefore in Unsorted quality may appear surprising at first, but it must be remembered that these are the maximum defects permitted in the grade, which must also contain a fair proportion of higher grade pieces. In addition, two major defects must not usually occur simultaneously.

These 1960 Grading Rules include a section covering sixth quality, schaalboards and 'Halvrena'. In addition, there are colour photographs of the defects mentioned and of sawn goods of various dimensions to illustrate the quality of the various grades.

TABLE 16.2 FINNISH GRADING RULES: Size and number of dead, bark-ringed and rotten knots allowed in proportion of sound knots

Grade	Dead		Barkringed		Rotten	
	size	no.	size	no.	size	no.
I	$\frac{2}{3}$	$\frac{3}{4}$	—	—	—	—
II	$\frac{2}{3}$	$\frac{3}{4}$	—	—	—	—
III	$\frac{2}{3}$	$1/1$	$\frac{1}{2}$	$\frac{2}{3}$	—	—
IV	$\frac{2}{3}$	$1/1$	$\frac{1}{2}$	$\frac{2}{3}$	$\frac{1}{3}$ *	$\frac{1}{3}$ *
V	$\frac{3}{4}$	$1/1$	$\frac{3}{4}$	$\frac{3}{4}$	$\frac{2}{3}$	$\frac{2}{3}$

* Knots partly damaged by rot.

16.3 Sweden

In 1960 the Association of Swedish Sawmillmen issued a publication entitled *Guiding Principles for Grading of Swedish Sawn Timber for Export*. These rules resulted from the work done by a committee appointed in 1957 which was charged with the task of unifying and revising the former rules published in 1926, which described the sorting of wood goods followed in the Härnösand district since 1880. A second edition was published in 1976 which changed all Imperial units to metric.

The Preface of this publication refers to the collaboration with Finland and states: '. . . the guiding principles were to apply to sawn timber for export and they were to indicate the lowest limit allowed for each grade. The relative composition of qualities was to depend on the circumstances with regard to the raw material available to each mill.'

Unfortunately, it is not possible to quote from these 1976 Rules, which are obtainable from the publishers, AB Svensk Trävaru–Tidning, Stockholm. However, the rules are comprehensive and closely follow the pattern of the Finnish rules already mentioned, including colour photographs.

16.4 Poland

The Swedish system of grading has been adopted in Poland.

16.5 Russia

The grading rules applicable to Russian exports are not officially published or released outside the USSR. The rules are strictly adhered to, and consequently there is little cause for complaint about the bracking. The redwood from all the loading ports is graded to Leningrad bracking and the whitewood to White Sea bracking. The goods are sorted into three grades: Unsorted, fourths and fifths. The Unsorted grade consists of first, second and third quality; the fourths can be regarded as being similar to a high-class Finnish fifth but not allowing for the inclusion of discoloured, as in Finnish fifths. The fifths are the equivalent of sixth quality or Utskott.

Sales are made on c.i.f. terms based on the amended Russian Contract Form 1952, the Soviet Charter party and Black Sea and Baltic Insurance. In common with Baltic shippers, the goods from the various loading places are identified by the marking on one end of each piece in red paint as indicated in Table 16.3.

16.6 Canada — West and East Coasts

Previously these two regions of Canada were covered separately in so far as grading was concerned. In recent years the rationalisation of all the various

TABLE 16.3

Port	Unsorted	Fourths	Fifths
Kara Sea Ports:			
Igarka	E**1	E*1	E – 1
White Sea ports:			
Archangel	E**AR	E*AR	E – AR
Onega	E**O	E*O	E – O
Mesane	E**M	E*M	E – M
Petchora	E**P	E*P	E – P
Kem	E**KM	E*KM	E – KM
Kovda	E**KV	E*KV	E – KV
Oumba (Umba)	E**U	E*U	E – U
Baltic ports:			
Leningrad	E**L	E*L	E – L
Petrozavodsk	E**PT	E*PT	E – PT
Pudoj	E**PD	E*PD	E – PD
Riga	E**RG	E*RG	E – RG
Ventspils	E**VS	E*VS	E – VS

grading rules has resulted in Standard Grading Rules for Canadian Lumber published by the National Lumber Grades Authority and known as the NLGA Rules. These are very comprehensive and apply to all the different species grown in the two regions; they also cover visual stress grades which allow stress ratings to be established for each size and grade. Because these Rules are so comprehensive, only limited detail can be given here under the general heading 'All Species'. The current Rules are in Imperial measure.

CLASSIFICATION

'The National Grading Rule (Canada) for Dimension Lumber classifies dimension into 2 width categories and 5 use categories. Dimension up to 4 inches wide is classified as Structural Light Framing, Light Framing and Studs. Dimension 6 inches and wider is classified as Structural Joists and Planks. In addition, a single Appearance Framing grade of 2 inch and wider dimension is designed for those special uses where a high bending strength ratio coupled with high appearance is needed.

2–4 in Thick   2–4 in Wide
Structural Light Framing

67%	Bending Strength Ratio	–	Select Structural	(1)
55%	Bending Strength Ratio	–	No. 1	(2)
45%	Bending Strength Ratio	–	No. 2	(3)
26%	Bending Strength Ratio	–	No. 3	(4)

(Bending strength ratio applies only to 2 x 4, 3 x 4 and 4 x 4)

Light Framing

34%	Bending Strength Ratio	—	Construction	(5)
19%	Bending Strength Ratio	—	Standard	(6)
9%	Bending Strength Ratio	—	Utility	(7)
			Economy	(8)

Studs

| 26% | Bending Strength Ratio | — | Stud | (9) |

2–4 in Thick   6 in and Wider

Structural Joists and Planks.

65%	Bending Strength Ratio	—	Select Structural	(10)
55%	Bending Strength Ratio	—	No. 1	(11)
45%	Bending Strength Ratio	—	No. 2	(12)
26%	Bending Strength Ratio	—	No. 3	(13)

2–4 in Thick   2 in and Wider

Appearance Framing.

| 55% | Bending Strength Ratio | — | Appearance | (14) |

'Except as otherwise provided herein, the above grades shall constitute the dimension grades included in rule books of certified rule writing agencies and are the only dimension grades which may be grade-stamped as Canadian Standard Lumber or American Standard Lumber. Modification of these descriptions may only be made by the National Grading Rule Committee.'

GENERAL

'The major characteristics encountered in grading of softwood lumber are listed for each grade. Not all the listed characteristics will occur in lumber of any particular species. Some minor characteristics unique to a single species may be encountered, but may not be listed in the grade descriptions. All grade descriptions set forth the limiting characteristics that may occur in lumber in each grade. Hence, the rules can be said to describe the poorest pieces allowed in a grade. All or nearly all of the permissible characteristics of the grade are never present in maximum size or number in any one piece. Any piece with an unusual combination of characteristics which seriously affects the normal serviceability is excluded from the grade. The grading of lumber cannot be considered an exact science because it is based on either a visual inspection of each piece and the judgment of the grader or on the results of a method of mechanically determining the strength characteristics of structural lumber. The National Grading Rule (Canada) for Dimension Lumber is, however, sufficiently explicit to establish a maximum of 5% below grade as a reasonable variation between graders.'

GRADE DESCRIPTION

Structural Light Framing

(1) *Select Structural*. Dimension lumber of this quality is limited in characteristics which affect strength and stiffness values to provide a fibre stress in bending value of 67 per cent of that allowed for clear, straight-grained wood and to provide a recommended design value for modulus of elasticity of 100 per cent of that allowed for clear wood average. This grade is recommended for use in applications where both high strength and stiffness values and good appearance may be required.

Characteristics permitted and limiting provisions shall be:

Checks: Surface seasoning checks not limited. Through checks at ends are limited as splits.

Knots: Sound, firm, encased and pith knots, if tight and well spaced, are permitted in sizes not to exceed the following, or equivalent displacement:

Nom. width	At edge wide face	Centreline wide face	Unsound and loose knots and holes (any cause)	
2 in	⅜ in	⅜ in	⅜ in	one hole or
3 in	½ in	½ in	½ in	equivalent
4 in	¾ in	⅞ in	¾ ft	smaller per 4 linear ft

Manufacture: Standard 'E'. Admits torn grain, raised grain, very heavy loosened grain, medium machine bite, machine gouge, medium machine offset, chip marks, knife marks, light wavy dressing, light mismatch.

Pitch and pitch streaks: Not limited.

Pockets – pitch or bark: Not limited.

Rate of growth: Limited to medium grain in Douglas Fir and larch, which means an average of approximately four or more annual rings per inch.

Shake: On ends limited to half the thickness. Away from ends several heart shakes up to 2 ft long, none through.

Skips: Hit and miss skips in 10 per cent of the pieces.

Slope of grain: 1 in 12.

Splits: Equal in length to the width of the piece.

Stain: Stained sapwood. Firm heart stain or firm red heart limited to 10 per cent of the pieces.

Wane: One-quarter the thickness, one-quarter the width. Five per cent of the pieces may have wane up to half the thickness and one-third the width for one-quarter the length.

Warp: Half of medium classification, which includes bow, crook and cup.

(2) *No. 1*. This grade differs from 'select structural' as follows:

Bending value 55 per cent of modulus of elasticity of 100 per cent.
Knots: Larger in size, as follows:

Nom. width	At edge wide face	Centreline wide face	Unsound and loose knots and holes (any cause)	
2 in	½ in	½ in	½ in	one hole or
3 in	¾ in	¾ in	¾ in	equivalent
4 in	1 in	1½ in	1 in	smaller per 3 linear ft

Slope of grain: 1 in 10.
Stain: Stained sapwood. Firm heart stain or firm red heart.

(3) *No. 2*. This grade differs from 'No.1' as follows:

Bending value 45 per cent of modulus of elasticity of 90 per cent.
Knots: Well-spaced knots of any quality are permitted not to exceed the following or equivalent displacement:

Nom. width	At edge wide face	Centreline wide face	Holes (any cause)	
2 in	⅝ in	⅝ in	⅝ in	one hole or
3 in	⅞ in	⅞ in	⅞ in	equivalent
4 in	1¼ in	2 in	1¼ in	smaller per 2 linear ft

Manufacture: Standard 'F'. Admits very heavy torn grain, raised grain, very heavy loosened grain, heavy machine bite, machine gouge, heavy machine offset, chip marks, knife marks, medium wavy dressing, medium mismatch.

Shake: On ends limited to half the thickness. Away from ends through heart shakes up to 2 ft long, well separated. If not through, single shakes may be 3 ft long or up to one-quarter the length, whichever is greater.

Skips: Hit and miss, and, in addition, 5 per cent of the pieces may be hit or miss or heavy skip not longer than 2 ft.

Slope of grain: 1 in 8.

Splits: Equal in length to one and a half times the width of the piece.

Stain: Stained sapwood. Firm heart stain or firm red heart. Not limited.

Unsound wood: Not permitted in thicknesses over 2 in, but in 2 in thickness, heart centre streaks not over one-third the width or thickness, or small spots or streaks of firm honeycomb or peck equal to one-sixth the width are permitted.

Wane: One-third the thickness, one-third the width. Five per cent of the pieces may have wane up to two-thirds the thickness and half the width for one-quarter the length.

White Speck: Firm, one-third the face or equivalent.

(4) *No. 3*. This grade differs from 'No. 2' as follows:

Bending value 26 per cent of modulus of elasticity of 80 per cent.

Knots: well spaced knots of any quality are permitted in the following sizes or their equivalent displacement:

Nom. width	At edge wide face	Centreline wide face		Holes (any cause)
2 in	¾ in	¾ in	¾ in	one hole or
3 in	1¼ in	1¼ in	1¼ in	equivalent
4 in	1¾ in	2½ in	1¾ in	smaller per 1 linear ft

Shake: Surface shakes permitted. If through at edges and ends, limited as splits. Elsewhere through shakes one-third the length. Several such scattered along the length.

Skips: Hit or miss, and, in addition, 10 per cent of pieces may have heavy skip.

Stain: Stained wood. Not limited.

Slope of grain: 1 in 4.

Splits: Equal to one-sixth the length of the piece.

Unsound wood: In spots or streaks limited to one-third the cross-section at any point along the length. Must not destroy the nailing edge.

Wane: Half the thickness, half the width. Five per cent of the pieces may have up to seven-eighths the thickness and three-quarters the width for one-quarter the length.

Warp: Medium.

White speck and honeycomb: Firm.

Light Framing

(5) *Construction*. Lumber of this grade is recommended and widely used for general framing purposes. Pieces of this grade are of good appearance but are graded primarily for strength and serviceability.

Characteristics permitted and limiting provisions are:

Checks: Surface seasoning checks not limited. Through checks at ends are limited as splits.

Knots: Sound, firm, encased and pith must be tight and are permitted in the following sizes or their equivalent displacement:

Nom. width	Anywhere on wide face	Unsound or loose knots and holes	
2 in	¾ in	⅝ in	one hole or
3 in	1¼ in	¾ in	equivalent
4 in	1½ in	1 in	smaller per 3 linear ft

Knots spiked entirely across the wide face are limited to a displacement of approximately one-quarter the cross-section.

Manufacture: Standard 'E'. Admits torn grain, raised grain, very heavy loosened grain, medium machine bite, machine gouge, medium machine offset, chip marks, light wavy dressing, light mismatch.

Pitch and pitch streaks: Not limited.

Pockets – pitch and bark: Not limited.

Shake: Several heart shakes up to 2 ft long, similar to seasoning checks, none through.

Skips: Hit and miss on 10 per cent of the pieces.

Slope of grain: 1 in 6.

Splits: Equal in length to the width of the piece.

Stain: Stained sapwood. Firm heart stain or firm red heart.

Wane: One-quarter the thickness, one-quarter the width. Five per cent of the pieces may have wane up to half the thickness and one-third the width for one-quarter the length.

Warp: Half of medium classification, which includes bow, crook and cup.

(6) *Standard*. Lumber of this grade is customarily used for the same purposes as or in conjunction with 'construction' grade. Characteristics are limited to provide good strength and excellent serviceability. This grade differs from 'Construction' as follows:

Knots: Not restricted as to quality and permitted in the following sizes or their equivalent displacement:

Nom. width	Anywhere on wide face	Holes	
2 in	1 in	¾ in	one hole or
3 in	1½ in	1 in	equivalent
4 in	2 in	1¼ in	smaller per 2 linear ft

Knots spiked entirely across the wide face are limited to a displacement of approximately one-third the cross-section.

Manufacture: Standard 'F'. Admits very heavy torn grain, raised grain, very heavy loosened grain, heavy machine bite, machine gouge, heavy machine offset, chip marks, knife marks, medium wavy dressing, medium mismatch.

Shake: On ends limited to half the thickness. Away from ends through heart shakes up to 2 ft long, well separated. If not through, single shakes may be 3 ft long or up to one-quarter the length, whichever is greater.

Skips: Hit and miss, and, in addition, 5 per cent of the pieces may be hit or miss, or heavy skip not longer than 2 ft.

Slope of grain: 1 in 4.

Splits: Equal in length to one and a half times the width of the piece.

Stain: Stained sapwood. Firm heart stain or firm red heart. Not limited.

Unsound wood: Heart centre streaks not over one-third the thickness or width, or small spots or streaks of firm honeycomb or peck equal to one-sixth the width are permitted.

Wane: One-third the thickness, one-third the width. Five per cent of the pieces may have wane up to two-thirds the thickness and half the width for one-quarter the length.

Warp: Light.

White speck: Firm, one-third the face or equivalent.

(7) *Utility*. Lumber of this grade is recommended and widely used where a combination of good strength and economical construction is desired for such purposes as studding, blocking, plates, bracing and rafters. This grade differs from 'Standard' as follows:

Knots: Not restricted as to quality, and permitted in the following sizes or their equivalent displacement:

Nom. width	Anywhere on wide face	Holes	
2 in	1¼ in	1 in	one hole or
3 in	2 in	1¼ in	equivalent
4 in	2½ in	1½ in	smaller per
			1 linear ft

Knots spiked entirely across the wide face are limited to a displacement of approximately half the cross-section.

Shake: Surface shakes permitted. If through at edges or ends, limited as splits. Elsewhere through shakes one-third the length. Several such scattered along the length.

Skips: Hit or miss, and, in addition, 10 per cent of the pieces may have heavy skips.

Splits: Equal to one-sixth the length of the piece.

Stain: Stained wood, not limited.

Unsound wood: In spots or streaks limited to one-third the cross-section at any point along the length. Must not destroy the nailing edge.

Wane: Half the thickness, half the width. Five per cent of the pieces may have wane up to seven-eighths the thickness and three-quarters the width for one-quarter the length.

Warp: Medium.
White speck and honeycomb: Firm.

(8) *Economy*. Lumber of this grade is suitable for temporary or low-cost construction, such as crating, bracing, cribbing, dunnage, blocking and other similar uses. It is permissible at shipper's option to ship 'Economy' framing in mixed species. On any order calling for one of these species, any combination may be shipped unless the order specifically excludes the other species.

This grade permits the following:

Honeycomb
Shake
Splits: One-third the length.
Wane: Three-quarters width, if through, equivalent to holes allowed; if across the face, half width must not exceed ¼ in scant for one-third length or equivalent.
White specks
Knots and holes (*unsound wood*): Seventy-five per cent of cross-section.

All characteristics which do not interfere with use of the piece full length are permitted. In pieces over 8 ft long characteristics which interfere with use of the piece full length are permitted if not located within 2 ft of either end; at least 75 per cent of such piece, however, must be usable after it has been cut into two or three pieces. Pieces 8 ft and shorter are usable full length. Quarter-inch scant in thickness and/or width is permitted.

(9) *Studs*. Lumber of this grade is limited in characteristics that affect strength and stiffness values, so that the grade is suitable for all stud uses, including use in load-bearing walls. The grade has a fibre stress in bending value of 26 per cent of that allowed for clear, straight-grained wood and a recommended design value for modulus of elasticity of 80 per cent of that allowed for clear wood average. There is only one grade of 'Studs'.

Characteristics permitted and limiting provisions are as follows:

Checks: Seasoning checks not limited. Through checks at ends are limited as splits.
Knots: Not limited as to quality but are well spaced and are permitted in the following sizes or their equivalent displacement:

Nom. width	At edge wide face	Centreline wide face		Holes
2 in	¾ in	¾ in	¾ in	one hole or
3 in	1¼ in	1¼ in	1 ¼ in	equivalent
4 in	1¾ in	2½ in	1½ in	smaller per
				1 linear ft

Manufacture: Standard 'F'.

Pitch and pitch streaks: Not limited.

Pockets – pitch or bark: Not limited.

Shake: If through at ends, limited as splits. Elsewhere through shakes one-third the length.

Skips: Hit or miss on any face. In addition, 10 per cent of the pieces may have heavy skips on wide faces only.

Slope of grain: 1 in 4.

Splits: Equal in length to twice the width of the piece.

Stain: Stained sapwood. Firm heart stain or firm red heart.

Unsound wood: In spots or streaks limited to one-third the cross-section at any point along the length. Must not destroy the nailing edge.

Wane: Half the width and one-third the thickness without length limit, or equivalent more for 2 ft if not exceeding three-quarters the width and half the thickness.

Warp: Half of medium classification, which includes bow, crook and cup.

White speck and honeycomb: Firm.

Structural Joists and Planks

(10) *Select Structural*. Dimension lumber of this quality is limited in characteristics that affect strength and stiffness values to provide a fibre stress in bending value of 65 per cent of that allowed for clear, straight-grained wood and to provide a recommended design value for modulus of elasticity of 100 per cent of that allowed for the clear wood average. This grade is recommended for use in application where both high strength and stiffness values and good appearance may be required.

Characteristics permitted and limiting provisions shall be:

Checks: Surface seasoning checks not limited. Through checks at ends are limited as splits.

Knots: Sound, firm, encased and pith knots, if tight and well-spaced, are permitted in sizes not to exceed the following, or equivalent displacement:

Nom. width	At edge wide face	Centreline wide face	Unsound or loose knots and holes (any cause)	
6 in	1⅛ in	1⅞ in	1 in	one hole or
8 in	1½ in	2¼ in	1¼ in	equivalent
10 in	1⅞ in	2⅝ in	1¼ in	smaller per
12 in	2¼ in	3 in	1¼ in	4 linear ft
14 in	2⅜ in	3¼ in	1¼ in	

Manufacture: Standard 'E'.

Pitch and pitch streaks: Not limited.

Pockets – pitch or bark: Not limited.

Rate of growth: Limited to medium grain in Douglas fir and larch only.

Shake: On ends limited to half the thickness. Away from ends several heart shakes up to 2 ft long, none through.

Skips: Hit and miss skips in 10 per cent of the pieces.

Slope of grain: 1 in 12.

Splits: Equal in length to the width of the piece.

Stain: Stained sapwood. Firm heart stain or firm red heart limited to 10 per cent of the piece.

Wane: One-quarter the thickness, one-quarter the width. Five per cent of the pieces may have wane up to half the thickness and one-third the width for one-quarter the length.

Warp: Half of medium classification, which includes bow, crook and cup.

(11) *'No. 1'*. This grade differs from 'Select Structural' as follows:

Bending value 55 per cent of modulus of elasticity of 100 per cent.

Knots: Sound, firm, encased and pith knots, if tight and well-spaced, are permitted in sizes not to exceed the following or equivalent displacement:

Nom. width	At edge wide face	Centreline wide face	Unsound or loose knots and holes (any cause)	
6 in	1½ in	2¼ in	1¼ in	one hole or
8 in	2 in	2¾ in	1½ in	equivalent
10 in	2½ in	3¼ in	1½ in	smaller per
12 in	3 in	3¾ in	1½ in	3 linear ft
14 in	3⅛ in	4 in	1½ in	

Slope of grain: 1 in 10.

Stain: Stained sapwood. Firm heart stain or red heart.

(12) *No. 2*. This grade differs from 'No. 1' as follows:

Bending value of 45 per cent of modulus of elasticity of 90 per cent.

Knots: Well-spaced knots of any quality are permitted in sizes not to exceed the following or equivalent displacement:

Nom. width	At edge wide face	Centreline wide face	Holes (any cause)	
6 in	1⅞ in	2⅞ in	1½ in	one hole or
8 in	2½ in	3½ in	2 in	equivalent
10 in	3¼ in	4¼ in	2½ in	smaller per
12 in	3¾ in	4¾ in	3 in	2 linear ft
14 in	4⅛ in	5¼ in	3½ in	

Manufacture: Standard 'F'.

Shake: On ends limited to half the thickness. Away from ends through heart shakes up to 2 ft long, well-separated. If not through, single shakes may be 3 ft long or up to one-quarter the length, whichever is the greater.

Skips: Hit and miss, and, in addition, 5 per cent of the pieces may be hit or miss, or heavy skip not longer than 2 ft.

Slope of grain: 1 in 8.

Splits: Equal in length to one and a half times the width of the piece.

Stain: Stained sapwood. Firm heart stain or firm red heart not limited.

Unsound wood: Not permitted in thicknesses over 2 in, but in 2 in thickness, heart centre streaks not over one-third the thickness or width, or small spots or streaks of firm honeycomb or peck equal to one-sixth the width, are permitted.

Wane: One-third the thickness, one-third the width. Five per cent of the pieces may have wane up to two-thirds the thickness and half the width for one-quarter the length.

Warp: Light.

White speck: Firm, one-third the face or equivalent.

(13) *No. 3*. This grade differs from 'No. 2' as follows:

Bending value of 26 per cent of modulus of elasticity of 80 per cent.

Knots: Well-spaced knots of any quality are permitted in the following sizes or their equivalent displacement:

Nom. width	At edge wide face	Centreline wide face		Holes (any cause)
6 in	2¾ in	3¾ in	2 in	one hole or
8 in	3½ in	4½ in	2½ in	equivalent
10 in	4½ in	5½ in	3 in	smaller per
12 in	5½ in	6½ in	3½ in	1 linear ft
14 in	6 in	7 in	4 in	

Shake: Surface shakes permitted. If through at edges or ends, limited as splits. Elsewhere through shakes one-third the length. Several such scattered along the length.

Skips: Hit or miss, and, in addition, 10 per cent of the pieces may have heavy skip.

Slope of grain: 1 in 4.

Splits: Equal to one-sixth the length of the piece.

Stain: Stained wood, not limited.

Unsound wood: In spots or streaks limited to one-third the cross-section at any point along the length. Must not destroy nailing edge.

Wane: Half the thickness, half the width. Five per cent of the pieces may have wane up to seven-eighths the thickness and three-quarters the width for one-quarter the length.

Warp: Medium.

White speck and honeycomb: Firm.

Appearance Framing

(14) *A*. There is only one grade of appearance framing. Lumber of this grade is intended primarily for exposed use in housing and light construction where knotty-type lumber of high strength and finest appearance is required. Characteristics that affect strength and stiffness are limited to provide fibre stress in bending value of 55 per cent of that allowed for clear, straight-grained wood and to provide a recommended design value for modulus of elasticity value of 100 per cent of that allowed for clear wood average.

Characteristics permitted and limiting provisions are:

Checks: Seasoning, medium — not over $\frac{1}{32}$ in wide and not over 10 ft long.
Free of heart centre (*FOHC*).
Knots: Sound, tight and well-spaced, are permitted in the following sizes or their equivalent displacement:

Nominal width	Anywhere on wide face
2 in	½ in
3 in	¾ in
4 in	1 in
6 in	1½ in
8 in	2 in
10 in	2½ in
12 in	3 in
14 in	3⅛ in

Ten per cent of the pieces may have one 1 in hole through a corner, but not through thickness based on 12 ft length.

Manufacture: Standard 'C'. Admits medium torn grain, light raised grain, light loosened grain, very light machine bite, very light machine gouge, very light machine offset, light chip marks if well scattered, occasional medium chip marks, very slight knife marks, very light mismatch.

Pitch: Light.

Pitch streak: Small — One-twelfth the width and one-sixth the length of the piece.

Free of heart centre (*FOHC*).

Pockets: Medium, well-scattered.

Rate of growth: Limited to medium grain in Douglas fir and larch. Approximately four or more annual rings per inch.

Skips: Two very light, 6 in long, based on 12 ft lengths.

Slope of grain: 1 in 10.

Splits: Equal in length to the width of the piece.

Stain: Stained sapwood, medium. Firm heart stain or firm red heart.

Wane: One-twelfth thickness, one-twelfth width for one-sixth the length.

Warp: Very light.

NON-STRUCTURAL GRADES

In the preceding pages structural grades are covered — these being load-bearing grades to satisfy the UK requirements for all softwood commonly known as carcassing. Needless to say, Canada supplies a wide variety of superior lumber suitable for joinery where appearance is of greater importance than strength. As with other exporting countries of softwood, it is anomalous that the better-quality goods are generally of greater strength, on account of fewer strength-reducing defects, but the fact remains that appearance is the deciding factor and has to be regarded more in the light of economics and end-use.

There are a number of Canadian grades covered under the heading of 'Industrial Clears'. These are included in the NLGA Rules and provide for all species except Western red cedar. These can be supplied rough or surfaced, kiln-dried or air-dried, or unseasoned. The Rules provide tolerances in size between seasoned and unseasoned goods.

There are three grades of Industrial Clears:— 'B and Better', 'C' and 'D'.

B and Better. A supreme grade recommended and widely used for interior and exterior trim, cabinet work, garage doors and similar uses, where the finest finish is important.

Characteristics or their equivalent smaller which may appear on pieces in this grade and their limiting provisions are:

Checks: Four small — no limit in number if surface is rough.
Cup: Light.
Pitch streak: One small.
Pockets: Three very small.
Rate of growth: Average 6 rings per inch.
Sapwood: Bright, one-third the width or equivalent.
Slope of grain: Not to exceed 1 in 8.
Splits: Short, in 5 per cent of the pieces.
Torn or raised grain: Very light.
Warp: Very light in occasional pieces.
(It should be noted that knots are not mentioned but they are to a limited extent in Grades 'C' and 'D'.)

C. This grade is recommended and widely used for interior and exterior trim, cabinet work, garage doors and similar uses, where a high-quality finish is important.

This grade differs from 'B and Better' as follows:

Heart stain: Firm.
Sap stain: Medium, 25 per cent of piece or equivalent of lighter stain.
Skips: Occasional, very light on face, light on edges and reverse side.
Slope of grain: 1 in 6.

Knots: Two sound tight small, or three equivalent smaller, or *Pitch streak*, one small, or *Pockets*, four small.

D. A grade recommended and widely used where general utility purposes are of more importance than appearance. Characteristics on reverse face may be 25 per cent larger or more numerous.
This grade differs from 'C' as follows:

Checks.
Cup: Medium.
Knots: Four fixed, approximately 1 in or eight equivalent smaller.
Pin holes: Limited
Pitch streaks: Medium.
Pockets: Four medium.
Skips: Hit and miss, approximately $\frac{1}{8}$ in scant on edge.
Splits: Short.
Stained wood.
Turn or raised grain.
Wane: One-eighth the width, one-quarter the length or equivalent, one-quarter the thickness, 50 per cent more on reverse face.
Warp: Light.
White specks: Firm, one-quarter the width or equivalent.
Cutout: Ten per cent of the pieces in a shipment may have a 3 in cutout 3 ft or more from either end in pieces 12 ft and longer.

There is another grade of Industrial Clears under the heading of 1 in and thicker and 3 in and wider. Like the Clears already mentioned, they are based on a piece 8 in wide and 12 ft long. Their characteristics for larger dimensions are proportionally adjusted — that is, the permissible defects are slightly extended.

The size of a knot is expressed by taking the average of its maximum and minimum diameters unless otherwise specified.
Reference should be made to the Export 'R' List published by the Pacific Lumber Inspection Bureau in 1951 covering the various species of lumber exported from the west coast. A certain volume of lumber is still graded and exported under these rules, and, in fact, the Pacif contract implies that this is acceptable. These rules provide strict limits for the various grades of Clears, Merchantable and Common. Certain tolerances and variations are permitted, not only in quality but also in dimension. Unlike most other exporting countries' procedures, west coast goods are usually shipped green or unseasoned though anti-stain treated, and the rules permit shrinkage during subsequent seasoning and variation in sawing. The various grades are designed to provide a range to satisfy all reasonable constructional requirements.
In the general notes the following statement qualifies the application of the rules:

'The inspection of timber is the analysis of the quality of the product. Inflexible rules for the inspection of timber are impossible, therefore variations determined by practical experience must be allowed. The analysis being visual, mathematical precision is impossible and therefore a reasonable difference of opinion between inspectors must be recognised.

The grade of timber, as determined by the inspector, applies to size, form, condition or seasoning at time of original inspection. Any subsequent change in timber must be disregarded in determining the accuracy of original inspection. Suitability for construction purposes, in the shapes and sizes in which timber is ordered and shipped, will be taken into consideration in grading material according to the grades contained herein. It is not intended to supply material guaranteed to be suitable for re-manufacturing into smaller sizes.'

The preamble to each grade describes its suitability as follows:

No. 2 Clear and Better (Clears). Shall be sound timber, well manufactured.
Selected Merchantable. Shall be sound, strong timber, well manufactured and suitable for high-class constructional purposes.
No. 1 Merchantable. Shall be sound, strong timber, well manufactured and suitable for good, substantial constructional purposes.
No. 2 Merchantable. Shall be sound timber suitable for ordinary constructional purposes without waste.
No. 3 Common. Suitable for general utility purposes.

It could be thought that these descriptions do not give the intended end-user a very clear appreciation of quality. Each of the grades is further qualified by thickness – the defects being proportional to dimension. These are defined in the following manner and one grade is given here as an example.

The grading of west coast softwood differs from European grading mainly in six ways:

(1) Attention is paid to the growth of the wood expressed in terms of annual rings to the inch.

(2) The dimensions are much larger on the average.

(3) Pitch pockets and/or pitch blisters are more to be expected.

(4) Attention is paid to the proportion of sapwood as against heartwood in the top grades (but bright sap is not limited when treated with anti-stain solution).

(5) The slope of grain is taken into account; whether the sawing is edge, flat or random grain.

(6) There is no restriction on the number of knots in Constructional grades.

It should be noted that the NLGA Rules are more explicit in their description and limitation of defects in the various grades than the 'R' List.

The general description of *No. 1 Merchantable Douglas fir* 1½–2½ in thick is as follows:

'Shall be sound strong lumber, well manufactured and suitable for *good sound constructional purposes*. Must be medium grain, *i.e.*, an average on either one end or the other of the piece of not less than 4 annual rings per inch over a 3 inch line measured at right angles to the rings.

Will admit the following or their equivalent:–

Knots – sound and tight, ranging from approximately 1½" in 4" widths to 3" in 12" widths. Proportionate in wider widths.

Knots – not firmly fixed, approximately two-thirds diameter of allowable tight knots.

Spike knots – equivalent.

Pitch pockets and/or pitch blisters – medium.

Pitch – streaks.

Sap – half width or equivalent (other than black).

Heart stain – firm, limited.

Split – approximately width of piece.

Wane – ⅙ width, ⅓ length of the piece or equivalent. Approximately ¼ thickness.

Wormholes – pin, occasional, scattered.

Variation in sawing – occasional, slight.

When planed.

Skips – occasional, 1/12 deep, 3 ft. in length; 1/16 deep by ⅓ length on edge.

Sap – bright or discoloured (other than black).

Edge or surface irregularities – slight, due to machining.'

In order to meet the requirements for something slightly better than '*good sound* constructional purposes' there is the *Selected Merchantable* grade which is suitable for '*high-class* constructional purposes'; this must be close grained and the defects allowed are less than those in the same dimensions of No. 1 Merchantable.

There are superior Clear grades and also inferior grades, *No. 2 Merchantable* and *No. 3 Common*, which together provide a range to satisfy all reasonable requirements. In addition to these, there are a number of special grades for ceiling, door stock, pipe stock, ship decking and cutting grades – for example, factory flitches, factory selects and ship's stagings.

16.7 USA Softwoods

The west coast softwoods are of course identical with those of Canada. On the southern Atlantic coast there was a time when the most important softwood was pitch pine but, as mentioned elsewhere, this is now virtually non-existent. This is illustrated by the fact that the Gulf Coast Classification covering this species was printed in 1923 and has not been amended since then.

There is now a substantial new source of southern yellow pine which is subject to the Southern Pine Inspection Bureau Rules of 1977 (SPIB). A study of these rules will show that their requirements in respect of permissible defects which determine the grade are almost identical with those of the NLGA Rules already outlined for Structural Light Framing, Light Framing, Studs, Structural Joists and Planks and Appearance Framing. The one exception under these headings is that 5 in width is included, whereas the NLGA Rules commence at 6 in width. For this reason it is not intended to quote these rules in detail, but it is worth noting that there was a Supplement No. 4 in August 1978 which gave the Machine Stress Graded ratings.

16.8 Brazil

The grading rules of Parana pine are quite different from those of Scandinavia and Canada. They are formulated by government decree and were revised on 21 December 1951, the revision making them less strict than formerly, so that

Prime grade consists of 80 per cent 1 and 20 per cent 2.

Grade 1 now permits some wane on one edge and small knots on one side.

Grade 2 now permits some wane on both edges, knots on both sides and a few wormholes.

Grade 3 now permits still greater defects, including some sap-rot on one side.

Grade 4 approximates to Scandinavian sixths (or Wrack or Utskott).

16.9 Czechoslovakia

Whitewood is exported to the UK in unsorted quality, and is to be compared with the better Central European productions. The Czechoslovakians are usually able to include in their offers a large quantity of wide widths, and are therefore in great demand for scaffold boards.

16.10 Austria

Grading rules are entitled *Sorteneinteilung von Nadelschnittholz*, 1951, Form D 252, and are obtainable from: Osterreichischer Agrarverlag, Wien, I, Bankgasse 3. These are quite comprehensive and give, in German, details of all grades and respective defect limitations.

16.11 South Africa

Although South Africa is a relatively new source of softwoods for importation into the UK (see chapter 2), it is considered to be a growth area by many. Domestic grading rules exist but goods are exported on a 'mill-run' basis and, as with 'saw-falling' goods from other countries, receivers are expected to make their own assessment and selection as to quality and suitability for use.

16.12 UK Standards

The authoritative guidance on the use of softwood for constructional purposes in the UK is afforded by British Standard Code of Practice CP 112.19, *The Structural use of Timber in Buildings*. It is based on the principles of engineering design and on data established through research carried out both in the UK and elsewhere, and it deals with methods of calculating the sizes of softwood components required to sustain loads under various conditions of service.

All structural materials are in some degree variable in quality and performance. This is particularly true for a natural product such as wood, and in the establishment of definite values for working stresses it has been necessary to make ample allowance for defects and for variations in strength properties due to the number of different causes. Recommendations in the Code of Practice are based on the performance of different species under laboratory tests, the observed strength values of clear specimens being reduced by the effect of natural characteristics such as knots, shakes, splits, sloping grain, etc. It is the size and number of these which determines the strength of a particular piece; consequently a schedule of maximum sizes is incorporated in the Code. The measurements are described in detail in BS 4978, *Timber Grades for Structural Use* (amended 1978).

TRADA have produced an excellent booklet which summarises this information.

16.13 Moisture Content of Softwoods

The Albion and Uniform contracts state that the timber shall be 'properly seasoned for shipment to the United Kingdom and Republic of Ireland' but no definite moisture content is specified.

In Scandinavia the following definitions are accepted by exporters as to moisture content. This is calculated in the same way as in the UK – that is, amount of water expressed as a percentage of the dry weight of the wood.

(a) *Shipping dry*. Loose goods: 20/24 per cent. Discoloration on passage is then unlikely unless the goods get superficially wet. Packaged goods: In order that no discoloration should be allowed to develop, it is desirable to ensure that the maximum moisture content of 18/19 per cent is adhered to.

(b) *Planing dry*. 15/18 per cent. This is simply for successful surfacing, as the wood will normally regain moisture content on exposure. Kiln seasoning is required for this, except during summer months.

(c) *Outdoor joinery dry*. 10/14 per cent. Doors, windows, etc.

(d) *Furniture dry*. 7/10 per cent (in houses which are central-heated and very dry).

Pacific coast softwoods are usually sold green without any guarantee as to seasoning (except when kiln-dried) and dimensions are subject to any natural shrinkage, whether 'green' or partially or wholly seasoned, the intention being to manufacture all rough lumber full size when green, but occasional variations in sawing are allowed.

For *Eastern Canadian spruce* the Maritime Lumber Bureau Grading Rules make this definition:

'(a) All the provisions of these rules shall apply to 'dry' lumber, that is, lumber having a moisture content not exceeding 25 per cent (based on the oven dry weight of the wood) at the time of shipment.

'(b) Lumber of which the moisture content exceeds 25 per cent at the time of shipment shall be classed as 'green' lumber, in which case it shall be graded on the basis of those defects which occur in freshly sawn wood and not those which develop in the process of seasoning or weathering.'

16.14 Hardwoods

The most important hardwood grading rules are those published by the National Hardwood Lumber Association (USA). These are very comprehensive, yet possibly clearer to understand than the West Coast softwood grading rules. For this reason they are often used outside the USA as a basis for local grading of hardwoods.

In the general instructions the following instructions are given concerning the measurement of the goods.

'Measurement and Tally
16. Board measure is the term used to indicate that a board foot is the unit of measurement of lumber. A board foot is 1 foot long, 1 foot wide and 1 inch thick or its equivalent. In surfaced lumber the board foot is based on the measurement before surfacing, and all lumber less than 1 inch thick is counted face measure and taken as 1 inch.

In lumber measured with a board rule, random width pieces measuring to the even half foot shall be alternatively counted as of the next higher and lower foot counts; fractions below the half foot shall be dropped and fractions above the half foot shall be counted as of the next higher foot. On pieces measuring to the even half foot, the grade requirements shall be based on the lower foot count. Fractional lengths in standard grades shall be measured as of the next lower standard length.

Note: Unless otherwise specified, reference to percentages applies to board feet and not to the number of pieces.

17. Tapering lumber in standard lengths shall be measured one-third the length of the piece from the narrow end.

18. Random width lumber of standard grades and thicknesses shall be tallied surface measure and this tally shall be the number of feet, board measure, of 1 inch lumber. In lumber thicker than 1 inch the tally so

obtained is multiplied by the thickness as expressed in inches and fractions of an inch. Except squares, lumber less than 1 inch thick shall be counted surface measure.

Tallying on 12 feet Basis
21. The terms "export tally", "width and length tally" and "tally on 12 feet basis" are synonymous. The term "tally on 12 feet basis" is more definite because the width of 12 feet lumber is the same as the surface measure on the board rule. On this basis, the lengths are tallied separately. In tallying the widths, pieces measuring to the even half inch are alternatively counted as of the next higher or lower width count, fractions below the half inch are dropped and fractions above the half inch are counted as of the next higher width. After the tally is figured up, the proper fraction is added or subtracted in order to obtain the correct measure, thus: for 4 feet lengths, divide the total by 3; for 6 feet divide by 2; for 8 feet subtract 1/3; for 9 feet subtract 1/4; for 10 feet subtract 1/6; for 11 feet subtract 1/12; for 14 feet add 1/6; for 15 feet add 1/4; for 16 feet add 1/3; for 5 feet and 7 feet multiply by the length and divide by 12.

This method of tallying should not be confused with tallying stock widths such as 1 in. x 6 ins., 1 in. x 8 ins., etc.'

The rules then define a 'cutting' as: 'a portion of a board or plank obtained by cross cutting or ripping or both'.

A 'clear face cutting' is stated to be: 'a cutting having one clear face (ordinary season checks are admitted) and the reverse side sound as defined in sound cutting, etc.'.

A 'sound cutting' is stated to be: 'A cutting free from rot, pith, shake and wane. Texture is not considered. It will admit sound knots, sound bird pecks, stain, streaks or their equivalent, season checks not materially impairing the strength of a cutting, pin, shot and spot wormholes, etc., etc.'.

Standard defects are laid down as follows:

'(Apply to the grades established on a "defect basis.")
36. One knot $1\frac{1}{4}$ inches in diameter is a standard defect.

When located away from edges and ends they cannot be admitted as the equivalent to wane defects, the following shall be considered as standard defects:

Four pin wormholes or their equivalent equals one defect.

Three spot wormholes or their equivalent equals one defect.

Two $\frac{5}{8}$ inch diameter knots or their equivalent equals one defect.

Not more than two standard defects of this character can be admitted to the piece; each additional pin wormhole or spot wormhole or $\frac{5}{8}$ inch knot shall be considered one additional standard defect.

Defects larger than one standard defect, excepting wane and split, shall be considered on the following average diameter measurement: $2\frac{1}{2}$ inch knots or their equivalent shall be two standard defects; $3\frac{3}{4}$ inch knots or their equivalent shall be three standard defects; 5 inch knots or their equivalent shall be four standard defects.

One split equal in length in inches to the surface measure of the piece in feet and diverging not more than 1 inch to the foot in length.

Wane or its equivalent in other defects, 1 inch wide, one-sixth the length of the piece along the edges, or its equivalent at one or both ends. In the wane defect, wane may extend through the full thickness of the piece showing on both faces.

Worm, grub, knot and rafting-pin holes, not exceeding in extent one standard knot defect described above.

Equivalent defects are:

37. Pith and other defects not defined as standard defects, that do not damage the piece more than the standard defects allowed, are equivalent defects and must be so considered by the inspector.'

From the measurement of the timber, and the standard defects present, the amount of 'cutting' in a board is assessed. That is the amount of clear timber if all defects were cut out. This amount of 'clear face cutting' is expressed as a percentage or fraction of the total face measure. The rules lay down a method of making these calculations working on units of 12 square inches.

This gives the clear cutting in fractions of $\frac{1}{12}$ or alternatively a straight percentage if preferred. This percentage of 'clear face cutting' is a major item in the definition of each standard grade.

The cuttings required by each standard grade are:

Firsts, 91⅔ per cent (or 11/12).   No. 1 Common, 66⅔ per cent (or 8/12).
Seconds, 83⅓ per cent (or 10/12). No. 2 Common, 50 per cent (or 6/12).
Selects, 75 per cent (or 9/12).   No. 3A Common, 33⅓ per cent (or 4/12).
              No. 3B Common, 25 per cent (or 3/12).

As an example, a board 9⅜ in wide x 16 ft long may contain the following clear face cuttings: 8½ in x 6 ft (4.25 ft²), 3 in x 9½ ft (2.38 ft²), 4 in x 2¾ ft (0.92 ft²), 3 in x 3⅓ ft (0.83 ft²); total 8.38 ft².

The full face measure of the board is taken as 9 in x 16 ft = 12 ft². The clear face cutting is therefore 8.38/12 = 69.8 per cent. Since the board contains more than 66⅔ per cent (8/12) cutting, it grades as *Standard No. 1 Common*, subject to certain other requirements.

In practice these calculations are made on a simple unit basis and not in the manner shown above, which has been adopted to make the calculation easy to follow. In the above calculation there are said to be four cuttings.

The *Standard No. 1 Common* grade permits up to five cuttings to be made, depending on the surface measure of the board. The lower the surface measure, the smaller the number of cuttings permitted and the higher the cutting yield required to make the grade, – that is,

Surface measure	Required cutting yield		Number of cuttings
1 ft	12/12	100%	
2 ft	9/12	75%	1
3 ft and 4 ft	8/12	66⅔%	1
	9/12	75%	2
5–7 ft	8/12	66⅔%	2
	9/12	75%	3
8–10 ft	8/12	66⅔%	3
11–13 ft	8/12	66⅔%	4
14 ft and over	8/12	66⅔%	5

Each standard grade has its own schedule of cuttings.

The Standard Grades: National Hardwood Lumber Association, USA
The standard grades are:

Firsts ⎫
Seconds ⎬ usually combined as F.A.S.

Selects ⎫
No. 1 Common ⎬ sometimes combined as No. 1 Common and Selects.

No. 2 Common

No. 3A Common ⎫
No. 3B Common ⎬ sometimes combined as No. 3 Common.

The following requirements for each grade are set out: (a) minimum widths; (b) lengths – giving admissible proportion of shorts; (c) limits for pith and other defects; (d) the minimum cutting size; (e) the percentage yield of clear face cutting.
For instance:

Firsts (a) widths 6 in and wider; (b) lengths 8 ft–16 ft admitting 30 per cent of 8 ft–11 ft, of which one-half may be 8 ft and 9 ft; (c) limits for pith, wane, splits and diameter of knots, etc., and other defects; (d) minimum cutting – 4 in wide by 5 ft long, or 3 in wide by 7 ft long; (e) cutting yield, to admit 91⅔ per cent (11/12), clear cutting face as follows: 4 ft–9 ft surface measure, in one cutting; 10 ft–14 ft in two cuttings; 15 ft and over in three cuttings.

It will be seen that the cutting yield figure is the basis of the grading. The standard grades are summarised in table 16.4.
Having laid down the conditions and requirements for the standard grades, the NHLA rules then give the grading rules for each separate class of hardwood by reference to the standard grade.

TABLE 16.4 CUTTING REQUIREMENTS FOR STANDARD GRADES: NHLA USA

	Widths	Lengths	Surface measure	% clear face	Cuts	Minimum cutting
Firsts	6 in and up	8−16 ft	4−9 ft	91⅔	1	4 in x 5 ft
			10−14 ft	91⅔	2	or
			15 ft and up	91⅔	3	3 in x 7 ft
Seconds	6 in and up	8−16 ft	4 and 5 ft	83⅓	1	4 in x 5 ft
			6 and 7 ft	83⅓	1	or
			8−11 ft	83⅓	2	3 in x 7 ft
			12−15 ft	83⅓	3	
			16 ft and up			

6 to 15 ft surface measure will admit one additional cut to yield 91⅔% clear face

	Widths	Lengths	Surface measure	% clear face	Cuts	Minimum cutting
Selects	4 in and up	6−16 ft	2 and 3 ft	91⅔	1	4 in x 5 ft
						or
			Reverse side cutting sound			3 in x 7 ft

4 ft and up shall grade on one side as required in seconds with the reverse side not below No. 1 Common or reverse side of cuttings sound

	Widths	Lengths	Surface measure	% clear face	Cuts	Minimum cutting
No. 1 Common	3 in and up	4−16 ft	1 ft	clear	−	4 in x 2 ft
			2 ft	75	1	or
			3 and 4 ft	66⅔	1	3 in x 3 ft
			5−7 ft	66⅔	2	
			8−10 ft	66⅔	3	
			11−13 ft	66⅔	4	
			14 ft and up	66⅔	5	

3 to 7 ft surface measure will admit one additional cut to yield 75% clear face

	Widths	Lengths	Surface measure	% clear face	Cuts	Minimum cutting
No. 2 Common	3 in and up	4−16 ft	1 ft	66⅔	1	3 in x 2 ft
			2 and 3 ft	50	1	
			4 and 5 ft	50	2	
			6 and 7 ft	50	3	
			8 and 9 ft	50	4	
			10 and 11 ft	50	5	
			12 and 13 ft	50	6	
			14 ft and up	50	7	

2 to 7 ft surface measure will admit one additional cut to yield 66⅔ clear face

For instance:

Ash, Beech, Birch
   Firsts   }   standard, except 40 per cent 8 ft–11 ft lengths admitted
   Seconds }   in ash and 30 per cent in other species.
   Selects, standard, except 40 per cent 6 ft–11 ft lengths admitted in
                 ash.
   Other grades, standard.

The NHLA rules cover many other specialised grades, squares, furniture, kiln-dried lumber, wagon building, cabinet, constructional, etc. The last section deals with veneers, and gives definitions, basis of measurements and grading, and tables of weights.

Grading rules have been established for Malayan timbers and these are also based on a system of 'cuttings'.
In terms of grade and cutting yields they are as follows:

Prime, 10/12.
Select, 9/12.
Standard, 8/12.
Serviceable, 6/12.

It will be seen that these do not vary much from the NHLA rules, except that the grade is different. Also, it should be noted that they do contain provision for a separate rule based on the marketing of borer-infested timber.
The grading rules for home-grown hardwood are covered by BS 4047: 1966. This sets out four grades, 1, 2, 3 and 4, defined in terms of the cutting system, and four grades, A, B, C and D, based on the defects system. This standard is not frequently applied, since most of the home-grown hardwood is sold for a specific end-use. In terms of grade and cutting yield, they are as follows:

Grade 1, 10/12 (unedged, 11/12).
Grade 2, 8/12 (unedged, 10/12).
Grade 3, 6/12 (unedged, 9/12).
Grade 4, 3/12 (unedged, 8/12).

16.15 Plywood

There are not many set grading rules for plywood and there are quite significant variations between individual shipper's productions. Basically, the European grades are as follows:

A: Specially selected grade with surfaces as free from blemish as it is possible to obtain. No joints permitted on veneers and generally machine-sanded on both sides to give a better finish.
B: Ordinary first-class production veneers practically free from defects.

In certain timbers, such as beech, occasional plugging permissible. No joints permitted in veneers.

BB: Sound material with small knots, unsound knots replaced by plugs. Some discoloration and well-made joints permitted.

WG: Signifies that the plywood merely requires to be well glued.

Very often it is only necessary to have one good face to the sheet, the reverse side being of a lower grade. The grade of such sheets is indicated by a combination of the various symbols, such as B/BB.

It must always be remembered that the bonding media used in the manufacture of plywood are of the utmost importance, since their properties determine the characteristics and end-usage of the final product. For example, plywood used for internal application such as furniture needs to be well bonded but does not need to be highly resistant to moisture or water. Conversely, plywood used externally and exposed to adverse weather conditions requires an adhesive of high durability. This subject is described in greater detail in chapter 19.

Finland produces the following grades of birch plywood:

A: Practically free from knots except some small ones (some open) up to 5 mm in diameter. A few brown streaks, swirls and slight variation in colour permitted.

B: Allowing a few knots (some open) up to 8 mm in diameter, some brown streaks, swirls and slight discoloration. Joints to be glued and adjacent strips matched for colour.

S: Good paintable quality. Knots (some open) up to 10 mm in diameter and discoloration permitted. Joints are glued.

BB: Knots are plugged except such small ones as are permitted in B quality; joints and discoloration allowed.

WG: Guaranteed to be well glued, admits knots, plugs and joints in any number and some manufacturing defects.

Plywood panels are obtainable in the following qualities: A/BB, B, B/BB, B/WG, S/BB, BB, BB/WG and WG.

Blockboard and Laminboard have BB quality faces — B, B/B and S/BB quality are available on special order.

In addition, Finland produces many sophisticated panels with various overlay face finishes for special uses in the building industry and other end uses.

The USSR produces the following grades: A, B, BB, CP and C. CP is an improved grade of C, with some large knots replaced by plugs or inserts. In addition to birch, a certain amount of softwood species is also produced. Its production is exported in the following combinations: B/BB, BB, BB/CP, BB/C and C (C/C).

Central Europe: Germany, Czechoslovakia and Romania produce, in the main, beech plywood, and their grades are: B/BB, BB and Standard. In Germany B/BB is often described as 1/11.

Far Eastern grades are not as diverse as might be supposed. Commercial plywood is exported to Europe mostly in B/BB quality with a small proportion of B/C.

The B/BB grade is described as follows:

Face side: Minimum 20 per cent unjointed, balance permitting one or two skilfully executed and well-matched joints. Permitting *occasional* minor defects such as small sound knots, slight natural discoloration. Permitting not more than two tight or neatly repaired splits not exceeding ⅓ in width and 6 in length.

Reverse side: Permitting up to four joints skilfully executed. Permitting up to four neatly repaired splits not exceeding 8 in length by ¼ in width. Permitting occasional small knots or slight natural discoloration.

Brazil produces both plywood and blockboard, which is manufactured principally in the Parana region close to the Parana pine growing area. Owing to increasing shortages of peeler logs of Parana pine some mills are now producing plywood and blockboard of 'Folhoza', which is a vernacular name for several mixed species of hardwood which have been found suitable for peeling.

The usual grade for plywood is B/BB with a small amount of C quality. Blockboard uses the same species for cores and veneers.

North America: Canada and the USA have always been traditionally associated with Douglas fir plywood. This species has declined in recent years and other coniferous species have been marketed as Canadian softwood plywood. This latter plywood has been proved to be acceptable, especially in sheathing grades. In recent years Canada has simplified the grading mainly by eliminating the solid grades in sanded plywood. The basic rules are as follows at the time of writing.

1. *GENERAL NOTES*

'(a) *Species*. Plywood conforming with the grade requirements listed in this Section shall be manufactured from Douglas fir veneer; veneers of other species shall not be admitted.

(b) *Interior Plies*. Interior plies of grades listed in this Section shall be of a quality equivalent to or higher than that specified for the back of a Good one Side panel (see para. 4 below).

(c) *Gluelines*. All panels conforming with the grade requirements listed in this Section shall be of the EXTERIOR type, bonded with approved phenolic formaldehyde resin glue, and shall fulfil the requirements for moisture resistance specified in Appendix A of this Grading Standard.

(d) *Size Tolerances*. A tolerance of 1/64 (0.0156) inch over or under the specified thickness shall be allowed on sanded panels. A tolerance of 1/32 (0.0312) inch over or under the specified length and/or width shall be allowed but all panels shall be square within ⅛ (0.1250) inch.

(e) *Marking*. Each panel conforming to grades listed in this Section may be marked on the end with the following registered Association mark: PMBC EXTERIOR.

2. *GOOD TWO SIDES GRADE* (*G2S*).

Each face shall be of one or more pieces of firm, smoothly cut veneer. When of more than one piece, it shall be well joined and reasonably matched for grain and colour at the joints. It shall be free from knots, splits, pitch pockets, and other open defects. Streaks, discolorations, sapwood, pitch, and neatly made wood inlays shall be admitted. This grade shall present a smooth surface suitable for painting.

3. *GOOD ONE SIDE, SOLID BACK GRADE* (*G/Solid*).

One face shall be equal to the face of Good two Sides. The back shall present a solid surface, free from open defects, but in addition to characteristics admitted in the Good face shall admit also neatly made repairs, as well as synthetic plugs that present solid level, hard surfaces, knots up to 1 inch if both sound and tight, tight splits, slightly rough but not torn grain, and other minor sanding and patching defects. The back shall be paintable.

4. *GOOD ONE SIDE GRADE* (*G1S*).

One face shall be equal to the face of Good two Sides. The back may contain knotholes not larger than 1 inch in least dimension, open pitch pockets not wider than 1 inch, splits not wider than 3/16 inch which taper to a point, worm or borer holes not more than ⅝ inch wide or 1½ inches long, knots if tight and not more than 1½ inches in least dimension, and plugs, patches, shims, sanding defects, and other characteristics in number and size that will not impair the serviceability of the panel. The back may be of one piece or of joined veneers.'

The two following grades are only produced by the USA, whereas Canada now only produces G1S and G2S.

'5. *SOLID TWO SIDES GRADE* (*Solid2S*).

Each face shall be equal to the back of Good one Side, Solid Back.

6. *SOLID ONE SIDE GRADE* (*Solid1S*).

The face shall be equal to the face of Solid two Sides. The back shall be equal to the back of Good one Side.

7. *SELECT MARINE GRADE*.

Both faces shall be equal to the faces of Good two Sides. All crossbanding and cores shall be equal to the face of Solid one Side. This grade is suitable for hull planking and all marine uses.

8. *CONSTRUCTION SHEATHING GRADE*.

Each face may contain knotholes not larger than 1 inch in least dimension, open pitch pockets not wider than 1 inch, splits not wider than 3/16 inch which taper to a point, worm or borer holes not more than ⅝ inch wide, or 1½ inches long, knots if tight and not more than 1½ inches in least dimension, plugs, patches, shims, and other characteristics in number and size that will not impair the serviceability of the panel. Each face may be of one piece or of joined veneers.'

16.16 Possible Changes in Grading Systems

As mentioned earlier in this chapter, some countries have given considerable thought to the modification of the long-existing grading rules. The emphasis is towards grading for 'end use' and in this respect Sweden has taken the initiative. It has long been recognised that the present system of grading has been somewhat anomalous. The classification of Unsorted, fifths and sixths means very little unless one is familiar with the shipper concerned. For example, an Unsorted grade from the north of Sweden or Finland is quite unlike the Unsorted from the south. Under the existing rules, a parcel of Unsorted from the south may only be equal to fifths from the north, and fifths from the south may only be equal to sixths from the north.

In 1968 the European Softwood Conference discussed the possibility of revising the classification of softwood from the point of view of end-use. Sweden volunteered to investigate this project and considerable work has been done through the research and development organisation Träinformation.

In 1977 the Swedish Timber Council in the UK held a seminar in London which was attended by all interested parties, such as shippers, importers, manufacturers, architects, building inspectors and agents. Tentative new classification proposals were outlined and discussed but no definite decisions were reached, even though it was considered that they did overcome many of the anomalies which exist under the present grading system.

It must be emphasised that while Sweden has taken the initiative, the aim is to produce a system which suits not only all exporting countries, but also all receivers. In other words, it must be internationally acceptable and it will be some considerable time before complete agreement is reached. At the time of writing, details of proposals are by no means finalised and it would be confusing to quote them. However, the subject is mentioned in order that it is recognised that action is being taken to produce a system which is considered by most trade members to be desirable.

Already in Sweden and Finland, some exporters have discarded the established system of Unsorted, fifths and sixths. They either sell on mark only or offer Grades 1, 2, 3 and 4. Broadly speaking, the latter means that Grade 1 contains goods suitable for first-class joinery — say firsts, seconds and better thirds. Grade 2 contains goods suitable for second-class joinery — say thirds and better fourths. Grade 3 contains goods suitable for carcassing — say fourths and fifths. Grade 4 contains goods suitable for packaging and pallet manufacture — say low-line fifths and sixths.

17   Softwood Surfaces

17.1 Sawing

The surfaces of imported sawn and planed wood goods are a matter of interest and may be of importance where there is an undertaking that the goods shall be produced in one particular way or another, but it is sometimes a little difficult to determine how they were produced from the appearance of the finished product.

In countries exporting timber there are mainly three types of saw used for converting logs into sawngoods: *bandsaws*, which may be single- or double-edged and may be vertical or horizontal, and of which the teeth may be spring-set or swage-set; *frame (or gang) saws*, which are usually spring-set; and *circular saws* of several different kinds.

(NOTE: In spring-setting every alternate tooth is bent out in the opposite direction, so that the cut or 'kerf' made by the teeth is greater than the thickness of the saw blade, giving the necessary clearance. In swage-setting every tooth has the point spread out equally, which has the same effect of providing clearance for the saw, but each tooth cuts both sides.)

BANDSAWS

A large bandsaw is capable of breaking down a very large log. The log is held firmly to a carriage which moves past the saw so that the projecting part of the log is sawn off in the form of a slab.

Valuable hardwood logs are usually converted to sawn goods on a horizontal bandsaw and the log may be cut into varying thicknesses through and through, or may be turned over on the carriage to produce desired effects in the way of figure. To obtain a smooth finish different woods require different shapes of tooth with a varying hook or rake or angle of cut, and not all woods will tolerate the same rate of feed.

In this country softwood logs are quite often converted on a rack sawbench, but in Canada (to which the following remarks mainly apply) usually on a vertical bandsaw, which, after removing a slab, may, if the saw is double-edged, make another cut in the reverse direction and the next cut in a forward direction and so on until only another slab is left. On the other hand, the log may be turned half-circle, or quarter-circle, on the carriage to produce various thicknesses according to the size of the log and the dimensions required.

The big bandsaw is capable of doing very fine work and the smaller bandsaw even finer, but the production of a fine finish is dependent upon very expert attention to the saws and their tensioning and setting by the saw doctor.

The carriage to which the log is held travels at a considerable speed. The turning of the log is done by a mechanical device which, in the hands of an expert, does superhuman work in turning the log and holding it until it is firmly held on the carriage.

Twin bandsaws are sometimes used, which are very useful for such operations as converting 75 mm deals into three boards of equal thickness by making two simultaneous deep cuts, or for converting 225 mm widths into three equal widths (a pile of boards can be cut simultaneously in this way) by making two flat cuts.

'Deep cutting', sometimes called 'deeping', is parallel with the wide surface, leaving widths the same. 'Flat cutting', sometimes called 'flatting' or 'ripping', is parallel with the edge, leaving the thickness the same.

Small bandsaws are very useful in the boxboard mill for dealing with small sizes requiring very accurate cutting and fine finish.

When the big bandsaw loses too much width by frequent sharpening, it comes into use as a horizontal resaw for converting the larger slabs into boards.

In recent years several large Scandinavian mills, particularly in Finland, have replaced their traditional framesaw lines with sets of large bandsaws which can be adjusted to cut the whole log into varying sizes in the same way as framesaw lines. This method of production gives an accurate and very smooth sawn surface to the timber coupled with a considerably increased output from each line. It is also common practice in some mills to convert top logs of smaller diameter into scantlings through a chipper or canterline machine. These machines pass the small logs through a chipping device which takes off the rounded parts of the log, the chips going to other uses – for example, chipboard, pulp, etc. The square thus produced can then pass through a circular saw or bandsaw which splits it into two scantlings. This method of production gives an extremely good surface finish far smoother than that given by the framesaw and is more economical, since it eliminates the extra operation of transporting the outside slabs to a separate chipper.

FRAMESAWS (OR GANG SAWS)

Frame or gang saws are still customary in the large mills of Northern Europe and these are now usually run in pairs in series, the first frame removing two slabs (and usually a couple of boards on each side of the log as well) and the second cutting the block, which has two sawn sides, into the required thicknesses, of which the first frame fixed the width. This is called block-sawing. By this system the bulk of the production, at all events in the larger sizes, will be frame-sawn on sides and edges, but any pieces cut waney will be edged by a circular saw, often known as a double edger.

The modern framesaw is very fast and very accurate, and although the sawkerf of the spring-set framesaw is greater than that of the swage-set bandsaw, it has the advantage of making several cuts at a time. In result the multiple production of the framesaw more than compensates for the greater feed speed of the bandsaw. Quite often the first frame will have six saws — three each side with a space of, say, 225 mm, 175 mm or 150 mm in the middle, according to the diameter of the log. The second frame often has nine saws, one in the middle for the centre cut and four each side of it to produce the thicknesses required — say 75 mm, 50 mm, 25 mm, 19 mm, in each case with sufficient excess measure to allow for shrinkage during seasoning.

CIRCULAR SAWS

Circular saws are of different types, according to the purpose for which they are to be used. There is the large log-saw used in south Sweden and eastern Canada, which is a fairly thick spring-set parallel-sided plate saw. The customary method is to take a slab off one side of the log, turn the log over half-circle, take another slab off and continue cutting the thicknesses required. Alternatively the log may be converted by several successive cuts without turning. Very large circular saws cutting frozen logs in freezing temperatures have a hard time of it, and the sawn product is frequently irregular in thickness; in fact, it is understood that if goods are described as circular-sawn they are not expected to be so regular and accurate in dimension as band-sawn or frame-sawn.

Particularly in the production of the small circular sawmills of eastern Canada there is a liability for occasional pieces to 'run off' or taper in thickness or width towards the end. This is not considered a serious fault in such productions, and it is customary to check for thickness and width a foot or two from the end and not at the extreme end.

In one of the most modern Canadian mills a big bandsaw is used for initially breaking down the logs and a pair of framesaws run in series for resawing.

In all three cases those of the sawn goods which are cut waney are edged by circular saws and the end trimming, or adjusting, is done by crosscut circular saws, several different types being used for the latter, some of them giving a very smooth finish, which is of great importance to appearance and consequently the value of the imported product, whether it has a paint-mark on the end or not.

The edger, which usually consists of two ordinary plate saws, one fixed and one movable on the same spindle, has a larger saw kerf than the recutting saw, but as this is at the expense of waste it is of little importance. Slatings, staves and laths are all cut on similar benches with multiple circular saws.

The recutting saw, principally used for 'cutting for planing', is usually a special type of circular saw, thickness perhaps 4 mm at the centre and tapering off to about 1 mm at the rim, so that the thickness of the cutting edge of the saw, plus the set of the saw, makes a saw kerf of only about 1.5 mm. The fineness of this recutting saw, in view of subsequent planing, is very important, so that the surface shall be as smooth as possible and the minimum of wood be lost by the cut. It is possible to recut deals and battens into boards and plane them, with a loss of less than 3 mm per cut.

'Ari-sawn' means that the goods have been cut on an improved type of circular-saw bench called the ARI, which has adjustable feed rollers enabling the wood to be sawn with much greater accuracy than on the old type of circular-saw bench. It has been claimed that Ari-sawn goods are equal in manufacture to frame-sawn: this largely depends on the respective saws themselves and how they are cared for, as well as on the skill with which they are operated.

The circular saw used for crosscutting, as in trimming or adjusting the ends, is of a different type from that used for straight cutting along the grain, as in edge trimming or ripping. The crosscut saw does not need so much set as the edging saw, as less clearance is required in cutting across the fibres than in cutting along them when they have a tendency to grip: it is also a shorter cut. The crosscut saw plate may therefore be thinner at the edge, with less set and smaller teeth, which has the effect of making the end look as if it were planed, thus adding considerably to the appearance and consequently the value of the shipment.

It may be very difficult to distinguish between well-sawn band-sawn and well-sawn frame-sawn surfaces, since the saw marks, which are practically always visible, are very similar. However, there is nearly always at least one tooth which runs fractionally out of line, making a defined scratch at regular intervals, and these scratches will be much wider apart in the band-sawn goods than the frame-sawn goods, as the bandsaw has so many more teeth than the framesaw.

One cannot necessarily judge from the edge of a pile whether the goods are band-sawn, frame-sawn or circular-sawn, as the edges may be circular-sawn however the other surfaces may have been worked. Circular-sawn goods practically always show the circular saw marks fairly clearly.

SHRINKAGE

When sawing logs into deals, battens and boards, allowances are made in Scandinavian mills (but not in Canadian and USA mills) for shrinkage in thickness and width. Shrinkage in length is so slight as to be negligible.

Shrinkage is greater in the direction of the annual rings than across them — in other words wood shrinks more tangentially than radially — and this fact is applied in the case of flooring blocks and flooring strips, which are usually cut 'rift-' or 'quarter-sawn' or 'edge grain', so that when laid not only do they have a harder wearing surface, but also any tendency to shrink will be more in thickness than in widths and so less likely to cause gaps between the blocks or strips.

It is estimated that Scandinavian sawn goods shrink, on the average, 3 per cent from green (unseasoned) to shipping dry. In practice a greater allowance is usually made, since it is most important that the wood hold up its nominal measure when shipping dry.

Boards cut from the outside of the log, consisting as they do mostly of sapwood, have a greater tendency to shrink than sizes consisting mostly of heartwood, and that also has to be taken into account. Furthermore, boards shrink more than deals and battens, being normally cut tangentially, and being thinner, they dry more thoroughly.

The allowance is made, when fixing the distance between the saw blades of the frame, by inserting blocks of wood which are the thickness of the deal, batten or board to be produced, plus the set of the saw to give the necessary clearance for the saw blade through the wood, plus the allowance for shrinkage.

In Canada and the USA softwood lumber is sold 'subject to natural shrinkage'. Douglas fir is estimated to shrink on the average 5 per cent, western red cedar 4 per cent, western hemlock and Sitka spruce 6 per cent. According to the British Columbian rules, Douglas fir shrinks approximately as follows:

Thickness	1 in, 1¼ in, 1½ in	2 in	3 in	4 in and thicker
Approx. shrinkage	$\frac{1}{16}$ in	$\frac{1}{8}$ in	$\frac{1}{16}$ in	$\frac{1}{4} - \frac{5}{8}$ in 12 in thickness

Width	3 in	4 in	6 in	8 in and 10 in	12 in	14 in and wider
Approx. shrinkage	$\frac{1}{8}$ in	$\frac{3}{16}$ in	$\frac{1}{4}$ in	$\frac{1}{2}$ in	$\frac{5}{8}$ in	$\frac{3}{4}$ in

It sometimes happens that sawn goods have ragged edges or ends, which is very detrimental to their appearance and consequently their value. This is a fault of the saws, which, if of the correct type for the job and properly sharpened and set, should be able to cut wood cleanly, whatever its moisture content or the temperature.

The amount to be allowed for the set of the saw depends upon the thickness of the blade and also the type and dimension of wood to be cut. The average framesaw blade is about 2 mm thick and the set about ½ mm on each side, making a total saw kerf of about 3 mm.

17.2 Planing

Planed boards have normally a face and a back and are produced on a machine which has a fixed knife, or series of knives, set in the bed, with a rotary cutter operating as thicknesser in advance of them and a rotary cutter or two operating above. The board to be planed normally goes through the planer face downwards on to the fixed knives while the upper side, constituting the back of the board, is thicknessed by the rotary cutter. The face of the board will thus have a perfectly smooth surface, but the back will show, however slightly, the ridges caused by the rotating knives of the cutter. Rotary cutting can be so beautifully done that it is almost impossible to tell the difference between the face and the back, but a wet finger wiped on the board will show up the rotary cutter marks. In some cases, as in the case of mouldings, the whole process is done by rotary cutters and not by a fixed knife, but the face can then never be quite so perfect, though commercially good.

The use of fixed knives for planing, although a standard practice in Scandinavian planing mills, is not so general in the UK or North America. In consequence, these planed boards generally have a surface slightly inferior to that of the Scandinavian imported planed boards.

18 The Home Grown Timber Trade

18.1 General

In the years up to 1939 less than 10 per cent of the timber consumed in the UK was home grown. During the Second World War over 60 per cent was home grown. These two figures express the relative importance commercially and economically of the home grown timber trade in peace and war. There was an immense increase in the home production of softwood, hardwood, pitwood and plywood during the war years. At the same time, it should be remembered that the proportion of land area, about 6.5 per cent, under forest in the UK is very low compared with the timber-producing countries of Europe (Sweden 56.5 per cent, Norway 23.8 per cent, France 19 per cent).

At one time the country mills producing timber from trees in England and Scotland held a proud position in the internal trade of the land. The growth of the imported timber trade during the nineteenth century, enabling bulk quantities of cheap timber to be put on the market to meet the expanding trade and population of the country, resulted in the decline of the home grown timber trade, which found itself unable to compete with the low prices of imported timber.

The home grown trade was in a depressed condition in the 1930s and as a result many firms further developed the sidelines carried on from time immemorial, such as agricultural work, gates, fencing, barrows, some extending into manufacturing of tool handles, mouldings, portable buildings and the like in order to have more than one source of income.

Wartime requirements changed the position immediately. From being the smallest supplier of timber of the country, the home grown trade became the largest. The trade was expanded greatly and the majority of sawmills previously handling only imported timber began to handle home grown timber, but of course at the first opportunity returned to the handling of the imported timber for which they were laid out.

The lack of any definite forest policy in the country until 1919, together with the excessively high rate of felling in both the World Wars, resulted in the forest areas of the country dwindling to a dangerously low level. For many years the rate of felling had to be drastically curtailed in order that these forest areas could regain a safe level. The immense effort made by the home grown trade during the war had been at the expense of their future livelihood.

During the Second World War the standing reserves of softwood became reduced by about 50 per cent and hardwood by about 40 per cent. This large-scale depletion was mainly from private estates, but some of the Forestry Commission's newly established plantations were also felled. The wartime experience was not a happy one for British softwood, as it was urgently required, with the result that logs of largely immature wood were converted with unsuitable equipment and delivered in an unseasoned condition. The situation did not improve substantially during the immediate post-war years, because supplies of coniferous sawlogs were then insufficient to justify the necessary investment in modern sawmilling equipment.

However, the situation today reflects an entirely different picture. The home-grown industry has been doubling its production roughly every twelve years or so and will inevitably continue to take a larger share of the market. It is estimated that there will be a steady increase until around the year 2025, when it is likely to level off unless planting on a wider scale than at present is undertaken.

18.2 The Forestry Commission

The Forestry Commission was set up in 1919 following the Acland Report of 1918, with these objects: (a) establishing and maintaining a national reserve of state-owned forests; (b) encouraging, advising and assisting privately owned forests and estates.

By the end of September 1951 – that is to say in the first 32 years of operation – the land areas under the control of the Commission amounted to 712 600 ha (1 781 500 acres). Ten years later, in 1961, this had increased to 1 018 240 ha (2 545 600 acres). In 1977 it had become 1 250 300 ha (3 125 750 acres) (see table 18.1).

In the year 1976–77 the Commission's income from the sales of timber amounted to over £22 million, which was some £5 million more than the year before.

There are few private landowners who can afford today to carry out ambitious forestry schemes. In operating a forest or woodland, the principal return comes to the landowner when the trees reach maturity and are felled. There is a yearly income from the sale of thinnings and other forest products.

TABLE 18.1

Total area (1000 ha)	Great Britain 1250.3	England 303.7	Scotland 785.4	Wales 161.2
Forest land, total	937.7	258.8	538.2	140.7
under plantations	840.9	247.3	459.8	133.8
to be planted	96.8	11.5	78.4	6.9
Other land	312.6	44.9	247.2	20.5

To assist and extend the development of private forestry, there are arrangements to grant financial assistance in the form of loans, planting and
maintenance grants. These arrangements are embodied in a project initiated in
1948 called the 'Dedication of Woodlands' scheme and there is also the
'Approved Woodlands' scheme − both of which amounted to a total
expenditure of £2.25 million in the year 1976−77. Needless to say,
landowners are expected to undertake certain responsibilities under these
schemes and the Commission exercises supervision and at the same time
makes advice available.

The Forestry Commission has its headquarters in Edinburgh, from where
eleven Conservancy areas are controlled − five in England, four in Scotland
and two in Wales. It employs over 8000 staff, of which over 70 per cent are
industrial. Its main research establishment is at Alice Holt Lodge, Farnham,
Surrey, and it has extensive education and training facilities in many areas. It
provides a wealth of publications on all aspects of forestry and the
subjects associated with it, and its advisory service is available to all. In recent
years there has been considerable emphasis placed on recreational facilities.
Camping sites and forest cabins, car parks and waymarked walks have been
fully appreciated by the public, who are encouraged to go into the forests
and see more for themselves. Figure 18.1 shows the boundaries of the eleven
Conservancy areas.

18.3 Structure of the Home Grown Trade

Landowner. In the UK roughly half of the productive woodland is currently
in private hands and half managed by the Forestry Commission. If one
considers all woodlands, the figures become private 57 per cent and Forestry
Commission 43 per cent. Since their inauguration in 1919, the Forestry
Commission have planted considerable areas of new forests and at the present
time have more than 840 ha of land under new plantation.

Agent or purchaser. The buying of standing timber requires considerable
skill and experience. Most home grown timber merchants are expert in this
phase of their business, carrying out surveys, valuations and purchasing by
means of their own staff. While it is unusual for them to employ outside
assistance, there are specialists in this work who will carry out a survey of the
standing timber and purchase it on behalf of the interested party, such as a
sawmill proprietor. Some of these agents may act on their own behalf and
buy standing timber, arrange for it to be felled and then sell the logs to the
sawmill proprietors, etc.

Harvesting contractors. Much standing timber is worked by harvesting
contractors who undertake the felling preparation and extraction of standing
timber. Sometimes they are employed by a woodland owner, sometimes by a
sawmiller and sometimes they also undertake the marketing of round timber
on their own behalf.

Hauliers. With the advent of the Second World War and the impetus given

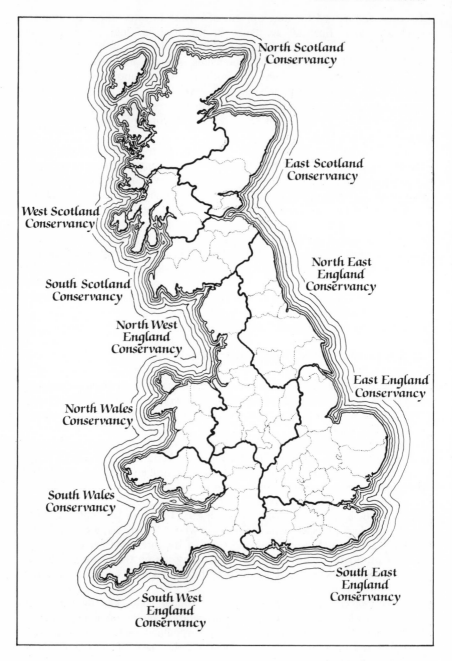

Figure 18.1 Forestry Commission Conservancy boundaries

to increased production, employment of haulage by contractors with their own haulage equipment developed. These generally work on contract, for which they move the logs from the woods and then haul them either direct to the sawmill or to a railway station. They are mainly concerned with roundwood, although today many sawmillers have their own specialised vehicles with hydraulic grapples.

Mills. In post-war years this has become a growth area and there are now a number of well-designed high-capacity mills which have come into production. The result of this is that it is now possible to obtain accurately sawn, stress-graded dry British softwood well suited for virtually all types of construction. Sawn softwoods have made considerable penetration into the packaging, pallet for material handling and mining markets, in addition to the former traditional use in farm building and fencing. The situation has now been reached where over 40 per cent of UK sawn sawlogs is converted by only 11 per cent of the mills. Indeed, as the production of logs exceeding 18 cm in top diameter will more than double before the end of the century, this trend towards conversion in larger modern mills will undoubtedly continue and the many smaller ones which are currently working below full capacity are likely to increase their production also.

18.4 The Future of Home Grown Timber

Without doubt, this industry is one which is continuing to flourish and in the long term will contribute very considerably to the country's demand for forest products. It is now reaping the benefits of long-term planning although, unlike most other industries, this is one which is slow to reach maturity; following the excessive depletions of the last war, a more fortunate situation exists today. Since 1959 there has been a joint programme of research by the Forestry Commission and the Building Research Establishment, with the result that the properties of all major species are now well known and widely publicised. Every home grown log assists in reducing the adverse import bill, which already exceeds £2000 million.

In recent years there has been a substantial revival in demand for roundwood, especially for particle board, which captured an increased share of the market by providing over 40 per cent of UK consumption in competition with imports. Associated with this demand was a strong recovery in the sawmilling industry but with only modest demand from the pulpwood sector. These improved market conditions have resulted in a substantial increase in the volume of timber harvested and have been accompanied by increases in prices in common with imported wood products. Figure 18.2 clearly shows the improved market conditions resulting from the increase in production – currently of the order of over 2 million m^3.

The entire timber industry in the UK has had to have second thoughts about grading for structural purposes. This has become mandatory, and with the introduction of BS 4978 in 1976 (*Timber Grades for Structural Use*)

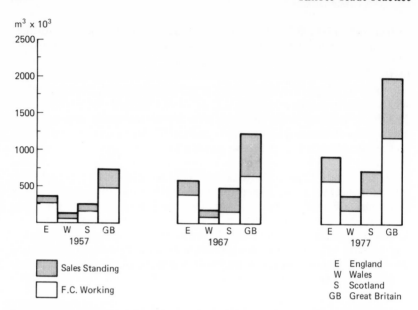

Figure 18.2 Wood production increases in the period 1957–1977 and the relative proportions sold standing and worked by the Forestry Commission

home grown softwoods are able to complement imported softwood, whereas they had been largely ignored on account of faster growth. BS 4978 specifies that timber with not less than four annual rings per 25 mm can be used provided that it satisfies the application of the knot area ratio (K.A.R.) by visual grading (see chapter 21, section 21.2). The advent of stress grading has had a profound effect on the marketing prospects of home grown softwood. Wood which was hitherto regarded as unsuitable for structural use on account of rapid growth can now compete with the traditional imported softwood.

It has been established – particularly with mechanical grading – that the yield of structural wood is raised from 43 per cent to 92 per cent for Scots pine and for Sitka spruce from 38 per cent to 98 per cent. In fact, Princes Risborough Laboratory has shown that 25 per cent of run of mill Sitka spruce could be machine graded to give wood with strength properties equivalent to those of the top grade (M 75) of imported redwood. Although it is not desired to overemphasise the position, it is felt that it should be considered seriously by those engaged in the imported softwood trade. It is estimated that home grown sawlogs will amount to a volume of 3 million m^3 by the end of this century – which is not so far off – and residues for other allied products will rise in equilibrium. This means that over 40 per cent of UK import could be replaced by natural resources. This, above all else, illustrates the estimated future of the home grown trade.

In regard to softwood, the most important contribution is Norway and Sitka spruce, which will dominate future sawlog production in all areas other than East Anglia, central south England, the Midlands and east Scotland — where the pines take over. Scots pine, which is the same species as Baltic redwood, has been proved to be equivalent to Lower Gulf redwood, which makes it slightly weaker than Polish redwood but stronger than that from Northern Europe. In the southern areas of Britain it is being replaced by the exotic Corsican pine, which gives a higher yield of straighter logs per hectare. In northern areas of Britain lodgepole pine has been widely planted, but it will be a decade before substantial production of sawlogs is available.

The larches, which occupy just under 10 per cent of the woodlands, are 'tailor-made' for farm use, with good strength properties, small knots and resistance to decay. Douglas fir has similar properties and, for most purposes, the two species can be regarded as interchangeable. However, machine grading tests have indicated that the strength properties of Douglas fir are slightly below those of the larches.

British hardwoods need no testimonial, but it is an undeniable fact that they cannot compete with the many species now being imported. Today the emphasis is on planting softwoods, on account of the advantageous commercial value and quicker crop rotation. This does not imply that hardwoods are being neglected, but it is perhaps fair to say that their importance is regarded as lying more in their aesthetic, nature conservation and amenity value. In the year 1976–77 the total planting of broad-leaved species occupied only 183 ha, whereas conifers occupied over 18 000 ha.

On the subject of hardwoods, it is appropriate to mention the effect that Dutch elm disease has had on prolific native elm. A Forestry Commission survey of southern Britain in 1976 indicated that about 6 million elms in the open countryside and in urban areas were dead or dying. When account is taken of elms in woodlands and trees felled over the past few years, it is estimated that 9 million have died during the present epidemic out of the original population of 23 million in the area surveyed. The result of this is that vast quantities of timber are available — most of which is usable — and the supply greatly exceeds the demand. The major outlet has been the possibility of its use for farm buildings but a cautionary note is necessary. It is not generally recognised that English elm is at the end of the strength spectrum, with values for stiffness and compressive strength lower than those of Sitka spruce. It follows that large sections will be required if used for load-bearing purposes, and since there is a high incidence of wild grain, careful selection is necessary to ensure that only straight-grained members are used.

To sum up, the home grown timber industry has no reason to be other than optimistic as to its role in Britain's contribution to its needs. It has opportunities of supplying structural timber for the construction industry and residues for the particle board, fibre building board and pulp industry, as well as making a very considerable contribution to meeting all the demands of allied industries such as farm buildings, fencing, palletisation and packaging. There are many Associations such as the Home Timber Merchants Association which co-operate in assuring that this will be achieved.

19 Specialised Branches of the Trade

19.1 Plywood and Veneer Trade

GENERAL

The word 'plywood' generally covers the following products.

(1) *Plywood.* A composite sheet material manufactured from veneers of wood arranged with the grain of adjacent layers running at right angles.

(2) *Laminboard,* sometimes known as laminated board. Here the centre core of the composite material is made of thin strips of wood not exceeding 7 mm wide glued to each other and laid at right angles to the grain of the outer layers or plies.

(3) *Blockboard.* A composite material of similar construction but where the centre core consists of blocks of wood not exceeding 25 mm wide.

(4) *Battenboard.* Again a similar construction of board but with battens of wood up to 75 mm wide as a core. This is known in America as lumber core.

Commercially, the most important are plywood and blockboard. In 1977 out of a total of all wood goods imported into the UK, these two amounted to 15 per cent of the c.i.f. value. In general, blockboard is the cheaper material than the equivalent thickness of plywood, but it must be remembered that particle board is a significant competing factor. In 1977 the imports of plywood and blockboard amounted to a volume of 867 800 m³, whereas the total volume of softwood amounted to 6 425 600 m³, including logs.

EXPORTING COUNTRIES

There was a time when plywood mills abroad were situated close to the forests which supplied their raw material. While this is still true for, say, northern European countries such as Finland and the USSR, it does not often apply to many of the countries which have significantly contributed to overall production in recent years — in particular, the Far East. It will be seen from tables 2.6 and 2.7 that the pattern of supply has drastically changed.

In 1977 Canada supplied 22 per cent of the UK import, the USSR 11 per cent, Korea 11 per cent, Finland 11 per cent, with Malaysia and Singapore jointly accounting for about 17 per cent.

As mentioned in chapter 16, the type of adhesive used in the manufacture of plywood is of great significance, since its durability determines suitability for specific end-use quite irrespective of the species of veneer or its quality. In other words, there is no point in using a veneer with high durability properties and bonding it with an adhesive of low durability. Therefore, it is essential for the user to understand the properties of the many types of adhesives. In very broad terms, the following types are used in order of increasing durability:

Interior use: Animal glues, blood albumen, casein and soya.
Moisture-resistant (M.R.): Urea—formaldehyde (UF).
Boil-resistant (B.R.): Urea—melamine formaldehyde (U.M.F.).
Weather- and boil-proof (W.B.P.): Phenol—formaldehyde (P.F.) and Resorcinol—formaldehyde (R.F.).

All British-made and most imported plywood is manufactured with synthetic resin adhesives in one form or another. It should be noted that synthetic resins can be extended to such a degree that they lose their moisture-resistant properties and may only be suitable for interior work. Extenders or adulterants are normally in powder form and are included to increase the spread of the adhesive, so reducing the cost. The term 'resin-bonded plywood' is in itself valueless, since adulteration can cause it to fall below the requirements of M.R. adhesives.

Plywood is manufactured in a very wide range of thicknesses, widths and lengths. It is impossible to quote the full range from all the countries involved, but the following is a guide:

Thickness range: 3—30 mm usually in 3 mm increments.
Sizes: 1220 mm width up to 3600 mm length, and there is a very considerable number of sheet lengths within that range, in both press and cut sizes.

HOME PRODUCED PLYWOOD INDUSTRY

The large-scale commercial production of plywood in the UK commenced in 1938, in direct competition with imports. It grew quite considerably and many new plywood factories were introduced to satisfy wartime requirements between 1939 and 1945. The UK industry has the disadvantage of being a long way from its source of raw material. Gaboon and other hardwoods have to be brought from West Africa, birch and maple logs from Canada, birch and beech veneers from Europe and Canada. The additional transport and handling costs made the production of home produced plywood uneconomical except in wartime, and for this reason the industry today has declined. In 1955 the home industry produced nearly 54 000 m^3, whereas it now only produces less than half that volume. Even this figure is made up of specialities in the main. While the industry was essential in an emergency, it now finds itself in a difficult position to compete with imports.

In 1977 the value of home produced plywood was £6 800 000, whereas the value of imports was £115 909 000.

STRUCTURE OF THE TRADE AND MARKETING

The imported plywood trade follows closely the structure of the other importing sections of the timber trade, with shippers, agents, importers and merchants.

The c.i.f. contract form follows the general terms of the timber contracts that have already been discussed, with the addition of special clauses applicable only to plywood. The contract specifies that all goods shall be shipped 'under deck' and protects the buyer against the occurrence of manufacturing defects such as:

(1) *Bad glueing* – for which claims may be made up to nine months from date of final delivery of the goods into stock (six months from Russia).

(2) *Manufacture damp* – being a defect in manufacture in which excess moisture is left in the core of the board. This may cause a fungal growth to develop which, if not arrested, will eventually destroy the glueline and finally the whole board and spread to the boards adjacent to it in the bundle. External water damage is sometimes mistaken for manufacture damp, but the difference is evident when a bundle is opened: in the case of external water damage the boards nearest the outside of the bundle will have suffered most damage, while in the case of manufacture damp the boards nearest the centre of the bundle will be the worst affected. In external water damage there is also usually a waterline mark on the boards which does not occur in the case of manufacture damp.

(3) *Metal clips* – wire or fastenings present in the board.

If either of the defects in (2) and (3) is discovered within twelve months of the final date of delivery of the goods into stock, the buyer may reject a part or the whole of the parcel as may prove necessary (nine months from Russia).

The grading of plywood is discussed in detail on page 374.

An important term used in the imported plywood trade is 'press size'. In the manufacture of plywood and, in particular, Finnish and Russian birch plywood, the plywood sheets when taken from the press are trimmed to the largest size that can be produced for the grade in question. Because of the natural characteristics of the veneers being used, some sheets have to be trimmed down further than others to maintain the grade. Where plywood is purchased in 'press sizes,' in addition to the stated size, a proportion of larger sizes and not more than one smaller size may be included in the shipment.

There is also a substantial business in 'cut sizes' – particularly for the furniture industry or for manufacturers who use large quantities of one size. As the name implies, cut sizes are sawn at the plywood mill to the specified size the UK consumer requires.

THE VENEER TRADE

Veneers may be put into two main classifications: decorative veneers (for furniture, panelling, etc.) and constructional veneers (for manufacture of plywood in the UK). A large amount of decorative veneers is imported, but there is an important difference between the import of these and the import of timber, since the buyer always inspects decorative veneers before buying, as it cannot be left completely to a full 'description of goods' in the contract.

As with other wood products, the pattern of the veneer trade has changed very considerably during the last number of years. Ten years ago Denmark was the source of the UK's highest import, accounting for about one-third of the total. At the present time West Germany takes precedence and accounts for about 18 per cent of the total import from as many as 30 countries. France is still an important source of decorative veneers, but Africa and the Far East have become increasingly predominant. It is not generally realised that the UK is a producer of veneers and that exports are quite considerable. More than four times the volume of ten years ago is now exported and the average f.o.b. value has more than trebled.

19.2 The Door Trade

In the last ten years this comparatively small section of the trade has undergone a change which can be described as remarkable. Whereas in 1969 the number of imported doors was of the order of 148 000, today it is well over 7 million. The traditional suppliers such as Sweden and Canada – although still in the market – have given way to entirely new sources. The most significant of these is Taiwan, which accounts for more than half our total import from over 30 countries. Both Spain and Denmark have overtaken even Sweden. The extremely high export of doors from Taiwan has brought about changes to our Customs and Excise Tariff, and such imports are now subject to an anti-dumping charge which is currently 30 per cent *ad valorem* in addition to normal import duty. As with some other commodities, this move is to protect the interests of home producers, who find it increasingly difficult to compete with cheaply produced goods.

Exported doors which come under the Tariff heading of 'Builders Carpentry and Joinery' are handled through normal trade channels in the UK.

19.3 The Fibre Building Board Trade

GENERAL

Wood fibre boards were originally a by-product of the mills producing sawn and planed wood cuts. They are marketed in the UK by the timber trade. The wallboard mills are usually found close to the sawing and planing mills. Waste from the latter, in the form of sawdust, planer chippings, edgings and 'drop offs', are fed to the wallboard mill by conveyor, either direct or after reduction to a condition ready for pulping.

The trade has now grown to such a size that there is insufficient waste produce at the sawmills, many of which are associated with wood fibre board plants. Manufacturers of wood fibre boards are now competing with wood pulp manufacturers for supplies of pulp logs and wood waste capable of conversion to pulp by mechanical processes. Pulp thus produced, mixed liberally with water and some additives, is fed into a machine not unlike a normal paper-making machine. From this a board is produced in one continuous length and crosscut to the length required.

This board is soft and porous and is known as 'insulating board' in both sheet and tile form. It has good thermal insulation properties and is widely used for wall, ceiling and roof linings. It is produced with a variety of surface finishes from smooth to dimpled, and one or both sides may have a mesh finish. Boards and tiles are available with painted, or paper-, plastics- or textile-faced surfaces, and there are flame-retardant types. BS 1142, *Fibre Building Boards*, defines all international Standards and gives procedure for sampling.

Sizes available are generally as follows:

Sheets: 610 mm x lengths up to 3660 mm; 1200 mm x lengths up to 3660 mm; 1220 mm x lengths up to 4270 mm. Thicknesses available are 9, 10, 12.7, 13, 16, 18, 19, 25 and 25.4 mm.

Tiles: 305 mm x 305 mm and 610 mm; 405 mm x 405 mm; 610 mm x 610 mm; 300 mm x 600 mm.

Weight varies according to brand but usually falls in the range 2.5–7.6 kg/m^2, and density ranges from 240 to 330 kg/m^3. BS 1142 gives a maximum of 350 kg/m^3.

If hardeners and binders are added at the pulp stage, and the board is formed under heat and pressure, the final product is known as 'hardboard'. Hardboard is produced in a wide variety of forms and is usually classified as standard, medium and tempered. It is an easily worked and consistent material which can be formed by hot- or wet-bending. It can be easily decorated with paint and any coating and faced with other materials. It is widely used for wall and ceiling linings, panelling, partitions, joinery, kitchen units, caravan interiors, floor coverings and flush doors, and in display and exhibition work. Tempered hardboard has higher strength properties and is suitable for external work, as it has superior durability. It is usually produced with a smooth finish on one side and a fine mesh pattern on the reverse. There are also varieties faced with plastics or other decorative surfaces or perforated in various patterns.

Sizes available are generally as follows:

Sheets: These vary between 1220 mm x lengths up to 5485 mm and 1700 mm x lengths up to 4800 mm. Thicknesses available are from 2.0 mm up to 12.7 mm. Weight varies from 3.0 to 7.3 kg/m² and density ranges from 400 to 1000 kg/m³.

Large quantities of hardboard are marketed as 'pegboard'. The board is perforated at regular intervals with holes and is widely used for display purposes. In its many forms and many decorative finishes this material has become a most important factor in the trade in recent years.

Acoustic boards and tiles are insulating boards which have been grooved or drilled to improve their sound-absorbing properties. Except for this modification, they are similar in size and characteristics to insulating board. They are used for ceiling and wall lining where reflected sound is to be reduced.

PRODUCING COUNTRIES

The main producing countries of wood fibre boards originally were Canada, USA, Sweden and Finland – countries with considerable softwood waste from their own large softwood and planing mills.

The world-wide expanding demand for this material has resulted in the setting up of wood fibre board mills in nearly every country in Europe. In 1976 the countries from which the UK imported the greatest amount of insulating board were, in order of volume, Norway, Poland, Sweden, France and Finland. For hardboard it was Sweden, Finland, South Africa, Poland and Belgium. In total, this amounted to 280 000 metric tons valued at £33.5 million. Home production amounted to a total of just over 30 000 metric tons or 10 per cent of UK consumption.

Some of the earliest wood fibre mills in Europe were established in the UK, and these mills have also expanded their production greatly, supplying a high proportion of the country's requirements.

STRUCTURE OF THE TRADE

The structure of the trade in wood fibre boards varies slightly from the structure of the timber trade. Until 1939 the wood fibre board industry was still growing and imported boards were sold in the UK through firms acting as concessionaires for the manufacturers. These concessionaires appointed local distributors and merchant stockists in the trade. They differed from the normal timber agents in importing stocks of board on their own account, taking them into warehouses and offering them as a 'landed stock', when required, to their distributors. They sometimes also permitted the distributors to import the board through them on normal c.i.f. terms. The position is now changed, since so many new mills have been established abroad. The recent tendency has been not to appoint concessionaires but to appoint agents in the normal way. At the present time, therefore, there are:

(1) *Agents* – for foreign shippers offering boards on normal c.i.f. basis to any importer capable of taking sufficient quantity at one time.

(2) *Concessionaires* – for the original foreign manufacturers. Offering boards either c.i.f. or from 'landed stock' imported by themselves.

(3) *Importer distributors* – merchants importing through agents or concessionaires on a c.i.f. basis. They may be appointed local distributors for a particular brand of board, but this practice is generally fading.

(4) *Merchant stockists* – merchants purchasing smaller quantities from importers or concessionaires for resale.

THE IMPORT AND HANDLING OF FIBRE BOARDS

In general wood fibre boards are shipped by liners, and so are automatically shipped under deck. If, however, a large quantity were shipped on a timber ship, it would be necessary to specify that shipment must be under deck.

The description of goods in the contract, together with any questions of quality, is much simpler. Wood fibre boards are manufactured articles with their own specification and trade name, so detailed description is unnecessary.

The principal cause of any claims on wood fibre boards is damage by crane hooks and slings. Imports of board must be closely inspected after receipt from the ship to see if this damage is present. A pair of chain slings carelessly placed on a crate of insulation board can damage every board in a crate.

The liability to damage in handling bulk quantities of board results in carriage rates being higher per ton than for timber. Road carriage rates for wood fibre boards are often nearly 20 per cent more than rates for carrying timber.

19.4 Particle Board Trade

Originally known as chipboard, this wood-based product was first produced in Germany and Switzerland in about 1941 and in the UK in 1946. The first particle boards were of wood chips, the forest areas of the initially producing countries representing a natural source of supply of raw material, but some countries had other raw material in the form of flax, hemp and bagasse from sugar cane plantations. Since these materials, like wood, are of lignocellulosic structure, they were found capable of producing boards with similar characteristics to those made of wood, and eventually the industry was widened to include these products. The description 'particle board' has been internationally recognised as the generic term for all boards having lignocellulosic particles bonded together with a synthetic resin adhesive.

Particle boards are important to all branches of the timber trade. They are complementary to other materials rather than competitive with them. In general, they are cheaper than plywood and blockboard, yet are self-supporting, whereas hardboard and thin plywood are not. Their homogeneous construction, with its absence of natural features, makes them immediately attractive to the engineer, manufacturer, etc., who is not concerned so much with natural beauty as with physical performance. Considerable quantities of particle board are supplied with wood veneers on each face; thus, in effect, the product is akin to blockboard but with a particle board core.

In 1963 the TTF introduced the Parcif contract form to cover the c.i.f. sale of particle boards. This is described in chapter 10.

Particle board is available in a variety of forms, and these fall broadly into four classifications — single-layer, three-layer, graded-density and extruded. With the exception of extruded board, all the others are platen-pressed. The single-layer board consists essentially of a relatively homogeneous mass of particles and varies in density according to the type of particle element used. The three-layer or sandwich construction board is recognised as offering some of the best opportunities for properties engineered to the most specific requirements and is the category where maximum versatility is found. This versatility is a factor traceable to the various ways in which surface materials may be combined with core materials. For example, fine particles may be applied to the top and bottom layers to produce a good paintable surface or to prevent showing through on overlays. Normally, three-layer boards consist of quite high-density surfaces between 1 mm and 3 mm thick composed of fine particles with a lower-density core of larger or coarser particles. The extruded boards, unlike platen-pressed boards, are made by extrusion through a die and their particles lie with their larger dimensions mainly at right angles to the direction of extrusion. The extrusion method allows much thicker material to be produced; often, metal tubes are inserted midway between the plates, and these have the effect of assisting the curing of the resin at the centre of the board. The extruded board is so formed with a series of holes running through the centre and the weight is considerably reduced. Unlike platen-produced boards, where the size is limited to the size of the press, in theory, extruded boards can be of any length, although this is limited by handling facilities.

Density is a factor which influences many properties of particle board, both physical and mechanical. It varies between 350 and 670 kg/m^3 and even higher and is usually classified as follows: low-density 350–450; medium-density 450–670; high-density 670 upwards.

Sizes are generally 2440 mm, 3660 mm and 4575 mm lengths and widths of 610 mm and 1220 mm. Thicknesses available are from 2 mm to 30 mm and sometimes thicker. The nature of the production process provides the manufacturer with opportunity to provide a multiplicity of sizes to meet special demands.

Particle board is broadly classified as general-purpose, interior structural and interior non-structural. Considerable work is being done in all producing countries to make available an exterior grade which will satisfy the most severe effects of exposure.

In 1976 the countries from which the UK imported the greatest amount of particle board were, in order of volume, Belgium, Finland, Sweden, West Germany, Norway and Austria. In total, the quantity imported from all sources was 674.5 million tons, valued at about £75 million. UK production amounted to a total of 452 million tons valued at about £37 million.

The use of particle board is now fully accepted in the furniture trade, which is probably the most important outlet for this material in the UK.

20   Trade Associations and Authorities

20.1 The Timber Trade Federation of the United Kingdom

Established in 1892, the Federation has long been recognised by governments, professional bodies, industry and commerce throughout the world as representing the interests of the UK imported timber trade.

Its membership of some 900 companies comprises agents, UK subsidiaries of Commonwealth and foreign shippers, importers, sawmillers and merchants through whose hands it is estimated passes over 85 per cent of UK imports; most companies belong to one or more of the Federation's Divisions/Sections, a list of which is given later. Most also belong to one or more of the approved Area Organisations listed, and in the case of importers and merchants this is obligatory.

The objects of the Federation as specified in its Rules cover all matters relating to the advancement and protection of members' interests, and include the support of a research and development organisation, The Timber Research and Development Association, referred to in more detail later.

The Federation has a Council comprising representatives of National Divisions and Area Organisations, headed by a President and Vice-president, who are elected annually; the Council determines the policy to be followed on all matters affecting the trade as a whole. The Divisions and their Sections are involved with the many and varied matters of particular concern to their own branches of the trade, while the Area Organisations deal with local problems, including the important aspects of port and transport facilities.

The Federation has a Director-general and a Secretary backed by a staff of more than 20. The service given to members extends from matters relating to the availability and purchase of timber from overseas right through to its delivery to consumers. Important links in this chain of service are regular statistical information providing background guidance in regard to purchasing; standard forms of contract appropriate to the type of commodity and source concerned; charterparties and insurance terms; matters relating to shipment, UK discharge and transport; and terms of resale. There is also a Legal Protection Committee to defend members' interests in disputes arising with shippers, shipowners, insurers, etc.

Through its relationship with other organisations the Federation is able to play an active part in all appropriate matters; of importance in this is its membership/representation on the Confederation of British Industry, British Shippers' Council, National Council of Building Material Producers, National Association of Port Employers, European Softwood Importers/Exporters

Conference, Union pour le Commerce des Bois Tropicaux dans la C.E.E. and some seven other Federations or Associations whose activities directly or indirectly affect the trade.

All members of the Federation are automatically also members of the Timber Research and Development Association (TRADA), which carries out and promulgates research into new or extended uses for timber, development of new methods of design in building and construction, measures to improve durability and resistance to forms of hazard such as fire and decay, etc. TRADA also carries out on behalf of the Federation the extremely important function of promotion so essential to the future well-being of the UK timber trade.

Members of the Federation who import timber under terms whereby they themselves have to bear the extra cost arising from vessels diverting to, and unloading cargoes at, other than scheduled ports of destination by reason of strike etc. clauses in their bills of lading are eligible to become members of the Diversion Insurance (Timber) Association Ltd, which covers the risk concerned on a mutual fund basis.

The Federation produces an annual handbook which gives particulars of all its Committees and names of members, Area Organisations, representation on BSI Committees, members of the Panel of Arbitrators and Umpires and its Rules.

TTF COMMITTEES AND AREA ORGANISATIONS

Federation committees
President's Advisory Board
Membership Committee
National Port Labour and Transportation Committee
Awards and Claims Committee
Legal Protection Committee
West Africa Shipping Committee
Far East Shipping Committee
Investment Committee

Divisional committees
Importers Division
Importers Division Documentary Committee
Agents Division
Merchants Division
International Division
National Sawmilling Association Division
National Sawmilling Association Safety Technical and Welfare Committee
National Sawmilling Association Wages Committee

Sectional committees
National Hardwood Importers Section
National Softwood Importers Section
Panel Products Importers Section
National Veneer Section
Sleeper and Pole Section
Softwood Agents and Brokers Section
Hardwood Agents and Brokers Section
Panel Products Agents and Brokers Section

Area Organisations of the Federation
Bristol Channel Timber Trades Association
East Anglian Timber Trade Association
East Midlands Timber Trades Association
Grimsby and Immingham Timber Importers Association
Hants and Dorset Timber Trade Association
Humber District Timber Trade Association
Irish Timber Importers Association
London Area Timber Trade Association
North East Coast Timber Trade Association
Northern Ireland Timber Importers Association
North West Timber Trade Association
Scottish Timber Trade Association
South East Timber Association
Western Counties Timber Trade Association
West Midlands Area Association
West Riding of Yorkshire Timber Trades Association

Affiliated association
British Wood Preserving Association

Other organisations
Timber Arbitrators' Association of the UK
Timber Drying Association
Diversion Insurance (Timber) Association Ltd

The functions of the local associations are as follows:

(1) Discussion and negotiation between members of the local association on local timber trade matters.

(2) Liaison and negotiation between the local timber trade as a whole and local organisations and bodies such as area officers of Board of Trade and other Government Ministries; local port and dock authorities; local offices of railway authorities, etc.

(3) Discussion of national matters affecting the local trade of the association and the forwarding of the considered and representative opinions of the local association to the TTF.

20.2 The Home Timber Merchants Association of England and Wales (HTMAEW)

The Home Timber Associations are the following:

English Timber Merchants' Association
Midland Home Timber Association
North Midland Home Timber Association
Northern English Timber Merchants' Association
Western and Southern Counties Home Timber Merchants' Association

The HTMAEW occupies the same position in the home grown timber trade as the TTF occupies in the imported trade. It is responsible for home grown timber trade matters on a national level, and has direct liaison with the TTF on matters of joint interest. The area home timber associations have responsibilities similar to those of the local imported timber trade associations, although the area covered by each home timber association is much larger.

20.3 The Timber Research and Development Association

HISTORY AND OBJECTIVES

The Timber Research and Development Association (TRADA) is an independent research and development organisation jointly financed by firms and individuals, the timber trade, the professions and industry; it is grant-aided by the Department of the Environment.

TRADA employs architects, engineers and technologists working in the interest of timber and wood-based sheet material users and specifiers. The mainstream of its work is directed towards the construction industry, but it also deals with timber and sheet materials in packaging, pallets and many other industries. Furniture applications are dealt with by the Furniture Industry Research Association.

TRADA has been established in its present form since 1962, when it became a recognised research association, but its roots go back to 1934, when it was first set up by the commercial timber trade under the name of Timber Development Association to co-ordinate development and promotion in the industry.

PREMISES

TRADA acquired its present premises at Hughenden Valley, near High Wycombe, Bucks., in 1967. The main building on site was the brick-built house which had been bought by a major insurance company early in the Second World War as its offices and for a safe depository for its records. To extend its accommodation the company had added two wings of hutments and these became the TRADA offices after acquisition. In 1974 TRADA commenced a programme of rebuilding using a system based on hardwood framing and meranti-faced plywood panels. By the end of 1976 the main two-storey office block was complete and this was followed by a new training wing and its associated dining facility. The office block was officially opened by HRH the Duke of Gloucester on 27 July 1978.

WORK PROGRAMME

TRADA's research programme has always been aimed at furthering the use of timber and wood-based products, and in the course of its work the Association has both created new markets and ensured the better utilisation of wood in its established outlets. TRADA has made important contributions in housing and building, timber engineering, industrial applications, fire research, timber drying, stress grading and testing of structures, components and finishes.

BUILDING DESIGN AND CONSTRUCTION

Consultancy services cover design and development work on timber constructions and components for housing, schools, hospitals, industrial and farm buildings. The timber frame housing appraisal service can authorise a certificate which provides warranty of structural stability acceptable for Building Regulation requirements. Advice is provided on all aspects of the use of timber in building, including production and economic matters.

TIMBER ENGINEERING

Advisory and structural design services involving timber engineering disciplines are provided by TRADA on a consultancy basis. The advisory service covers all aspects of the use of timber, including economic studies and structural calculations.

TRADA has available from past work a wide selection of standard and *ad hoc* designs which may quickly provide off-the-shelf structural solutions to problems.

TESTING OF STRUCTURES AND COMPONENTS

Testing is carried out on all kinds of timber structures and components, including roof trusses, beams, portal frames, joinery units, floor and roof panels, wall panels, pallets and packing-cases, as well as strength tests on mechanical fixings and timber joints. Testing and development of windows, doors, curtain walling units and gasket glazing systems is also undertaken.

TESTING OF PRODUCTS AND MATERIALS

Ignitability and fire propagation tests are carried out on wood-based lining materials and treatments. Full-scale fire-resistance tests are also conducted on elements of construction such as walls, floors, glazed partitions and ceilings to BS 476 and ISO 834 specifications. Service trials and comparative assessments of wood finishes, preservatives and flame-retardant treatments are undertaken. *Ad hoc* testing involving microscopic examinations, natural weathering and chemical analysis of specimens is carried out. A consultancy and advisory service is offered by the timber-drying section, which is concerned with the practical aspects of the drying of timber in relation to its utilisation.

ADVICE AND INFORMATION

TRADA maintains an advisory service network with offices at headquarters and industrial centres throughout the country (the addresses are given below). In 1977 over 52 000 technical enquiries from the professions, industry and timber users were answered. Enquiries cover all aspects of timber design, specification, end-use application and the identification of species, infestation and decay. The service also includes on-site investigations.

INDUSTRIAL CONSULTANCY SERVICES

The industrial department carries out a full range of consultancy services for timber companies. These include planning yard and sawmill operations, stock control and operational management.

QUALITY ASSURANCE

At the end of 1977 inspection schemes were offered by TRADA for visual stress grading, finger jointing and trussed rafters, and additions to this list were envisaged.

EDUCATION AND TRAINING

Courses are offered by TRADA at its Hughenden Valley headquarters and at schools of architecture, technical colleges, universities and other venues.

LIBRARY SERVICES

A comprehensive library is maintained by TRADA to provide a technical reference service on timber subjects. The collection consists of bibliographies, books and periodicals, films, film strips and slides.

PRESS AND PUBLICITY

Feature articles and supplements are organised in collaboration with editors. The work includes exhibitions, advertising, films and promotional literature. About 1500 people from many countries visit TRADA each year.

PUBLICATIONS

TRADA produces a stream of design aids, reference and general publications covering a very wide field of interests and subjects. A complete list is available on request.

LOCATION

The addresses of TRADA headquarters and regional offices, and their telephone numbers, are as follows:

Headquarters: TRADA, Hughenden Valley, High Wycombe, Buckinghamshire HP14 4ND. 0240 24 (Naphill) 3091
Scotland: TRADA, 6 Newton Terrace, Glasgow, G3 7PF. 041 221 0719
Northern: TRADA, 48 Dudley Court, East Square, Cramlington, Northumberland NE23 6QW. 0670 (Cramlington) 713238
North-west: TRADA, 115 Portland Street, Manchester M1 6DW. 061 236 3740.
North-east: TRADA, 18 Park Row, Leeds, LS1 5JA. 0532 457256.
Midlands: TRADA, Engineering & Building Centre, Broad Street, Birmingham B1 2BD. 021 643 1914
East: TRADA, 16 Trumpington Street, Cambridge, CB2 2QA. 0223 66287
South-west: TRADA, Building & Design Centre, Colston Avenue, The Centre, Bristol, BS1 4TW. 0272 23692
South-east: TRADA, The Building Centre, 26 Store Street, London, WC1E 7BU. 01 636 8761
Western counties: TRADA, Pearl Assurance House, High Street, Exeter EX4 3NS. 0392 54034

20.4 The Princes Risborough Laboratory

Princes Risborough Laboratory (PRL) is part of the Department of the Environment's Building Research Establishment. BRE carries out research and development relevant to the needs of central government, principally in the building and construction fields. PRL has been a centre of expertise on timber and its utilisation since it was formed over 50 years ago, but, additionally, it now directs a proportion of its effort to studying a wide range of building components, building maintenance and problems of environmental pollution. The Laboratory's work is divided between three Research Divisions.

Timber and Technology Division is concerned with the physical and mechanical properties and the performance in use of timber and wood-based sheet materials; the classification of timber usage on the basis of end-use performance requirements; the design and prototype testing of timber structures; the evaluation of the effects of forestry management on wood quality and yield from UK forests; the development of systems for computer-aided log conversion; and studies of the pattern and economics of timber usage and the design of building components in relation to life-cycle maintenance costs.

Components Division is responsible for the development of performance standards for doors, doorsets, windows and associated hardware; the establishment of performance requirements for prefabricated external walls and cladding; the development of test methods for measuring weathertightness of joints and the assessment of joint performance; the provision of data on the design and performance of flat roofs, including criteria for selecting materials of construction; and the evaluation of various methods for improving the utilisation of space in houses.

Protection Division has the role of providing information on the technical and economic aspects of the deterioration of wood products; of investigating remedial and preventative methods and treatments for combating biodegradation of wood; and of studying the performance of protective finishes for timber and wood-based sheet materials. This Division is also concerned with safety and environmental aspects of the use of pesticides in industry and in the home, and with some aspects of housing maintenance.

The expertise of the Princes Risborough Laboratory is made available through the Building Research Advisory Service, which offers advice on a wide range of construction topics. Staff at PRL give advice on problems encountered in the design and construction of timber- and wood-based building components, their durability and protection against biodeterioration. Advice is available by telephone, letter, consultation or as a result of a site visit or laboratory study. Enquiries that can be answered by reference to published information are free of charge, but when a problem has to be studied in depth, a charge is made. An organisation can become an Associate of the Building Research Advisory Service, which will provide them with a faster, cheaper, more efficient service. General and specialised information resulting from PRL's research is available through a large number of publications, many of which are free. Free publications are available from the Distribution Unit, Building Research Station, Garston, Watford WD2 7JR, Herts., together with a list of current publications; priced publications are available from HMSO.

20.5 The Institute of Wood Science

The Institute of Wood Science was formed in 1955, when it was incorporated under the Companies Act. The need for such an institute had been felt for a considerable time, both to maintain the interests and associations of all those students who had studied timber technology and to promote a much wider knowledge of wood science, which would be playing such a vital part in the continued and greater use of wood and allied products. The Institute numbers among its members leading names in wood science in the UK and throughout the world, those qualified by the Institute's examinations, students of wood science and representatives of professional and trade interests, all of whom are interested in furthering the knowledge of wood.

The purpose of the institute is to advance the scientific, technical, practical and general knowledge of persons interested in the study of wood and allied subjects. This aim is achieved by courses, lectures and seminars arranged nationally and through its many branches. The Institute is the recognised examining body in the timber trade. It examines in timber technology (including utilisation), timber economics and administration at the Intermediate (Certificate) level and in advanced timber technology at the Final (Associate) level.

The *Journal* of the Institute is published twice a year and contains original articles on all aspects of wood science and technology. It is accepted throughout the world as a leading journal in its field.

Membership is divided into six categories and the respective qualifications are as follows: Fellows (FIWSc), Honorary Fellows (Hon. FIWSc), Associates (AIWSc), Certificated Members (CMIWSc), Members and Students. In recent years a revised syllabus has been introduced and its subjects are taught at Colleges throughout the UK. This revised syllabus provides greater emphasis on the commercial aspects of the trade than on technology.

20.6 The British Wood Preserving Association

This Association was founded in 1929 for collecting, promoting and spreading knowledge of all methods of wood preservation and the protection of wood against fire, and to promote the standardisation of preservative specifications. It is not a trade development association or a propaganda organisation, but one which sponsors scientific research into the use of preservatives and makes available the results through leaflets, a technical advice service and specialist lectures.

Among its members are learned societies and research bodies in the UK and abroad, manufacturers of all types of preservatives and fire retardants, users of timber (for example, British Transport Commission, Electricity Boards, etc.), firms operating all forms of treating plants, specialists in the remedial and curative treatment of timber, manufacturers of plant, architects and surveyors.

Its committees, dealing with such matters as health, safety and environmental interests, specifications and technical problems, maintain close liaison with government departments, the British Standards Institution, the British Tar Industry, the Building Research Establishment through the Princes Risborough Laboratory and Fire Research Station, the Timber Research and Development Association and the principal consuming industries. Each year it holds a convention at which specialist papers are presented by experts from all over the world, and following the annual convention it publishes in book form a *Record* containing copies of the papers and a report of the discussions thereon.

20.7 The Fibre Building Board Federation

The Fibre Building Board Federation (City Wall House, 14–18 Finsbury Street, London EC2) was formed in 1957 for the purpose of co-ordinating the interests of those firms concerned with the import of fibre building board. It consists of three sections: (1) agents for the overseas manufacturers; (2) the original concessionnaire importers (also often acting as agents) for overseas manufacturers; and (3) importers. There are approximately 124 importers, 27 agents and 11 concessionnaires. It is financed by a straightforward annual subscription. The Federation's aim is to encourage and develop the use of imported fibre building board; to support FIDOR (see below); to collect and disseminate statistical and other information to the trade; to form a common ground for joint action and co-operation among all those concerned with the imported fibre building board trade; and to act as a watch-dog, and if necessary a mouthpiece, for the trade with regard to legislative measures which might affect its interests.

20.8 The Fibre Building Board Development Organisation Limited (FIDOR)

FIDOR (6 Buckingham Street, London WC2) was founded in 1953 to promote and develop the market for fibre building boards in the UK. This is still its aim today. Its international aspect has steadily widened and now embraces 25 countries. Throughout its 27 years, FIDOR has maintained high standards of technical objectivity and the strictest impartiality between different brands. Its objectives are pursued by means of technical development and sponsored research, a technical advisory service to all board specifiers and users, a comprehensive range of general and technical publications, educational programmes and a range of educational aids. Coupled with its development role, FIDOR also has a considerable task in maintaining and protecting existing markets. This involves constant monitoring and scrutiny of legislation, regulations, standards and advisory specifications and publications affecting the use of fibre building boards. As the market has developed, with annual consumption having risen to some three times the level of 1953, so its role has increased in complexity. FIDOR is concerned with hardboard, insulating board and accoustic boards — all in a variety of grades. These are described in detail in chapter 19.

20.9 Chipboard Promotion Association

The Chipboard Promotion Association (7A Church Street, Esher, Surrey) was formed to provide a recognised and authoritative source of information on chipboard and to promote its proper and potential use for those applications which it best satisfies. Chipboard is formed from particles of wood bonded together with a synthetic resin to give a smooth-surfaced rigid board, the carefully controlled manufacturing process ensuring a uniform and reliable product. It is available in a wide range of board sizes and thicknesses. These include flooring boards, moisture-resistant and fire-retardant grades, a variety of surfaced boards for easy painting and boards faced with plastics laminate, vinyl sheet, wood veneer and textiles. Details of the various grades and their properties are given in chapter 19.

21 Developments in the Timber Trade

21.1 Timber Preservation

INTRODUCTION

There has been tremendous expansion in the timber preservation industry in the UK during the post-war years. The increased importance of timber preservation as an ancillary industry to the timber trade and to the timber-using industries has been due to a number of reasons. Timber is no longer a cheap material and has been subjected to intense competition from other materials, such as steel, concrete, aluminium, etc., so that the user now demands the maximum possible life from timber with the minimum expenditure on maintenance. With the shortages of timber during the Second World War and the post-war years timber was used very much more scientifically than in the past. This helped it to compete more successfully with other materials and opened up new markets, but it meant also that if used untreated under conditions where there was a danger of insect or fungal attack, there was no longer the safety margin which had existed in the past when normally far larger timber sizes had been used than were actually required for a specific end-use in the constructional industries. In addition, whereas in the past much of the softwood for constructional purposes had come from the natural forests where the trees had taken from 200 to 600 years to grow and where there was a small proportion of sapwood, in the post-war period most of the softwood has come from plantations where the aim has been to produce a marketable tree in 90–120 years or less. This timber has a very much higher percentage of sapwood, which is more susceptible to fungal and insect attack than the heartwood.

There has also been since the war a far wider study of timber technology and, in particular, of research work on timber preservatives and their application. Before the war much of the timber preservation carried out in the UK was with creosote and related to railway sleepers and transmission poles, with a certain volume of timber for marine and agricultural uses. To-day in the UK there are as many pressure impregnation plants carrying out treatment with the water-borne preservatives as with creosote. There has also been a great increase in the use of preservatives of the organic solvent type, particularly for the *in situ* curative treatment of timber.

WOOD PRESERVATIVES IN COMMON USE IN THE UK

The effectiveness of any substance for the preservation of wood depends on a number of factors, of which the most important are:

(1) Toxicity towards wood-destroying fungi, timber-boring insects and other destructive organisms.
(2) Permanence — that is, resistance to leaching, evaporation and chemical decomposition.
(3) Penetrating power — for example, low viscosity at temperatures at which the product is normally applied.
(4) Freedom from undesirable effects on timber, metals and operatives.

The materials described below are the most commonly used preservative substances in the UK, and most of the proprietary preservatives are based on one or more of them, with or without additional substances for other purposes, such as water-repellents, insecticidal materials and antibloom agents.

THE MAIN TYPES OF PRESERVATIVE FOR USE AGAINST DECAY AND INSECTS

Substances used for the preservation of timber against fungi, insects and marine borers are usually classified under the following three headings:

(1) Creosote and heavy tar oil preservatives.
(2) Water-borne preservatives.
(3) Organic solvent preservatives.

Many of the materials covered under these three headings are formulated solely to prevent attack by biological agents. Fire-retardant chemicals must, therefore, be considered separately; the majority of these are soluble in water, but intumescent paints are also used.

Creosote and Tar Oil Preservatives

Creosotes, used in wood preservation for over a century, consist of blends of the distillate oils of coal tar. They are complex mixtures with high activity against fungi, insects and marine borers, and thus have found extensive use in the treatment of timbers exposed to the most severe hazards such as marine and freshwater piling, railway sleepers, telegraph and electricity transmission poles, fencing, farm and estate timber. Creosote conforming to BS 144 is formulated for hot application by vacuum pressure impregnation, although provision is made for a more fluid grade suitable for cold application by steeping, brushing or spraying. A more mobile creosote conforming to BS 3051 is, however, more suitable for use without heating, although it can be — and is — applied in a heated condition.

There are a number of proprietary preservatives based on coal tar oil, mainly used for surface application, which impart a measure of fungal resistance and water repellency as well as colour to articles such as woven fencing, garden sheds, etc.

It is generally impracticable to overpaint creosoted timber and for most interior work in inhabited premises creosote is unacceptable owing to its odour and its liability to stain adjacent plaster or paper. Creosoted timber should not be brought into direct contact with food products.

Water-borne Preservatives

A large number of water-soluble chemicals have been used during the past century for the treatment of timber, but many of the preparations to the early formulae were liable to be washed out if the treated timbers were exposed to the weather.

The present tendency is to use combinations of chemicals which become fixed in the timber and are therefore usable for a wider variety of purposes. These preservatives are based on a combination of copper, chrome and arsenic. In the UK the preservatives of this type are proprietary and are covered in BS 4072. They are applied by pressure impregnation and are used for a number of purposes, ranging from railway sleepers, structural timbers, horticultural timbers and timbers used in shipbuilding. The main advantages are that they have no smell and that the treated timber can be glued, painted or varnished, once the timber has been redried after treatment, and does not discolour or taint adjacent articles.

Since these preservatives are water-soluble, the treatment causes the wood to swell, but dimensional changes can be minimised by careful attention to drying before and after treatment.

A second type of water-soluble preservative is based on boron and must be applied to green timber by a diffusion process. It is not suitable for severe leaching situations and generally is used for internal timbers only. Most timbers are imported already treated, and the process is used to a very limited extent in the UK for home grown spruce.

Organic Solvent Preservatives

This type of wood preservative includes various compounds, the most commonly used being pentachlorophenol and its derivatives, tributyl tin oxide and metallic naphthenates. They also contain insecticides such as dieldrin and gamma hexachlorocyclohexane. Most of the preservatives of the organic solvent type are covered by BWPA or BSI Standards. They are seldom soluble in water to any extent and are thus resistant to leaching.

Advantages of this type of wood preservative are that they can be applied without causing change in dimension in the wood and there is no need to redry after treatment. When the solvents have evaporated, the treated timber can be glued, painted or varnished.

Some organic solvent preservatives contain, in addition to the fungicides and insecticides, water-repellent additives to increase the dimensional stability of the timber in use.

Application normally is by double-vacuum impregnation and time-controlled immersion for the treatment of new and replacement timbers, and by spray and brush application for the remedial treatment of infested timber *in situ*.

Modified forms: (1) Mayonnaise-type paste emulsions. These consist of active chemicals, similar to those used in organic solvent type preservatives, mixed into a paste form. They can be used where organic solvent preservatives are used, except in situations where 'creep' of the chemical is a problem − for example, joists above ceilings.

(2) Water-repellent preservative stains. These are organic solvent preservatives as above, often with colouring added. They are used to preserve the appearance of timber and to prevent the ingress of water.

There are also insecticidal smokes which can be used as a method of treatment against insect attack in enclosed spaces.

Fire Retardants

No known treatment is capable of entirely preventing the destruction of wood by fire and the main purpose of applying fire-retardant chemicals is to reduce the spread of flame. This can be accomplished in two ways: first, by treating the wood so that ignition is delayed, or second, by preventing the treated timber from flaming. To achieve the former objective, fire-retardant paints are often used; these contain chemicals which melt at low temperatures, thereby forming a cover over the timber.

To prevent flaming, an ingredient in common use is monammonium phosphate, which is generally applied by vacuum/pressure impregnation. With this treatment the wood may be carbonised if the temperature is high enough, but there will be little or no flaming. With some of the salts there is a further advantage in that when flames from other materials have died down, the treated timber immediately becomes inert and does not glow.

The main purpose of fire-retardant treatments is to delay the spread of the fire long enough for occupants to escape and also for effective measures to be taken for the extinction of the fire before it has grown to unmanageable proportions.

SELECTION OF A WOOD PRESERVATIVE

In selecting a wood preservative there are a number of considerations to bear in mind, although in practice certain overriding factors such as cost, colour, smell, subsequent painting and swelling effects may necessitate a compromise over other desiderata. Much useful information on this subject and on the characteristics of the various types of preservatives will be found in the booklet *Timber Preservation,* published jointly by the British Wood Preserving Association and the Timber Research and Development Association; in BWPA Leaflets 8, 'The use of creosote oil for wood preservation', 9, 'Organic solvent wood preservatives', and 10, 'The treatment of timber with water-borne preservatives'; and in BS 5268: 1977 Part 5 *Preservative Treatments for Constructional Timber.*

WHEN SHOULD TIMBER BE PRESERVED?

Preservative treatment of timber should be employed under certain conditions of use or service, of which the following are typical examples:

(1) in contact with the ground;

(2) at or below damp-proof course level in buildings and structures;

(3) wholly enclosed in brickwork, concrete or masonry;

(4) in any situation in which adequate ventilation cannot be provided;

(5) in any situation in which the equilibrium moisture content of the timber is likely to exceed 20 per cent;

(6) timber classified as of low durability, or with a fair amount of sapwood, and used in circumstances in which there is a reasonable doubt of service conditions in regard to temperature, ventilation and humidity;

(7) in special cases in areas where fungal or insect attack is known to be prevalent; and

(8) where subject to attack by marine or other water-borne organisms.

CONCLUSION

The principles given above provide a useful guide on the subject of the proper treatment of timber. It should further be remembered that should either fungal, insect or marine borer attack occur in any structures large sums of money will have to be spent on remedial and replacement work. It is not merely a matter of treating certain timber *in situ* or of purchasing replacement timbers, for often heavy labour charges are incurred in carrying out the work.

The precise conditions under which timber is to be used should be carefully studied and should then be related to the advisability of using pretreated timber at the time of erecting a structure. Timber is pre-eminent as a constructional material, and timber which is efficiently treated can be used with confidence. The small additional cost of treatment should be regarded as an insurance premium paid once to ensure immunity from fungal and insect attack during the lifetime of a building.

Today sawn timber and plywood are facing increasing competition from other materials. The use of these other materials has to some extent been due to changes in forms of construction but on occasion due to the assumed superiority of other materials under certain conditions of use. Such competition may intensify as new materials are developed, existing ones improved or cheapened by mass production, automation, better components and cheaper processes. It is therefore not sufficient to point out the many virtues of wood. It is wiser in the long run to face up to the inherent defects in natural wood and prove to the consumer, engineer and architect that these can be corrected. Proper and efficient timber preservation can do a great deal to maintain existing markets and even develop new ones for timber and can at the same time help to restore confidence in timber as a material of construction. Although preservative treatment will increase the initial price of the timber, it is still justifiable and even economical to the user if it gives longer trouble-free service life with reduced maintenance charges.

21.2 Stress Grading of Timber

GENERAL

Stress grading, or the selection of timber for structural work by assessing load-bearing properties of each piece, has been the subject of experiment for many years, but it is only during the last decade that it has become a commercial reality. In the past all timber was assessed on the basis of a 'commercial' or 'appearance' grade (that is, Unsorted, fifths, Merchantable, etc.), these qualities being dictated by the number and size of visible defects. While this grading may be satisfactory for joinery and non-structural uses, it is not wholly satisfactory for load-bearing structural use. It is surprising that this development has not become mandatory before, since the Forest Products Research Laboratory of the UK produced a specification as far back as 1941. In those days it was not realised that economy of import volume and cost was to become significant as it is today.

The number and size of defects may reflect the actual strength of a piece of timber but does not give any accurate appraisal in engineering terms. Various important factors are not accounted for by such methods:

(1) Density is a fundamental factor affecting strength.

(2) Unless the precise end use of a piece of timber is known, it must be considered to be only as strong as its weakest point.

(3) The position of a defect in a cross-section of a piece may vary its strength, particularly in bending.

(4) Certain distortions of shape, if moderate, do not in themselves reduce strength.

(5) No special consideration is given to likely areas of loading or fastening.

The various methods of stress grading seek to take account of these factors and furthermore to calculate, in engineering terms, the strength attributable to a given piece. Appearance, therefore, is not of primary importance, and occasionally a piece which would have a high-grade appearance would be rejected by stress grading. Conversely, a very knotty piece could well make a reasonable stress grade. Basically there are two ways in which timber is stress graded at the present time.

MECHANICAL STRESS GRADING

For some years now computerised machines have been available, the best-known being the Plessy Computermatic, capable of assessing the suitability of a piece of timber for a definite end-use. These machines are necessarily complex and bulky, but despite their complexity the basic principles are simple – that is, they can measure the stiffness of a piece more or less continuously along its length. They can measure and record visually its strength at several points as well as indicating its overall grade. Researchers are satisfied that the stiffness bears a close relation to ultimate breaking strength. The feed speed of current machines is comparable with that of many planing machines in use in the UK and as such makes continuous bulk production possible and economical. Reliability and consistency are features, as the risk of human error is eliminated, provided that the machine is correctly programmed. It is still necessary visually to inspect the timber for fissures, wane, distortion, etc., which might render the machine-graded timber unsuitable.

VISUAL STRESS GRADING

By adopting standards wherein the strength-reducing features in a piece of timber are clearly laid down and limited, it is possible for a visual grader to assess the stress grade of the piece. For the most part, the defects are capable of accurate measurement in relation to the code or standard to which the grader is working. Certain aspects, however, are subject to his discretionary interpretation or common-sense. Visual stress grading from existing stock is necessarily a slower process than mechanical, and unlikely to be economical for a continuous bulk production. A visual grader, however, has greater flexibility of movement and is invaluable where small parcels of timber need grading – perhaps many miles from a machine – and while he is not actually engaged in grading can perform other duties. Experienced visual graders in producing countries are able to stress grade almost as quickly as they graded for appearance previously.

It should be borne in mind that material which is stress graded, either mechanically or visually, must be regraded if sawn to a different section. The principle of visual stress grading is clearly defined in BS 4978: 1973, and explanatory notes on this Standard are obtainable from TRADA in a special publication dated January 1974.

The system of visual stress grading ultimately chosen for general use in the UK and the trade was that based on the knot area ratio (K.A.R.). In this system a grader has to decide when looking at a piece of timber which knots are to be considered as being in any one cross-sectional area. He then has to visualise the projected pattern formed by these knots. To understand what is meant by 'the projected pattern of knots', it may help to imagine the selected

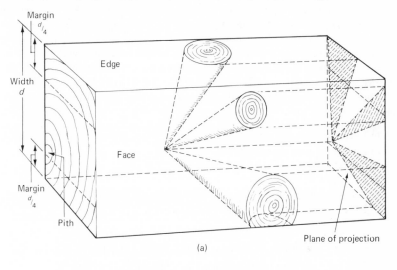

(a)

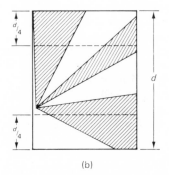

(b)

Figure 21.1 (a) Axonometric view showing three-dimensionally a group of knots in a piece and their projection on a cross-sectional plane. (b) Front view of projection plane, showing projection of knots (hatched)

cross-sectional area as if it was made of glass with only the knots themselves made of wood. The disposition of the wooden knots as viewed from one end of the 'glass box' is the projected pattern. It is upon this projected pattern of the knot formations that the various grading assessments are made. The ability to visualise this projection with accuracy can only be gained with practice. This system is known as the 'Knot Area Ratio Method', or K.A.R. Method, and is illustrated in figure 21.1.

When a piece of timber is subject to a bending load, it is the knots which are formed nearer the edges of a piece that are more critical than those which are through or nearer the centre part of the width. In practice, therefore, it is with the two quarters of the width nearest each edge that the grader is chiefly concerned. These are known as the 'margin areas', and if the knot formation in either margin area is more than half of that margin area, a 'margin condition' is said to exist. Under these conditions, it is necessary for the grader to make a closer examination of the whole cross-sectional area, as on an assessment of the total area of knots at this point will depend whether the piece is Special Structural (SS), General Structural (GS) or a reject.

Other defects than knots can well affect the grading of a piece, these being:

(1) Excessively quick growth – that is, not less than 4 rings per 25 mm.
(2) Fissures – excessive shakes or splits.
(3) Excessive slope of grain.
(4) Excessive wane.
(5) Excessive distortion – that is, twist, spring or bowing.
(6) Excessive resin pockets, insect damage, etc.

Regarding the use of stress-graded timber, the British Standard already mentioned gives comprehensive load tables and the Building Regulations give span tables but these are really outside the scope of this book.

As practically all structural softwood used in the UK is imported, and the most economical method of stress grading is to do it at the producing mill, it has been necessary to reach agreement with other exporting countries on the same rules for stress grading. A European standard largely based on BS 4978 has been recommended by the Timber Committee at Geneva, and this probably will be introduced by the members of the Importers/Exporters Conference in the early 1980s. It is intended to have three visual grades instead of two. S6, the lowest, will be approximately equal to GS; the next, S8, will be approximately equal to SS; and the high engineering grade, S10, will be further graded out from S8, with special attention to density.

21.3 Packaged Timber

Packaged timber consists of steel- or plastics-banded bundles of pieces, all of one length and dimension and of an overall size and weight which can be handled conveniently. Truck-bundled timber is different, because it consists of varying lengths instead of all the pieces being of the same length – this being the only difference.

The benefits of packaged timber have been the subject of discussion even before the Second World War, but it is only in the last decade that it has become the general practice to ship timber in this way. Packaging and truck-bundling is the logical result of the uneconomical method which was employed in handling timber from the mill overseas to the ultimate receiver in the UK or any other country. The handling of timber piece by piece at the shipper's yard, into the ship at the port of loading, from the ship at the discharging port and into the ultimate buyer's yard, had, with ever-increasing costs, become entirely uneconomic and unitisation in some form or other was therefore essential.

Packaging and truck-bundling is now in most sawmills a completely automatic operation. Various types of length-sorting machinery are in use in all timber-producing countries, but all achieve the same ultimate result – namely a well-formed, tightly packed and strapped package of a size capable of easy handling. Modern heavy handling equipment is now in general use in nearly all timber yards, such as forklift trucks, side loaders, etc., but it is most important to remember that the size and weight of the package shipped from the mill must not exceed the handling facilities along the line of passage.

The introduction of packaging has not been without its problems, and one of the greatest in the early stages was the breaking open of packages in transit, chiefly during loading and discharge. This has been largely overcome by the general use of cross 'ties' consisting of narrow slats of wood placed at intervals across the width of the packages at two or three levels. This, coupled with strapping of the package under considerable mechanical pressure, has resulted in a much more stable package in recent years.

Another problem which quickly became apparent with packaged goods was the question of discoloration of timber kept in packaged form for any length of time. It was found that provided both redwood and whitewood were kiln-dried down to a moisture content of around 18 per cent, close-packaged and kept completely dry throughout the journey from the mill to buyer's yard, such packages could be kept indefinitely, under cover, without risk of discoloration developing. To keep packages in this perfectly dry condition throughout a long sea journey, with the inevitable delays when packages are lying unprotected on the quayside or on lorries, is almost impossible. For this reason it was obvious that, at least for the better qualities of timber, some form of protection was necessary. Rainwater falling on the tops of packages or driven in to the sides and ends is drawn in to the centre of the package by capillary action, and the tighter the packages are made when being strapped up, the stronger this capillary action appears to be. The surface and sides of the packages dry out very quickly but the centre holds the water and discoloration swiftly starts to develop.

In order to overcome the problem of discoloration in packages, producing mills have experimented with various antistain preparations, one of the more successful being the Finnish solution Ky5. This is based on sodium pentachlorophenate or tetrachlorophenate and is applied in various ways by the mills. The most popular method appears to be by dipping the packages when they have been made up with the cross-piling sticks in position prior to kilning. Other mills arrange for each piece at some stage to pass through a trough containing the antistain solution and yet others spray the pieces as they pass through a special spray booth. Whichever system is used, there is some risk of the chemical coming into contact with the skin of the workers in the mill despite the use of protective clothing. This has been found to cause a form of dermatitis and there has been considerable pressure brought to bear in both Sweden and Finland to have the use of antistain treatment stopped, but at the time of writing, most mills are using some form of treatment. It has been found that in the case of the lower-quality carcassing timber, particularly that shipped from southern Sweden, provided that a fairly strong solution is used, the timber can be kept packaged for quite long periods without serious deterioration.

Antistain treatment may, and probably does, prevent serious discoloration for a fairly limited period, but really there is no substitute for properly dried timber well protected during transit. Many methods have been tried using plastics or paper covering and shippers have developed their own methods of using these materials. Some merely place the sheet over the tops of packages before putting the straps round, but the covering material quickly becomes damaged while the goods are in transit and a hole in the top of a package merely seems to 'funnel' the water through, giving a more pronounced wetting to a small area of the package. From experience, the more satisfactory way of protecting the timber is to put the covering under the top layer of the package, and although the top layer is unprotected, the covering is much less likely to become damaged during transit and the bulk of the goods is properly protected. Yet another way of protecting packages used by some mills is by enclosing the top, ends and sides in a kind of plastics 'cocoon'. Without doubt, this prevents the possibility of water penetrating, but some importers maintain that unless this plastics covering is removed soon after arrival, sweating takes place within the package, with consequent discoloration.

Length packaging, while popular with some of the larger importers, has the disadvantage that few smaller customers require a whole package all of one length, which necessitates breaking open packages in order to supply a fair spread of lengths. The savings which have been made through the ease of handling packages enabling turnround times of vessels to be reduced to a matter of hours, as opposed to days in the past, are incalculable. Vessels which in the past carried loose timber were not really suitable for packaged goods, but these have now more or less been replaced by vessels which have been constructed with the packaged timber trade in mind.

21.4 Finger Jointing

Although the subject of finger jointing has been included in this chapter, it is by no means a new development, even though it has become commercially common since the previous edition of this book was published.

There are three main advantages to the end-jointing of timber. The limitation of available length is eliminated, the quality of low-grade timber can be upgraded by removal of defects such as knots, and short lengths which would normally be discarded as waste can be converted into usable material. The conventional finger joint is produced by cutting tapered fingers on the ends of the pieces to be joined, and interlocking and gluing the two pieces together under pressure. By varying the length and pitch of these fingers and the width of their tips, joints of different characteristics can be produced. As a general rule, the longer the fingers and the narrower the tips, the stronger the joint. It has been proved that a joint with fingers 50 mm long with a pitch of 12 mm and a tip width of 1.5 mm will be sufficiently strong for all structural purposes.

BS 5291, *Finger Joints in Structural Softwood,* specifies requirements for the manufacture of finger joints in load-bearing members designed in accordance with CP 112, *The Structural Use of Timber,* Part 2, 'Metric Units', and Part 3 'Trussed Rafters for Roofs of Dwellings'. This Standard does not cover non-structural use such as joinery, for which BS 1186, Part 2 is applicable. Neither does it cover the die-formed joint (often called the mini-joint).

BS 5291 gives profiles of joints and a guide to their efficiency ratings in terms of bending. These are shown in figure 21.2 and table 21.1. Manufacturing requirements, joint spacing, type of adhesives, moisture content and strength tests for quality control are all given in detail.

Returning to the advantages to be gained by finger jointing, these should be further clarified in the light of present-day developments in the trade as a whole. The removal of length limitation is particularly important in the field of structural laminated timber used for long-span beams, arches and roof

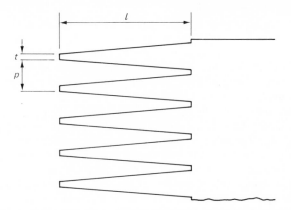

Figure 21.2 Typical profile of a finger joint: the profile is determined by the shape of the fingers in terms of their length, *l*, pitch, *p*, and tip width, *t*

TABLE 21.1 GUIDE TO EFFICIENCY RATINGS OF SOME FINGER PROFILES IN BENDING

Finger profile			Efficiency in bending, $R\%$
Length, l (mm)	Pitch, p (mm)	Tip width, t (mm)	
60	15.0	2.7	80
55	12.5	1.5	75
50	12.0	2.0	75
40	9.0	1.0	65
40	10.0	1.6	60
30	6.5	1.5	55
30	11.0	2.7	50
25	5.0	1.5	50
12.5	4.0	0.7	65
12.5	3.0	0.5	65
10	3.7	0.6	65
7.5	2.5	0.2	65

trusses. The use of long-length members brings the prospects for timber engineering closer in competition with other structural materials. End-jointing techniques introduced at the exporter's sawmill can effect the production of high-grade material by cutting out the worst defects and so producing clear grades of associated higher value. The small amount of cutaway material or waste can be better utilised by the exporter, especially if the mill is integrated and produces other allied products requiring chips. Additionally, length control resolves many of the problems arising with packaged timber in a limited range of precut lengths.

From the end-use point of view, the advantage of reclaiming short offcuts is very considerable. In joinery works the wide range of products or components creates an inevitable source of such pieces which were normally wasted. It will be seen that both the exporter and the importer can benefit from this form of end-jointing — which has proved to be superior to any other form, such as butt and scarf joints.

There are now available many types of fully automated machines for producing finger joints. These can be fed with a continuous supply of pieces of timber of equal moisture content. The machine cuts the matching fingers, applies the glue to the joint, sets the glue by high-frequency heating and ejects a continuous piece which can be automatically crosscut to the desired length. Crosscutting facilities before the piece enters the machine can remove major defects such as knots, etc. The glue most commonly used is of the P.F. and R.F. types which give the highest degree of durability (see chapter 19 under 'Plywood').

21.5 Laminated Timber

The use of laminated timber beams in constructional work is an example of the modern conception of timber as an engineering material. Laminated timber beams are built up from laminations of small sections of timber, the completed beam being considerably stronger than the equivalent beam in one piece of timber. Although the timber used for the lamination does not require to be of such a high structural grade as a solid piece would be, it is not possible to use very low grades throughout, lower grades being limited usually to the central core of the member.

Laminated timber at present is rather expensive, since each lamination must be machined before the whole is bonded together, but a little of the labour cost is offset by a saving in the cost of the timber, since the value of the timber laminations will generally be less than the equivalent in solid timber.

The advantages of laminated timber may be summarised as follows:

(1) The production of long lengths and large sections.

(2) The production of curved shapes.

(3) The improvement of the structural quality of timber by a controlled distribution of the weaker structural characteristics of timber (such as knots, etc.).

(4) In certain applications a reduction in cost where cheaper material can be used in the core.

(5) Increased fire resistance by the use of large-sized sections.

(6) Low weight for given strength, reducing erection costs.

(7) Reduced maintenance and finishing costs.

(8) Pleasing appearance.

As part of trusses, such as bow string girders, spans of up to 230 ft have been built with laminated timber. It is also used to form edge beams in timber shelves, where an economical structure can be produced.

It is probable that in the future production costs will be reduced, possibly by making only standard sizes of laminated timber sections, so that laminated timber could become competitive with other materials for long-span joists, purlins, beams, etc.

21.6 Timber Connectors

The many improvements in timber connectors and advances made in design standards in recent years have contributed greatly to the increased use of timber for every conceivable type of building, irrespective of its size or function.

Joints using timber connectors are now designed with the same degree of mathematical accuracy as other parts of the structure, which results in a balanced design, providing both an economic and a structurally sound building. A wide variety of connectors are available, ranging from the 2 in diameter round toothed-plate connector, capable of carrying a load in the region of 1000 lb, to the larger 4 in diameter double-bevelled split-ring, or shear-plate connector, which will take care of loads up to 2½ tons. Each type of connector has its own distinct advantages, and joint details should no longer be left to unqualified on-site judgement.

The toothed-plate, split-ring and shear-plate connectors are used essentially for joining together timber members forming a frame, such as a roof truss or girder. In order to obviate the use of tusk tenon and similar carpentry joints, which nowadays are time- and labour-consuming, special pressed metal framing anchors may effectively be used. These anchors eliminate the difficulties and uncertainties of skew nailing, toe nailing, etc., and provide a strong and efficient shear connection.

The toothed metal plate has largely superseded other types of connectors, especially for the manufacture of trussed rafters or roof trusses.

21.7 Trussed Rafters

The most significant development in domestic roof construction in recent years has been the factory-manufactured roof truss. This is a lightweight truss which is used to replace the rafters, purlins and ceiling joists. It has a number of advantages over the traditional roof construction methods, which involve *in situ* cutting to size and nailing. This latter form of construction is seldom seen these days in the public sector of house building and only very rarely in the private sector.

Being factory-produced, the truss is subject to greater control in materials and construction. The timber is stress graded, the volume used per truss is considerably less and erection time can be reduced to almost a quarter of the time. In production the members are cut to length, butt jointed and secured with 18 or 20 gauge galvanised steel plates with integral teeth. The whole component is laid in a combined jig and press which forces the toothed plate into the timber components, so forming a complete truss of adequate strength and stiffness.

There are two commonly used types of roof trusses which are called fink and fan. Both have symmetrical configuration but with different centre spacing (see figure 21.3). BSI CP 112, Part 3 covers *Trussed Rafters and Roofs of Dwellings*, as mentioned in the section on finger jointing. This Code of Practice covers all aspects of roof trusses, including species of timber, grades, loading, fabrication, joints, permissible stresses and spans, handling and erection.

One of the main hazards with the prefabrication of roof trusses lies in handling, transportation and storage. The nature of the structure, which is produced in a horizontal plane and designed to be used vertically, has to be

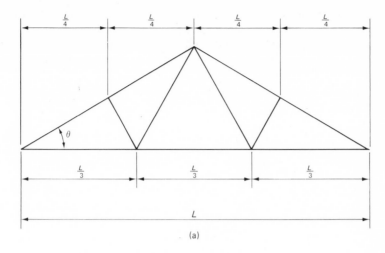

(a)

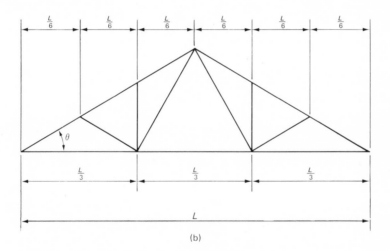

(b)

Figure 21.3 (a) Fink or 'W' trussed rafter; (b) fan trussed rafter. θ = pitch

adequate to resist normal handling or, alternatively, provision has to be made
to ensure that means of handling are adopted that are not injurious to the
truss. Transportation from the factory to the building site should be made on
road transport specially designed with cradles to support the trusses, and this
is usually done by banding the units together in the cradle with the ridge
down. Storage at the site is particularly important and too often one sees
trusses delivered to the site well in advance of requirement and left

in the open without adequate protection. Since the above-mentioned Code of Practice states that the moisture content of the timber should not exceed 22 per cent at time of fabrication, and green western hemlock is so often used, this aspect requires close control in order to satisfy the Building Regulations.

Glossary of Timber Trade Terms

Compiled by T. F. O'Reilly of Price & Pierce Ltd.

ENGLISH	SWEDISH	GERMAN	FRENCH	FINNISH
across the grain	tvärs över fibrerna	quer zur Faserrichtung	sens perpendiculaire au fil, (sens transversal)	poikkisyin
afforestation	skogsodling	Aufforstung	afforestation, boisement	metsittäminen, metsänviljely
air drying	lufttorkning	Lufttrocknung	séchage à l'air	ilmakuivatus
alder	al	Erle	aune	leppä
allowance for shrinkage in seasoning	torkmån	Schwindmass	surmesure pour retrait au séchage	kuivumisvara
allowance for trim(ming), extra length	stötmån,-fot, justermån	Justierungsmass, Messzuschlag, Übermass	surlongueur	tasausvara
along the grain	i fibrernas riktning längs fibrerna	in der Faserrichtung	sens du fil, (sens axial)	pitkin syitä, syiden suuntaan
annual ring, growth ring	årsring	Jahresring	cerne d'accroissement, couche annuelle	vuosirengas, vuosilusto
approximately, about	cirka, omkring	ungefähr, cirka	environ, approximativement	lähes, suunnilleen, noin
arbitration	arbitration, skiljemannaförfarande	Arbitrage	arbitrage	välimiesmenettely
arrival advice	ankomstmeddelande	Ankunftsmeldung	avis d'arrivée	saapumisilmoitus
as falling	fallande	wie es kommt	tombant, qualité tombante	lankeavasti

ENGLISH	SWEDISH	GERMAN	FRENCH	FINNISH
ash (common)	ask	Esche	frêne (commun)	saarni
aspen	asp	Espe	tremble	haapa
assistant	biträde, assistent	Assistent	aide, assistant	apulainen
average (subst.)	medeltal	Durchschnitt	moyenne	keskimäärä, keskiarvo
award	skiljedom	Arbitrage-Zuerkennung	réfaction	välitystuomio
axe	yxa	Axt	hache	kirves
Baltic redwood	furu	Kiefer	sapin rouge du Nord	mänty
band saw	bandsåg	Bandsäge	scie à ruban	vannesaha
barge	pråm	Leichter	chaland, péniche	proomu
bark	bark	Rinde, Borke	écorce	kuori
bark (to) peel, remove the bark	barka	entrinden	écorcer	kuoria
bark stripping machine, barker, peeler	barkningsmaskin	Entrindungs-machine	machine a écorcer	kuorimakone, kuorimiskone
bast	bast	Bast	liber	nila
battens	battens	Battens	bastings	soirot, battensit
baulk	bjälke, timmer	Balken	billon	hirsi, pelkka, parru
beech	bok	Buche	hêtre	pyökki
belt conveyor	remtransportör	Laufband, Förderband	courroie-convoyeuse, -transporteuse	hihnakuljetin
bending strength, resistance to static bending	böjhållfasthet	Biegungsfestigkeit	résistance à la flexion	taivutuskestävyys

English	Swedish	German	French	Finnish
bill of exchange	växel	Wechsel	effet de commerce	vekseli
bill of lading	konossement	Konossement	connaissement	konnossementti
birch	björk	Birke	bouleau	koivu
blade	blad, klinga	Blatt	lame, couteau	terä
blockboard	blockboard	Tischlerplatte	panneau latté	rimalevy
blue stain	blånad	Bläue	bleuissement	sinistyminen, sinistymä
board (timber)	bräda	Brett	planche	lauta
board foot	plankfot	Brettfoot	pied de planche	lautajalka
bole, stem, trunk	stam	Stamm	tige, grume, tronc	runko
boom of logs	flottbom	Schwimmkette, Baumkette, Ringfloss	train de bois flotté	puomi
botany	botanik	Botanik	botanique	kasvitiede
box-board	lådbräda	Kistenbrett	bois de caisserie	laatikkolauta
bracking	sortering	Sortierung	classement	lajittelu
broadleaved tree	lövträd	Laubbaum	arbre feuillu	lehtipuu
broker	mäklare	Makler	courtier	kaupanvälittäjä
bundle	bunt	Bund	paquet de billes cerclé	nippu
bundling	buntning	Bündlung	cerclage	niputus
butt-end	rotända	unteres Stammende	gros bout, culée	tyvipää
buyer	köpare	Käufer	acheteur	ostaja
by-product	biprodukt	Nebenprodukt	sous-produit	sivutuote
caliper (tree	klave	Kluppe	compas forestier	mittasakset, kaulain
cambium	kambium, savring	Kambium	cambium, assise génératrice	jälsi

ENGLISH	SWEDISH	GERMAN	FRENCH	FINNISH
cancellation	annullering	Annullierung	annulation	peruutus
capacity (performance)	arbetsförmåga	Leistung	puissance, rendement	suorituskyky, kapasiteetti
cargo	last	Ladung	chargement, cargaison	lasti
casehardened	yttorkad, ythårdnad	äusserlich trocken, oberflächentrocken	cémenté en surface	pintakuiva
ceilings	(inman-) takbräder (hyvlade)	gehobelte Deckenbretter	lambris de plafond	sisäkattolaudat
cellulose	cellulosa	Zellulose/Zellstoff	cellulose	selluloosa
cell-wall	cellvägg	Zellwand	membrane cellulaire	solunseinä
chain conveyance	kedjetransport	Kettenförderung	transport par chaine	kettinkikuljetus
chain saw	kedjesåg	Kettensäge	scie à chaine coupante	kettinkisaha
charcoal	träkol	Holzkohle	charbon de bois	sysi, puuhiili
chartering	befraktning	Befrachtung	affrètement	rahtaus, laivan vuokraus
charter party	certeparti	Frachtvertrag, Charterpartie	chartre-partie	rahtauskirja, sertepartia
chemical (adj.)	kemisk	chemisch	chimique	kemiallinen
cheque	check	Scheck	chèque	sekki, shekki
chief, director-general	generaldirektör	Generaldirektor	directeur général	pääjohtaja
chief forester	skogschef	Ober-Forstmeister	chef d'exploitation forestière	metsäpäällikkö
chips (wood) for pulp making	flis	Hackspäne	copeaux (de papeterie)	hake
chlorophyll	klorofyll	Blattgrün, Chlorophyll	chlorophylle	lehtivihreä

c.i.f. (cost, insurance and freight)	cif (kostnad, försäkring, frakt)	cif (Kosten, Versicherung, Fracht)	C.I.F., caf (coût, assurance, fret)	cif (kulut, rahti ja vakuutus)
circular saw	cirkelsåg	Kreissäge	scie circulaire	pyörösaha, sirkkelisaha
claim	reklamation	Reklamation	réclamation	reklamaatio, valitus, moite
clean barked and basted	bastbarkad	weissgeschält (entbastet)	écorcé à blanc, blanc-blanc	täysipuhtaaksi kuorittu
coarse-grained	frodvuxen, grovringad	schnellwüchsig, grobringig	à grain grossier, à croissance rapide	hyötykasvuinen, leveälustoinen
cold press	kallpress	Kallpresse	presse à froid	kylmä paino
compression wood	tjurved	Druckholz	bois de compression	lyly
compressive strength	tryckhållfasthet	Druckfestigkeit	résistance à la compression	puristuslujuus
condition (of goods)	kondition	Trockenheitsgrade	état (de la marchandise)	kunto
conifer	barrträd	Nadelbaum	conifère, résineux	havupuu
coniferous wood	barrträdsvirke	Nadelholz	bois résineux	havupuu
consumer	konsument, förbrukare	Konsument, Verbraucher	consommateur	kuluttaja
contract	kontrakt	Kontrakt, Vertrag	contrat	sopimus, myyntisopimus
conversion table	omräkningstabell	Umrechnungstabelle	table de conversion	muuntotaulukko
convert (to) (figures, measurements, etc.)	omräkna	umrechnen	convertir, (les chiffres, les mesures etc.)	muuntaa
conveyor belt	transportband	Transportband	courroie transporteuse	kuljetushihna
cordwood	travat virke, klenvirke	Schichtholz	bois d'industrie	pinotavara, ohutpuu

ENGLISH	SWEDISH	GERMAN	FRENCH	FINNISH
cost(s)	kostnad(-er)	Kosten	frais, dépenses	kustannus, kustannukset
crane	kran	Kran	grue	nosturi
crosscut (to)	kapa	kappen	tronçonner, découper	katkoa, katkaista katkominen, katkaiseminen
crosscutting	kapning	Zersägung, Absägung	tronçonnage	
cross-grained (spiral-grained)	vresig, vresfibrig	drehwüchsig, drehfaserig	contrefil, (fil tors)	kierresyinen, kierosyinen
cubic foot	kubikfot	Kubikfuss	pied cube	kuutiojalka
cubic metre	kubikmeter	Kubikmeter	mètre cube	kuutiometri
Customs	tull	Zoll	douane	tulli
cutting (felling)	avverkning	Hieb, Schlag	coupe, abattage	hakkaus, hakkuu
dead freight	dödfrakt	Leerfracht	fret mort, fret à vide	kuollut rahti
deal (dimension of sawn timber)	planka	Planke	madrier	lankku
decay	röta	Fäule, Fäulnis	pourriture	laho
deciduous tree	lövträd	Laubbaum	arbre à feuilles caduques	lehtipuu
deckload	däckslast	Deckladung	pontée	kansilasti
defect	fel	Fehler, Defekt	défaut, vice	vika
demurrage	överliggetid, överliggedagsersättning	Überliegezeit, Überliegezeitsentschädigung, Liegegelder	surestaries, frais de stationnement	lisäseistontapäivät, lisäseisonta-aika, lisäseisontakorvaus
density	täthet	Dichtigheit	densité (du peuplement)	tiheys, sakeus

English	German	Swedish	French	Finnish
description	Beschreibung	beskrivning	description	kuvaus
deviation	Abweichung	avvikelse	déviation	poikkeus
diameter at stump height	Durchmesser in Stockhöhe	stubbdiameter	diamètre sur souche	tyviläpimitta
diameter, breast height (d.b.h.)	Brusthöhendurchmesser	brösthöjdsdiameter	diamètre à hauteur de poitrine	rinnankorkeusläpimitta
dimension	Dimension	dimension	dimension	koko
discharge (to)	entladen, löschen	avlasta, lossa	décharger, débarquer,	purkaa lasti
discoloured	verfärbt, blau	färgad, blå	décoloré, bleuté	värivikainen, sininen, sinistynyt
discount	Diskonto, Abzug	diskonto	escompte, rabais	diskontto
dispute	Streit	tvist	différend, contestation	riita
dock	Dock	docka	bassin, dock	satama-allas, telakka, laituri
documents (shipping)	Verschiffungsdokumente, Verladungspapiere	skeppningsdokumenter	documents (d'embarquement)	laivauspaperit
Douglas fir	Douglasie, Douglastanne	douglasgran	sapin de Douglas	douglaskuusi
dovetail	Schwalbenschwanz	laxstjärt, sinka	queue d'aronde	lohenpyrstö
down-grade (to)	abstufen	nedsätta, nedsortera	déclasser	luokitella huonommaksi, sijoittaa alempaan luokkaan
drawing date	Ziehungstag	indragningsdag	date du tirage (d'un effet de commerce)	perimispäivä
drum barker	Entrindungstrommel	barkningstrumma	écorceuse à tambour	kuorimarumpu
dry	trocken	torr	sec	kuiva
dry weight	Trockengewicht	torrvikt	poids à sec	kuivapaino

ENGLISH	SWEDISH	GERMAN	FRENCH	FINNISH
drying shed	torkskjul	Holztrocknungs-schuppen	hangar de séchage	kuivausvarasto
duty (import)	införseltull, importtull	Einfuhrzoll	droit/taxe d'importation	tuontitulli
edge (to)	kanta	abkanten	déligner	syrjätä
edger	kantsåg	Abkantsäge, Besäumungssäge	déligneuse, scie à déligner	syrjäyssaha
elm	alm	Ulme	orme, ormeau	jalava
end check	ändspricka	Endriss	fente en bout	pään halkeama
endorsement	endossering	Indossament	endossement	siirto, nimikirjoitus selkäpuolella
ends	kortlängder	Enden	coursons	pätkät
examination, inspection	inspektion, besiktning	Inspektion, Untersuchung	inspection, examen	tarkastus
export duty	exporttull	Ausfuhrzoll	droit(s) de sortie, – d'exportation	vientitulli
f.a.s. (free alongside ship)	F.A.S. (fritt vid fartygets sida)	F.A.S. (frei an Schiffsseite)	F.A.S., (franco de long du navire, franco quai)	vapaasti laivan sivulla
fast-growing	frodvuxen	schnellwüchsig	à croissance rapide	nopeakasvuinen
felling	avverkning	Hieb, Schlag	coupe, abat(t)age	hakkaus, hakkuu
felling season	avverkningssäsong	Einschlagszeit	saison d'abattage	hakkauskausi
fifths	kvinta	fünfte Qualität, Quinta	cinquième (class ou choise)	kvinta
finish (to), plane (to)	hyvla	hobeln	raboter	höylätä

English	Swedish	German	French	Finnish
fireproof	eldfast, eldsäker	feuerfest, feuerbeständig	resistant, -e au feu, à l'epreuve du feu	tulenkestävä
firewood	brännved	Brennholz	bois de feu	polttopuu
first open water	första öppet vatten	erstes offenes Wasser	l'ouverture de la navigation	ensi avovesi
firsts	prima	erste Qualität	première (classe), Iere	priima
floated wood	flottved	Flössholz	bois flotté	uittotavara
floating	flottning	Trift	flottage, transport par radeaux	uitto
floorings	golvbräder	Fussbodenbretter Dielenbretter	frises à parquet	lattialaudat
F.O.B., f.o.b. (free on board)	fritt ombord (fob)	Frei an Bord (F.O.B.)	F.O.B. (franco à bord)	vapaasti laivassa
foot (ft)	fot (f) (mått)	foot (f)	pied	jalka
F.O.R., f.o.r. (free on rails)	fritt banvagn (f.o.r.)	frei Waggon (F.O.R.)	franco sur wagon	vapaasti vaunussa
force majeure	force majeure	höhere Gewalt	force majeure	ylivoimainen este
forest	skog	Wald, Forst	forêt	metsä
forest resources	skogstillgångar	Waldvorräte	ressources forestières	metsävarat
forest officer	jägmästare, forstmästare	Forstmeister	ingénieur des eaux et forêts	metsänhoitaja
forest worker	skogsarbetare	Forstarbeiter	ouvrier forestier, bûcheron	metsätyöläinen
forestry, forest management	skogsbruk	Forstwirtschaft	gestion forestière	metsätalous, metsänkäyttö
forklift truck	gaffeltruck	Gabelstapler	chariot elévateur à fourche	haarukkanosturi
forwarding agent	speditör	Spediteur	transitaire	huolitsija

ENGLISH	SWEDISH	GERMAN	FRENCH	FINNISH
fourths	kvarta	vierte Qualität, Quarta	quatrième (classe ou choise)	kvarta
frame saw	ramsåg	Gattersäge	scie à châssis, scie alternative verticale	kehäsaha, kehyssaha
free from decay	fri från röta	fäulnisfrei	sans pourriture	lahoton
freight	frakt	Fracht	fret	rahti
freight advance	fraktförskott	Frachtvorschuss	fret payé d'avance	rahtiennakko
fungus	svamp	Schwamm	champignon	sieni
gang	arbetslag	Mannschaft	équipe	työryhmä
girth	omkrets	Umfang	circonférence	ympärys
glazed board	glanspapp	polierte Pappe	carton glacé	silitinlevy
glue, to	limma	leimen	coller	liimata
gluing machine	limspridare	Leimauftragmaschine	encolleuse	liimauskone
goods	varor	Waren	marchandises	tavarat
grade (to)	sortera	sortieren	classer, séparer	lajitella, luokitella
grading	sortering	Sortierung	classement	lajittelu
green timber	rätt virke	Frischholz	bois vert	tuore puu
green weight	råvolymvikt	Frischgewicht	poids en vert	tuore paino
grooved and tongued board	spontbräde	Nut-und Federbrett,	planche rainée, à rainure et languette	ruoteinen lauta, ruoditettu lauta
	spontad bräde	Spundbrett		
gross weight	bruttovikt	Bruttogewicht	poids brut	bruttopaino
growth ring	årsring	Jahresring	cerne, couche annuelle	vuosirengas, vuosilusto

English	Swedish	German	French	Finnish
hammer	hammare	Hammer	marteau	vasara
handling	hantering	Handhabung	manutention	käsittely
hardboard, wallboard	fiberplatta, hardplatta	Faserplatte	panneau de fibres	kuitulevy, kovalevy
hardwood timber	lövvirke	Laubholz	bois feuillu	lehtipuu
hawthorn	hagtorn	Weissdorn	aubépine	orapihlaja
hazel	hassel	Haselstrauch	coudrier, noisetier	pähkinäpuu
heart shake	kärnspricka	Kernriss	cadranure	sydänhalkeama
heart rot	kärnröta	Kernfäule	pourriture du coeur	sydänlaho
heartwood	kärnved	Kernholz	bois de coeur	sydänpuu
hemlock	hemlock, kanadensisk tsuga	Hemlock	Hemlock, Pruche (Canadian French)	hemlok-kuusi, tsuga
hewn timber	tillyxat virke, bilat timmer, bilat virke	behauenes Holz	bois équarri à la hache	veistetty tavara
hornbeam	avenbok	Weissbuche	charme	valkopyökki
horse-chestnut	hästkastanje	Rosskastanie	maronnier d'Inde	hevoskastanja
horsepower (HP)	hästkraft	Pferdestärke (PS)	puissance en chevaux	hevosvoima
hot press	varmpress	Warmpresse	presse à chaud	kuuma paino
humidity	luftfuktighet	Luftfeuchtigkeit	humidité de l'air	ilmakosteus
ice	is	Eis	glace	jää
import duty	importtull	Einfuhrzoll	droits d'entrée, – d'importation	tuontitulli
importer	importör	Importeur	importateur	tuoja
impregnation (chemical treatment)	impregnering	Imprägnierung	imprégnation	kyllästys
inch	tum	Zoll	pouce	tuuma
increment	tillväxt	Zuwachs	accroissement	lisäkasvu

ENGLISH	SWEDISH	GERMAN	FRENCH	FINNISH
incur expenses (to)	nedlägga kostnader	Umkosten aufwenden	encourir des dépenses, des frais	joutua maksamaan kustannuksia
information	upplysningar	Auskunft, Information	informations, renseignements	tieto
insect damage	insektskada	Insektenschaden	dommages causés par les insectes	hyönteisvahinko
inspection	inspektion, besiktning	Inspektion, Untersuchung	inspection, vérification, contrôle	tarkastus
insulating board	porös board	Isolierplatte	panneau isolant	huokoinen kuitulevy
insurance	försäkring	Versicherung	assurance	vakuutus
interest	ränta	Zins(-en)	intérêt	korko
invoice	faktura	Rechnung, Faktura	facture	tavaralasku
item (of timber)	virkesparti, post	Holzposten	lot (de bois)	puuerä, erä
jig-saw	lövsåg	Laubsäge	scie à chantourner, scie sauteuse	lehtisaha
joiner	snickare	Tischler	menuisier	puuseppä
joinery quality	snickerikvalitet	Tischlerqualität	qualité "menuiserie"	puusepänlaatu
joinery shop	snickerifabrik en	Tischlerei	menuiserie (atelier de)	puusepäntehdas
juniper		Wachholder	genévrier	kataja
kiln	torkugn	Darrofen	sécheri	kuivaamo
kiln-dried timber	ugnstorkat virke	darrofengetrocknetes Holz	bois séché artificiellement	uunikuiva puu
knife-barking machine	knivbarkningsmaskin	Entrindungsmachine	écorceuse à lames	veitsikuorija
knot	kvist	Ast	noeud	oksa

English	Swedish	German	French	Finnish
knot, bark/encased	barkdragande kvist	eingewachsener Ast	noeud entouré d'écorce	kuorioksa
knot, black/dead	svart kvist	schwarzer Ast	noeud noir, noeud mort	musta oksa, kuiva oksa
	torr kvist			oksa
knot, loose	löskvist	Ausfallast, lockerer Durchfallast	noeud non adhérent, noeud "bouchon"	irto-oksa
knot, rotten	rötkvist	verfaulter Ast	noeud pourri	laho-oksa
knot, sound, tight	frisk kvist	gesunder Ast	noeud sain	kiinteä oksa, terve oksa
knot cluster/whorl	kvistvarv, kvistkrans, kvistring	Astkranz	noeud adhérent, couronne de noeuds, verticille	kehäoksat
knot-free	kvistfri, kvistren	astrein	sans noeuds	oksaton
knot-hole	kvisthål	Astloch	trou de noeud	oksanreikä
knottiness	kvistighet	Astigkeit	densité des noeuds	oksaisuus
knotty timber	kvistigt virke	astiges Holz	bois noeueuse	oksainen puutavara
labour force	arbetskraft	Arbeitskraft	main-d'oeuvre	työvoima
laminated wood	trälaminat, skiktat virke	Lamellenholz	bois lamellé, lamellé collé	kerrostettu puu
landed goods	lossade varor	Schichtholz / entlöschte Waren	marchandises débarquées	puretut tavarat
larch	lärkträd	Lärche	mélèze	lehtikuusi
lath (plasterer's)	läkt	Latte	latte, lattis	päre, rappausäle
law	lag	Gesetz	loi	laki
laydays	liggedager, liggetid	Liegetage	estaries	seisontapäivät, odotuspäivät
lb (pound)	pund	Pfund	livre	naula
licence	licens	Lizenz	licence, permis d'importation	lisenssi

ENGLISH	SWEDISH	GERMAN	FRENCH	FINNISH
lien	retentionsrätt	Eigentumsvorbehalt	droit de rétention	pidätysoikeus
lighter (barge)	pråm	Leichter	allège, barge	proomu
lime tree	lind	Linde	tilleul	lehmus
linear foot	löpfot	laufendes foot	pied linéaire	juoksujalka
loading	lastning	Ladung	chargement	lastaus
log blue	stockblånad	Verbläuen der Sägeblöcke	bleuissement de la grume	tukkisinistymä
log storage pond	timmermagasin	Langholzmagazin	bassin de stockage	tukkiallas
logging season	avverkningssäsong	Fällzeit, Einschlagszeit	saison d'abatage	hakkuukausi
logging volume	avverkningsbelopp	Hiebsmenge	volume de la coupe	hakkuumäärä
longitudinal direction	längdriktning	Längsrichtung	sens longitudinal	pituussuunta
lorry	lastbil	Lastkraftwagen	camion, truc(k)	kuorma-auto
lumber	sågade trävaror, virke	Schnittholz	bois scié	sahatavara
mahogany	mahogny	Mahagoni	acajou	mahonki
manipulation	hantering	Handhabung	manutention, manipulation	käsittely
managing director	verkställande direktör	leitender Direktor	directeur, gérant	toimitusjohtaja
manufactured timber	trävaru	aufgearbeitetes Holz	bois manufacturé	puutavara
maple	lönn	Ahorn	érable	vaahtera
margin	marginal	Spielraum	marge	marginaali
mark (shipping brand)	märke	Marke	marque, estampille	leima, merkki
market conditions	marknadsförhållanden	Marktlage, Absatzverhältnisse	conditions du marché	markkinatilanne

English	Swedish	German	French	Finnish
matched board	spontbräde, spontade bräde	Nut-und Federbrett, Spundbret	planches appareillées, planches à rainure et languette	ponttilauta
M.B.F. (thousand board feet), M.B.M. or M ft b.m.	tusen plankfot	tausend Brettfuss	mille pieds-planche (Canadian French)	tuhatlautajalka
mean diameter	medeldiameter	Durchschnittsdurchmesser	diamètre moyen	keskiläpimitta
mean (average) value measurement, measuring	medelvärde mätning	Durchschnittswert Messung	valeur moyenne mesurage du bois, cubage, toisage	keskiarvo mittaus
measuring tape, band mechanical (wood) pulp	måttband slipmassa, trämassa	Messband Holzschliff	mètre à ruban pâte mécanique	mittanauha puuhioke
metre modulus of elasticity moisture content	meter elasticitetsmodul fuktighetshalt	Meter Elastizitätsmodul Wassergehalt, Feuchtigkeitsgehalt	mètre module d'élasticité teneur en humidité, pourcentage d'humidité	metri kimmomoduli kosteuspitoisuus
moisture-resistant	fuktbeständig	feuchtigkeits-beständig	résistant, -e à l'humidité	kosteuttavastustava
moulding mycelium	listverk mycel(ium)	Leistenwerk Myzel, Pilzmyzel	moulure mycélium	lista rihmasto
narrow-ringed, close-ringed, fine-ringed	finringad	engringig	à couches minces, -cernes étroits, -accroissements fins	kapealustoinen
natural reproduction, natural regeneration	självföryngring	natürliche Verjüngung, Naturverjüngung	régénération naturelle, reensemencement naturel	luontainen nuorentuminen

ENGLISH	SWEDISH	GERMAN	FRENCH	FINNISH
natural resources	naturtillgångar	Naturvorräte	richesses naturelles, ressources naturelles	luonnonvarat
needle (of a conifer)	barr	Nadel	aiguille (d'un résineux)	havu
negotiations	förhandlingar	Verhandlungen	négociations	neuvottelut
nominal measure	nominellt mått, nominell kubik	nominelle Masse, nominelle Kubikmasse	dimension nominale	nimellinen mitta, nimellinen kuutio
Norway spruce	gran	Fichte	épicéa	kuusi
oak	ek	Eiche	chêne	tammi
offer	offert	Angebot	offre	tarjous
operating costs	driftskostnader	Betriebskosten	frais d'exploitation	liikekustannukset
option	option, valrätt	Option, Wahl	option	valinta
Oregon pine	douglasgran	Douglasie, Douglastanne	sapin de Douglas, pin d'Oregon	douglaskuusi
output, production	produktion	Produktion, Ertrag	production	tuotanto
oven-dry	ugntorkad	ofengetrocknet	anhydre, désseché	uunikuiva
over-bark (o.b.)	på bark (p.b.)	mit Rinde (m.R.)	sur écorce, écorce comprise	kuoren päällä
overheads, overhead costs	omkostnader	Verwaltungskosten	frais généraux	yleiskustannukset
overlying goods	överliggande varor	überliegende Waren	marchandises en souffrance	noutamatta jääneet tavarat
overmature	överåldrig	überjährig	suranné, depérissant	yli-ikäinen
overside	över bord	Über Bord	pardessus bord, bord à bord	yli laidan
overshipment	överskeppning	Mehrlieferung	excédent embarqué, surplus embarqué	ylilaivaus

English	Swedish	German	French	Finnish
overtime	övertid	Überstunde(n)	heure(s) supplémentaire(s)	ylityö
overtime, work (to)	arbeta på övertid	Überstunden machen	faire des heures supplémentaires	tehdä ylityötä
panel	panel	Wandtäfelung	panneau (de cale)	paneeli
paper	papper	Papier	papier	paperi
paper mill	papersbruk	Papierfabrik	papeterie, fabrique de papier	paperitehdas
paper pulp	pappersmassa	Papierbrei	pâte à papier	paperimassa
parcel of timber	virkesparti	Holzpartie, Holzposten	lot (de bois)	puuerä
part shipment	delskeppning, dellast	Teillieferung	livraison partielle, expédition partielle	osalaivaus, osalasti
particle board, chipboard	spånplatta	Spanplatte	panneau de particules	lastulevy
payment	betalning	Zahlung	paiement	maksu
peel (to)	barka	entrinden	écorcer	kuoria
peeling machine, peeler, barking drum	barkningsmaskin	Entrindungsmaschine	machine à écorcer, écorceuse, tambour écorceur	kuorimiskone
photosynthesis	fotosyntes	Kohlensäureassimilation	photosynthèse	hiilihapon yhteyttäminen
piece work	ackordsarbete	Akkordarbeit	travail à la pièce	urakkatyö, kappaletyö
pile	trave, stapel	Stoss, Stapel	pile	pino, tapuli
pile (to), to pile in stacks	stapla, trava	aufschichten, stapeln, in Ster aufsetzen	empiler, enstérer	kasata, kasata kokoon (taaplata)
pile of wood stacked crosswise	korslagd stapel	über Kreuz geschichteter Stapel	tas empilé en croix	ristitapuli

ENGLISH	SWEDISH	GERMAN	FRENCH	FINNISH
piled wood	travat virke	Schichtholz	bois empilé	pinotavara
pit-props, props	props, gruvstolpar	Grubenholz	bois de mines, poteaux de mines	kaivospuu
planed wood	hyvlat virke	gehobeltes Holz	bois raboté	höylätavara, höylätty tavara
planing machine	hyvelmaskin	Hobelmaschine	raboteuse, machine à raboter	höyläyskone, höyläkone
plywood	kryssfanér	Sperrholz	(panneau) contre-plaqué (bois) contreplaqué	vaneeri
pole, post	stolpe	Pfosten	poteau	pylväs
policy (insurance)	försäkringsbrev, – polis	Versicherungsschein, Versicherungspolice	police d'assurance	vakuutuskirja
poplar	poppel	Pappel	peuplier	poppeli
port of discharge	lossningshamm, lossningsplats	Löschhafen, Entladungshafen	port de déchargement	purkaushamina
port of shipment	skeppningshamn	Ladehafen, Verladehafen	port d'embarquement	laivaussatama
power saw	motorsåg	Motorsäge	scie à moteur, scie mécanique portative	moottorisaha
price (to), to fix the price(s) of	prissätta	Preis festsetzen	fixer le(s) prix de	hinnoitella
price level	prisnivå	Preisniveau	niveau des prix	hintataso
private forest	privatskog, enskild skog	Privatwald	forêt particulière, forêt privée	yksityismetsä
properly seasoned	skeppningstorr	verschiffungstrocken	correctement séché	laivauskuiva

protest	protest	Protest	protêt	protesti
pruning	uppkvistning	Aufästung	élagage, émondage	karsiminen
pulp	massa	(Holz) Masse, Zellstoff	pâte (de bois), pulpe	massa
pulp mill	pappersmassefabrik	Zellulosefabrik	usine de pâte, usine de cellulose	paperimassatehdas
pulpwood	massaved	Papierholz, Faserholz	bois à pâte, bois de râperie	paperipuu
quality	kvalitet	Güte, Qualität	qualité	laatu
quantity	kvantitet	Menge, Quantität	quantité	määrä
quarter-sawing	kvartersågning	Viertelspaltsägen, Kreuzholzschneiden	sciage sur quartier	neljännessahaus
quay	kaj	Kai	quai	laituri
radius of curvature	krökningsradie	Krümmungsradius	rayon de courbure	kaarresäde
raft	flotte	Floss	radeau, train de bois (flotte)	lautta
rafter	taksparre	Dachsparren	chevron	kattoparru
railway	järnväg	Eisenbahn	chemin de fer	rautatie
random, falling	fallande	wie es kommt	tout venant, tombant	lankeava
rate of growth	tillväxthastighet	Wachstumsrate	vitesse de croissance, rapidité - -	kasvunopeus
rate of interest	räntefot	Zinsfuss	taux d'intérêt	korkokanta
rayon	konstsilke	Kunstseide	soie artificielle, rayonne	tekosilkki, raijon
ready date	redodagen	Bereitschaftstag	date de disponibilité	valmiuspäivä
redwood (Baltic)	furu	Kiefer, Rotholz	sapin rouge du Nord, bois rouge	mänty

ENGLISH	SWEDISH	GERMAN	FRENCH	FINNISH
reforestation, reproduction, regeneration	skogsreproduktion, skogsföryngring	Wiederaufforstung, Waldverjüngung	reforestation, reboisement, régénération	metsittäminen, metsänuudistus, metsänviljely, metsännuorennos
reject (to) (timber)	vraka	ausscheiden, aussortieren	rejeter, rebuter	hylätä
rejection, refusal to accept	refusering	Annahmeverweigerung	rejet, refus d'accepter	hylkääminen
report	redogörelse	Bericht	rapport	kertomus, selostus
resaw (subst.)	klyvsåg	Spaltsäge	scie à refendre, scie à dédoubler	halkaisusaha
research	forskning, undersökning	Forschung, Untersuchung	recherche	tutkiminen, tutkimus
resin	harts, kåda	Harz	résine	hartsi, pihka
ring-bark (to)	ringbarka	ringsum entrinden	anneler, ceinturer	kaulata
rip saw	klyvsåg	Spaltsäge	scie à refendre	halkaisusaha
risk	risk	Risiko	risque	vastuu, riski
rot	röta	Fäule, Fäulnis	pourriture	laho
rot, dry	torr röta	Trockenfäule	pourriture sèche	kuiva laho
rot, heart	kärnröta	Kernfäule	pourriture du coeur	sydänlaho
rot, soft, loose	lösröta	lose Fäule, weiche Fäule	pourriture molle	pehmeä laho
rotary-cut veneer	svarvat faner	Schälfurnier	placage déroulé	sorvattua vaneria
round timber	rundvirke	Rundholz	bois rond	pyöreä puutavara
revolutions per minute (r.p.m.)	varv per minut	Tourenzahl pro Minute, Umdrehungszahl pro Minute	tours par minute (t.p.m.)	kierroksia minuutissa, kierrosluku minuutissa

St Petersburg standard	S:t Petersburg standard	St. Petersburger Standard	Standard de Saint Petersbourg	pietarin standartti
salvage (to)	bärga	bergen	repêcher, récupérer	pelastaa
sap	sav	(Baum) Saft	sève	mahla
sapwood	splintved, ytved	Splint, -holz	aubier	mantopuu, pintapuu
saw	såg	Säge	scie	saha
saw (to)	såga	sägen	scier	sahata
saw blade	sågblad	Sägeblatt	lame de scie	sahanterä
saw cut, kerf	sågskär, -spår	Sägeschnitt, Schnitt, Kerfe	trait de scie	sahausrako
saw timber, saw log	sågtimmer, -stock	Sägeholz	grume à sciage	sahatukki
sawmill	sågverk	Sägewerk, -mühle	scierie	saha
sawdust	sågspån	Sägemehl	sciure de bois	sahajauho
sawing	sågning	Sägen	sciage	sahaus
sawn timber, sawn goods	sågat virke, sågade trävaror	Schnittholz	bois scié, sciages, bois débites	sahatavara, sahattu tavara
sawyer	sågare	Säger	scieur	sahrui
scaffolding	byggnadsställning	Baugerüst	échafaudage	rakennusteline
scant measurement	undermål	Untermass	mesure par défaut, sous-dimension	alamitta, vajaamitta
scantling	scantling	Scantling	volige	kaitasoiro, piensoiro, scantling
schaalboard	förskalningsbräde	Schalbrett	planche étroite	pintalauta
schedule, scheme (of operations), process charts(s)	schema, schema över arbetsförlopp, tidstabell	Schema, Schema für Arbeitsverlauf	programme, horaire, plan de déroulement des opérations, – de travail	kaavio, aikataulu
Scots pine	tall, furu, fura	Kiefer, Rotholz	pin sylvestre	mänty, petäjä, honka

ENGLISH	SWEDISH	GERMAN	FRENCH	FINNISH
seasoning	torkning	Trocknung	séchage (à l'air)	kuivaus, kuivaaminen
seasoning check, -crack, -shake	krympspricka	Schwindriss	gerce de séchage, fente de retrait	kutistumisrako
seconds, 2nds	sekunda	Sekunda, zweite Qualität	deuxième, 2ième (classe)	sekunda
seller	säljare	Verkäufer	vendeur	myyjä
shake	spricka	Spalt, Riss	fente	halkeama
shake, cross	tvärspricka	Querriss	fente radiale	poikittainen halkeama
shake, cup, ring	ringspricka	Ringriss	roulure	rengashalkeama
shake, heart	kärnspricka	Kernriss	fente de coeur	sydänhalkeama
shift	skift, arbets-	Schicht	relève	työvuoro
shingle	takspån	Schindel	bardeau	kattopäre
shipbrokers	skeppsmäklare	Schiffsmakler	courtiers maritimes	laivanselvittäjä, meklari
shipment	skeppning	Verschiffung	chargement, livraison	laivaus
shipowner(s)	skeppsredare	Schiffsreeder	armateur	laivanvarustaja
shipper	avlastare	Ablader	expéditeur	laivaaja
shipping	skeppning	Verschiffung	expédition	laivaus
shipping dry	skeppningstorr	trocken zur Verschiffung	commercialement sec pour éxpedition	laivauskuiva
shorts	korta längder, kortlängder	Enden, Stauholz, kurze Sägeware	coursons, coupures, levées courtes	pätkät
shrinkage	krympning	Schwinden	retrait	kutistuminen
sinkers	sjunkvirke, dykare	Sinkholz	grumes tombant au fond	uppopuu, juoppopuu
sixths, 6ths	sexta	sechste Qualität	sixième (classe) 6ième	seksta

English	German	French	Swedish	Finnish
skirtings	Fussleisten	plinthe	fotlister	jalkalistat
slab	Seitenbrett	dosse	bak, kantbräde	kelles, pintaosa
slating batten	Dachlatte	latte pour couverture, latte à panne	takläkt	rimalauta
sleeper	Schwelle, Eisenbahnschwelle	traverse (de chemin de fer)	sliper	ratapölkky
sliced veneer	Schnittfurnier	placage tranché	knivskuret fanér	veitsileikattua vaneria
slide rule	Rechenschieber	règle à calcul	räknesticka	laskutikku
smooth	glatt	lisse, scié fin	slät	sileä
snow conditions	Schneeverhältnisse	état de (la) neige	snöförhållanden	lumiolosuhteet, lumitilanne
soaked through with water	durchnässt, nass	imbibé, -e d'eau, trempé, -e (—) imprégné, -e (—)	vattendränkt	vettynyt
softwood forest	Nadelwald	forêt de conifères, – résineuse	barrskog	havumetsä
softwood timber	Nadelholz, -ware	bois résineux	barrträdsvirke	havupuu
sorting	Sortierung	classification, classement	sortering	lajittelu
specific gravity	spezifisches Gewicht	poids spécifique, densité	specifik vikt	ominaispaino
specification	Spezifikation	spécification	specifikation	erittely
spiral grain	Drehwüchsigkeit	fil tors, fil spirale	vresfibrighet, vridvuxenhet	kierteisyys
split	Spalt, Riss	fente	spricka	halkeama
spring wood	Frühjahrsholz, Frühholz	bois de printemps	vårved	kevätpuu
spruce timber	Weissholz, Fichtenware	bois d'épicéa, bois blancs	granvirke	kuusitavara, näre

ENGLISH	SWEDISH	GERMAN	FRENCH	FINNISH
square timber	fyrkantvirke	Kantholz	bois équarri	nelisärmäinen puutavara
square cut, -sawn	vinkelrätt avsågad vinkelrätt avkapad	gerade geschnitten	scié d'équerre	kohtisuoraan katkaistu
stack of logs	välta, timmer-	Langholzstapel, Stamm-	pile de grumes, tas de billes	tukkikasa
standing timber	rotstående virke	stehendes Holz	bois sur pied	pystymetsä
statement	uttalande	Angabe	déclaration	selonteko
statistics	statistik	Statistik	statistiques	tilasto
stevedore	stuvare	Stauer	stevedore, arrimeur	ahtaaja
storage defect	lagringsskada	Lagerungsschaden	défaut occasionné par l'empilage	varastoimisvahinko
storage method	lagringsmetod	Lagerungsmethode	methode d'empilage	varastoimismenetelmä
straddle truck	grensletruck		chariot cavalier	hajasäärirukki
straight grain	rätfibrighet	gerade Maserung, Geradmaserung	fil droit, de droit fil	suora syy
stress grading	bärmodul	Tragmodul	classement par contraintes admissibles	kantojännite
strike	strejk	Streik	grève	lakko
stump, stool	stubbe	Stumpf	souche, pied	kanto
stump height	stubbhöjd	Stockhöhe, Stumpfhöhe	hauteur de souche	kantokorkeus
sulphate pulp	sulfatmassa,-cellulosa	Sulfatzellstoff, -zellulose	pâte au sulfate	sulfaattiselluloosa
sulphite pulp	sulfitmassa, -cellulosa	Sulfitzellstoff, -zellulose	pâte au sulfite	sulfiittiselluloosa

summary	sammandrag	Zusammenfassung	résumé	yhteenveto
summer felling	sommarfällning, sommaravverkning	Sommerfällung	abattage en sève	kesäkaato, kesähakkuu
supply and demand	tillgång och efterfrågan	Angebot und Nachfrage	l'offre et la demande	tarjonta ja kysyntä
surface (to)	hyvla	hobeln	raboter, planer	höylätä
surface check	ytspricka	Oberflächenriss	gerce superficielle	pintahalkeama
surplus	överskott	Überschuss	excédent, surplus	ylijäämä
tally (to)	pricka	Zählen	dénombrer, pointer	vastakirjata, laskea
tannin, tanning substance, tanning material	garvämme	Gerbstoff	tanin, tannin	parkkiaine, parkkihappo
tapered	avsmalnad	spitz zugelaufen	conique, effilé	kavennettu
tapering	starkt avsmalnande	schlank zulaufend	à forte décroissance	kapeneva, katolatvainen
tax	skatt	Steuer	impôt(s), contributions, taxe	vero
teeth, serration	tänder	Zähnung	denture	hampaat
temperature	temperatur	Temperatur	temperature	lämpötila
tensile strength	draghållfasthet	Zugfestigkeit	résistance à la traction	vetolujuus
terminology	terminologi	Terminologie	terminologie	ammattisanasto
testing apparatus, testing instrument	provningsapparat	Prüfungsinstrument	appareil d'essai, instrument d'essai	koettelukone
thermoplastics	termoplastiker	thermoplastisches Kunstharz	matières thermoplastiques	termomuovit
thirds, 3rds	tertia	Tertia, dritte Qualität	troisième (class), 3ième	tertia

ENGLISH	SWEDISH	GERMAN	FRENCH	FINNISH
timber	timmer, virke	Bau-und Nutzholz, Langholz, Holz	bois d'oeuvre, de service, de construction, de charpente	puutavara, puu
timber agent	trävaruagent	Holz (waren) agent	agent en bois, représentant en bois	puutavara-asiamies puutavara-agentti
timber contract	trävarukontrakt	Holzwarenkontrakt, Holzwarenvertrag	contrat d'achat de bois	puutavarasopimus
timber market	trävarumarknad	Holzmarkt	marché du bois	puutavaramarkkinat
timber trade	trävaruhandel	Holzhandel	commerce du bois	puutavarakauppa
timber yard	brädgård	Holzhof	chantier de bois	lautatarha
time charter	tidsbefraktning	Zeitbefrachtung	affrètement à terme	aikarahtaus
tongue and groove	spont och not	Spund und Nut, Feder und Nut	reinure et languette	ruodesauma
tool(s)	redskap, verktyg	Gerät, Werkzeug	outillage, équipement, matériel	työkalu(t)
torsion(al) strength, twisting strength	vrid(nings)-hållfasthet	Drehungsfestigkeit, Torsions-	résistance à la torsion	vääntölujuus
total	(slut-) summa	Summe, Gesammtbetrag	somme, total	summa, kokonaismäärä
tow (to)	bogsera	schleppen, bugsieren	remorquer	hinata
transfer (to)	överföra	übertragen	transférer	siirtää
transport(ation)	transport	Transport	transport	kuljetus
tree	träd	Baum	arbre	puu
trim (to) (round timber)	avkvista	entästen, ausästen	ébrancher	karsia
truck	lastbil	Lastkraftwagen	camion	kuorma-auto

trunk	stam	Stamm, Schaft	tronc	runko
tugboat	bogserbåt	Schlepper, Bugsierboot	remorqueur, toueur	hinaaja
turnover	omsättning	Umsatz	chiffre d'affaires	liikevaihto
under-bark (u.b.)	under bark (u.b.)	ohne Rinde (o.R.)	sous écorce, sans l'écorce	kuoren alta
undershipment	underskeppning	Minderlieferung	expédition déficitaire, expédition insuffisante	vajaalaivaus
unedged	okantad	unbesäumt	flacheux, non deligné	särmäämätön, kanttamaton
uneven	ojämn	holperig, uneben	rugueux, inégal, -e	epätasainen
uniformity	jämnhet	Ebenheit, Gleichmassigkeit	uniformité	tasaus
unload (to)	lossa, avlasta	entladen, abladen, löschen	décharger	purkaa
unseasoned (wood)	rått (virke)	frisches (Holz)	bois vert, bois frais	tuore (puu)
unshipped	oskeppad	unverschifft	non embarqué	laivaamaton
unsorted, U/S	osorterad (o/s)	unsortiert	non classé, inassorti	lajittelematon
upgrade (to) (quality)	uppsortera	aufstufen	surclasser (la qualité)	luokitella paremmaksi, sijoittaa ylempään luokkaan
valuation	värdering	Abschätzung, Taxierung	inventaire, évaluation, estimation	arvio, arviointi
value (to)	värdera	Abschätzen, taxieren	estimer, évaluer	arvioida
veneer	fanér	Furnier	placage	viilu
volume	kubikmassa, kubikinnehåll	Kubikmasse, Kubikinhalt, Festgehalt	cube, volume	kuutiomäärä, kuutiosisältö

ENGLISH	SWEDISH	GERMAN	FRENCH	FINNISH
voyage	resa	Reise	traversée, voyage (en mer)	matka
wages	arbetslöner	Arbeitslohn	salaire	työpalkat
wagon (railway)	vagn	Wagen, Waggon	wagon, (de chemin de fer)	vaunu
wallboard, hardboard	fiberplatta, wallboard	Faserholzplatte	panneau de fibre	kuitulevy
wane	vankant	Wahnkante, Schal-, Wald-	flache	vajaasyrjä
				vajaasärmä
waney	vankantig	wahnkantig, nicht voll-	flacheux, -euse	vajaasärmäinen
warehouse	magasin	Lagerhaus	entrepôt	varasto
warped timber	skevt virke	verzogenes Holz, verkrümmtes Holz	bois gauchi	käyristynyt puutavara
water (to)	vattna	tränken	faire eau	kastella
water-soaked	vattendränkt	durchnässt, nass	imbibé,-e d'eau, trempé,-e (—), impregné,-e (—)	vettynyt
wavy grain	flammighet, vågfibrighet	wellige Maserung, Flammenzeichnung Wimmerwuchs	fil sinueux, -ondulé	lainemuodostuma
weatherboard	snedkluvet foderbräde	schräg spaltgesägtes Verschalbrett, Futterbrett	auvent, bardis	limilauta
weathering	gråyta, vädergrånad	Verwitterung, grauwerden (infolge von Wettereinfluss)	vieillissement, décomposition	ilmoittuminen

English	Swedish	German	French	Finnish
wedge	kil	Keil	coin	kiila
whitewood	granvirke	Weissholz, Fichtenware	bois blanc	kuusitavara, näre
wide-ringed	bredringad, frodvuxen	breitringig, weit-, mit breiten Jahresringen	à couches d'accroissement larges, à ceines larges	leveälustionen
without prejudice	utan förbindelse, utan förfång för	ohne Präjudiz	sans préjudice	menettämättä oikeuttaa johonkin
wood	trä, virke	Holz	bois	puutavara
wood consumption	virkesförbrukning	Holzverbrauch	consommation en bois	puutavarakulutus
wood flour	trämjöl	Holzmehl	farine de bois	puujauhe
wood pile	trave, stapel	Scheiterholz	pile de bois	pino, tapuli
wood product	träfabrikat	Holzfabrikat	produit dérivé du bois	puuvalmiste
wood waste	träavfall, sågavfall	Holzabfälle, Sägeabfall	déchets de bois	puujäte, sahausjäte
wood-wool	träull	Holzwolle	laine de bois (fibre de bois)	lastuvilla
wooden goods	träsaker	Holzware	articles en bois, ouvrages en bois	puuesineet
wood yard	brädgård	Holzniederlage, Holzhof	dépôt de bois, chantier de bois	lautatarha
woodworking, wood fabrication, wood processing	träförädling	Holzveredelung	industrie du bois, de transformation, mécanique du bois	puunjalostus
wood-working industry	träförädlingsindustri	Holzindustrie	industrie du travail mécanique du bois	puunjalostusteollisuus
working capital	driftskapital, rörelse —	Betriebskapital	capital d'exploitation, fonds de roulement	liikepääoma

ENGLISH	SWEDISH	GERMAN	FRENCH	FINNISH
working conditions	arbetsförhållanden	Arbeitsumstände, Arbeitsverhältnisse	conditions de travail	työolosuhteet
working day	arbetsdag	Arbeitstag, Werktag	journée de travail	työpäivä
workshop	verkstad	Werkstatt	atelier	työpaja
yew	idegran	Eibe	if	marjakuusi
yield of the forest	skogens avkastning	Waldertrag	rendement de la forêt	metsäntuotto, metsänsato
yielding a profit	räntabel	rentabel	rentable, laissant un bénéfice, un profit	kannattava
young growth, seedling stand	ungskog, plantbestånd	Jungwald, -bestand, -holz	jeune peuplement	taimisto, nuori metsä

Index

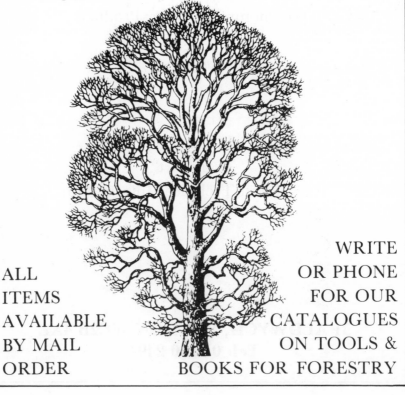

From wood chips to micro- chips.

We've come a long way since beginning our service to the trade.

Building timber, sawmilling and preserving still form vital parts of our business. But these days they're complemented by all the refinements of up-to-date "timber engineering" technology.

Refinements like a computer installation that masterminds the design of trussed rafters to your own specifications.

And sophisticated mechanical stress-grading for the assessment of load-bearing timber.

Plus a range of modern sheet materials ideal for roofing, ceiling lining, flooring, partitioning and wall lining.

Southerns Evans: everything you want from a traditional timber company. And more.

Southerns Evans Ltd.
WIDNES, CHESHIRE. TELEPHONE: 051-424 5500.

Magnet 🔷 Southerns